Green Belts

Green Belts

Conflict mediation in the urban fringe

Martin J. Elson

HEINEMANN : LONDON

William Heinemann Ltd
10 Upper Grosvenor Street, London W1X 9PA

LONDON MELBOURNE TORONTO
JOHANNESBURG AUCKLAND

First published 1986

British Library Cataloguing in Publication Data
Elson, Martin J.
Green belts.
1. Greenbelts 2. City planning 3. Regional planning
I. Title
711 HT166

ISBN 0 434 90532 1

Photoset by Rowland Phototypesetting Ltd
Bury St Edmunds, Suffolk
Printed in Great Britain by
Redwood Burn Ltd, Trowbridge, Wilts

To Ben and Katy

Contents

Tables

Illustrations

Foreword

Between the idea
And the reality
Between the notion
And the act
Falls the shadow
T.S. Eliot, *The Hollow Men*

Simple concepts are appealing. But simplicity in expression is not necessarily conducive to ease of application; and the green belt may be a case in point. The nature of the gulf between theory and practice is debatable, but the clarity of the image of green belts is beyond doubt: it is firmly rooted in the public mind. Green belts form an integral part of the culture of a crowded island striving to make the best use of land by means of a statutory planning system. This breadth of recognition deserves to be matched by a comparable depth of understanding. Unfortunately, there has been no single comprehensive overview of the idea and the reality of green belts to assist our appreciation of the subject. Martin Elson's book fills that gap.

The evolution of the green belt is inextricably linked to that of town and country planning generally in Britain. Although the role of planning is again the subject of political debate, there is no real sign of a challenge to the postwar consensus about the need for planning to strike a balance between the pressures for development and the interests of conservation. The green belt is a symbol of that balancing act and of the conflicts which make it a political issue. Such symbols inevitably have their supporters and detractors and, as with the overall machinery for plan-making and controlling development, the British have a love–hate relationship with green belts. At a time when the prevailing mood favours deregulation and planning control is itself subject to criticism, one of the most restrictive tools of planning, the green belt, attracts much popular support. Why is this so?

Part of the reason for the popularity of the green belt concept undoubtedly lies in the very greenness of the metaphor, rather than the image of the 'belt'. The trickle of green thinking evident in the 1960s and 1970s has turned into a flood in the 1980s. Whether, as some have argued, the green outlook is ingrained in the English character, with its roots derived from the gardening revolution of the seventeenth century, and the traditional fondness of the English for countryside leisure pursuits is of academic interest. But the current political enthusiasm for green politics is real. The environmental rhetoric, if not the environmental cause, has been espoused by all major parties, and one party has changed its name to the Green Party. Such nostalgia and current fashion for greenery, alongside a debate about the proper role of planning, have done much to increase the attention paid to green belts and this book could not, therefore, have been more timely. In looking forward as well as back, Martin Elson traces the main themes which are essential to any assessment of the contemporary significance of the green belt.

In this context, Martin Elson's comprehensive analysis of the uses of green belts covers a wide and topical canvas. First, and most generally, it gives a valuable insight into the whole issue of changing central–local relations in the postwar years. Second, the book serves to reinforce a justifiable concern about the growing institutionalization of planning. At a time when the rate of change demands an increasingly responsive planning process if plans are not to become irrelevant, the statutory machinery of plan-making looks increasingly cumbersome. In that drift towards a quasi-legal framework of land-use policy, the apparent rigidity of green belts have played a part. Third, this story of the green belt pinpoints the dilemma facing the planning system itself, namely, it is expected simultaneously to provide for both certainty and flexibility. While the virtue of the latter in planning is much extolled, it is the stability and durability of green belts which explains why they retain public confidence and support. The final and current conflict highlighted by green belt policy is Government's wish to see more weight given to market demand for housing land while protecting open countryside. Since the areas with highest demand are in and around green belts, it is not surprising that this has resulted in mixed signals between central and local government! Ironically, this policy conflict has promoted a dialogue among government, local planning authorities and builders which has helped improve central–local communications and understanding.

Evidence on the effectiveness of green belts is less clear-cut than the perception of planners and the public often suggests. The book attempts to identify the diverse consequences of the implementation of green belt policies in a wide variety of situations. There are two problems in doing this, both of which are faced squarely by Martin Elson. The first is the general difficulty of isolating the effects of the green belt from other land-use policies when considering streams of costs and benefits. The other is the large number of claims made for green belts, including managing decentralization, achieving economy in service costs, maintaining separation between towns, preserving farmland and open space close to cities and assisting urban regeneration. Each of these is examined in the context of the green belt experience.

Even if precise causal links with policies can be established, measures of success in planning are hard to devise. If the green belt has helped avoid some problems becoming worse – does that represent success? Quite apart from the effectiveness of green belts there are good reasons for continuing to evaluate the practical results and future potential of these policies. In particular, social objectives are rarely constant – witness, for example, the shift of policy from relieving city congestion in the 1960s to stimulating urban investment in the 1980s – in both of which green belts play a part.

The Royal Town Planning Institute has rightly been anxious to give as much encouragement as possible to a balanced account of the green belt since it forms a key strand in planning history and a major component of current planning practice. Martin Elson's book is most timely, looking forward as well as backward. A complex plot has been unravelled into a readable saga. It was Dr Johnson who remarked that heaven would contain the amenities of the town and the pleasures of the country – and perhaps that is why green belts have such a wide appeal beyond the planning profession. An understanding of this tool of planning is essential to the formulation of future policy, and this book is to be commended to all with a concern for the management of change.

Martin Shaw, Norwich
January 1986

Preface

Green belts are the most long-standing policy instrument used by local authorities and central Government to shape patterns of urban development. Promoted nationally by Ministerial Circular in 1955 approved belts now cover nearly 11 per cent of England, an area similar to that devoted to urban development, and greater than is covered by National Parks, or Areas of Outstanding Natural Beauty. Over the last ten years the area of fully approved green belts had grown by over 100 per cent as part of a process of renegotiation of green belt aims, locations, and policy wording through their incorporation into new development plans. The aim of this book is to provide a systematic national assessment of green belts in the new planning system. In doing this it focuses on three factors; the upsurge of interest in the use made of land within green belts including leisure and agricultural uses; the effects of unprecedented increases in unemployment since 1979 which may cause reappraisals of attitude to greenfield development in the search to maintain local economies; and the pressure from housebuilders to obtain continuing supplies of marketable land in areas where green belt policies apply.

The text has three main subdivisions. The first traces the origins of green belt policy, its enthusiastic reception by local authorities in 1955, and its survival and adjustment through a period of rapid growth in the 1960s. The process of redefinition, at its height in the middle of the 1980s, is then assessed. The second discusses the detailed implementation of policies within green belts including those for settlements of varying size, for wealth-creating uses such as mineral production and agriculture, and for restorative and appreciative needs such as recreation and conservation. The third evaluates the intense national debate surrounding the issue of the latest Green Belt Circular (Circular 14/84) and how far its advice was influenced by the deliberations of the House of Commons Environment Select Committee earlier in the same year. An assessment is also made, in the context of changing social and economic conditions, of the status of green belt policy in the 1980s, stressing outstanding issues for the implementation of the policy and how it may evolve in the future.

Central themes within this book include continuity in the structure of central–local relations, the use of physical policies in an attempt to achieve social and economic ends, the interdependence of green belt with other urban restraint policies, and the use of regulatory development control approaches to land use, in contrast to the persuasive and exhortatory approaches used in green belt land management. However the reader will discover a wide variety of subsidiary themes running through the text. These include the motives and actions of local community, environmental and other pressure groups, the activities of the development industry, and the negotiative roles of planners as they tread the ill-defined line between conservation and development in local situations. Therefore to the student of rural or urban planning, geography, environmental studies, recreation, agriculture or land management, the renegotiation of green belts is an instructive case study of structures and relationships within the planning system.

There is also a need for greater dissemination of the experiences and outcomes of current practice both within the planning profession and between planners and other groups concerned with the use of land. Green belts have a powerful hold in the minds of the general public, with private developers, and among those concerned with the conservation of our natural resources. However, many of the more strident voices appear to misrepresent (inadvertently and otherwise) the concept and its use. If this book clears away some of the cultural 'fog' surrounding the use, and as often the misuse, of the term green belt it will have achieved its second main objective.

The subject matter of the book arises from a programme of research entitled *The Implementation of Land Use Policy* being carried out at the Department of Town Planning, Oxford Polytechnic, which commenced in 1978. Setting out to catalogue the transfer of green belts into the new system of development plans, a group of researchers became interested in the survival of the concept over more than 35 years of changing ideas about land use planning, local needs and the release of land for development in green belt areas, and the leisure use of green belts and urban fringes. The concept appeared to draw together insights about the nature of planning practice at many levels and the specific place of plans in the ever-changing spectrum of local authority policies. Other stimuli came from the authors' brief period of secondment to the Countryside Commission in the late 1970s, from research on land release in restraint areas and on the leisure use of green belts funded by the Economic and Social Research Council (including its Leisure and Recreation Panel); also, more recently, from work for the Department of the Environment on the implementation of development plans.

A study on this scale cannot emerge without the encouragement and assistance of many people. The early sequence of working papers on green belts owes much to the work of Michael Hebbert, Iain Gault and Sheila Terry. In the later stages the implementation–research team of Paul McNamara and Andrew (Joe) Doak read various chapters and made valuable comments. Liz Hill and Sean O'Grady, as linked research students, have collected case study evidence which they have graciously allowed me to adapt for use in the text. A large number of planners in practice across the length and breadth of England have, despite severe pressures on their time, granted me interviews and have responded to written requests for material. David Rose at the Royal Town Planning Institute has proved a constant help in progressing the book through its various stages in conjunction with Martin Shaw and other members of the Editorial Panel. Chris Topley drew the excellent maps and diagrams with great skill and an affable good nature. Above all I must record my gratitude to Patsy Healey for her persistent encouragement of this venture (and of its author), and for extensive comments on the material at various stages of production. The continuous torrent of ideas, concepts and theoretical propositions produced by Patsy have done much to provide a stimulating research environment for the twenty or more persons who have been closely involved in the programme of work on planning implementation at Oxford over the last six years.

Finally I must record my gratitude to my family for their tolerance in adjusting their lifestyle to the demands of authorship. My wife Clare understood the need. Ben and Katy wondered why. This book is dedicated to them so they may come to understand.

Martin Elson,
Charlbury,
Oxford

Acknowledgements

The author and publisher would like to thank the following for permission to reproduce copyright material: Weidenfeld and Nicholson, London for Figure 1.1; Controller of Her Majesty's Stationery Office for data in Tables 1.1, 2.2, 4.1, 4.2 and 7.3; The London and South East Regional Planning Conference for data in Table 2.1; Greater Manchester Council for data in Table 4.3; University of Aston Management Centre for data in Tables 6.2 and 8.1; Hertfordshire County Council for data in Tables 6.5, 8.2, 8.3 and 8.4 and Allen & Unwin for Table 7.2.

Introduction: Policy Survival and Policy Adjustment

We consider Green Belts have a broad and . . . positive planning role: that of open spaces whose presumption against development can better shape urban areas, particularly on a regional scale

House of Commons Environment Committee 1984

In the first major public reassessment of green belt policy since its inceptión the House of Commons Environment Committee recommended strong support for sacrosanct green belts. In this, it reaffirmed the case for firm policies to intervene in market processes in order to shape and channel urban development. It has the strongly-expressed support of local authorities keen to retain policy control at local level, as well as the support of articulate suburban residents and local and national amenity societies. Yet, at the same time, the central thrust of Government policy is to make the planning system more responsive to market demand. It is prompted in this by the housebuilding industry, and by other groups keen to loosen locational controls on employment-related uses.[1]

This book investigates the most important dimensions of this conflict of interests, through studies of the attempts made by local authorities to renegotiate green belts during the decade to 1984. By an analysis of the major 'actors' involved in the definition of green belts, and the operation of green belt controls and management, it seeks to provide an assessment of the role played by the policy as a response to contemporary social and economic conditions.

A green belt is a special policy defining an area within which only a highly restrictive schedule of changes constituting development under the planning acts will normally be permitted. The purposes for which a green belt may be defined are governed by advice in Government Circulars. They are:

1. to check the further growth of a large built up area;
2. to prevent neighbouring towns from merging into one another; and
3. to preserve the special character of a town.

To be fully effective green belts must be incorporated in structure (county level) plans approved by the Ministry,[2] and in local plans approved by county authorities. Green belt does not have the status of a designation such as an Area of Outstanding Natural Beauty or National Park (both designated by the Secretary of State directly on the recommendation of the Countryside Commission, with the support of local authorities). It is thus on a par with other local authority policies but is normally several kilometres wide and therefore has implications for the regional distribution of land use. By far the majority of green belts in Britain cover parts of more than one local authority area.

Within green belts the intention is to retain the open rural character of the environment. To this end the purposes for which new buildings and changes of use will be permitted are agriculture and forestry, sport, cemeteries, institutions standing in large grounds, or other uses appropriate to a rural area.[3] Although this implies severe restriction it does not imply no development of any sort, and there are circumstances in which green belt policies can be overridden for national and urgent regional need, and other considerations. In general the presence of green belt places the onus of proof on the applicant to show how proposed developments will not infringe green belt criteria. The policy therefore invites negotiation and admits the possibility of accommodation of some proposals which may result in a material improvement in the appearance of a green belt or the economy of an area.

Contrary to popular belief green belts do not exist around all cities. Neither are their boundaries literally permanent. Even where green belts do exist their detailed boundaries in over 50 per cent of cases have *never* been formally approved in development plans. This rather confused situation is a product of the powers over planning decisions vested in local and central Government by Parliament. It is also a consequence of the different policy concerns of the centre and the locality. These produce the different views on the function, definition, and use of green belts which brought forward the need for Government to introduce new advice in 1984.[4]

The Quest for Policy Control

British land use planning is a system of response to change. It operates by guiding a predominantly private development market, and it is a political system.[5] The planning acts define an area of discretion within which local authorities can act to formulate and operate policy. This discretion is narrowed by the supervisory and reserve powers of the Ministry to protect the national interest and secure consistency in policies. Whilst this national interest is ill-defined, the actions of Governments have stressed three rationales; the need to protect nationally-scarce kinds of land; a wish to avoid putting Governments' own economic, social or environmental policies at risk through local political control of land; and a wish to avoid disparities in the nature and quality of development between localities becoming too extreme.[6] These aims are pursued through advice, persuasion and direct influence brought to bear by Ministry officials, by the issue of Circulars and Advice Notes, and in Ministerial speeches. Also modifications may be made to development plans prepared by local authorities, and by intervention in specific cases to 'call in' major proposals for Ministerial decision. Circulars are of particular importance as they attempt to define the scope of planning action open to local authorities and to advise on the balance to be struck between competing interests in land at the local level. Disputes over the *interpretation* to be given to advice in Circulars remain, however, and they have loomed large in the green belt 'debate' over recent years.

Local authorities thus make their choices between competing claims for development and conservation in a constrained and insecure environment. As most planning decisions are made by elected councillors policies must be politically tenable for implementation to occur. At the same time the process of policy formulation has to take account of powerful influences and pressures from outside the locality in the form of the policies of sectoral agencies such as the Ministry of Agriculture (MAFF), the Department of Industry (DoI), or nationalized industries. The financial and other resources required to implement policies are usually in other hands.[7] Planning, it has been argued, is thus reduced to performing a number of functional tasks such as supplying land for development by private housebuilders, co-ordinating development, and reducing the extent of adverse effects of one use upon another at local level.[8] Yet planning policies need to be derived through a process which is accountable to local populations, who may want far less development than that proposed by outside interests; and this in a situation where local economies are both dependent on the market and are seeking to control its effects.[9,10]

Within this combative framework green belt policies assume particular importance. No other policy has such a strong presumption against development. This unique quality gives it the potential to shift the initiative in central-local relations from the centre to the locality. Once approved in plans green belts may only be altered in exceptional circumstances. Although central Government has the final say over what is exceptional, convention, and the history of decisions made, suggest that this criterion has been broadly adhered to over the years. Once formally approved, green belts have not been systematically dismembered by individual decisions. For example, in the West Midlands Green Belt only 23 hectares of land a year were lost to non-conforming uses in the eight years to 1983, and only 11 hectares a year were lost from the Green Belt *within* the Greater London Council area between 1970 and 1981.[11] Green belt is therefore a very *desirable* policy for a local authority seeking to retain or enhance its power to affect local events. A strong position is created from which to negotiate, and arrive at accommodations with those interests promoting development.

Central Government has historically shown itself loath to enter into widespread binding commitments of this sort, preferring to keep its ability to exercise discretion in decision-making at future dates. Hence its stress on the idea that green belts should be set back from urban boundaries to what are termed the long-term limits of development. This clash of central and local interests is fundamental to an understanding of the extent, form, and development of control policies within green belts in England (as Mandelker noted 20 years ago),[12] and is thus detectable in each of the subsequent chapters.

The Main Themes

It is important in assessing the present scale and operation of green belts to understand their origins in statutory planning. Green belts arose as a response to specific social and economic changes, and assumptions about the role that could be played by a comprehensive system of land use controls. It has been argued that the policies developed in the 1940s and 1950s owed their origins to Victorian philanthropists and the promptings of major figures in the 'town planning movement'.[13] Lobbying groups such as the (then) Council for the Preservation of Rural England (CPRE) and the Town and Country Planning Association (TCPA) also had strong environmental and other reasons for wishing to see green belts established. It was implausible that the Government of the day would adopt any of the prescriptions put forward uncritically. As a result there has been widespread misunderstanding of what the ministerial pronouncements of the time implied. Chapter 1 therefore investigates, more closely than has hitherto been attempted, the events surrounding the production of the 1955 Circular. It also seeks to move beyond the words in Circulars to study how the green belt concept was interpreted by central Government across the country.

During the 1960s it seemed inconceivable, in a period of rapid urban growth and accelerating decentralization, that the apparently static green belt concept could survive. Previous writers have focused almost exclusively on the less than typical history of the London Green Belt,[14] whereas outside the South East the conurbations were diagnosed as suffering from different problems, and the operation and effects of green belts are likely to have varied as a result.[15] One of the reasons green belts survived outside the South East appears to have been their adaptability to local conditions. Alternatively it might be argued they were only a pale imitation of the full green belt ideal as, apart from small exceptions, no green belts were formally approved in development plans in such areas until after 1970. So how, and in what form, did green belts survive a period when local authorities were continually exhorted to free more land for development, and a variety of attempts was made to alter the fiscal and regulatory processes involved in the development of land? The various forms of negotiated compromise arrived at between central and local government are discussed in Chapter 2 where a number of factors are adduced which favoured the survival of green belts and their re-emergence after 1970.

These insights allow a more comprehensive assessment to be made of the pattern of green belts appearing in the 1980s.[16] Local authorities have always tested the limits of the policy tools handed down to them by central Government. In the case of green belts this took the form of widening the justifications for green belts to those of protecting agricultural land and rural landscapes, making provision for recreation, and aiding regeneration of the inner city. The process of redefinition is discussed in Chapter 3 and comments are made on the coverage sought by local authorities, and the consistency of the central Government response. The new green belts have been put in place at a time when the discretion available to local planning authorities has been under attack. The structure and influences of the various conservation and development interests on planning in local areas is vastly different to that of 1955. With reductions in the pace of decentralization from cities, and far lower levels of population growth, it might be expected that the reassessment and redefinition of green belts would be an uncontentious process. In the most recent study of the London Green Belt, Munton suggests that 'pressures for peripheral urban expansion are weak and the . . . (green belt) . . . debate can be conducted in the absence of strong demands for building land'.[17] However recession has led to strong demands by organized interests concerned with production,[18] such as housebuilders and industrialists, for incorporation at an earlier stage *within* the planning process, as well as for a more relaxed attitude to the conversion of greenfield land for development, to help them out of their financial problems.[19] By contrast the much-discussed *numerical* growth of conservation and local environmental interest groups may not have been accompanied by an increase in their *power* to influence rates of development, even if some marginal effects on locational decisions may be detected.[20] There have also been conflicts between counties and districts over the extent and form of green belts. Such disagreements may have increased the power of central Government over green belt definition by allowing it more extensive use of the available reserve powers to mediate conflicts.

Perhaps the central issue for local authorities is the question of definition of detailed green belt boundaries. It is around such decisions that questions of central control versus local discretion, and the public interest view of planning (as expressed by planning policies) and private profit, crystallize. The greatest confusion has arisen over the interpretation of the central Government view that green belt boundaries should be long-term, that is, drawn back far enough to allow for possible development for an unspecified period beyond the time horizon of statutory plans. This had occurred around London in the 1940s and 1950s when detailed boundaries were fixed in the old-style development plans. Translated into the 1980s this appeared an open invitation to housebuilders to speculate in the white land areas which would need to be indicated in local planning documents. However to avoid this, local authorities have preferred to draw tight green belts to retain local control over where and when future land would be released for development. Central Government, aware of the need to keep housebuilding production moving ahead, has disagreed with this approach. If negotiation and persuasion fail, the only way their will can be expressed in *local* policy in plans prepared by districts, is by objecting at a public local inquiry. Distaste for this process led to the production of draft advice in 1982 on the matter,[21] and to a draft Circular on green belts in 1983 which placed clear emphasis on their policy approach.[22] Chapter 4 discusses how local authorities are dealing with these problems of boundary definition and the permanence of green belts.[23] In order to indicate the complexity of the process of boundary definition, and the interests being articulated *within* it, case studies from different parts of the country are presented.

Although green belts may in the past have been defended as an end in themselves, they are only one of a number of measures used by local authorities to restrain development. An understanding of the interaction of locational restraint policies such as green belt with other policies designed to regulate the level of activity and the ordering, phasing and timing of new development, is essential to any realistic assessment of the implementation of restraint.[24] The locally-derived political consensus in the late 1970s was expressed as a need to balance population, housing, and jobs so as to minimize land take for new development. Since 1980 this appears to have shifted to reflect local needs for economic growth, but at the same time it seeks to retain control over the scale of peripheral development for housing. The extent to which restraint policies can be pursued locally in the face of the central Government tendency to intervene, in order to revise locally-derived balances between restraint and new development, is an explicit test of the limits of policy discretion in planning.[25] The 'policy-implementation gap' has been much discussed. Cloke sees policy preparation and policy implementation as obscure stages in the process of planning,[26] and Herington (in a confused exposition) sees the way in which policies emerge locally as 'complex'.[27] Chapters Four and Five penetrate this area to reveal how the major interests concerned with restraint policy exert their influence both on policy formulation and its implementation.

Land Uses Within Green Belts

Inside green belts local authorities are faced with such issues as the management of small-scale change in villages and areas of more scattered residential development, and pressures for the change of use of country houses in large grounds to institutional and office uses. The guidelines on land use control in such situations issued by central Government are general, allowing apparently wide discretion to local authorities and planning inspectors in deciding appeals.[28] The exercise of development control, governed as it is by planning law, functions as a system of administrative discretion and does not lead to an automatic outcome in any particular case. The law itself is an uneasy compromise between attempts to avoid what are seen as burdensome infringements on private property rights, whilst also catering for the public interest (in reality, many public interests), and allowing a defensible level of public participation in decisions.[29] Therefore although decisions must take account of green belt policies in development plans, they also take account of other material considerations. As the scope of material considerations is unclear, a straightforward fit between policy and decisions is unlikely to occur. Because of these factors, and the knowledge that restrictive policies enhance the *rate* of profit realizable on permitted schemes (thus reinforcing pressures for development), local authorities have sought to elaborate 'or codify' development control policies. Special pleading by a wide variety of sectoral interests, all wishing to be excepted from green belt restraint, has occurred during this process. Policies have also sought to achieve wider aims, for example, discrimination in favour of local people in the housing market. Codification, insofar as it makes the criteria for decisions more precise, can reduce the discretion exercisable by central Government and Inspectors. At the same time local authorities may not wish to be *too* precise in the presumptions they lay down in plans, as there may be local political reasons for wishing to approve specific proposals, even in green belt. These tensions and their outcomes are discussed in Chapter 6.

The green belt prescription is only a selective restraint on development. Two important space-extensive uses are present in all green belts. Agriculture, largely exempt from land use planning controls, is seen as one of the most appropriate uses of green belt land. The extraction of minerals is considered acceptable, although there is constant pressure from local parish councils and environmental groups to restrict the extent of operations and the scale of external effects. Under pressure at the urban fringe (the areas of intruded farmland near towns) agricultural interests seek particular outcomes from the operation of planning.[30] How far *planning* decisions can reduce speculative pressures, modify the direct effects of urban proximity, and improve the day-to-day problems of survival for owners and tenants under pressure, is discussed in Chapter 7. Mineral companies are a powerful production interest whose concerns have become well integrated at early stages in the planning process. The methods by which land for mineral production is secured in green belts by the aggregates industry offer a useful insight into the workings of corporate power.[31]

The potential of green belts as a recreation and leisure resource has been a major plank of green belt philosophy, at least since the early proposals of Unwin around London.[32] Agencies such as the Countryside Commission have enthusiastically promoted green belt recreation despite the reservations of the National Farmers Union, other landed interests, and local residents over the conflicts which might occur.[33] Recreation planning, as reflected in levels of commitment and expenditure, is a Cinderella of local government activity. Severe problems of access and management are manifest close to urban areas, but there are few criteria by which to judge the adequacy of provision. Local authorities have taken a number of strategic and local initiatives towards new forms of provision but the 'recreation interest' appears weak in the absence of improved powers over access to private land. Many of the sports and recreations with the greatest potential for growth appear to infringe a strict application of the criteria for green belt development control.[34] Chapter 8 critically evaluates the main arguments for provision and the problems of implementation.

The gap between policy and implementation in recreation provision forms a stark contrast with the close alliance of intention and action in the development control of other uses in green belts. It has long been suggested that landscape, recreation, conservation and agricultural policies should be concerted by special means within defined geographical areas.[35] However, present planning powers do not allow a comprehensive approach to be taken. They need to be complemented by the judicious use of an esoteric mix of powers scattered among countryside legislation. As a result of these shortcomings, a wide variety of *ad hoc* ways of concerting action have emerged. These methods, which may be seen as alternative or complementary *modes of action*, include grant aid, persuasion, demonstration and advice, and attachment to other expenditure programmes with wider aims. These and the advantages and drawbacks of such mechanisms as standing conferences, joint county-district working, and environmental trusts are discussed in Chapter 9.

The basic green belt concept has remained unaltered since 1955. Apparently simple at first glance, it has retained the support of Governments of both political persuasions. Administrations have stressed over the years that new advice or fine tuning was not required lest the idea became devalued or public confidence was lost. More realistically they have eschewed change because of an awareness that the green belt prescription strikes a delicate balance between competing interests in the use of land. To interfere would bring forward howls of protest from vested interests and watchdog organizations many of whom regard green belt as a central symbol of land use planning. This non-interventionist attitude was valid on the part of central Government as long as the logic of its advice on green belts did not have to be argued through to the formal approval of boundaries on the ground. Why then did the Government decide in 1983 that new advice was needed? How did the various interests arrange themselves in the argument preceeding the approval of Circular 14/84 and what effect did they have on its final form? These matters are discussed in Chapter 10.

It is the basic premise of this book that only by investigation of these wide-ranging issues – strategic and local planning, policy-making and implementation, urban and rural planning, and the wealth-creating and appreciative interests in society – that a *balanced* assessment can be made of the relevance of green belt policy to modern conditions. Evaluation of this sort does not suggest that the British predilection for consensus will necessarily provide easy answers, any more than will the slide-rules or micro-computers of economists. It has recently been suggested that to study current struggles over green belt is to indulge the British predilection for fighting yesterday's battles.[36] Is this necessarily true? If we did not have green belts perhaps we would have to invent something similar around which to reach the local accommodations over land use that society suggests are necessary.

Part I. The Emerging Pattern

1. City Sprawl and the Early Response

the preservation of green belts is the very *raison d'être* of town and country planning.

Desmond Heap
TPI Presidential Address 1955

The concept of a clear cut physical boundary between large cities and their surrounding countryside has been central to town planning since its inception. Some have traced it further back. Osborn saw echoes of later town-hinterland ideas in More's '*Utopia*',[1] and others have seen the proclamation of Elizabeth I restricting development outside the gates of the City of London as a precursor of green belts.[2] A healthy debate even arose in the columns of the Town Planning Institute Journal in 1955 as to which part of the Old Testament most clearly put forward the green belt ideal![3] The green belt concept, introduced by Government Circular in 1955 and still in use today, is only one of a number which had been discussed with increasing urgency over the previous fifty years. Each prescription was a creation of its era. Overcrowding in Victorian cities prompted the work of Howard; the recreational needs of London's residents preoccupied Unwin; and the horrors of urban sprawl into the countryside were the mainspring of Abercrombie's response. The first post-1955 green belts outside London were severely circumscribed by the decisions of central Government. Any understanding of the pattern in the 1980s can only be derived from close inspection of the original decisions.

Differing Concepts

Howard's version of the green belt must be seen in the context of his cellular 'social city'. He envisaged a series of small towns separated by narrow belts of open country forming a green background. The green background would be functionally part of the social city containing facilities such as hospitals, children's homes and sports grounds, and also acting as a source of agricultural produce (Figure 1.1). The individual towns would range in size from 30–60,000 people, separated by no more than three kilometres of open

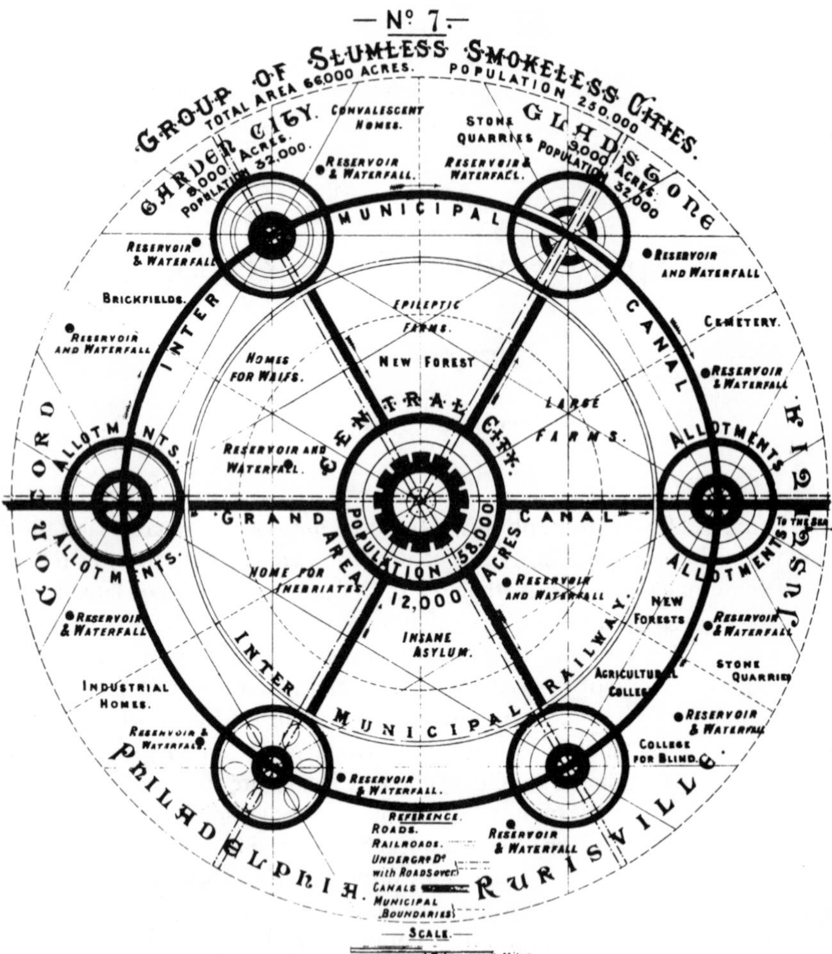

Figure 1.1 Howard's Social City
Source: Hall, P. *The World Cities,* 2nd ed. (Weidenfeld and Nicholson: London, 1984)

country.[4] Howard's proposals allowed for the addition of other towns within the green backcloth with land owned and managed by the towns contained within it. Such ideas applied to South-East England would have resulted in a widespread scatter of small towns a few kilometres apart, and a higher general density of development close to the edges of London than has subsequently occurred. Howard was proposing overall conurbation growth at densities similar to those of subsequent new towns but in the form of small, relatively high density units on a green background.

Concern about the physical spread of London and the need to preserve access to areas for recreation had been expressed in 1901 by the London

Society, and Sir George Pepler had been concerned to introduce a zone of green space into the future planning of London following the model of the Chicago parkway system.[5] Raymond Unwin, who was advisor to the Greater London Regional Plan Committee from 1929, saw the green belt as providing open recreation land on the edges of large urban areas to compensate for the lack of space within city boundaries. In his first report to the Regional Plan Committee he estimated that 250 square kilometres of open space was required on the edges of London to serve its nine million inhabitants.[6] He later proposed that land be purchased by the local authorities to form a 'green girdle', preferably a continuous tract of land three or four kilometres wide, around London (Figure 1.2). This concept thus

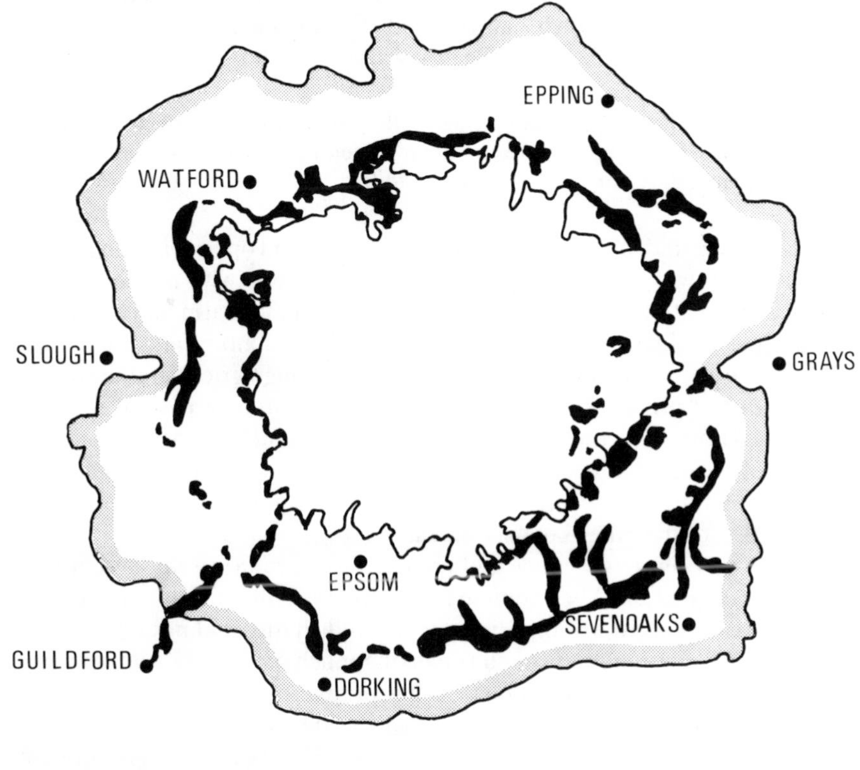

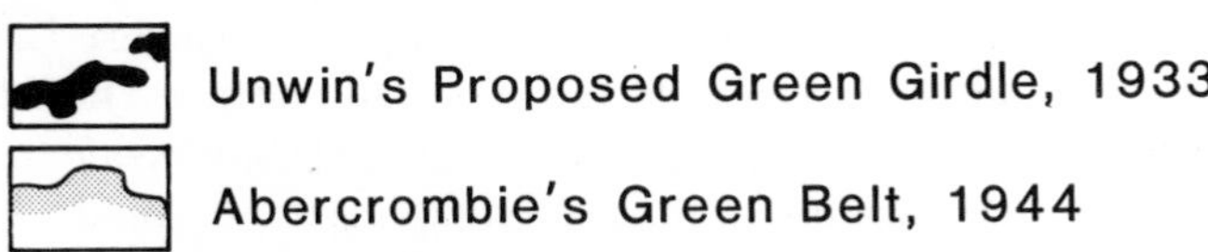

Figure 1.2 Unwin's Green Girdle
Source: Adapted from House of Commons Environment Committee *Green Belt and Land for Housing*, HC 275-II (HMSO: London, 1984), p. 4

defined the extent of green belt in terms of open space and recreation needs.

A further perspective on the green belt concept was supplied by the Council for the Preservation of Rural England (CPRE), and largely reflected the findings of the wartime Scott Report on Land Utilisation in Rural Areas. The CPRE was alarmed by the physical spread of urban areas and ribbon development, which they saw as posing a severe threat to agriculture and the rural landscape. They were opposed to the type of green belt proposed by Howard, which was actively pursued by his disciples, the influential Town and Country Planning Association (TCPA), as they felt it would increase pressures on agriculture and the rural landscape. The Scott Report recommendations saw it as a function of the local planning authority to determine when a town had reached its maximum size and should be limited by a zone of open land. They saw a green belt as:

> a tract of ordinary country, of varying width, round a town . . . where the normal occupations of farming and forestry should be continued so that here, as elsewhere in rural land, the farmer is the normal custodian of the land.[7]

The area would 'naturally' include golf courses and open common land for the use of townspeople. Its extent should be agreed with the Ministry of Agriculture with the object of conserving good quality farmland and woodland which could be both scenically attractive and economically productive. This concept thus stressed the primacy of retaining agricultural use of the belt within a private custodial framework guaranteeing natural resource quality. At the same time it was realized there would be a special duality of interest between the urban dweller and the farmer, each of whom might need to modify any claims to the exclusive enjoyment of the land in recognition of the other's expectations.

These varying perspectives and approaches were taken up, and at least partly reconciled, by Abercrombie in his important Greater London Plan of 1945.[8] According to Thomas he was inspired by the findings of the Scott Committee.[9] Certainly, through traversing much of London's urban fringe by motor car with his assistants during preparation of the Plan, he was alarmed by the visual erosion of the countryside and what he saw as urban exploitation through development pressures. He argued for development on a green background, proposing a *family* of green belts (Figure 1.3). The first, a 'cordon sanitaire' (The Green Belt Ring) would surround the City to a depth of 10–16 kilometres to 'separate the threatened countryside from the threatening town'. This was the stopper. Beyond this there would be 'lesser girdles' for existing and new towns in the Outer Country Ring. These would be two or three kilometres wide with much of the land in recreation use. The third type of green belt would protect the setting and approaches to 'scenic areas', such as the Chilterns and North Downs, by restricting development

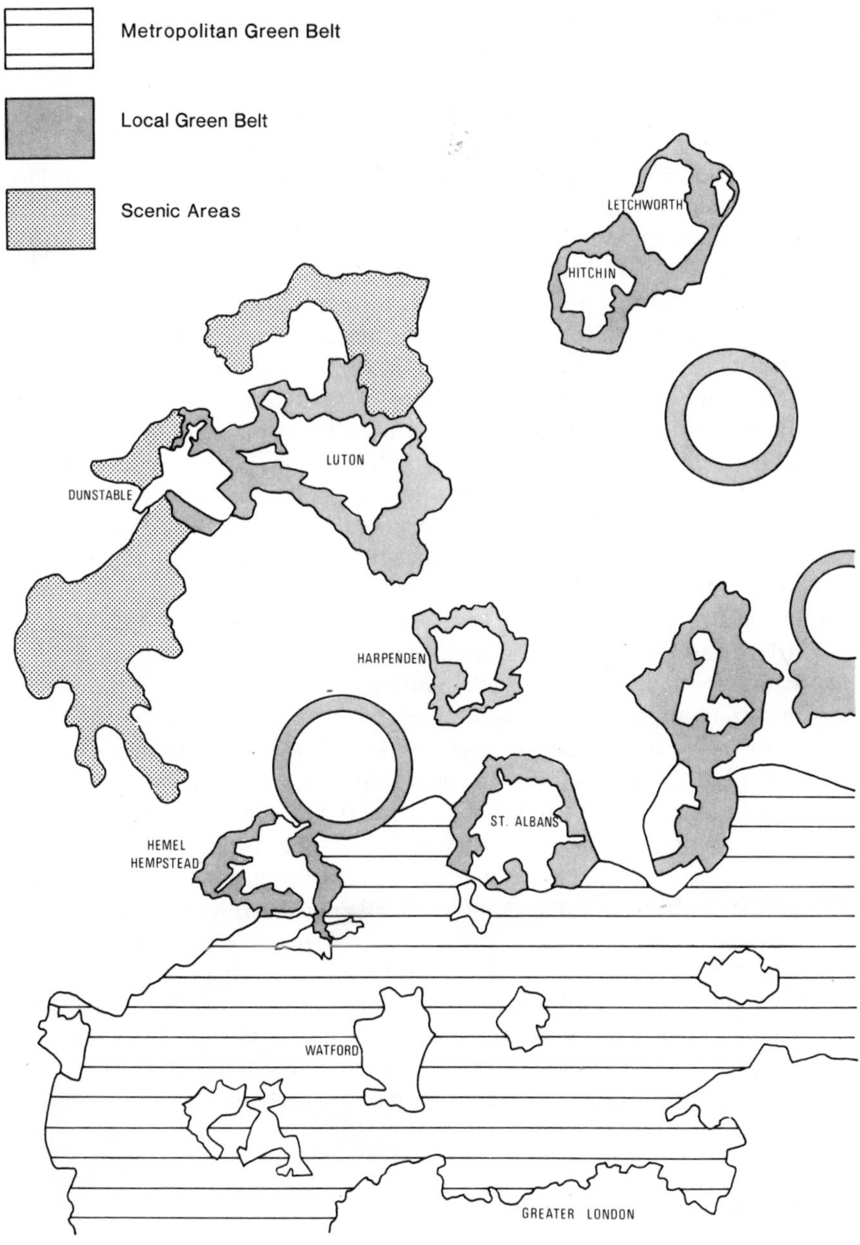

Figure 1.3 Abercrombie's London Region Green Belts
Source: Adapted from Abercrombie, P. *Greater London Plan: 1944*, (Master Plan, HMSO: London, 1945)

on their foothills and immediate surroundings. The three types of belt were to form parts of a park system with 14 components beginning with the urban playground and reaching to 'the threshold of Rural England'. The green background idea was repeated in the West Midlands where an independent group (the West Midlands Study Group) in their proposals *Conurbation* recommended a stop line and a green setting for the main urban areas. The 'green setting' would act as a separating and shaping device, as well as providing for recreation space. This was feasible at the time (the late 1940s), as over half of the area of the conurbation was open land.

The concept of the green belt ring was closest to that propounded by the CPRE and the Scott Report, which was unsurprising as Abercrombie was Chairman of CPRE at the time. He was motivated by a concern to shape the form of the urban area by the control of development. The green belt ring was part of a strategy to disperse over 600,000 people from the congested London County Council area, and 415,000 from the rest of the built-up area of London. The concept not only achieved an acceptable compromise between the various proponents of new city forms, but also between the opposing political groups involved; the shire counties broadly represented private land-owning interests, the countryside protectionists, and the Fabian–Socialist urban reform lobby, as represented by the TCPA.[10]

Early ideas about the green belt thus had a variety of antecedents and motives. Howard was trying to maximize accessibility and environmental quality simultaneously *in a situation of growth* at the end of the Victorian era. Unwin's proposals can be traced back to Neville Chamberlain's tenure as Minister of Health and his chairmanship of a Committee set up to deal with the problems of unhealthy urban areas. Abercrombie saw the need for a clear separation of town and country as a concomitant of his professed broad objectives for planning – beauty, health and convenience. He was, in the Greater London Plan, attempting to redistribute activities by decentralization *assuming no growth in overall population*. The cordon sanitaire fitted into the Scott Report theme of the protection of agricultural land in the national interest, and the view that 'every acre mattered'. In terms of method the ideas were physical designs or blueprints specifying desired outcomes. The green belt concept therefore fitted well into the language of the time representing an apparently simple idea, rich in promise and easy to grasp.

Green Belt Land Purchases

The earliest example of green belt land purchase on a large scale was associated with the founding of Letchworth Garden City, in line with Howard's principles, in 1909. An area in excess of 500 hectares situated between Hitchin and Baldock in Hertfordshire was purchased by the Letchworth Garden City Corporation with a view to forming a green backcloth and to yield produce for the town. This has remained unintruded upon to the present day and, in the late 1970s, was added to by further purchases.

The idea of preserving rural land from development by purchase and of providing for the recreation needs of urban dwellers, took firm hold among local authorities in the 1930s. The need for purchase was occasioned by the compensation position in planning schemes submitted under the 1932 Town and Country Planning Act. Compensation was payable on open land shown on 1932 Act maps for preservation at full market value. Early schemes had attempted to circumvent the problem by zoning land at one dwelling per four or eight hectares or, as in Worcestershire,[11] delineating areas of 'Great Landscape Value'. But the position was far from satisfactory. In 1931, at the request of the Greater London Regional Planning Committee, the London County Council convened a meeting to discuss the possibility of acquiring land to preserve it from development and for recreation use. However, financial problems restricted activity until 1935 when the London County Council obtained £2 million from the Government towards a scheme to 'provide a reserve supply of public open space lands, not necessarily continuous, but readily accessible to Londoners'.[12] This was the Unwin concept in practice. London County Council made grants to adjoining county and urban district councils of up to 50 per cent of acquisition costs. This scheme complemented the earlier efforts of Middlesex County Council who, in the early 1930s, had assisted some 15 urban and rural districts to acquire 'regional open spaces'.[13]

The London County Council Scheme was most active in the early years. By mid-1936 some 7,300 hectares of land had been purchased or was in the process of purchase. Land was acquired for its recreation value and natural beauty as well as its position in relation to other purchases, the aim being to join up the areas acquired to form a belt. The need to protect the land purchased from possible future development more effectively led to the 1938 Green Belt (London and Home Counties) Act.[14] Its objectives were to preserve land in and around London from 'industrial or building development' in order to enhance the amenities of London. These were to be achieved by:

1. declaratory deeds whereby a private owner, local authority or parish council could covenant to restrict the uses of land to those listed in the Act (basically recreation or agriculture); and
2. acquisition of land by purchase, gift, lease or exchange, but not by compulsory purchase.

Once so reserved such land was known as 'Green Belt Land' and specific permission of the Minister was required for its release for development. By 1956 some 10,731 hectares of Green Belt Land existed in London and the Home Counties.[15] Some of this land was outside green belts as defined in subsequent statutory development plans (for example land in Aylesbury, and at Brill Hill in Buckinghamshire).

Other large cities were pursuing similar courses. Following the work of a sub-regional advisory body, the Midland Joint Town Planning Council, set up in 1923, the concept of reserving some peripheral land from development was accepted by the Birmingham City Council. This was prompted by the acquisition of land in the Lickey and Waseley Hills to the south west of the City by Cadbury Bros Ltd. Cadbury's had set up a Trust in 1935 to purchase land for preservation as Green Belt. Apart from land directly purchased by the Trust, other areas were transferred to the City with covenants, and money for the purchase of Green Belt Land was also given to the City. Some 282 hectares were purchased at this time by these means.[16] On 1 June 1938, Sheffield City Council approved a 'Green Belt Scheme' designed to 'secure the permanent preservation of the City's unique surroundings'. The scheme, according to a booklet produced by the CPRE Sheffield and Peak District Branch in 1945,[17] was a logical extension of the policy of retaining for public enjoyment the special features of the Sheffield landscape. The scheme had

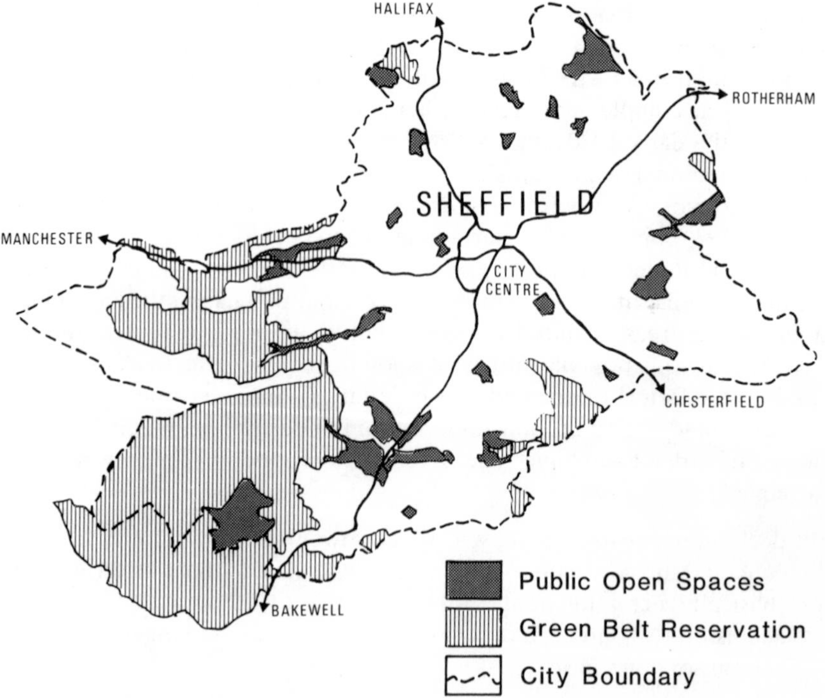

Figure 1.4 The Sheffield Green Belt Scheme
Source: Adapted from Council for the Preservation of Rural England Sheffield and Peak District Branch *Sheffield's Green Belt* (CPRE: Sheffield, 1945), p. 2.

recreation and landscape aims. The land preserved would provide 'a satisfying and varied background for the leisure time of a great industrial population engaged for the most part in work which involved complete exclusion from nature amid surroundings of noise, smoke and grime'. Most of the Green Belt (1895 hectares in 1938) was in the south west of the City including the Don, Rivelin, Loxley and Porter Valleys running from what was to become the Peak District National Park. Much of the land was given to the City by its eminent citizens and other owners including an ex-mayor Alderman Graves, a Mr. Walter Hall, Sir John Bingham, and the Duke of Norfolk. Some was purchased following public subscription and 405 hectares were acquired through the auspices of the National Trust (Figure 1.4). Around Oxford some 200 hectares of land were acquired prior to 1939 by the Oxford Preservation Trust, and covenants were made and understandings reached with other owners to keep land open. The land represented 'key sites to be saved from housing development' and areas which were important parts of the visual setting of the City.[18] These types of purchase were common among the large and powerful provincial authorities in the 1930s and were made possible by low agricultural land values consequent upon the agricultural depression. A mixture of civic pride and a wish to provide healthy open air surroundings for the working population motivated some authorities (as in Sheffield, Manchester and Leeds); the urge to preserve attractive landscape areas near to cities and to halt sprawl spurred others to action (as around London and Oxford).

The 1955 Circular

Circular 42 of 1955 *Green Belts* apparently represented an extension of the principle involved in the acceptance in 1946 by the Government of the Abercrombie principles for the planning of London. It was made possible by the provisions of the 1947 Town and Country Planning Act. The Act comprised three important elements in a system designed to make decisions on the use of land in the public interest. The first was nationalization of the right of landowners to develop land as they saw fit. Compensation was to be paid on a once for all basis for lost development rights from a £300 million fund set up for the purpose. Second, local authorities, who were charged with operating the system, were obliged to prepare development plans looking 20 years ahead. These would show the manner in which land in their areas was to be used, which areas were to be developed for housing or industry, and which were to be kept for agriculture or open space. The third element was a set of rules determining when owners proposing development would need to apply for planning permission. The system would operate by local authority council committees making decisions on proposals, guided by the advice of their planners, and having regard to the provisions of the plans they had drawn up. Although characterized by the wide discretion accorded at local level, the system incorporated a number of checks and balances from the outset. Landowners, for example, had a right to have their objections heard before development plans were finalized. Persons refused planning permission could appeal to the Minister and have the material facts of the case re-examined by an Inspector. The Act was a broad enabling power, and to assist in securing consistency in the operation of the system in the national interest, circulars giving information on how policy should be interpreted at local level were issued from time to time.

The compensation provisions were of prime importance to green belts.[19] Landowners were to be compensated for lost development value as it existed in 1948, and in order to establish a right to compensation a claim had to be registered with a body known as the Central Land Board. The total to be paid out was limited to £300 million and owners were to receive whatever proportion of their established 1948 development value the fund would allow. At the same time increases in development value consequent on planning approval were to go to the government by way of a Development Charge. However the totality of the system was compromised by the Town and Country Planning Acts of 1953 and 1954 which removed the Development Charge and restricted compensation to cases where planning permission had been refused. Most importantly, compensation for refusals was frozen at 1948 prices. As the Government paid compensation, this made it possible to include green belts in development plans at no direct cost to local authorities.

Green Belts were also made feasible by attitudes to urban policy in the early years of post-war reconstruction. The Barlow Commission had recommended the urgent need for dispersal (but in the case of London only) and the New Towns Act had been passed in 1946. In assessing their post-war housing needs the local authorities were contemplating, without exception, ambitious public-sector programmes which, because of land purchasing policies, would involve a new wave of peripheral extensions. The London out-county estates – Borehamwood, Oxley, Harold Hill and Debden – were vivid examples of such opportunistic purchasing and had already used some of the land in the proposed Abercrombie Green Belt. Applications for the removal of covenants under the 1938 Act were being received by the Minister.[20] In response Ministry officials prepared a map of the suggested London Green Belt as a guide to local authorities in the area in the preparation of their development plans.

The arrival of a Conservative Government in 1951 saw approval of the Town Development Act in 1952, designed to speed the process of accommodation of overspill. Under this Act agreements were to be made between the major exporting authorities (London, Birmingham, Liverpool) and receiving authorities whereby the latter purchased land, built houses, and laid out industrial sites using financial assistance from the Government and exporting authorities. However progress in concluding agreements was extremely slow despite the urgency of the Macmillan housing drive which led to 340,000 new houses being constructed in 1954.

Outside the South East similar problems of overcrowding and housing shortage were evident. In 1952 Sheffield City Council estimated that 49,000 new houses would be needed in a twenty year period. Spurning an offer by Derbyshire to take overspill, Sheffield promoted a private bill in Parliament to annexe part of the West Riding of Yorkshire. When this was unsuccessful they turned to the land suggested as Green Belt in the 1930s,[21] approval for its compulsory purchase being sought from the Ministry. The CPRE booklet had foreseen this situation, warning 'It would be a blow to the City's prestige if the . . . (Green Belt) . . . scheme were abandoned and sacrificed'.[22] Few local authorities outside London saw any need to halt the 'normal' processes of peripheral expansion at this time.

The immediate precursor of the Circular was the threat of a wave of peripheral urban development on a scale rivalling that of the 1930s. Over the 1952–4 period a considerable upsurge in private housebuilding was experienced, with private developers carrying out almost half of the building by 1955. The TCPA, concerned by the scale and location of this new development, conducted a vigorous lobby of Government. In a paper entitled *Dispersal: A Call for Action*, sent to the Minister in March 1955, they estimated the overspill needs of the major conurbations to 1971 as follows: London 472,100, Birmingham 203,600, Manchester 226,650, and Liverpool 112,200 dwellings.[23] In a survey conducted among planning officers it was noted that ribbon development had re-emerged as a significant problem,[24] and Ian Nairn's *Outrage* provided vivid illustration of the sterility of 'subtopia' and the desecration of the countryside as well as the town.[25] The Ministry of Housing and Local Governments' (MHLG) Report of 1955 noted that County Boroughs were seeking an increase in the area of their jurisdictions of 25 per cent to provide more land for housing, and were proposing frequent boundary extensions to make this possible.[26] Watson reports further inroads into the Worcestershire 'Green Belt' in the 1952–4 period.[27]

On 26 April 1955, Duncan Sandys made his statement inviting local authorities to submit green belt proposals:

> I am convinced that for the well-being of our people and for the preservation of the countryside, we have a clear duty to do all we can to prevent the further unrestricted sprawl of the great cities.
>
> The development plans submitted by the local planning authorities for the Home Counties provide for a Green Belt, some seven to ten miles deep, all around the built-up area of Greater London . . . These proposals, if strictly adhered to, should prove most effective. For this the authorities in the Home Counties deserve much credit.
>
> In other parts of the country, certain planning authorities are endeavouring, by administrative action, to restrict further building development around the larger

> urban areas. But I regret that nowhere has any formal green belt as yet been proposed. I am accordingly asking all planning authorities concerned to give this matter further consideration, with a view to submitting to me proposals for the creation of clearly defined green belts, wherever this is appropriate.[28]

Five days later at a speech in Welwyn Garden City, the Minister stated a wish to see green belts around not only big cities but around all towns, linked with the dispersal of population from 'overcrowded places'.[29] At the TCPA Annual Meeting a few weeks later he requested the Association's advice on the functions and form of the green belt provisions. F. J. Osborn immediately set up a Green Belt Committee of the TCPA to this end.

Circular 42/55 in August asked planning authorities outside London to consider establishing clearly defined green belts, where desirable, in order:

a) to check the further growth of a large built up area;
b) to prevent neighbouring towns from merging into one another; and
c) to preserve the special character of a town.

A green belt should be several miles wide so as to ensure an appreciable rural zone all around the built-up area concerned. Within green belts there would be severe restrictions on development. Approval would not be given, except in very special circumstances, for the construction of new buildings or for the change of use of existing buildings for purposes other than agriculture, sport, cemeteries, institutions standing in extensive grounds, or other uses appropriate to a rural area. Within towns and villages in a green belt 'strictly limited' infilling and rounding off would be allowed but such settlements should not be allowed to expand further. In particular, within urban areas thus defined, every effort should be made to prevent further building for industrial or commercial purposes since if this was allowed, further demands for the release of housing land would occur. The Circular made clear that green belts were to be justified and defined as part of *urban* policies; all three basic objectives looked inwards towards the town.[30] There was no mention of amenity or recreational criteria, and nothing to suggest the encouragement of agriculture or other positive uses of the land so protected.

The green belt proposals met widespread acclaim. Desmond Heap in his presidential address to the Town Planning Institute in 1955 adjudged green belts one of the fundamentals of planning control. He went on to say:

> There should be a clear-cut line where the pavement ends and the green fields begin. Such a state of affairs is . . . of the very essence of good town and country planning and is, moreover, one of the things by which its success or failure is most likely to be judged by popular opinion

adding prosaically:

> the preservation of green belts is . . . the very *raison d'être* of town and country planning.[31]

But Mandelker has noted that the Circular was issued by the Minister against the advice of his senior civil servants.[32] Dame Evelyn Sharp, the Ministry's Permanent Secretary at the time, echoed this in discussion of Heap's presidential paper, stating that it was easy to preserve green belts but the problem was where was the development to be? The implication of a green belt was decentralization and development in the areas beyond.[33] Ministry officials had been involved in seemingly endless negotiation with local authorities on overspill and it seemed that 'the game would never be worth the candle'. Silkin noted the limitations of the Circular in his criticism that its major regional functions had been omitted.[34] It is significant that on the day of Sandys' first parliamentary statement he also announced increased financial assistance to receiving authorities under the Town Development Act.

The TCPA pronounced: 'one great nation has officially adopted one of the major principles of the garden city idea formulated by Sir Ebenezer Howard in 1898'.[35] Of course this was not the case, as the limited 'stopper' conception outlined by Sandys differed in virtually all respects but name from that put forward by Howard. However, despite its narrow definition, and possibly due to the emotive force of the very term 'green belt', the concept was immediately popular with county councils seeking to protect themselves from the expansionist intentions of urban districts. In 1957 Ernest Doubleday, Hertfordshire's County Planner noted, 'probably no planning circular and all that it implies has ever been so popular with the public. The idea has caught on and is supported by people of all shades of public interest'.[36] The County Planning Officer for Middlesex noted 'The very expression Green Belt sounds like something an ordinary man may find it worthwhile to be interested in who may find no appeal whatever in the "Distribution of Industrial Population" or "Decentralisation" . . . Green Belt has a natural faculty for engendering support'.[37]

At the end of 1956 Wilfred Burns ventured the view that there was no accepted definition, even among professional planners, of what a green belt was. He saw it as 'simply a technique to show the limits for town growth'.[38] A green belt should have a line for a boundary which is respected by all. The line would divide the rural areas from those required for urban development. It should be unassailable and demonstrably logical so that fringe incursions would be accepted as just as impossible as attempting to locate pockets of development in the middle of the green belt area. For example green wedges, open spaces, and allotments penetrating urban areas need not necessarily be in the green belt to ensure their protection; they must defend themselves on their own basis of need.

Others took different views. The TCPA's 1956 Memorandum to the Minister proposed that the green belt should have twin purposes, to limit the outward extension of a town, and to preserve a rural area in which the town dweller could enjoy the 'pleasures' of the countryside.[39] Lord Chorley, Chairman of the CPRE, saw the green belt as central to issues of amenities and planning. It had been arrived at 'by an historical process in which amenities have been the *leitmotif*'.[40] Herein lies the emergence of the division between central Government's utilitarian view of the green belt as an urban stopper and the populist views of the green belt as either a dual-purpose instrument to halt urban sprawl and protect agriculture, or the more urban idea of providing for recreation, and amenity. The distinction has loomed particularly large because, to become effective, the Sandys conception required incorporation into statutory development plans and consequent approval by Government. Only the three justifications in Circular 42/55 could be used to ensure such admission and there was wide scope for Government to interpret whether green belt was needed in a particular form at a particular time.

Green Belts and Development Plans

An important duty under the 1947 Town and Country Planning Act was the *requirement* placed on planning authorities (counties and county boroughs) to submit a development plan to the Minister for approval. This plan was a written statement, and a map (in the case of a county at one inch to the mile scale) 'indicating the manner in which the local planning authority propose that land in their area should be used'. Prior to 1955 the majority of counties had submitted their first county development plans, termed by the polemicists 'the new Doomsday Books of Britain', and the process of checking against the regulations and the holding of public inquiries was underway. Prior to the 1955 Circular the Home Counties (Kent, Surrey, Buckinghamshire, Berkshire, Hertfordshire, Middlesex and Essex) had submitted Green Belt proposals modelled on those of Abercrombie. Following considerable detailed work by Ministry planners to amend boundaries, especially the inner boundaries bordering London, these had been approved as a basis for development control.

In his parliamentary announcement, and in Circular 42/55, the Minister indicated that local authorities seeking formal approval to define green belts were first to submit to the Ministry a 'sketch plan'. These plans were to indicate the approximate boundaries of proposed green belts. Local authorities, before submitting such proposals, were first to consult with neighbouring authorities and discuss the proposals with the Ministry. This procedure was to act as a holding operation. If the Ministry, following examination of a proposal, considered it to be soundly based (that is, in apparent accord with Circular 42/55 guidance) the authority could proceed to put forward a formal proposal for an amendment of the development plan.

During 1956 planners were experiencing a number of difficulties in defining rules for drawing green belt boundaries and green belt insets around villages, and in deciding on the criteria to be applied in development control. In response to this, Circular 50/57 explained how sketch plans should be adapted and detailed for inclusion in development plans. Submissions were to take the form of a map showing the boundaries on an Ordnance Survey base at a scale of one or two and a half inches to the mile, together with a justification for the establishment of the green belt forming part of the Written Statement of the Amended development plan. The Statement was therefore to include the reasons, chosen from those in Circular 42/55, for defining the belt, the types of development the authority would permit within the green belt, development control criteria for areas of 'white land', and policies for settlements inside the green belt where infilling, rounding off or other forms of development would normally be permitted.[41]

This second Circular contained a number of important elaborations on the advice of 1955. It advised that the inner boundary of the green belt should mark 'a *long-term* boundary for development'. The term 'white land' was introduced and explained:

> There may be some pockets of land, between the town and the Green Belt, which are not to be developed within the present Plan period but which could be developed later without prejudice to the Green Belt. It would be misleading to allocate such areas now, but to include them in the Green Belt for the time being might give rise to difficulties and undermine public confidence in the Green Belt at a later date if it were then decided to allocate the land for development. Such areas may well be left as pockets of 'white land'. They are then bound to be especially attractive to developers and it will be desirable to set out in the Written Statement the authority's policy for such areas in order to make it clear that they are not available for development at the present time.[42]

In the Appendix listing draft paragraphs for insertion in amended plans, it was suggested that white land might be covered by the phrase, 'these areas may later be allocated to meet demands for development beyond the present period of the Plan. Meanwhile the authority will permit only such development there as would be appropriate in the neighbouring Green Belt'. In addition local authorities were invited to include references to the attention to be paid to visual amenity in considering proposals in the green belt, or conspicuous from it. The position as regards industrial buildings remained firm. The suggested wording for settlements within the green belt read 'No new industrial buildings will be permitted in any of the settlements in the Green Belt'.[43]

The issue of the 1955 Circular led to a rapid scramble to assemble sketch plans and by the end of 1955, only eight months later, nearly twenty sketch plans had been submitted. They included proposals for:

1. a large swathe of land in South Lancashire from Rochdale in the east to Southport in the West;
2. land on the Wirral, and South of Manchester in Cheshire;

3. a seven to twelve kilometre Belt around Birmingham and Coventry, and separating the two towns;
4. an area separating Derby and Nottingham;
5. a wide Green Belt around Southampton, and
6. areas in the northern part of Derbyshire, and around Bristol and Sheffield.

Less well-known proposals were made for:

7. a comprehensive system of Green Belts throughout County Durham;
8. Green Belts north and south of the Tees in the Middlesborough–Stockton area, and
9. a Green Belt around Scarborough.

This wave of submissions clearly alarmed the Ministry who were at pains to point out in their 1957 Report the *special circumstances* in which green belts were appropriate. Clearly worried at the implications of the Sandys brainwave, the Report states:

> the establishment of a green belt is a step which calls for most careful deliberation. The strict control that needs to be exercised in green belt areas . . . cannot be justified except where the position *urgently* demands it, that is, in the *limited number of cases* falling within the three categories . . . (in Circular 42/55).
>
> Elsewhere, around smaller towns and in the countryside as a whole, it will be the duty of local planning authorities to prevent wasteful and sporadic development, but this task can be carried out without the need for a green belt. . . It is important that selection and definition should be carried out to avoid possible amendments to what are thought to be permanent features of a development plan.[44] (Author's emphases).

As a result the Ministry deferred approval of some sketch plans, and altered the extent of others before allowing them to go forward to the formal stage. Some were turned down altogether. In 1956 the flood continued with proposals for further parts of the Bristol Green Belt, for Oxford, a wide range of extensions (over 1600 square kilometres) to the London Green Belt already provisionally approved by the Minister, North Staffordshire, additional areas around Derby and Nottingham (including parts of the Derbyshire–Nottinghamshire coalfield), Cambridge, York, Doncaster and North Tyneside.[45] In 1957 notable proposals included an extensive system of Belts on the Hampshire Coast; Green Belts around a number of further towns in Essex; around Chester linking with the Wirral proposal; and parts of the West Riding of Yorkshire between Leeds, Barnsley and Dewsbury. In 1958 the full West Riding proposals were submitted, Wiltshire proposed Green Belts around Salisbury and Swindon, and additions were proposed around Trowbridge and Bradford-on-Avon forming part of the Bristol –Bath Green Belt.

It was only at the end of 1960 that the flood began to abate with proposals from Bedfordshire, Kent, Gloucestershire, and Berkshire; and later for Flintshire (part of the Chester Green Belt), and from East Sussex, for a Green Belt adjacent to Crawley. The Ministry was able to announce in 1961 that from August 1955 to December 1960 some sixty-nine sketch plans had been received, including six for extensions to the London Green Belt (see Table 1.1). Preliminary decisions had been issued on all but eight proposals by this time.

Table 1.1 Land Subject to Green Belt Policies 1963

Location	*Square kilometres*	*Local authorities involved*
Birmingham–Coventry	2,022	8
Bristol–Bath	632	3
Cambridge	141	1
Cheltenham–Gloucester	54	1
Hampshire South Coast	973	1
Merseyside–Manchester	973	6
London	2,166	6
London Extensions	3,064	6
North Tyneside	353	1
Nottingham–Derby	640	2
Oxford	343	3
South Tyneside	36	1
Sunderland	51	1
Durham City	31	1
Stoke-on-Trent	410	3
West Riding of Yorkshire	2,048	7
Wirral–Chester	282	2
York	246	4
Total	14,465	57

Sources: Adapted from MHLG *Report of the Ministry of Housing and Local Government*, 1963. Cmnd. 1976, table 11, pp. 44–5; MHLG *Handbook of Statistics 1967* (HMSO; London, 1968) table 29, pp. 22–3.

The Ministry Decisions

Following its declared intentions to be strict in interpreting the Circular 42/55 criteria, the Ministry pruned, and in some cases turned down the proposals. Those turned down before the end of 1960 were for Salisbury, Swindon, Scarborough, Teesside, and the Flintshire proposals west of Chester. The East Sussex proposals were turned down in 1963, following a public inquiry which established that none of the Circular 42/55 justifications applied, but only after their acceptance at sketch plan stage. The Durham proposals were severely pruned, and a significant part of the Essex proposals rejected (see Figure 1.5).

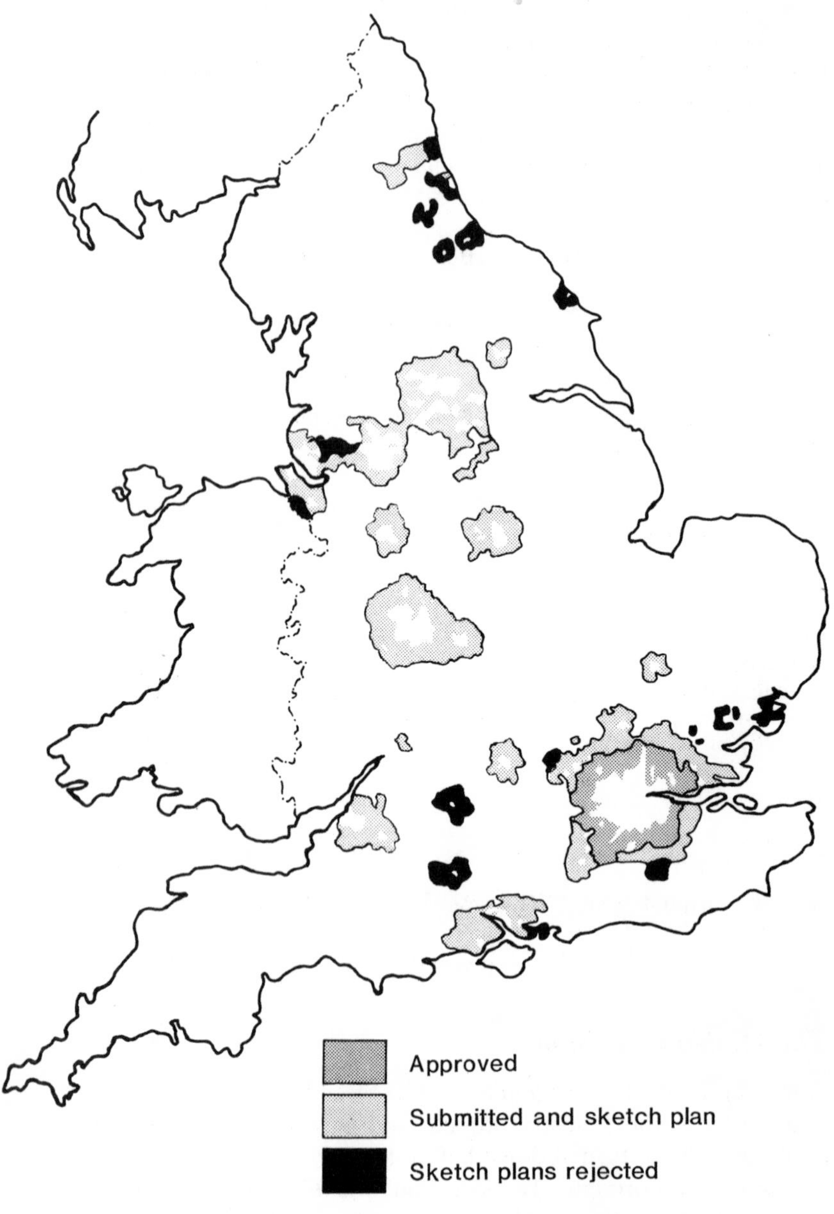

Figure 1.5 Green Belt Plans Submitted 1955–62

The decisions on this first round of bids appear to reflect five important criteria:

1. *green belts should not apply to 'small' towns.* Despite the Sandys pronouncements, on this basis the Ministry accepted sketch plans for additions contiguous with the approved London Green Belt in Essex but rejected the idea of a number of small Green Belts around Witham, Chelmsford, Braintree, Colchester, and the coastal towns of Clacton, Frinton, Walton on the Naze and Harwich. Also turned down was the 'fairly extensive' system of Green Belts surrounding towns in County Durham, but it was suggested there might be a case for some 'pieces' of Green Belt around Durham, and a narrow strip of land to separate Easington from Peterlee New Town. This latter would be under the 'separating' justification in Circular 42/55. The refusal to allow the North Riding (Yorkshire) County Council to proceed with the Scarborough proposal also falls under this heading.
2. *green belts are unnecessary where growth pressures are not strong.* This reason, often related to size of town (above), suggests that a judgement was made as to whether development pressures were too strong or not to be dealt with by normal (that is, non-green belt) restraint policies. Thus in the cases of Salisbury and Swindon it was stated that 'the firm application of normal planning controls' was sufficient to check their growth. In the case of the Cheshire proposal it was not considered that areas to the south and east of Chester were 'seriously threatened with development'. In Teesside the Ministry considered that the 'extent of development' north of the river did not call for a Green Belt and, although the built-up area to the south was larger, the application of Green Belt would be premature.
3. *green belts are inappropriate where there is uncertainty over the pattern of future development.* This relates to the concern over permanence; green belts should not be reviewed frequently as this would lead to loss of public confidence and defeat their objectives. Because of the extent of future coal working, the possibility of industrial development, and the likely need for population relocation, the proposed North Tyneside Green Belt was cut back to an area north west of Newcastle. The central part of the proposed Lancashire Green Belt around St Helens was deleted 'until the industrial prospects of the area as a whole could be seen more clearly'.
4. *green belts should not be too large for the purpose they are intended to serve.* Under this criterion the Ministry recommended reductions to the 'extensive' area comprising the Hampshire Coast Green Belt. The agreed purposes of the Belt were to prevent the coastal towns from spreading too far inland, and to keep the main built-up areas separate from each other. The proposed Belt, covering the Southampton–Portsmouth–Bournemouth area was reduced by omitting areas on the northern edge

in the Havant area, and between the Southampton boundary and the River Hamble. In the case of a proposed 35,600 hectare extension to the London Green Belt in Buckinghamshire the Ministry deleted a proposed area in the Oxford plain beyond the Chilterns as far as Aylesbury but extended the Belt west of High Wycombe.

5. *there should be room left for some increases in population in towns surrounded by green belt.* Here, for example, in approving the submission of the Buckinghamshire extension in 1960, the Ministry stated there was room for a further 40–50,000 people in the newly-surrounded towns of Amersham, Beaconsfield, Chesham and Marlow. In the case of High Wycombe 'considerable room' for expansion (over 800 hectares) had been left.[46] In approving further progress on the sketch plan for the Bristol–Bath Green Belt the Ministry suggested that greater provision for the development of Avonmouth should be allowed for in the formal plan. It was also noted, in the 1960 Ministry Annual Report, that within the area enclosed by the proposed eight kilometre-wide Green Belt surrounding Oxford there was room for a population increase of 32,000 to 1971.

These early decisions set the pattern for green belt restraint which has endured to the present day. The concept of an urban-oriented checking or stopping device was thus formalized. As Henry Brooke, Sandys successor, stated in 1961:

> The very essence of a green belt is that it is a stopper. It may not all be very beautiful and it may not all be very green, but without it the town would never stop, and that is the case for preserving the circles of land around the town.[47]

One reason, or a different combination of the three Circular 42/55 reasons, was considered relevant for their establishment in each case. Not all the areas were belts in the sense of continuous tracts of land completely surrounding urban areas. Where belts existed they were of differing width to suit local circumstances. Thus the London Green Belt as agreed prior to 1955 was 10–15 kilometres wide and the proposed extensions would, if approved, result in a 20–25 kilometre Belt. In the West Midlands the Belt was 10–15 kilometres wide, around Bristol and Oxford 8 kilometres, and around Cambridge 3–5 kilometres. The best example of a separating Green Belt or green barrier was that for Cheltenham–Gloucester, a narrow band of land covering 54 square kilometres between the two towns. Whilst the primary aim of the London Green Belt was to check the growth of the built-up area it was also, in places, to prevent the coalescence of towns within the Belt. A good example of a combination of reasons is the West Riding (Yorkshire) Green Belt, the second largest area subject to green belt controls in 1960. The reasons were, to limit the outward spread of the West Riding conurbation; to prevent further coalescence of the towns comprising it; and to protect the area of land between the conurbation and Sheffield, Rotherham and Doncaster. The Green Belts around Oxford and Cambridge were to preserve the special character of those towns but the early Belt around Chester was to prevent coalescence with towns to the north.

The process of submission, initial decision, and formal incorporation into development plans was however proving time-consuming. The pattern of local government organization with large numbers of County and Municipal Boroughs involved meant that processes of consultation were lengthy in what was a new endeavour for many. By the end of 1962 some eight local authorities had formally submitted parts of the West Riding Belt to the Minister. The scale of the problem in the West Riding was daunting with 89 local authorities, including 11 County Boroughs, potentially involved, Bates describes the process whereby the Technical Sub-Committee of the West Riding Joint Advisory Committee in 1957 reached a wide degree of agreement on land requirements for the future, including agreements with York, Leeds, Wakefield and Doncaster on their expansion needs and possible boundary revisions. Having identified the specific land needed for ten years ahead they then allowed for further 'elbow room' before defining and submitting Green Belt boundaries. The West Riding thus had a 'loose' Green Belt, as opposed to the rather tighter 'fit' around London. Bates described it this way:

> . . . unless the Green Belt is . . . properly measured and fitted to allow for proper growth it cannot be worn without constant pain and chafing . . . we have tried to make sure . . . our customers get a good fit.[48]

In hindsight this approach seems to have worked well in the circumstances of the West Yorkshire Conurbation. Succeeding years saw far less wrangling and soul searching over land needs and overspill than in the other major conurbations.

Thus by the end of 1962, around 14,600 square kilometres of the country was subject to green belt policies. Although 20 of the 56 authorities involved had submitted formal amendments to their development plans it was, in many cases, to be over ten years before full confirmation was achieved. Large tracts of green belt were to be operated for a quarter of a century on what was effectively an interim basis. Three categories of green belt were to be found in England by 1962. They were:

1. *approved green belt;* green belts which were contained in an approved development plan (the London Green Belt);
2. *formally submitted green belt* (the largest category); these were proposals included in a development plan which had been submitted to the Minister but which had not yet been approved (for example the extensions to the London Green Belt and the Green Belt in the West Midlands); and
3. *sketch plan green belt;* proposals which had been approved in principle as

the basis for formal submission and in which green belt policies operated with the tacit approval of the Minister (for example the North Staffordshire and Nottingham–Derby Green Belts) (see Figure 1.6).

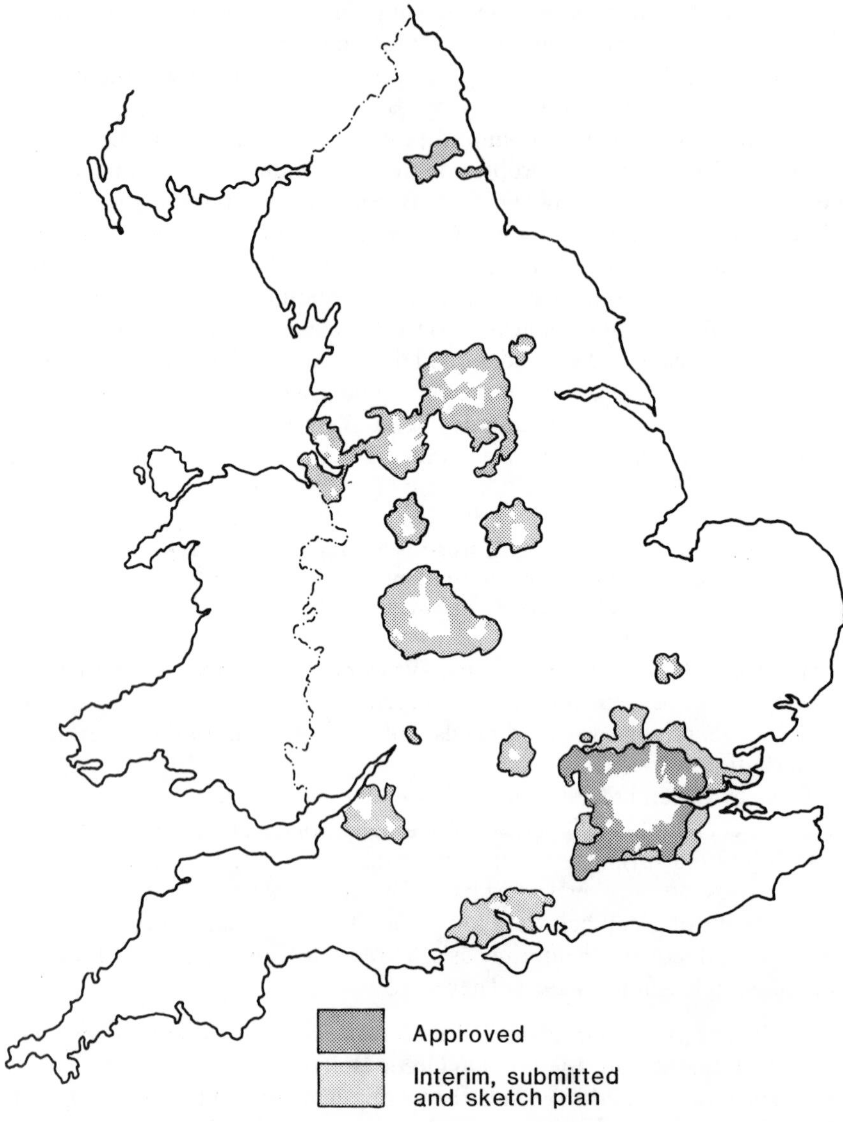

Figure 1.6 Green Belts in 1962
Source: Adapted from James, J. R. 'City Regions' Town and Country Planning Summer School, *Report of Proceedings* (TCPSS: London, 1962), p. 17

Lessons of the First Round

This early 1945–60 period ended, apparently, with the green belt concept fully embedded in the day to day process of development control and decision-making. Brief reflection, however, suggests that green belts were posited on a narrow range of justifications. Further, these restricted the form that green belts could take on the ground. In theory a green belt policy could be based on a wide number of single or combined objectives and could restrict uses in different ways. For example a green belt designed to create compact and cost-effective patterns of urban development could be a 'stop line' or relatively narrow band around a town pulled back at five- or ten-year intervals as the need for physical expansion was demonstrated. A belt performing the function of a recreation lung for an urban area might again be narrow, have a wider range of uses, but might place more emphasis on the protection of green wedges penetrating urban areas to maximize the possibilities of access to open country. A belt to protect agriculture would be defined in relation to the quality of agricultural land and farm unit boundaries, and would have a highly restrictive set of uses. One to preserve a green setting to a town might be wide in extent and be defined by reference to important topographical features, with uses restricted to those fitting the rural scene.

The Ministry concept was not that of a rolling green belt. As their 1962 booklet states 'the object of including land in a green belt is to keep it permanently open'.[49] It was to remain open in appearance and the land within it was to be devoted predominantly to agriculture. The public had no extra rights of access as a result of its delimitation and there was no intention of public acquisition of the land. It was thus closest to the Scott Committee's description in terms of its character and the form of land management expected within it. However, its presence at all and its shape were to be determined by subjective judgements based on the three criteria of the Circular. For example, given the need to half the spread of a city or town how wide should a belt be? The TCPA in its memorandum to the Minister had suggested a width defined by daily commuting distance in order to encourage the growth of self-contained communities away from the old centres. The Government came down in favour of widths fitted to desired patterns of decentralization. The new towns around London were thus on the edge of the original London Green Belt, and the green belt was part of a *positive* strategy for dispersal.

In terms of the separating function no specific width was desirable beyond that which would retain the physical and psychological separation of towns with a tendency to merge. A gap of two or three fields was enough, particularly if the local topography meant that two adjoining towns were not visible one from another. Green belts justified in this way were narrow, for example between Newcastle and Sunderland, or Gloucester and Cheltenham.

Green belts based on the need to retain the special character of a town were designed to suit a particular range of circumstances. As a stopper they would avoid increased pressures on historic town centres as a result of peripheral development, they would retain attractive 'gateways' or approaches to a town and its green setting which, combined with its historic built form, combined to produce its physical attractiveness. In no instance, it should be noted, were the characteristics of the natural resources (such as woodland, landscape or agriculture) of an area on their own the determinant of the size or extent of a belt.

What should be noted in the context of this set of subjective decisions is the power of central Government. All proposals by local authorities were in the nature of bids and all were subject to the closest scrutiny by Ministry officials who would walk the ground before the plan inquiries, designed to hear objections, were heard. Ministers, advised by their officials, thus decided which belts should exist and what form they should take. A number of proposed sketch plans were never sent to the Ministry following informal consultations. As has been seen a number of submitted schemes were rejected and all of the remainder were modified in major or minor ways. Following the Tribunals and Inquiries Act of 1958, any substantial modifications to plans, and those proposed in the course of approval, were to be submitted to a second public inquiry. However even in this case the Minister was not bound by the findings of Inspectors. In the case of the Buckinghamshire proposed extension, following a first public inquiry in 1958, the Ministry's proposal to delete an area beyond the Chilterns to the southern edge of Aylesbury was tested at a second inquiry in 1961. Although the Inspector found in favour of the local authorities seeking to create this extension, it was not subsequently approved by the Minister.[50] Most crucially the success of the early green belts was tested in the first few appeal decisions. Local authorities may not have liked the extent of Ministry powers but they were dependent on the consistency of Ministry support at appeal in making what they were left with a reality.

The enthusiastic take-up of the concept by counties was not surprising. Many had felt threatened by the physical expansion of the cities and urban districts and, as today, urban-rural conflicts of interest had dominated local politics in many areas. In the 1940s and 1950s these had often been accompanied by lengthy inquiries into sequences of boundary extension proposals. The counties were frankly seeking to use the green belt to protect the environments of their ratepayers from outsiders, and to protect valued landscapes, as well as to safeguard recreation and food producing areas. The green belt was the most powerful planning tool invented which made this sequence of local political objectives potentially attainable. Its existence invited authorities to use it to resist urban encroachment.

Green belts rapidly became defended territory and a plethora of local green belt, environmental and amenity groupings at different scales of organization evolved. Around London a Metropolitan Green Belt Council, which was the forerunner of the South East Standing Conference of Local Authorities was founded in 1958. The Wirral Green Belt Council was active from the late 1950s in what is now Merseyside. Umbrella organizations such as the Surrey Amenity Council fostered alliances of local environmental groups forming dense and effective lobbying networks. The Oxford Preservation Trust was active in bringing together Oxford City, and Oxford and Berkshire Counties to make a Green Belt submission for the area around the City in 1956. Many of the larger groups were affiliated to the CPRE. Green belts were a catalyst for large parts of what has developed over recent years to be termed the 'environmental lobby'.

Green belts were also popular with professional planners. They promised a clear framework for expressing local authority intentions in respect of development and a chance to control sporadic development in the countryside. They potentially clarified discussions with developers who could clearly be shown the areas for development and those where it was prohibited. In the long term they promised some continuity over and above the swings in attitudes to land and development resulting from local political changes. In short they appealed to a profession and to a Ministry who, in the early 1950s, had been recruited largely from the ranks of engineers and architects, and who saw the solution to many urban problems as residing in effectively applied policies of physical arrangement of town and country.

The Green Belts were highly circumscribed by a need to be permanent. By 1962 no proposals, apart from the original London Green Belt, had been formally approved in development plans. The idea of a permanent restriction fitted well both with a static population and in cases where it was a policy intention to disperse population more widely within a region. When the scale of growth became evident after 1955 this position was increasingly difficult to sustain. Green belts outside London therefore operated by courtesy of the MHLG in less than fully approved form. In many senses therefore, they created an illusion of permanence, with local authorities highly dependent on central Government attitudes at any point in time.

2. Green Belts and Regional Planning

the idea that at some time a city becomes too big for comfort and must be prevented from spreading by a green belt seems now altogether too rigid

Dame Evelyn Sharp 1969

By 1963 the first round of green belt submissions had been vetted by the Ministry and the controls were in operation around most of our major cities. To the Government they represented an *instrument of policy*, a means to assist in the orderly dispersal of population. To many of the other interests they represented an ideal, the physical expression of a commitment to countryside and landscape protection, a *policy in its own right*. This chapter traces the development and survival of the green belt concept during the 1962–76 period, one of hectic regional planning activity, the impetus of which only reduced with the reorganization of local government in 1974. Government attitudes and actions in respect of green belts are discussed, and developments in planning in the South East and West Midlands Regions are used to indicate briefly the fortunes of green belt during the period. In 1963 the portents were not good. How would the essentially static Sandys concept, conceived in an era of low growth, fare in a period of rapid growth and development?

The Sandys Concept in Operation

The process of incorporation of green belts into 1947 Act development plans was overtaken by events. The 1947 Act system had been posited on large public sector development programmes; thus their name 'development plans' and the requirement for a programme map of the local authorities' intentions for development. However, the removal of the Development Charge in 1953 led to the creation of divergent prices for land with or without the benefit of planning permission. This was particularly true of green belt zones where building land was, by definition, restricted. The attention of speculative developers therefore focused on the edges of green belt towns, especially those with no town map, or maps which might be argued to be out of date.

Local public inquiries into green belt amendments to development plans were dominated by landowners, using the 'white land' paragraph of Circular 50/57, to argue that if *any* doubt existed about the future extent of a settlement then boundaries should be drawn back. Local authorities in the South East were alarmed that if the high (20 to 40 per cent) population growth commonly experienced in green belt settlements over the decade to 1961 were to be repeated the whole concept of checking sprawl would be prejudiced. The white land should be kept for local needs.[1] Ministry planners were however clear on the *intended* solution; firm green belts to help shape the regional pattern of decentralization. The 1962 booklet *Green Belts* stressed firstly the permanence of green belts – 'an area of land which is kept open by permanent and severe restriction on building' – and secondly the view that boundaries should be drawn so as 'not to include land which it is unnecessary to keep permanently open for the purpose of a green belt'.

The regional role of green belts was also made more explicit. Green belts should not be too narrow otherwise development, merely forming dormitories to the major cities, would leapfrog. A green belt which was too wide would result in alternative locations for development not sufficiently attractive to housebuilders and industrialists:

> The problem is to reduce employment in the heart of the conurbation and to encourage its growth in towns which, though partly dependent on the great city, are independent to the extent of providing sufficient local employment for the people who live there, as well as shops and opportunities for entertainment and recreation. Looked at in this way, a green belt is seen as a means of shaping the expansion of a city on a regional scale and not just an attempt to combat the forces which make for growth.[2]

The problem from the Government's point of view was to secure rapid provision of more land in development plans. J. R. James, the Ministry Chief Planner at the time, noted that the forecast of growth for the 1961–81 period was 4.7 million, yet the first round of approved plans only allowed for a 2.5 million increase in population.[3] Shortages of land and high land prices led to the issue of Circular 37/60. This urged local authorities to update plans to match the new forecasts. Land was to be identified which did not conflict with 'important planning objectives' such as green belt, and fuller use was to be made of land within towns. Where a town was encircled by a green belt, adequate land should be selected *beyond* the belt to encourage decentralization. Densities in areas allocated for development should be increased to levels consistent with retaining good layout and design.[4]

But development beyond the belts was not easy to secure. In the early 1960s the dispersal programme was producing only a trickle of new housing, and there was criticism that insufficient financial resources had been devoted to town expansion schemes. Whilst this factor had deterred exporting and receiving authorities alike, more profound conflicts of interest emerged.

Some of the conurbation authorities in the remainder of England outside London were not convinced of the need for dispersal beyond green belts on the South East pattern. Potential receiving authorities were reluctant to enter into agreements to take population from cities due to the poor financial terms offered by the Government. There was also concern over the effects of large numbers of new arrivals, particularly in the smaller receiving communities. Faced with these difficulties, urban authorities could either redevelop at higher densities within the cities, or seek peripheral land. The latter represented a good alternative economic proposition, especially as many of the large cities owned land immediately beyond their boundaries purchased at pre-war prices. The green belts were therefore put in place at a time of considerable inter-authority conflict over decentralization against a backcloth of rapid land price escalation.

The principles outlined in the Green Belt booklet of 1962 were soon to be tested. A Cabinet Committee on population and employment, convened two years after the James pronouncement, estimated a growth of six million in the population of England and Wales by 1981, with three quarters of this likely to take place in the South East and the West Midlands. The Government were determined on a pro-growth strategy and wanted to reduce the cost of new land for development to this end. Accordingly, Keith Joseph, the Minister at the time, persuaded his cabinet colleagues that the only way to improve the land prices problem was to make greater supplies of land readily available for development. Ministry officials embarked on long-term comprehensive studies for each region designed to secure a balanced provision of the necessary land. As a result progress on the approval of the first round of green belts was halted around the major conurbations in 1962, leaving the majority less than fully confirmed for over a decade.

The outlook in the South East was gloomy. There was a shortage of land for housing, there were high land values on each side of the London Green Belt, and the number of London's homeless was growing. The relief offered by overspill schemes had been nullified by an increase in jobs in the City and congestion was spreading to dormitory towns within and beyond the Belt. Government philosophy was to accept growth in the Region (indeed, they were probably powerless to stop it). As Joseph noted at the time, this 'necessarily involved a review of the London Green Belt'. The Government came to the view that there was no alternative to the use of some Green Belt for housing. It was appreciated that this would give rise to strong objections, but Joseph was convinced this could not be avoided. Cullingworth's analysis of Government papers at the time reveals the following insight into the Minister's attitude:

> I think it is time that I started to clear the air. Nobody intends to destroy the Green Belt. On the other hand, the pressure for housing land within easy reach of London is tremendous.[5]

The 1963 White Paper, *London: Employment, Housing, Land* suggested, allowing for redevelopment and building within London and the overspill programme, that there remained a need for 200,000 houses in a ten-year period outside London.[6] Some of this land would have to be found within the London Green Belt and its proposed extensions. Some modest expansion of existing towns and villages could take place on land not necessary to the purposes of the Green Belt, nor of high amenity value. However, the Government maintained support for the London Green Belt as a permanent feature of planning policy for London. It would be maintained without *substantial* change and, in due course, extensive additions would be made. Local authorities were invited to consider development needs and to suggest appropriate land to the Minister which would be the subject of local public inquiries. It was suggested that land in Hertfordshire and Essex could be released as the railway lines servicing such areas had spare capacity for commuters. One result of the White Paper was the identification of a 160 hectare area of disused glasshouses in the upper Lea Valley as a residential area upon which permission for development was granted three years later in 1966.[7] However, this instruction was not generally well received by the Home Counties around London and little action was taken.[8]

The West Midlands

In the West Midlands the Abercrombie–Jackson Plan of 1948 had proposed a mixture of decentralization *and* peripheral development around Birmingham.[9] The Green Belt proposed would aid dispersal but would not necessarily be a permanent feature of the Region. Rapid inward migration combined with natural population increase had, by the early 1960s, utilized the allocated peripheral land. It was estimated in 1961 that the overspill requirement up to 1981 would be 300,000 persons.

Birmingham City Council, not convinced of the need for dispersal, sought more housing land adjacent to the conurbation. They made application in 1959 for a boundary extension in the Wythall area of Warwickshire to the south-east of the City. The aim was to develop housing for 42,000 people on five square kilometres of land. The Inquiry which resulted is a vivid illustration of the irreconcilable clash of arguments raging at the time. During the Inquiry Sir Herbert Manzoni, the City Engineer of Birmingham, sought to establish the imperative need for development on what was City-owned land. The City's obligations under the Housing Acts necessitated City centre redevelopment at lower than existing densities; development on this peripheral land was the only alternative. The Midlands New Towns Society, a regional pressure group set up in 1956, sought to establish that effective and assiduously pursued policies of dispersal would avoid the need for hasty decisions leading to peripheral development.[10] The encounter was mainly a political one. Peripheral expansion would cost the City least in the short term and would probably lead to boundary extensions at a future date. Worcestershire County, essentially representing environmental, agricultural, and local property owning interests, had found in the Green Belt a perfect spatial expression of their interests. In this situation decisions on the confirmation of the Green Belt were deferred pending a resolution of the City's housing land problem and discussion of new town proposals. Therefore unlike London, Birmingham did not have a fully approved Green Belt during the 1960s. Like the South East the Region had severe land shortages by 1964, with even less success in the field of negotiating housing overspill arrangements. Industry had not decentralized on the pattern of the South East and the conurbation authorities were unwilling to build houses at long distances from people's work.

Thus at the end of their 1951–64 term of office, Conservative Governments had signally failed to solve the land problem. The formal development plan system was not capable of responding speedily enough to the need to release more land and processes of exhortation through Circulars had proved weak. Local authorities in green belt zones, responding to the wishes of their electorates, were unwilling to compromise green belts and they could use Ministerial affirmations of support for the policy and its permanence in the acrimonious dealings with urban authorities and Ministry officials which developed. The form of local government organization, with a multitude of large and small urban authorities short of land within their own boundaries, surrounded by Counties operating green belt policies, was a recipe for stultifying chaos. The mass of minor *ad hoc* revisions to local government boundaries during the period presented no permanent solution to the problem. Only two additional areas of green belt had become fully approved between 1959 and 1964, an area of 353 square kilometres in Northumberland along the Upper Tyne Valley, and 23 square kilometres surrounding the Saddleworth villages in what is now Oldham District. Both were uncontentious. It thus appears that a concept suited to the spatial rearrangement of population was unable to stand up to the unforseen forces and agents of growth emerging in the 1960s. The allowances of white land in many of the submissions of the late 1950s had provided some breathing space, but this had now been virtually exhausted.

The Decline of Green Belts

The arrival of a Labour Government in 1964 led to a number of innovations. Regional Economic Planning Councils and Boards were set up and an experiment in advisory regional economic planning commenced. The Ministry created a full pattern of regional offices in 1965 to reflect this new impetus, and the Land Commission, one of whose main duties was that of bringing land forward for development in areas of development pressure, was created. Whilst reaffirming central Government's belief in green belts

Richard Crossman, the new Minister, was soon beset by the demands of urban authorities for more development land.[11] With the birth-rate continuing to rise until 1966, as did the numbers in manufacturing employment, there was no abatement in the pressures for land release.

In the South East the first Regional Study, and the Government's response, were published in 1964.[12] Land to accommodate nearly one and a quarter million people to 1981 was to be found in a second generation of new and expanded towns well beyond the London Green Belt in areas such as South Hampshire, in the Bletchley (Milton Keynes) area, and around Newbury in Berkshire. However, the Study suggested that the 2,560 square kilometres of proposed *extensions* to the London Green Belt should be looked at again in the light of the increased population projections, with a view to finding more land for development. For this reason the proposed extensions would not necessarily be proceeded with in their existing form. The original approved Green Belt would, however, be retained and there would be no general extension of the London built-up area.

The South East Study of 1964 also discussed two possible changes to the London Green Belt.[13] The first was to push back the boundary one kilometre from the edge of the conurbation all the way round. The second was to sponsor radial development from the City leaving the London Green Belt as a series of giant open spaces between the axes of development, a theme taken up by housebuilders at the time.[14] The former was dismissed as too arbitrary, and the latter as negating the benefits of the hard fought battle to establish green belt principles outside London. The Study concluded that locally arising needs for new housing should be met in towns in the London Green Belt, and that some proportion of London's demand should also be met in the towns surrounded by submitted Green Belt extensions (see Figure 2.1 for these distinctions). These would be accommodated by modest adjustments to land allocations by taking small amounts of land on the fringes of existing towns, increasing densities (particularly by modest increases at the lower end of the range), and by speeding up redevelopment where this would result in extra housing being accommodated. Also Counties were encouraged to re-examine the fringe of London to see if sites could be released which would avoid the need to take open country further out. When considering changes in the submitted Green Belt areas, boundaries should be drawn with proper regard to 'the long-term needs' for development, that is, having allocated land for the period to 1981, and after leaving a margin of unallocated or white land. Proper justifications for extensions would include maintenance of the separate identity and physical separation of country towns, or the prevention of building on fine landscapes, especially those close to towns which acted as 'rural rings' for town dwellers. Thus restraint in the approved London Green Belt was to be tighter than in the proposed extensions, and a new criterion relating to the character of the land to be protected was suggested. At the same time the Green Belt was to be a

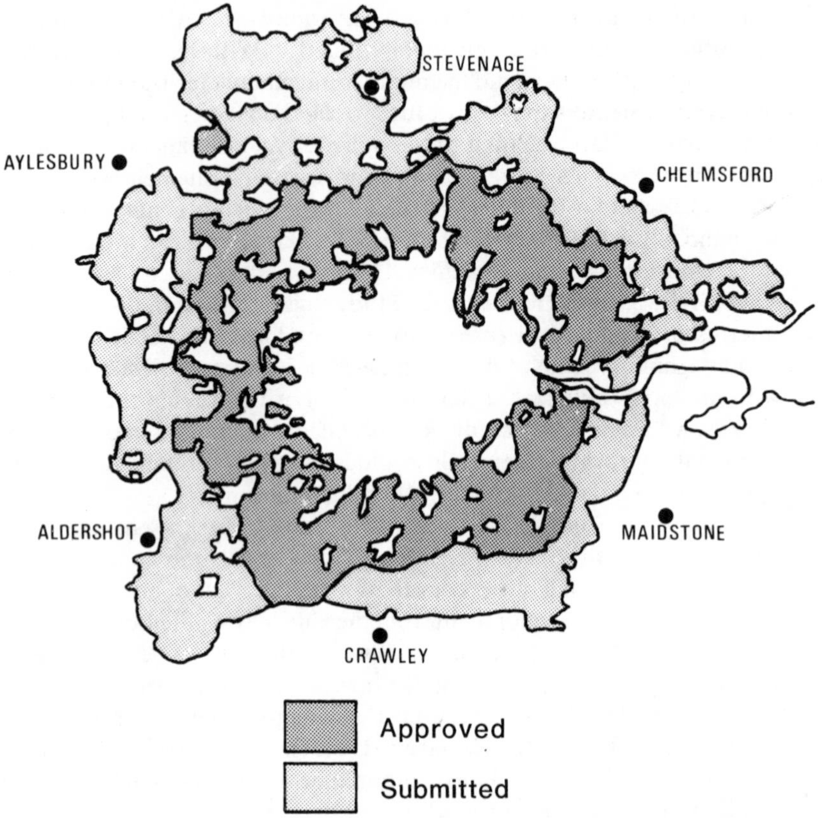

Figure 2.1 The Approved London Green Belt and Submitted Extensions 1963
Source: Adapted from Thomas, D. 'Green Belt Attitudes', *Town and Country Planning* (1963), vol. 31, p. 387

permanent feature of the region's planning (according to the 1962 MHLG Booklet), *but not literally inviolable* according to the South East Study, a nicety which has dominated much of the debate in the early 1980s.

A Strategy for the South East, the first assessment of the Regional Economic Planning Council published in 1967,[15] saw a need to find room for four million more people in the Region by the year 2000. This was to be accomplished by promoting a pattern of sectors of growth radiating from *beyond* the London Green Belt. The Study suggested retention of the original approved Green Belt with the proposed extensions treated as 'country zones'. These would be a more positive concept than that of green belts circling urban areas. Country zones would be applicable over wide areas of the Region wherever there was a need to emphasize a clear and recognizable distinction between town and country. They would protect the rural economy in the areas between the main corridors of growth. Criteria for definition would include the extent of pressures for development on the area concerned, the aesthetic quality of the countryside, and the recreation and amenity needs of local populations. The Strategy map shows such areas in pale green. In some ways they were to be a second (some would say second class) category of Green Belt, but falling under the heading of 'countryside policy'. They established the idea of categories of restraint of which fully-approved London Green Belt was the most severe.[16]

The three years to 1970 in the South East were dominated by discussion of the locations for future growth. They all had implications for the proposed extensions of the London Green Belt. The Standing Conference on London and South East Regional Planning, acting to support and defend shire county interests, proposed development should be at a small number of locations well away from the outer edge of an extended Green Belt. The Town and Country Planning Association favoured growth at locations less distant from London, for example in the Reading–Basingstoke and Luton

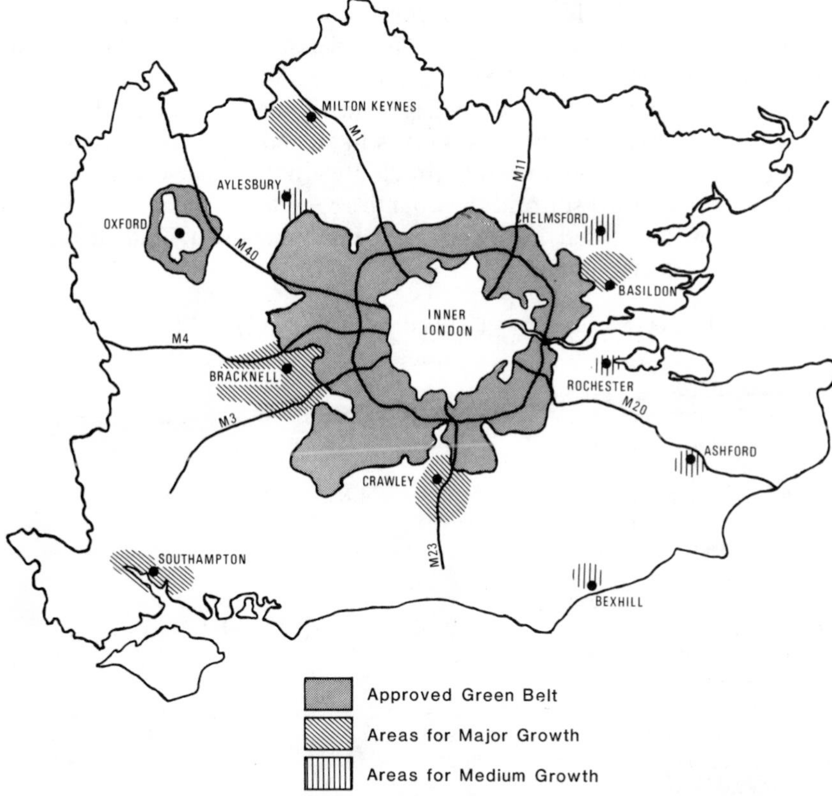

Figure 2.2 Green Belts, Growth and Restraint Areas in the South East 1976
Source: Adapted from DoE *Government Statement on Strategic Plan for the South East* (HMSO: London, 1978), p. 33

–Dunstable areas. The Government, accepting none of the schemes, commissioned a further Regional Study which reported in 1970. This, an amalgamation of previous proposals, proposed a limited number of major growth areas in South Hampshire, Milton Keynes–Northampton, Reading–Wokingham–Aldershot–Basingstoke, South Essex, and at Crawley–Gatwick. One of the major aims of the Plan was the preservation of extensive areas of open country. This would be achieved, in part, by the continued application of green belt controls. The London Green Belt would remain an important element defining the regional structure but strict controls would deflect development pressures to the growth areas. An extended London Green Belt, and the towns encompassed within it, would accommodate 1.71 million people by 1981, over double its 1974 population (see Figure 2.2).

The outcome thus represented a victory for the Home Counties, the intention being to deflect development pressures beyond the approved London Green Belt. Alarmed by suggestions that changes might be made to urban boundaries in the approved Belt, the County Councils Association lobbied the Ministry for clarification of the decisions made. In March 1969 they obtained a Ministerial letter suggesting new white land areas need not be found adjacent to towns and villages surrounded by approved London Green Belt.[17] Accordingly the Counties tightened their Green Belt maps taking out 'insets' and drawing Green Belt notation over many small settlements. Table 2.1 suggests the Counties were successful in their aims, as little land was released from approved London Green Belt during the 1964–70 period, and up to 1974.

Table 2.1 Land Use Changes in the London Green Belt 1963–74

	1963		*1974*		*% change*
Land use	*ha*	*%*	*ha*	*%*	
Villages, groups of houses and land where other surface development predominates	8,000	3.5	9,050	3.9	+13.1
Airfields, WD land, reservoirs and waterworks, mineral workings, tips and other land uses of a predominantly open character	11,100	4.8	10,850	4.7	−2.3
Institutions in extensive grounds, cemeteries, playing fields and other land uses appropriate to a green belt	16,950	7.4	17,750	7.7	+4.7
Public open space	17,300	7.5	18,400	8.0	+6.4
Remainder, mainly agricultural land and woodland	176,250	76.8	173,500	75.7	−1.6

Source: Adapted from SCLSERP *The Improvement of London's Green Belt*, SC 620, (SCLSERP: London, 1976) tables 2 and 3.

Peripheral Development or Decentralization?

In the West Midlands the six years to 1970 were ones of continuing dispute over Regional strategy and the Green Belt. Through a process of re-zoning open space and by building on white land, virtually all new development to 1965 had been within the Conurbation. It became clear by the mid-1960s that industry remained stubbornly within the Conurbation, and although a pattern of redistribution inside urban areas was going on, there was little scope for decentralization beyond the Green Belt. The provision of housing land at distances from the Conurbation would merely create longer journeys to work. The 1967 Strategy, faced with this dilemma, sought to *balance* peripheral development with provision for planned overspill.[18] By this time Government planners were at the centre of the stage arbitrating between the different interests. They accepted, crucially, that job mobility was not likely to occur on the scale desired to create a balance between housing and employment beyond the Green Belt. The Ministry's Chief Planner rejected the feasibility of an inviolate Green Belt of the sort apparently operated around London in the West Midlands situation.[19]

The 1960s in the West Midlands were a period of fiercely-contested peripheral expansion. In 1964 a development for 52,000 persons at Chelmsley Wood was approved, followed in 1968 by developments at Moundsley (35,000), Hawksley (11,000) and in 1969 at Pirton, west of Wolverhampton. All were granted by Government Ministers on appeal, attracting the unedifying sobriquet of 'underspill' from the Midlands New Town Society.[20] Some of the pre-war covenanted land south of the City was also used for housing.[21]

Thus although the principle of a Green Belt survived, in practice extensive peripheral development was approved. The need to keep up the impetus of Birmingham City's housing programme was used to sustain some decisions, but in reality the failure of the overspill programme bottled up such forces in the Conurbation that the Green Belt had to give way.[22] Significantly this was only achieved by the active intervention of central Government. Although the Regional Council had warned of the adverse social and economic consequences of not adhering to the Green Belt in 1967, the actions of the following two years directly contradicted this view. No 'consensus' on Regional strategy was to be reached until 1974; meanwhile the Green Belt remained a chessboard across which the main actors moved their pieces with the Ministry intervening to state the rules at various stages.[23] David Saunders, the Ministry's Chief Regional Planner, in summarising the West Midlands experience, has noted:

> The end result . . . was in theory a strategy of containment but increasingly in practice a pragmatic combination of limited (belated) overspill into new and expanded towns plus, on the grounds of expediency, as well as for social and economic reasons, some substantial development in selected peripheral locations.[24]

Out of Favour

The 1964–70 period marks the nadir of the fortunes of the green belt concept in England. Major doubts were expressed as to its utility given the urgent housing pressures of the 1960s. Others saw pursuit of the 'old' philosophy of containment as a barrier to creative thought about new forms of urban development. The South East Study in 1964 was roundly condemned by Hall, who was convinced of the merits of the growth corridor model of regional development popular in the USA and Western Europe at the time:

> the Study specifically rejects . . . radical solutions such as the replacement of the present (green) belt by a series of green wedges running in less developed land between the main transport lines. Though this form of development is *almost certainly preferable* for a rapidly growing Metropolis like London, the Study points out that London has been planned on the basis of a green belt for twenty years and it is now almost impossible to change.[25] (Author's emphasis).

At the Town Planning Institute Summer School in 1966 J. R. Allison questioned the conventional wisdom of containment using green belts, seeing it as a 'psychological barrier' to looking at new city region forms. The 1962 Booklet had said green belts were necessary where towns had grown too large. But was urban misery related to town size? Was city life so unbearable that people needed to be decentralized in such numbers? Would not a pattern of restraint based on Ministry of Agriculture protection of good agricultural land, and Countryside Commission protection of valued landscapes, free much useful land for building? Size had nothing to do with the unattractiveness of cities; this was due to the *forms* of urban development and redevelopment being implemented. 'If we really wish', it was concluded 'to re-fashion our environment we must be ready to sacrifice ideas that protect a small part of the population from change'.[26] Periodicals such as *Town and Country Planning*, and *The Housing and Planning Review*, published articles similar in tone at this time. In the latter case the County Planning Officer of Hampshire commented on the abandonment of the eastern part of the proposed South Hampshire Green Belt in the face of a large sub-regional planning study to assess the feasibility of major urban growth in South Hampshire.[27]

The 1968–70 period was occupied by a plethora of sub-regional planning studies. With hindsight they appear labrynthine in their arguments and extravagant in their use of computerized techniques. The findings of those studies covering areas of sketch plan and submitted green belt are instructive.[28] In the recommendations of the *Nottinghamshire–Derbyshire Study* a 'countryside policy' was to protect the resources and assets of the *rural* areas. It was therefore open to the local authorities concerned to choose whether to continue with the Green Belts or to rely on these new policies to achieve similar objectives. In the *Coventry–Solihull–Warwickshire Study* in the West Midlands the expression 'Green Belt' was studiously avoided but a permanent boundary to a buffer of countryside was recommended. The *South Hampshire Study* did not recommend a green belt but a fluid concept of open space in and around the built-up area, and 'a total approach' to the design and management of all land. Jackson, the reviewer of these studies, concluded 'from the evidence of the studies it would appear that inviolable green belts are no longer an essential element in the formulation of planning policy for urban growth'. Dame Evelyn Sharp noted in 1969 that 'cherished' policies such as the green belt appeared to have come full circle: 'the idea that at some point a city becomes too big for comfort and must be prevented from spreading by a green belt seems altogether too rigid'.[29]

Another important event, local government reorganization, also loomed ahead. The findings of the Recliffe–Maud Commission were of major importance to green belts. The prolonged wrangles over green belt land, repeated in every major conurbation, were also arguments about local government boundaries. In 1969 the Commission suggested the redrawing of boundaries based largely on the concept of 'unitary' authorities, all-purpose bodies covering town and country, each containing populations of between a quarter and one million. In the cases of Birmingham, Liverpool and Manchester a two-tier system was proposed but with the top tier having planning powers and covering wide areas of land on a city region scale. The implication in the West Midlands was that Staffordshire would disappear and large tracts of Worcestershire and Warwickshire would come under the control of a West Midlands Authority. In the North West, Cheshire, another 'Green Belt County' which had conducted a series of exchanges over the 1940–70 period with Manchester City on the West Midlands model,[30] would also disappear. Intense lobbying by Cheshire and Staffordshire was overtaken by the 1970 Election.

With the South East, West Midlands and North West Green Belts 'in suspension' during the period, the only major approvals were for the West Riding of Yorkshire, and for the Bristol–Bath Green Belt, both in 1966. In the former case complicated overspill arrangements were not thought to be necessary and, in the latter, overspill arrangements had been made and new land for housebuilding had been freed within the City boundary.[31] The only other Green Belts approved were for South Tyneside, to separate Newcastle and Sunderland in 1969, a very small area bordering Cambridge, and a small 'separating' Green Belt between Gloucester and Cheltenham. Thus only about 1840 square kilometres of Green Belt were formally approved between 1964 and 1970.

Green Belt Rehabilitated

The new Conservative Government of 1970, as one of its first acts, revised the scheme for local government reorganization and in a White Paper in 1971 proposed the creation of a two-tier system throughout the Country. The new system created smaller metropolitan areas and attempted to respect pre-existing local authority boundaries in the shire counties. As a result the West Midlands Metropolitan County had a boundary tightly drawn around existing built-up limits to the south and west, and Greater Manchester had its southern boundary with Cheshire drawn close to the limits of development south of the City. This new pattern represented, on the whole, a victory for the shire Counties. As Goldsmith notes, the original Maud proposals were urban-oriented and, if implemented, would have resulted in a concentration of local political power in town and city hands at the expense of rural areas.[31] The reforms introduced by the Conservatives both contained the urban areas and thus the scope of their political power, and largely maintained the power of the shire Counties and thus the green belts they had promoted.

The first incumbent at the new Environment Ministry, Peter Walker, announced at the Conservative Party Conference in 1970 his wish to clarify the position over green belts. Declaring strong support for the concept, he promised early decisions on existing proposals, the majority of which had been with the Ministry for nearly 10 years.[33] In the South East, consideration of the Strategic Plan for the Region had by 1971 clarified a number of issues sufficiently for large parts of the London Green Belt extensions to be approved.[34] In August 1972 it was announced that the Surrey extensions would be approved (adding 20 per cent by area to the original Belt), and in September, that additions in Buckinghamshire and Kent would also be approved (adding a further 15 per cent). These were to be areas of firm restraint in the long-term.

The intention to approve the West Midlands Green Belt was also announced in 1972 but it was to be three years before this took full effect. A Sub-Regional Strategy for the Coventry–Solihull–Warwickshire area had reported in 1971 suggesting major peripheral development on the south western edge of Coventry, in the Aldridge–Brownhills and Sutton Coldfield areas in the north of the conurbation, and at Solihull in the South.[35] During the 1972–4 period a further period of 'debate' between the Economic Planning Council, the shire Counties, and central Government ensued over the vexed question of the scale of long-distance dispersal. A 'balance' was again negotiated in 1974 by which significant peripheral development was to be allowed in the main conurbation, but in which the Coventry–Solihull–Warwickshire situation remained unresolved. Reflecting this the defined Green Belt (Figure 2.3) consisted of 1262 square kilometres of land of fully approved status, and 684 square kilometres of interim status (including

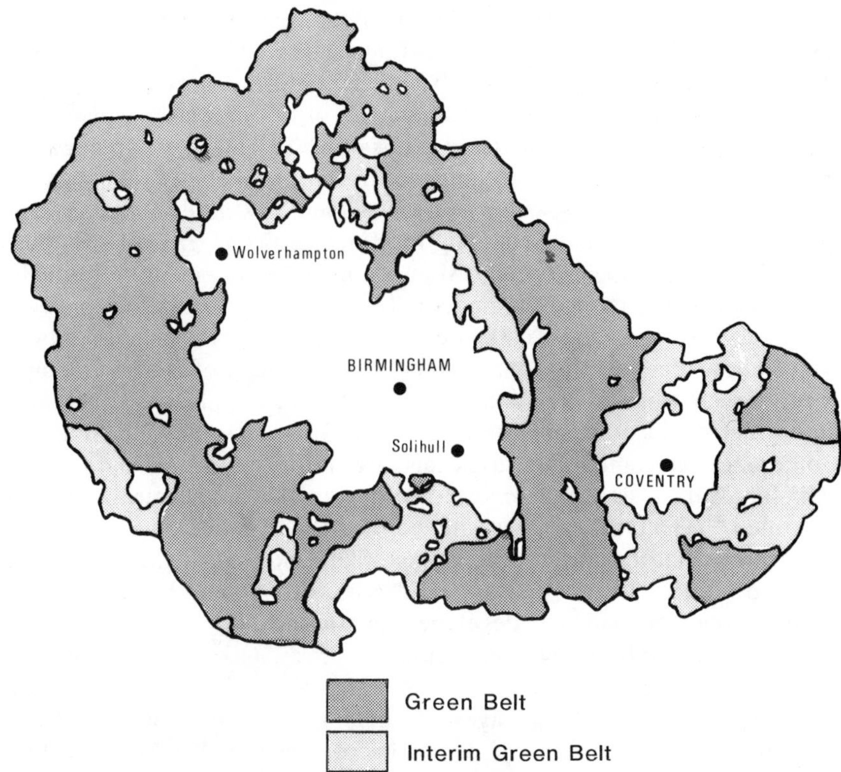

Figure 2.3 The West Midlands Green Belt 1975
Source: Adapted from Gregory, D. 'Green Belt Policy and the Conurbation', in Joyce, F. E. (ed.) *Metropolitan Development and Change* (Teakfield: Farnborough, 1977), p. 245

corridors north, south and east from Coventry), pending the preparation of structure and local plans.

Although by the early 1970s population projections had declined, and the amount of potentially mobile industry was reducing, the state of the property market belied such evidence. A relaxation of credit controls with consequent rapid wage and price inflation saw land become a precious investment commodity, and the well-known boom of 1972–3 developed. In the South East, and to a lesser extent in the West Midlands, there was renewed concern over the adequacy of land releases for housebuilding. Whilst this situation probably represented one of too much capital chasing the land available, rather than an increase in housing need, the Government were not slow to act.[36]

Circular 10/70 had asked local housing authorities to review their land holdings with a view to disposing of any surplus for private housing.[37] Geoffrey Rippon's White Paper *Widening the Choice: The Next Steps in*

Housing suggested the urgent need for more housing land in the South East and indicated that 800 hectares of undistinguished land in the London Green Belt, which were not contributing significantly to the aims of the policy, should be released for housing.[38] Circular 122 of 1973, *Land Availability for Housing*[39] altered the longstanding status of white land shown in development plans. These measures, redolent of the land availability debate which was to dominate planning with the arrival of the 1979 Conservative Government, caused consternation among local authorities in green belt areas. Assurances were sought from the Minister on the Government's attitude to green belts in the House of Commons in January 1974. The carefully phrased reply suggested that the '2000 acres exercise' (as it had become known) would allow the Government to protect the remainder of the London and other Green Belts all the better.[40] The Minister had asked the local authorities to identify sites and report back the results. The Standing Conference reluctantly undertook this task in the South East and in June 1975 John Silkin was able to report to Parliament that 385 hectares had been identified.[41] The balance, it was argued, had been granted on appeal since the exercise had begun and there was other land that might have to be released as a result of earlier appeal decisions (only one third of the 800 hectares 'released' had been developed for housing by 1979).

White land had been regarded, prior to 1973, as land where existing uses would remain undisturbed. Circular 122/73 stated the need to give planning clearance to substantial acreages of land in the South East, the West Midlands, and other areas of development pressure. Whilst green belt would constitute an 'exceptionally compelling' objection to the release of land for development, the same was not true of white land. White land should be regarded as suitable for housing where its development represented a *natural extension* of existing development and was compatible in size, character, location and setting with existing development. Extensions to settlements would be objectionable only if they entailed creating 'ribbons' or 'isolated pockets' of development. If, however, exceptional need could be established then the land may, nevertheless, be made available for development. Development in villages should be consistent with 'community capacity' and could involve expansion outside (but not divorced from) village envelopes, as well as infilling. Planning authorities were urged to approve developments for housing at significantly higher densities, and to set minimum rather than maximum density requirements in plans.

The Circular only referred to 'green belts'. No clarification was included in relation to submitted, interim or sketch plan green belts. This resulted in concerted attempts by county authorities and MPs to elicit clarification for areas where green belts had been operated on an interim basis for a number of years. The clarification, in a letter to the Association of County Councils in 1974, permitted the continuation of green belt controls in submitted, interim and sketch plan areas pending the approval of structure and local plans.[42] On this basis some 9,450 square kilometres of Green Belt continued to be operated until replaced by structure plans mainly in the 1978–82 period.

Thus by 1974 the total area covered by green belt controls had barely altered from that in 1962 (Table 2.2). The area of *fully approved* green belt had, however, grown from under 20 to 48 per cent of the total during the period. The main areas covered by the 6,900 square kilometres of fully approved belt under the old development plan system were:

1. the original London Green Belt of 1959;
2. extensions to the London Green Belt in Surrey, Kent and Buckinghamshire (1972–3);
3. the North Tyneside Green Belt (1963); and
4. the Bristol–Bath, West Riding of Yorkshire and Cheltenham–Gloucester Green Belts (all 1966).

Table 2.2 Land Subject to Green Belt Policies 1974

Green Belt	*Square kilometres*		
	Approved		*Other*
London	3,031		2,632
West Midlands	1,408		512
Greater Manchester			
Cheshire, Lancashire			
Merseyside–Wirral	15		1,226
Tyne and Wear	394		—
Nottingham–Derby	—		571
York	—		77
South and West Yorkshire	1,247		868
Oxford	141		108
Bristol–Bath	620		—
Gloucester–Cheltenham	54		—
Stoke on Trent	—		450
Cambridge	18		144
South West Hampshire	—		952
Totals	6,928		7,540
Grand Total		14,468	

Source: Adapted from House of Commons Environment Committee *Green Belt and Land for Housing*, HC 275-II, (HMSO: London, 1984), pp. 14–18.

With the approval of parts of the West Midlands Green Belt in 1974, and the Oxford Green Belt in 1975, the main Conurbation area outstanding was the North West. Apart from the approval of 23 square kilometres bordering Stockport, decisions on the remainder of submissions in this area had been deferred in 1962. In 1965 the first Regional Strategy for the North West had warned of loss of confidence in the Green Belt idea if the 1958–62 proposals were not speedily acted upon![43]

approvals were conservative in their definition of boundaries. …llands the 684 square kilometres of interim status constituted …ıd around settlements of all sizes in the Green Belt. Around …e kilometres of the outer part of the Green Belt had been …ut the innermost 60 square kilometres were left with interim …us, the boundaries drawn well back from a number of rural settlements (see Figure 4.5). These decisions were to leave scope for further discussion during the preparation of new policies by reorganized local authorities. The status of Green Belts at the end of the era is shown in Figure 2.4.

Why Did Green Belts Survive?

As has been demonstrated, green belt policy was a constant preoccupation of all levels of Government during the 1962–74 period. At national level it affected, and was affected by, land policy changes and the concerns of successive administrations to free land for development. At the regional level green belt was an essential complement of the decentralization strategies of the main conurbations in the 1960s. In areas covered by the policy its retention had, universally, strong local political support. There are perhaps six main reasons why green belts survived into the mid-1970s:

1. *a slackening of growth pressures in the late 1960s*

From 1966 the birth rate began to fall and projections for the overspill requirements of the main conurbations fell with them. This occurred early in the Northern Regions, but by 1970 it was clear in the South East that Regional planning was likely to involve a redistribution of a numerically stable future population. The 1969–72 period was one of rapid change in demographic indicators and a widespread realization of the presence of an 'inner city' problem. From 1972 attention has increasingly focused on regenerating activity inside the conurbations, rather than encouraging them to decentralize. As the targets for New Towns were reduced the pace of outward migration slackened, and the pressure was relieved to some extent in the green belts themselves. This was also assisted by the achievement of far higher housing densities on land allocated in plans than had been envisaged. The need to provide for the natural increase of population that had moved into green belt zones in the 1950s and 1960s however, loomed as a larger problem.

2. *continued support for the concept from central Government*

Governments of all political colours consistently expressed support for green belts. Whilst analysis of the statements made by different Ministers might suggest some disagreement over the purpose of the green belt, (for example in 1975 Antony Crosland saw it as 'a strategy for saving the countryside'),[44] there is no example of wholesale dismemberment of an

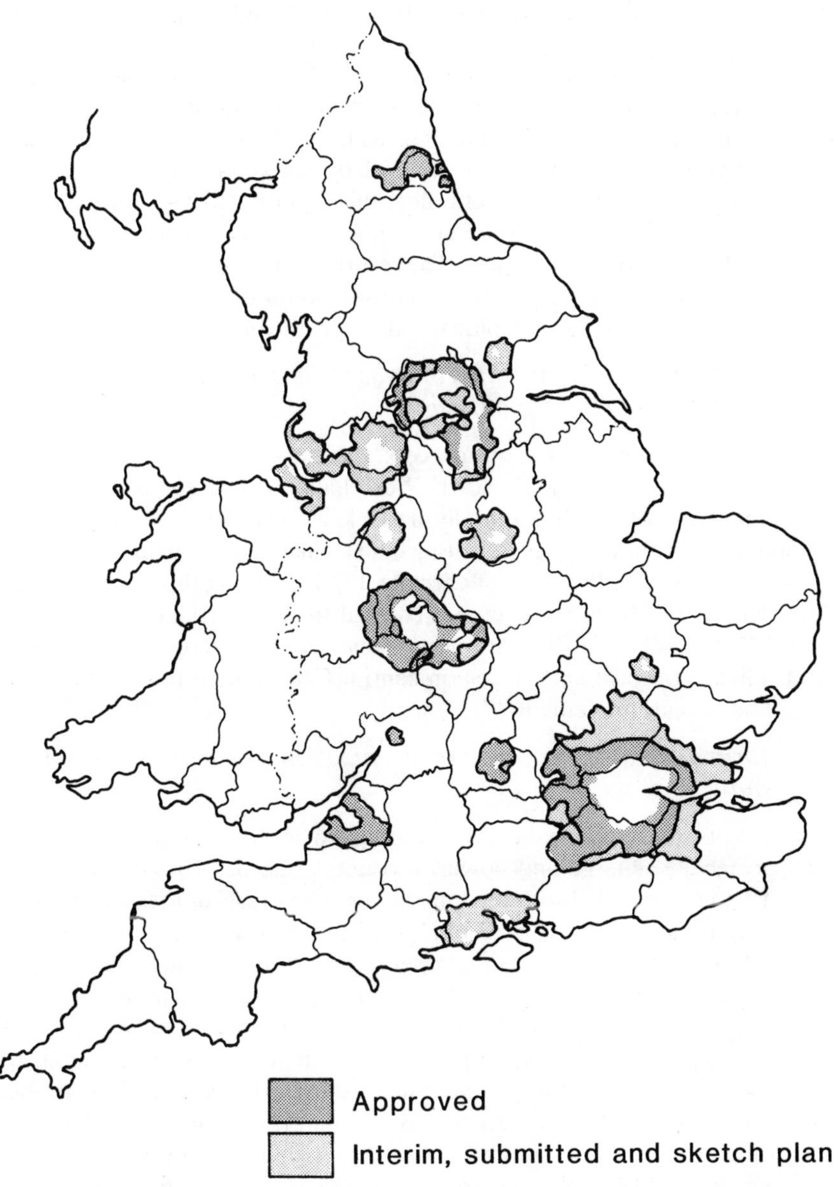

Figure 2.4 The Status of Green Belts in 1976
Source: Adapted from House of Commons Environment Committee *Green Belt and Land for Housing*, HC 275-II (HMSO: London, 1984), between pp. 6 and 7

approved green belt by Government decisions. In supporting green belt, Ministers were also lending credibility to the statutory planning system. Such support also reflected vocal public and pressure group attitudes. Any departures from green belt principles were highlighted in the national press and were matters of some discomfort to individual Ministers. The signs were that by the end of the 1960s civil servants in the Ministry did not share the politically-expressed views, and some of the decisions made in the West Midlands in the 1968–70 period reflect this. Conservative politicians were more convinced of the need to maintain green belts, reflecting their geographical base of political support. The return of the 1970 Government saw a marked revival of impetus towards consolidation of the pattern of green belts at a time when demographic trends were moving also in their favour.

3. *the emergence of some form of consensus over patterns of development in the major regions*

Although it was an acrimonious process, the 'regional debates' in the South East, West Midlands, and North West had reached some measure of agreement by 1974. Undoubtedly a slackening in the scale of overspill demands contributed, as the resulting land availability problems were easier to solve. However, the issue of Circular 122/73 altering the status of white land, and the '2000 acres' exercise, created fresh uncertainties and soured central–local relations. These episodes underlined the crucial importance, and reliance of local authorities on central Government resolve, to make green belt policy implementable.

4. *a form of local government reorganization which protected shire county interests*

Green belts survived into the new planning era because they were promoted and protected by large and powerful county councils. They could do this because they coincided with the long-standing interests of their electorates. Green belts had become a 'positional good' in their own right, defended also by local rate-payer, amenity and conservation groups. As an environmental 'totem' they also represented the best guarantee available for the continued pursuit of an urban way of life among rural surroundings. The green belt ideal had cross-party political support in the shire counties and no authority contemplated its voluntary abandonment during the period. The survival basically intact of the main Green Belt Counties (such as Cheshire and Staffordshire) following reorganization, and their retention of strategic planning powers, ensured that green belts would not easily be abandoned.

5. *the policy had a history of long and successful application in the South East*

Decisions on development had consistently taken account of Green Belt principles around London from 1947. Successive regional strategies had retained the concept of a 12 to 16 kilometre Green Belt around the Conurbation. The successful application of the concept in the area of most severe development pressure in Britain acted as an example to other areas. Planners were keen to operate a concept which was clear and uncomplicated and which established the 'rules of the game' early on in the process of negotiation with applicants. In a situation where development plans were outdated by the pace of demands for land it recreated some order where otherwise there would have been chaos. Its presence provided a set of ground rules at the interface of the public and private sectors. Local planners could also argue that because of central Government support it was the Minister's policy; a policy over and above that of local importance. No other restraint policy could be devised which commanded the same degree of support.

6. *green belt became a sign of Government commitment to the protection of the countryside*

Rightly or wrongly the green belt became a test of good intentions for successive Governments, applied by the emerging environmental lobby. The CPRE acted as a consistent watchdog over the creation and maintenance of green belts throughout the period, and the TCPA continued as a persistent advocate of the Green Belt–New Towns solution to regional problems. Organizations such as the Countryside Commission and the Ministry of Agriculture were also strong supporters of green belts, especially in the later part of the period.

The problems experienced in operating green belt policy over the 1962–74 period were rooted in the decisions of the post-war advisory planners. Conceived by the Scott Committee in a situation where population was to remain static according to all foreseeable predictions, green belts had been formalized as part of an instrument of dispersal. In the important '*Containment of Urban England*' Hall and his colleagues describe the relatively small contribution to dispersal made by the New and Expanded Towns Programmes. They had made up only 15 per cent of the dispersal effort over the 1945–71 period. Most development had been by peripheral accretions to existing settlements. The green belts had therefore compacted the pattern of urban development. Many of the pressures experienced in green belts over the period are attributable to failure to implement the formal mechanisms of dispersal, as well as lack of consistent direction, finance and impetus in city redevelopment. The green belt was one part of a triad of policies (Redevelopment–Green Belt–New and Expanded Towns) which were interdependent. It was the only one of the three that had been implemented. To this extent the fears of Dame Evelyn Sharp, expressed at its inception, dogged the process of incorporation into formally approved development plans.

Experience also showed that a Green Belt on the London model did not necessarily reflect the processes of social and economic change as experienced in other regions. The experience of the West Midlands thus contrasts with that of the South East and reflection on its effects during the period suggests it functioned as a crude device to manage the physical spread of the conurbation and to shape it. In the South East it had halted peripheral growth by the mid 1960s, and by the mid 1970s had slowed development in the London Green Belt zone. Here it had acted as a stopper and had diverted pressures to other areas. Green belts had not altered the rate of decentralization but they had produced a physically contained pattern of development at settlement level.

The increase in under-used land and dereliction problems in some green belts did, periodically, render parts of them vulnerable to development. The 1963 White Paper alerted counties to the need to make positive use of all green belt land as an additional mechanism for its defence. Ideas of a dual-purpose green belt, defined on the ground in terms of its recreation functions, however, also represented a potential weakness. A green belt for recreation need only be rather narrow and builders could argue that land should be developed if no demand or accepted use for recreation existed.

Green belts were criticized, particularly towards the end of the period as a 'civilised version of apartheid'.[45] The urban working classes remained in public-sector housing stock within the conurbations, whereas the more affluent and well-qualified sectors of the population migrated to towns beyond the green belt rings. Once there they strictly defended green belt environments which became enclaves of affluence contrasting starkly with inner city conditions. Analyses of trends in voluntary migration suggest this to be the outcome as more widespread city regions have developed.[46] However, this issue did not lead to any organized current of opposition. Many of those living in the major conurbations have consistently supported green belt as offering the promise, if not always the reality, of recreation and relaxation in natural surroundings.

3. Central Government and the New Pattern

The reorganization of local government marked the start of a new era for green belts. The two-tier system, with its division of responsibilities for land use planning between county and district, offered the opportunity to reconsider and clarify the position of green belts around our major towns and cities. Over 30 counties and 140 districts have been involved in this process during the decade to 1984. By the end of 1982 all of the county structure plans had been submitted to the Ministry; by mid-1984 some twenty-three alterations to the earlier approved plans had also been submitted. What changes have the resulting decisions made to the extent and form of green belts and their justifications? What form has this process of arriving at the new green belts taken?

The New Situation

Green belts have been reconsidered and recast against greatly changed social and economic circumstances. The 1974–8 period was one of major demographic change. Dramatic declines in the birth rate, and reduced migration between and within regions, led to the scaling down of forecasts of development needs in all the major conurbations. Since 1979 processes of intensification and technical change within industry, responding to a need to improve competitiveness in both declining and expanding sectors of the market, have had profound effects for local economies.[1] These have affected parts of the country, and areas within regions differently. The older industrial plants closed have tended to be in inner city areas and the northern conurbations, although the *rate* of decline in sectors such as engineering has been greatest in the West Midlands since 1980.[2] Even the South East outside London has lost more than 15 per cent of its manufacturing jobs since 1980, whilst the GLC area has lost nearly 25 per cent. The creation of new jobs in services has cushioned the effects of recession in the South East outside London, but this has not occurred elsewhere.

Although industry had been leaving the conurbations at an increasing rate from the early 1960s the process only received clear recognition in the mid-1970s as the amount of 'mobile' industry slowed to a trickle.[3] The structure of industry in cities in constrained urban locations with lack of space to expand, and high rates and land costs, have all contributed to dispersal as well as the demise *in situ* of many old urban-based industries. The 'outer city', including the green belt (now combining many of the attributes of accessibility and environment propounded by Howard at the turn of the century), is the investment environment most sought after by industrial developers. Here are to be found lower rates and land costs, higher accessibility, and a more highly skilled or easily trained pool of labour.[4] What has emerged is a sharper contrast in economic fortunes between the inner and the outer city overlying the older north–south differences of previous decades.

The population of England and Wales grew by less than half a million between 1971 and 1981 but, as in the previous decade, there were losses in the largest urban areas, and gains in many of the smaller towns. A pattern of the younger and more affluent members of the population exercising a choice to live in less congested areas, or seeking the elusive qualities of a 'rustic utopia' has typified the period.[5] Dispersed decentralization has occurred with minor growth recorded in many small towns beyond green belts. In the South East the population of the inner parts of the London Green Belt has grown little but housing development continues in many towns embedded in its outer edge and beyond. In the West Midlands and other conurbations the inner and outer edges of the Green Belts are the most dynamic parts of Regions. Pressures for housing within green belts continue, resulting from the natural increase of those already living there, and the tendency for household sizes to decline.

The operation of green belt policies since 1955 had contributed to within region differences in the commercial attractiveness and marketability of sites. Economic depression, and the conservative attitudes of the pension funds and insurance companies who finance development, have combined to focus attention on green belts as a profit-making environment.[6] The same has been true of housing where, in depressed market conditions, housebuilders have sought more attractive sites adjacent to green belts to secure a selling advantage over their competitors.

Thus in addressing the land use consequences of such social and economic changes the major conurbation planning authorities have reoriented their policies. In the mid-1970s all expressed concern, and pursued policies, for inner city regeneration. In land use terms this involved recycling inner city waste land, providing expansion space for existing firms, and freeing land for new employment. Authorities not wishing to hinder development which would only go to urban peripheries have had to make difficult decisions on the 'tightness' of green belts. Too tight and some activities might move away altogether; too loose and they would have no effect in the regeneration process. Since 1980 the emphasis has widened from inner city regeneration to attempts to maintain and regenerate whole city region economies.[7] This could imply a shift in the balance of restraint policies towards freeing more marketable peripheral land for development as one of the easiest actions open to local authorities wishing to attract development to their areas.

At the same time local authorities have experienced real reductions in funding. Thus local infrastructure support programmes for new development have been more difficult to maintain. As the new and expanded towns programmes have run down, a higher proportion of the servicing costs of new development have fallen on public authorities. In response to this, and for environmental and social reasons, the necessity of locating new development in and adjacent to large towns has not been seriously challenged during the period.[8] Containment has been increasingly a necessity if development is to proceed. Even then this has often been in the form of peripheral development resulting from negotiated 'partnerships' with private developers, with the latter providing large contributions to sewerage, water and road costs.

Authorities have thus seen a situation develop where over seven per cent of land in major cities is either derelict or vacant but where, despite much publicized inner city projects, private investors in land and property are predominantly interested in conurbation peripheries and beyond.[9] Authorities have also been concerned that the acceptance of such pressures might entail loss of agricultural land, countryside landscapes and wildlife habitats, and have sought to protect culturally-valued natural resources. The pressure from local residents in the outer city for such protection (forcibly expressed in the public participation forums created by the new planning system) has grown. The need particularly to preserve good quality agricultural land is as high as ever on the agendas of local authorities, despite evidence that land-take for urban development, running at 18,000 hectares a year from 1965–70 had reduced to 9,300 between 1975–80.[10] National and local politicians have seen green belts as an important response to these concerns for natural environments. Thus countryside protection, and associated recreation access arguments, have had a profound influence on the preparation of the new green belt submissions in plans.[11,12]

Governments have formed their own views about land use priorities in response to these social and economic changes. Advice has stressed the need to bring forward a five year supply of marketable sites for housebuilders (see Chapter 10) at the same time reiterating the need to protect good quality agricultural land. Circulars and other advice have urged a more lenient approach to industrial location and the need for a 'positive' response to infrastructure developments such as the M25, yet a need to maintain approved green belts. Thus local authorities must make sense of often ambivalent and conflicting advice as it applies to particular localities. They must also balance interests between counties and districts, and arrive at priorities for land use in the outer city in a constantly shifting situation.

Development Plans

The post-1974 development plan system arose from analysis of the deficiencies of its predecessor.[13] The Planning Advisory Group were concerned to bring only matters of major importance before the Minister for approval. As a result a new two-tier system of plans was introduced. The 'model' was hierarchical. Broad brush structure plans would interpret national and regional policies at county level and establish general proposals for housing, employment, transport, and conservation of the countryside. Within this framework local authorities would have discretion to produce local plans indicating detailed proposals for land use, but which would not have to be submitted to the Minister for approval. Structure plans would have a time horizon of fifteen or twenty years but the 'key diagram', showing the proposed disposition of development, would not have an Ordnance Survey (OS) base. Local plans would generally be of ten years' duration and would contain OS-based land allocations.

The process of preparing structure plans is complex. Policies are based on a survey of the area in question and, using Government predictions of population and migration, the preparation of forecasts of future economic activity and housing requirements. In the early stages this technical planning activity is complemented by consultation with important sectoral interests with land use concerns such as the Ministry of Agriculture, the National Coal Board and the Department of Industry. Draft proposals are open to comment by such statutory consultees and the public (see Figure 3.1). Following such consultations, and the approval of policies by the local authority, final proposals are submitted to the Ministry for approval.

The approval process involves the Ministry convening an Examination in Public (EIP) of the Plan. This consists of a searching examination of the main policies of a plan, or of those policies that have provoked substantial controversy, before a two or three person panel nominated by the Minister. Green belts have been discussed at the EIPs of thirty-one of the thirty-four structure plans which proposed the policy. In this rather incestuous forum, Ministry officials decide the agenda of issues, brief the panel before the proceedings, and can co-opt reluctant participants. They may even assist in writing the panel report, a document giving recommendations to the Minister to aid officials (often the same ones) in arriving at decisions to confirm or amend policies in the plan. The Ministry then issues a statement of proposed modifications and, following further negotiations with interested parties, approves the plan, usually with a variety of amendments. The plan preparation procedure thus allows for an element of public participation in its early stages but tends, in its later important stages, to be a dialogue between central and local government. The vetting and approval process allows central Government to intervene in order to alter policies in the national or regional interest, and to ensure a degree of consistency of policies in different parts of the country, or within regions.[14]

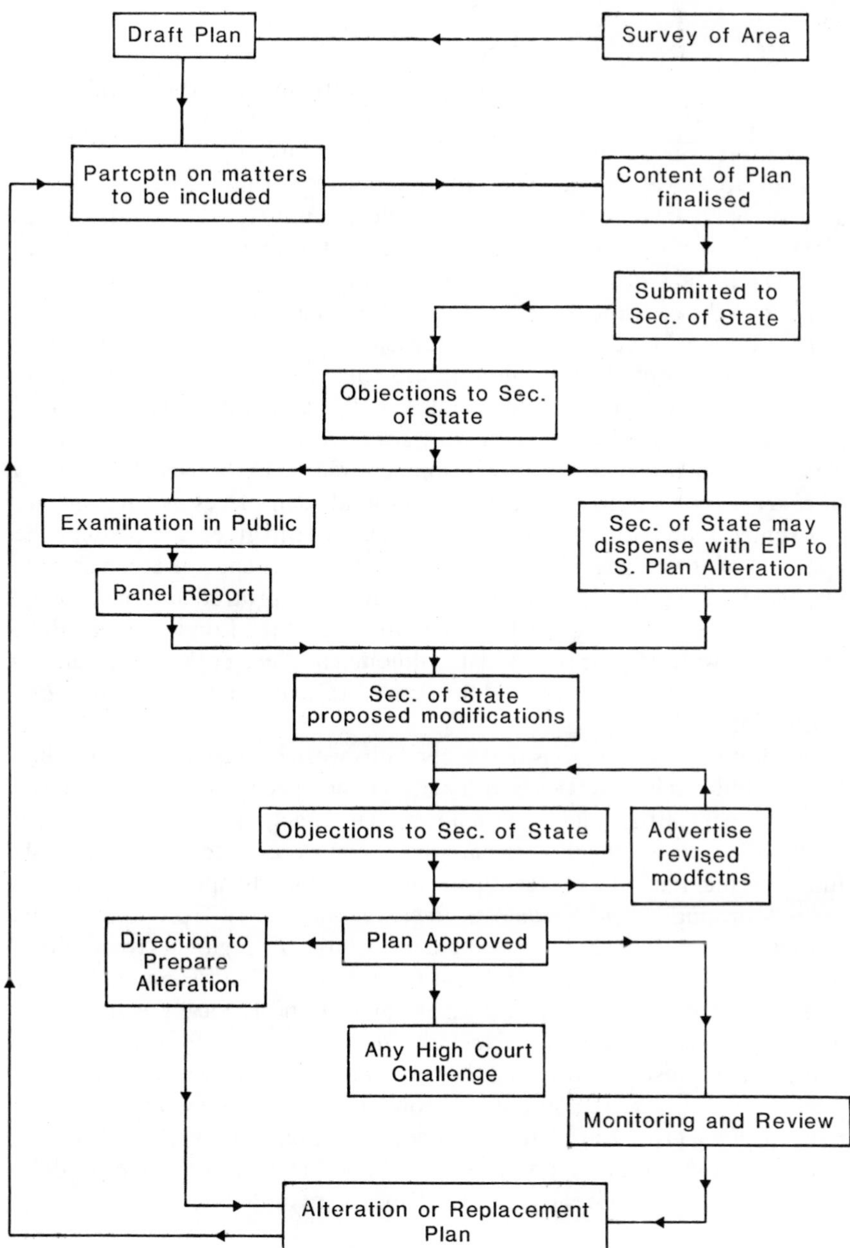

Figure 3.1 The Structure Plan Process
Source: Adapted from a diagram produced by DoE (1983)

The Green Belt Inheritance

Green belts inherited from the old system often appeared illogical in the context of post-1974 local government boundaries. Changes in a number of areas altered drastically the balance of urban and rural land potentially available for development. The City of Salford for example, by annexing an area of open land to the west of its old administrative boundary, was presented with new possibilities for locating housing requirements. Walsall's acquisition of the Aldridge–Brownhills area in the West Midlands resulted in the creation of a similar room for manoeuvre.

The status of much of the inherited pattern was, in addition, far from clear. A number of planning authorities such as Salop, around Telford, and Durham County south and east of Gateshead, had operated 'green belt type' policies with tacit Ministry approval, although no sketch plans had been cleared for incorporation into development plans. In the post-1972 period Ministry adjudications on green belts around such places as Birmingham–Coventry and Oxford had left much land as interim green belt pending the approval of structure and local plans. In other areas angular green shapes, representing green belts in approved town maps, protruded nonsensically into areas of submitted green belt. In most areas of the London Green Belt, town maps were 15 years out of date, although in West Yorkshire around 20 town maps had been approved at the time of a Government *Joint Green Belt Study* in 1974.

In addition, the functions that green belts were expected to perform had become blurred in practice. Green belts had been adapted to perform more all-embracing urban and rural management functions. The Government study in Yorkshire concluded that green belts were performing at least six functions including the protection of countryside landscapes and patterns of upland farming.[15] *The North West Regional Study* in 1973 proposed a dual purpose Green Belt where land would be included in 'regional green belts' if not required for urban use and also because of its landscape quality and recreation potential. Local authorities could propose 'local green belts' to add to those defined at regional level.[16] *The Strategic Plan for the South East* had gone farthest in suggesting that green belts should be used to delimit growth areas in the region outside London, and that they might even be needed *within* growth areas to shape and manage patterns of development.[17] Such variety attracted adverse comment. F. H. Layfield complained in 1974, in the context of the Greater London Development Plan:

> The deficiencies in aims and policies for the green belt are the product of drift . . . in not a single one of the green belt documents of this country is . . . (there) . . . any appraisal of the costs such a policy involves or any attempt to balance the advantages and disadvantages of retaining, amending or ending the present green belt provisions.[18]

The consideration of proposals in structure plans constituted this reassessment as all policies were required to be justified anew. The compromise that the old green belts represented was long overdue for renegotiation, but during the first round of structure plan approvals no new national advice was issued on how the inclusion of green belts in the new plans was to be justified.

The advice in Circulars 42/55 and 50/57 remained in place. Reconsideration of the provisions of the Circulars had occurred within the Ministry from time to time after 1970 but the need for new advice had, according to officials, never been established. The green belt, it was argued, is a simple concept well understood by the public and therefore supported by them. Changes could undermine this essential precondition for its continued use. Central Government has, however, wished to see:

1. simple, clear and unambiguous green belt proposals in structure plans justified by reference to only one or more of the three criteria (sprawl, coalescence, character preservation) of Circular 42/55;
2. proposals supporting regional strategies for appropriate patterns of development and restraint;
3. no large extensions to the areas covered by the policy lest these 'devalue' the concept; and
4. only one category of fully approved green belt, dispensing with interim and provisional green belts.

It was also clear from the *Joint Green Belt Study* that pre-existing green belt policies should neither entirely determine the location of new development, nor should they be a residual policy; 'the definition of green belts should be an integral part of the process'.[19] This implied that in the technical and political sieving process to find necessary land for new development local authorities should evaluate green belts to see if they were still performing valid Circular 42/55 functions, and were suited to doing so for the plan period. However if the extent of formally approved green belts had been correctly assessed at their inception, it was not expected that much land would be required to be withdrawn from the notation in new plans. Interim and provisionally approved green belts were in a far more fluid situation as subsequent events were to reveal.

The New Pattern

The legacy of the old system consisted of 6,930 square kilometres of fully approved green belt and 7,540 square kilometres of land where green belt policies of varying status applied. It is estimated that the thirty-four structure plans containing green belt proposals put forward new belts, and extensions to existing ones, totalling an additional 6,270 square kilometres. If approved in their entirety these would have constituted green belt coverage for 13.8

per cent of England and Wales. They involved proposals to extend green belts to the boundaries, almost without exception, of all the Metropolitan Counties. The main *new* areas proposed are given emphasis in Figures 3.2 and 3.3. They included South East Northumberland and Tyne and Wear; North Yorkshire (bordering Cleveland); and in the south of the County: North East Lancashire; the South-West Lancashire plain; the North Cheshire plain; South Yorkshire around Telford, Salop; Worcestershire and Warwickshire; South Cambridgeshire; and South East Dorset.

In terms of area covered the most striking proposals were in the North West and Northern Regions. A continuous Belt around Merseyside, Greater Manchester, West and South Yorkshire would, if approved, have given coverage from Chester in the west to York in the east, and from Preston in the north to south of Macclesfield. In the South East a Belt would have run from south of Reading to Canvey Island, and from north of Cambridge to the borders of Gatwick Airport. Other proposals included a number of small separating Green Belts in the Fylde Coast area, including one to separate Carnforth and Morecambe, areas bordering Crawley in West Sussex, and an area east of Yeovil within Dorset. As in the 1958–62 period, Ministry consideration has reduced the area of the proposed extensions. The broad areas of green belt actually approved in Plans (Table 3.1) totalled 15,815

Table 3.1 Estimated Area of New Green Belts 1984

Green Belt	*Area Sought in Plans*[1]	*Area Approved in Plans*[1]
	Square kilometres	
Birmingham–Coventry	3,430	2,534
Bristol–Bath[2]	666	660
Cambridge–South Cambridgeshire	448	161
Cheltenham–Gloucester	90	72
Hampshire Coast–Dorset	1,011	909
Tyneside–Northumberland	868	643
Nottingham–Derby	852	576
Oxford	356	354
Stoke-on-Trent	451	451
West, South and North Yorkshire	4,035	2,334
North East Lancashire and Fylde	243	243
Merseyside, Greater Manchester, Cheshire and South and East Lancashire	2,083	2,073
London[3]	5,791	4,454
Luton–Dunstable	351	351
Yeovil–West Dorset	64	—
Total	20,739	15,815

1. Indicative estimates made by the Author.
2. Formal approval of Structure Plan awaited at September 1984.
3. Including small areas in West Sussex.

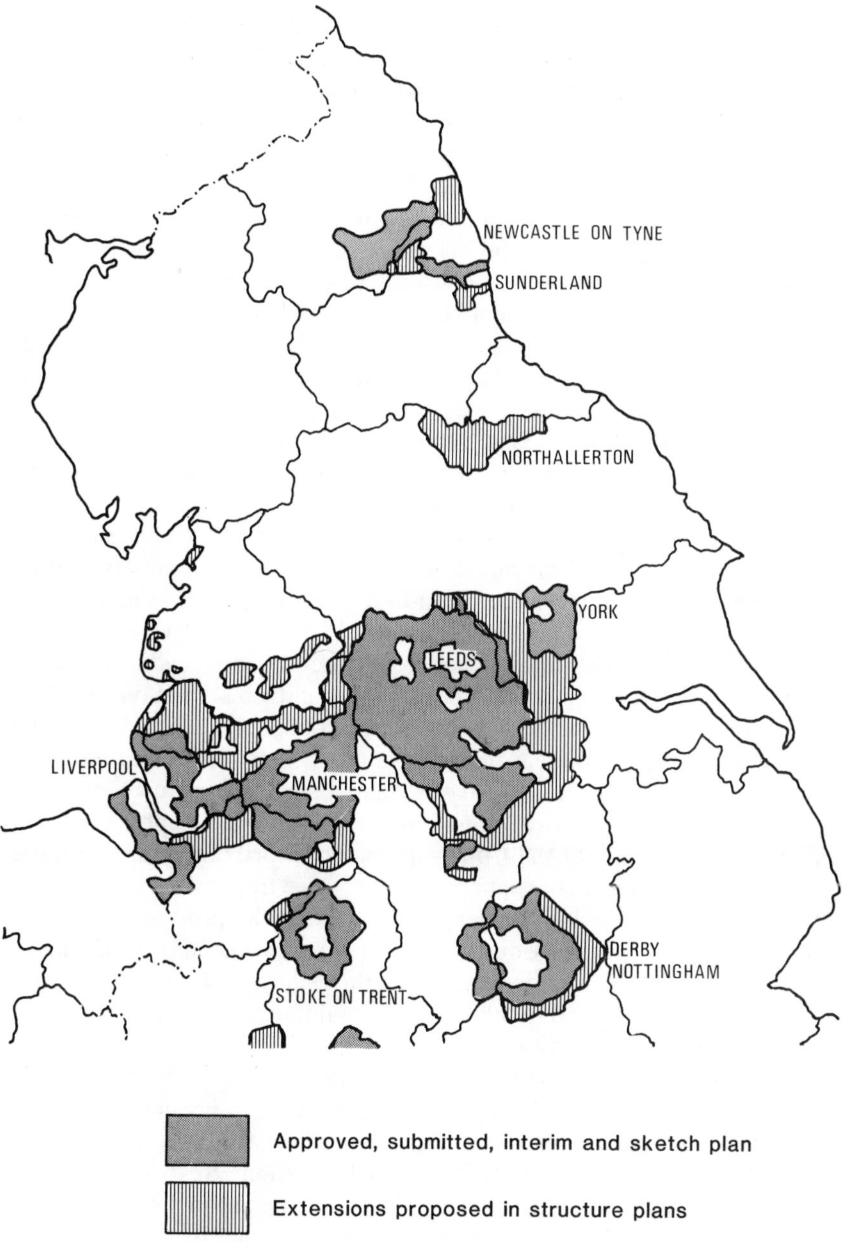

Figure 3.2 Green Belts Proposed 1974–84 (Northern England)
Source: Submitted and Approved Structure Plans

square kilometres in 1984, some 10.5 per cent of the land area of England and Wales.[20] This constitutes less than a 10 per cent increase in the land covered by *all types* of green belt policy in 1976 but a 110 per cent increase in the area of *fully approved* green belt. What then have been the main adjustments made in the five major conurbations?[21]

The Conurbation Green Belts

In *Tyneside/Wearside* the proposed Green Belt was to cover all land not required under any set of land release assumptions in the Metropolitan County area, and included a proposed eastward extension of the Northumberland Belt to the coast near Newbiggin.[22] In defining the Green Belt, Tyne and Wear County had taken the most optimistic regional assumptions regarding future economic activity, and added a contingent allowance of 1,500 hectares between built up areas and the proposed inner boundary.[23] However the Districts, in competition for new employment, and keen to keep room for manoeuvre to locate new housing, saw no reason for extending the old pattern of Green Belts. The Ministry therefore produced a compromise whereby some extensions were made to the old pattern in Tyne and Wear, but the new Belt would not reach the County boundary south of Gateshead and Sunderland, or north-east of Newcastle. In seeking urban regeneration, the Tyne and Wear Structure Plan proposed a concentration of housing provision in inner urban areas. The Ministry readjusted this to allow for a greater proportion of housing demands to be met on the urban peripheries. They added 60 per cent to the totals for housing land in the outer and intermediate areas of each District.[24] This support for decentralization and the market will involve land being taken from previously approved Green Belt between Sunderland and Newcastle upon Tyne, and on the northern edge of the Conurbation. The Northumberland proposal was rejected on grounds of vagueness. It appeared from evidence at the EIP that little detailed work had been done to justify the proposal, and there remained doubts over the County's attitude towards the approval of major employment-related development within the Belt if it was approved.[25] The new Green Belt is approximately 640 square kilometres in area, a 45 per cent increase on the area approved before 1974.

In *Yorkshire* extensive changes to the pattern of Green Belts were proposed (Figure 3.2).[26] North Yorkshire considered that policies of development restraint were necessary to resist commuter pressure from outside the County. They proposed a band of Green Belt, 14 kilometres wide, across the north of the County extending south to Richmond and Northallerton, and a large new area in the south of the County below a line from Harrogate to York. Both South and West Yorkshire proposed virtually complete green belt coverage outside urban areas, but to take advantage of locational factors in West Yorkshire, for example, two 'areas of search' totalling 225 hectares were proposed for removal from Green Belt around Morley and Rothwell in the M62 corridor in Wakefield District.

Neither of the North Yorkshire extensions received approval from the Ministry, who considered that Circular 42/55 reasons did not apply. The proposal north of Northallerton was reduced in size, following District Council opposition before the EIP, and was rejected by the Minister who considered that normal development control powers would be adequate to restrain development.[27] In South Yorkshire the eastern extension around Doncaster was opposed by the District and rejected by the Ministry. Normal development control policies were adjudged sufficient to control new development.

As was noted in Chapter 1, the old West Riding Green Belt was far looser than those for the West Midlands or Greater London; it was more of a 'green background' or 'blanket'. The EIP Panel for West Yorkshire concluded the Green Belt was too large but, despite objections to its 'indiscriminate use' from Rochdale District, considered there was insufficient objection from participants to suggest the need for a complete review. The Ministry approved a Belt which performs a shaping function around towns. They also accepted the view of Leeds City Council that there was insufficient land to solve the City's housing problems in the Plan, and extended the scope for peripheral development west and south of the City, and in the Morley area. Despite the views of the *Joint Green Belt Study* and the EIP Panel the extent of Green Belt in the Yorkshire and Humberside Region (2,330 square kilometres) exceeds that before reorganization by 11 per cent.

Around *Manchester and Merseyside* the advice of the 1973 Regional Study was also reflected in local authority proposals. In the southern part of Lancashire and in Cheshire, large new areas of Green Belt were proposed, in the latter case a Belt across the Cheshire Plain joining together the longstanding Wirral and north-east Cheshire areas and extending south around Macclesfield. (Figure 3.2).

Again discussion of the balance to be struck between peripheral development and inner city regeneration dominated discussion at both Metropolitan County EIPs. In Merseyside a relatively tight Green Belt was approved 'to check the outward spread of the built up areas . . . and to direct development into existing towns and encourage their regeneration.'[28] In Greater Manchester, approved policies reflect intentions to concentrate development in the centre of the Conurbation, although this has proved compatible with the allocation of substantial greenfield allocations in areas west of Salford and south of Bolton. Also a wide range of new peripheral industrial sites have been allowed for, mainly along the M62 corridor. The approved Green Belt is a *shaping* and *separating* device in the northern part of the County and a *restraining* and *diverting* device in the south on the edges of Stockport and Trafford. (Chapter 4 discusses Greater Manchester in more detail). In Cheshire the Green Belt extension across the north of the County was approved with the exception of an area bordering the Mersey Estuary (the Frodsham–Helsby Marshes) which has high potential for industrial development. The new contiguous Green Belt area in Merseyside, Manchester, Cheshire and Southern Lancashire is estimated to be 2,073 square kilometres, an increase of 63 per cent over the area subject to the policy before 1974.

The *West Midlands* Green Belt has the longest history under the new development plans system. Eleven structure plans for old local authority areas with Green Belt were submitted prior to local government reorganization. Only since 1981 have some of their proposals been consolidated into structure plans covering the new County area. In this Region the Green Belt has been most obviously defined with recreation needs in mind. The new proposals contain Green Wedges drawn closer to the centre of the Conurbation (for example in the Sandwell Wedge).[29]

In the remainder of the Conurbation both Warwickshire and Worcestershire proposed southward extensions of the Green Belt. (Figure 3.3) In the case of Warwickshire the extension to the northern edge of Stratford-upon-Avon was approved. The original Worcestershire proposals, south of Worcester towards Malvern, were seen as too extensive for Circular 42/55 purposes and likely to devalue the concept. The approved Belt was cut back to a line south of Kidderminster and Redditch, with an additional small area separating Droitwich and Worcester.[30] From 1971 Salop had operated a *de facto* Green Belt policy in a 16 kilometre radius of Telford New Town. This was to concentrate new development and economic activity in the designated area, and to avoid the surrounding villages becoming 'gentrified'. Although confirmation of this area as Green Belt was sought in the Salop Structure Plan (the proposal being included at the instigation of the Ministry) it was subsequently turned down. The measure was seen as possibly of limited duration, and would not be needed if development impetus in Telford increased.

The West Midlands Green Belt is thus larger than that submitted in the early 1960s in respect of its southern outer boundaries. Its inner boundaries penetrate further into the urban fabric in some areas, whilst withdrawal of Green Belt coverage in parts of Aldridge–Brownhills, Sutton Coldfield, South Staffordshire, and Solihull has taken place. In the latter case an attempt was made to adjust the *rate* of peripheral housing growth in line with progress in building in the urban priority areas. Virtually all new areas for employment and housing-related development have been found in land of Interim Green Belt status, 510 square kilometres of which was left open for further discussion in 1975. Thus around one per cent of the total 1,920 square kilometres shown in the 1975 map has been indicated for development and around 20 per cent has been added to its southern outer edges.

Around *London* the longstanding Green Belt extensions have now been reconsidered, as have new proposals in Cambridgeshire and West Sussex

(Figure 3.3). In arriving at the new broad Green Belt the influence of Government has again been paramount. In 1978 the proceedings of the House of Commons Select Committee on Regional affairs revealed that for 'normal' purposes the new Green Belt should be 19–24 kilometres (12–15 miles) wide from its boundary with the Greater London built-up area.[31] The major proposals included extensions to cover the whole of Hertfordshire and Surrey, and westwards to Wokingham District in Berkshire. Further Green Belt stretching east to Southend and Chelmsford and extending north of Stansted Airport was also proposed for confirmation. Two new proposals were made: an extension from the North Hertfordshire boundary to the southern boundary of the Cambridge Green Belt, and an area south from the Surrey County boundary around parts of Gatwick Airport in West Sussex. These proposals if approved would have extended the London Green Belt to a general depth of 40 kilometres, and in some cases, as in the North Hertfordshire–Cambridge direction, to between 55 and 65 kilometres.

The decisions made by Ministry officials since 1978 have cut back the

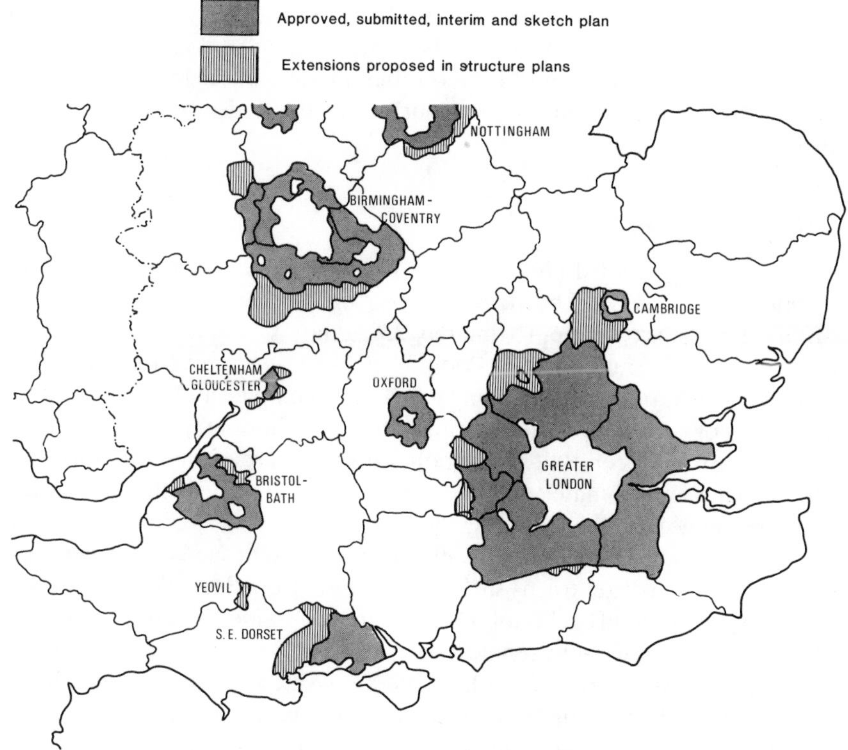

Figure 3.3 Green Belts Proposed 1974–84 (Southern England)
Source: Submitted and Approved Structure Plans

proposals by an average of eight kilometres around most of London. The Cambridgeshire proposal was turned down because other policies of development restriction were considered sufficient for the regional strategic purpose, intended restricting development to local needs arising in the area.[32] The Hertfordshire and Surrey proposals were reduced because blanket green belt coverage was seen as an inappropriate use of Circular 42/55 (see also page 70). The West Sussex proposal was considered not to have demonstrated why the special measure of green belt was necessary and, in view of amendments to the Green Belt in Surrey which would have left the Sussex proposal isolated, it was rejected. In Berkshire the proposal was cut back to a line east of Bracknell to allow all parts of the Central Berkshire 'growth area' to be considered in any search for new development land; this was also the rationale for a cut-back in the Surrey Heath District in western Surrey. In Essex the new Green Belt has been retracted to a line south of Stansted Airport and there is an M12 salient extending as far as the southern boundaries of Chelmsford. The Southend Green Belt, (originally proposed by Essex as a Local Green Belt) was approved, but as part of a specially justified extension beyond the normal London Green Belt.[33] If the South Cambridgeshire and West Sussex proposals are included there has been an increase of 58 per cent (from 3,030 to 4,810 square kilometres) in *fully approved* Green Belt around London, but a reduction of 15 per cent from the area (5,660 square kilometres) subject to full and interim controls at 1976.[34]

Other Green Belts

The main new Green Belts approved in plans are an area of 240 square kilometres around Blackburn, Accrington and Burnley in *North East Lancashire*, and an area of approximately 250 square kilometres in *South East Dorset* north of Bournemouth–Poole. The first was approved as part of an urban concentration theme seeking to maintain compact and separate towns in this part of Lancashire. The second area is one of more rapid development where a narrow Green Belt, and a policy of 'green areas' were put forward. The Ministry amalgamated these to form a Green Belt 7–8 kilometres wide and contiguous with that covering the New Forest.

Five small 'separating' Green Belts have been approved on the *Fylde* in Lancashire to separate towns such as Blackpool from St Annes, Fleetwood from Cleveleys, and Blackpool from Poulton-Le-Fylde (Figure 3.4). Further north, a Green Belt now separates Lancaster, Morecambe and Carnforth. The smallest approved areas in England and Wales are 'separating' Green Belts between Burton upon Trent and Swadlincote in South Derbyshire, and Rawtenstall and Bacup in Rossendale, Lancashire. A proposal for a Green Belt covering 64 square kilometres of land between Sherborne and Yeovil in Dorset in order to retain open land between the two settlements,

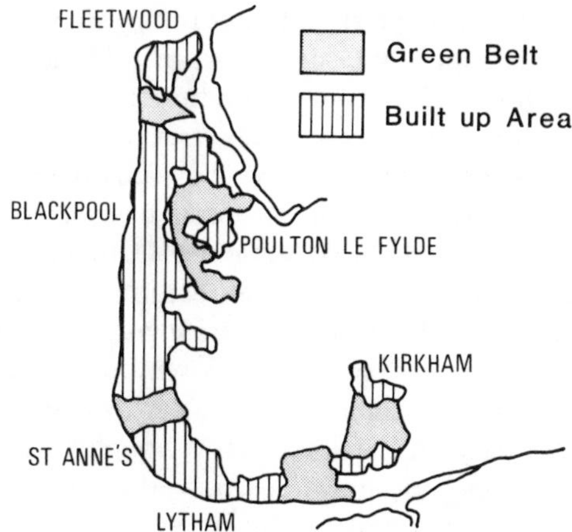

Figure 3.4 Separating Green Belts in the Fylde, Lancashire
Source: Adapted from DoE *Central and North Lancashire Structure Plan: Report of Panel* (DoE: Manchester, 1981)

and to preserve the character of two villages within the area, was rejected by the Ministry.

Structure Plan Alterations

Once approved in a structure plan a green belt should only be changed in 'exceptional circumstances'.[35] What constitutes these exceptional circumstances is, in the final analysis, left open to Government interpretation. In practice, assessment of the relevance of policies at local level is under continuous review and therefore a succession of alterations to green belts is likely. In some areas, such as South Staffordshire, alterations to approved Green Belt boundaries have been the consequence of changes in the housing requirements imposed by Government rewriting of structure plans.[36] Thus land in the 1975 approved Belt was taken for housing in 1980, and by 1984 the approval of the Alterations to the Staffordshire Structure Plan implied a similar exercise would be required.

In the West Midlands, it was argued at the EIP into alterations to the Structure Plan, such exceptional circumstances exist. A rapid deterioration in the local economy since 1979, with jobs being lost at a rate faster than any other region in the Country, dictates a reappraisal of land use policy. The need is to widen the focus from inner city regeneration to regeneration of the whole regional economy. This dictates a different attitude to peripheral restraint.[37] It is argued that as an 'essential first step' to restructuring the regional economy, an environmentally-attractive Green Belt location should be selected to attract modern companies using high technology. West Midlands County have thus proposed the most marketable location currently within the approved Green Belt adjacent to the M6 and M42 Motorways (and the National Exhibition Centre) for an intended high technology development, and the City have purchased the necessary land at little more than agricultural value. This approach reverses the conventional view that firm peripheral restraint by green belts will best aid urban regeneration. The Government decision to approve this proposal has provided the first test of the term 'exceptional circumstances' in the 1984 Circular.

The continuous nature of central–local relations over green belts is well illustrated by reference to Hertfordshire (see Figure 3.5). Here six 'changes' have occurred over a ten year period. The submitted Structure Plan of 1976 proposed coverage for the whole County after assessed development requirements to 1991 had been provided for. Although the EIP recommended approval, the first proposed alterations, issued under the stewardship of Peter Shore, suggested that neither the sprawl nor the coalescence arguments were valid north of the line on the 1977 map in Figure 3.5. Based on the statement in the Ministry letter that proposals to avoid the coalescence of settlements beyond the 19–24 kilometre band might be considered, councillors and officers from Hertfordshire met the Minister in London to press their case. The result was the approval of a northward salient of Green Belt to stop the coalescence of Hitchin, Letchworth and Baldock and to contain Stevenage.[38]

The controversial decision to omit Green Belt around Bishop's Stortford pending the outcome of the Stansted (Third London Airport) Inquiry was immediately countered by local proposals. East Hertfordshire District included a 'Local Green Belt' in their local plan and this was certified by the County as in conformity with the Structure Plan. Early drafts of the North Hertfordshire District Plan suggested complete coverage for the area deleted by the Minister in 1979. At the EIP into the Alterations to the Structure Plan in 1982, the Panel discussed Green Belt additions around Bishop's Stortford and in the west of the County near Luton Airport (Figure 3.5: 1980 map). The Panel recommended by two to one (with the Ministry's Regional Controller dissenting in each case) that appropriate conditions for green belt policy did apply, and recommended their approval.[39] The Regional Office accepted its own minority view and turned down the Bishop's Stortford proposal, because of the unresolved Third London Airport situation, but approved the small addition on the western boundary of the County.[40]

This sequence of events, typical of what is going on around the Country, shows the power of the centre. Even where, on a 'disinterested' technical assessment, a green belt is seen as justified, Government does not need to accept the recommendations of its own EIP Panels. Agreement on the areas to be covered by green belt thus emerges through a process which narrows, through time, to negotiation between county and Ministry officials. In this way 'regional policy', which now exists increasingly only in the heads of

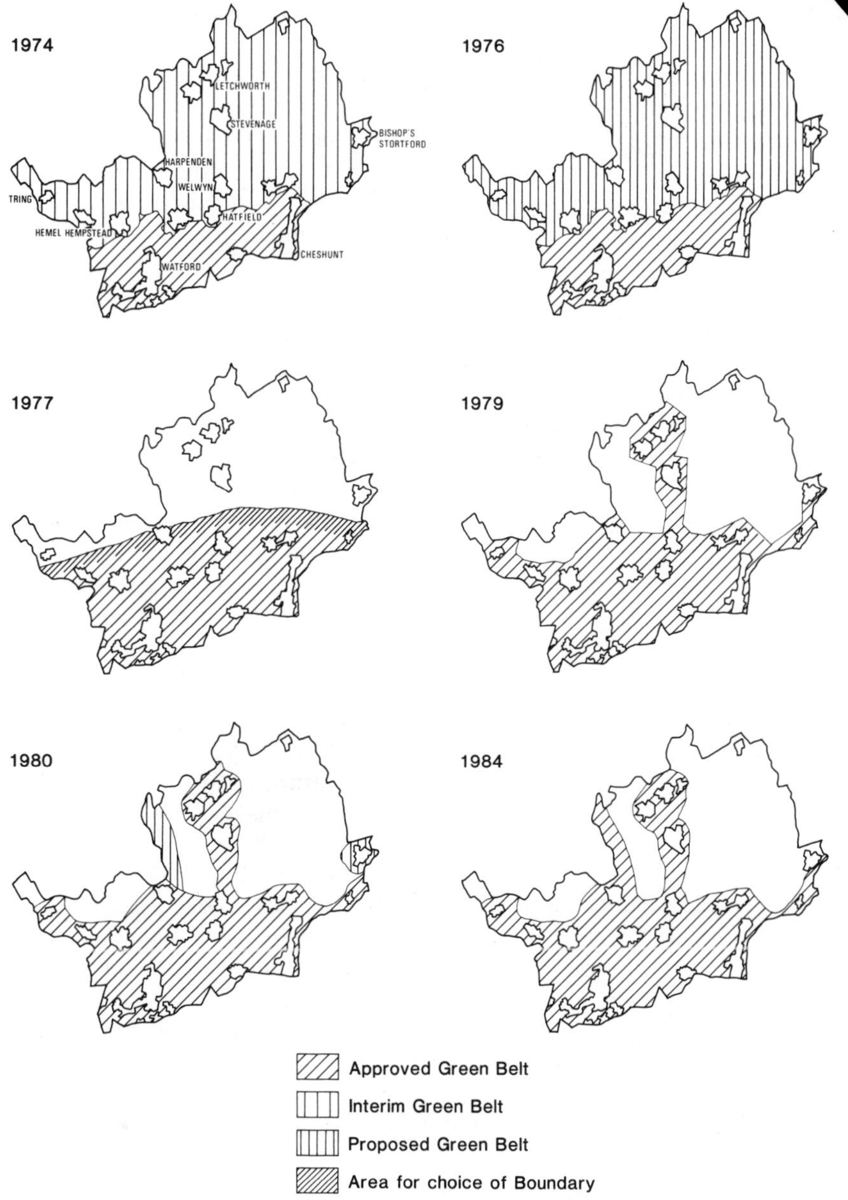

Figure 3.5 The Evolution of Green Belts in Hertfordshire
Sources: Adapted from Hertfordshire County Council (HCC: Hertford) (various): *County Development Plan* (1958); *First Review of the County Development Plan* (1971); *Hertfordshire 1981* (1973); *Structure Plan (Submitted)* (1976); *Structure Plan (Approved)* (1979); *Structure Plan – Alteration No. 1 (Submitted)* (1980); *Structure Plan – Alteration No. 1 (Approved)* (1984)

cials, can be rewritten by one-off decisions largely isolated from f public participation.

son of the new pattern at national level with that in 1976 shows t change (see Figure 3.6). The areas fully approved before local eorganization have virtually all been retained, but not all of the ..g submitted proposals, and even fewer of the new proposals, have been approved. The examinations by Ministry officials have focused on ensuring that adequate supplies of land are available for housebuilding. In each case the prospects and marketability of inner areas for building have been subjectively assessed and judgements made on the emphasis to be given to peripheral restraint. By 'playing safe' in seeking to maintain supplies of marketable housebuilding land there has been some 'nibbling' at the inner edges of the areas previously operating green belt policies around all the major conurbations except London. However only London has had a tight fully-approved Green Belt in place around all of its periphery for any length of time, and provision has been made in other towns in the South East. These decisions can thus be seen as the first time the principles of Circular 42/55 have been fully tested through to approval in plans outside London. What then do they say about the functions of green belts in the 1980s?

Green Belt Justifications

The process of deciding what is the proper use of green belt policy has been contentious and time consuming. Because green belts are seen as long-term, extending beyond the period of structure plans, Ministry officials have paid close attention to every proposal. The major discussions between Government and local authorities have stressed the determining influence of the Circular 42/55 justifications. Lack of Circular-based advice at this crucial stage in fixing the new broad areas of green belt has meant the costly reworking of many proposals, and the lack of public involvement in the 'behind-closed-doors' negotiations that have gone on is a feature of the decisions reached. The process of appreciation of the strictly limited situations in which green belt policy can validly be used has taken nearly a decade.

The negotiative process around the country appears to have established the following principles:

1. *green belts are not an agricultural land, landscape or general countryside protection device.*

Looking at the open land around major cities planners were faced not only with problems of urban sprawl and the merging of towns resulting from demands for increased urban living standards (even where populations were static); but also with those of agricultural land protection, landscape con-

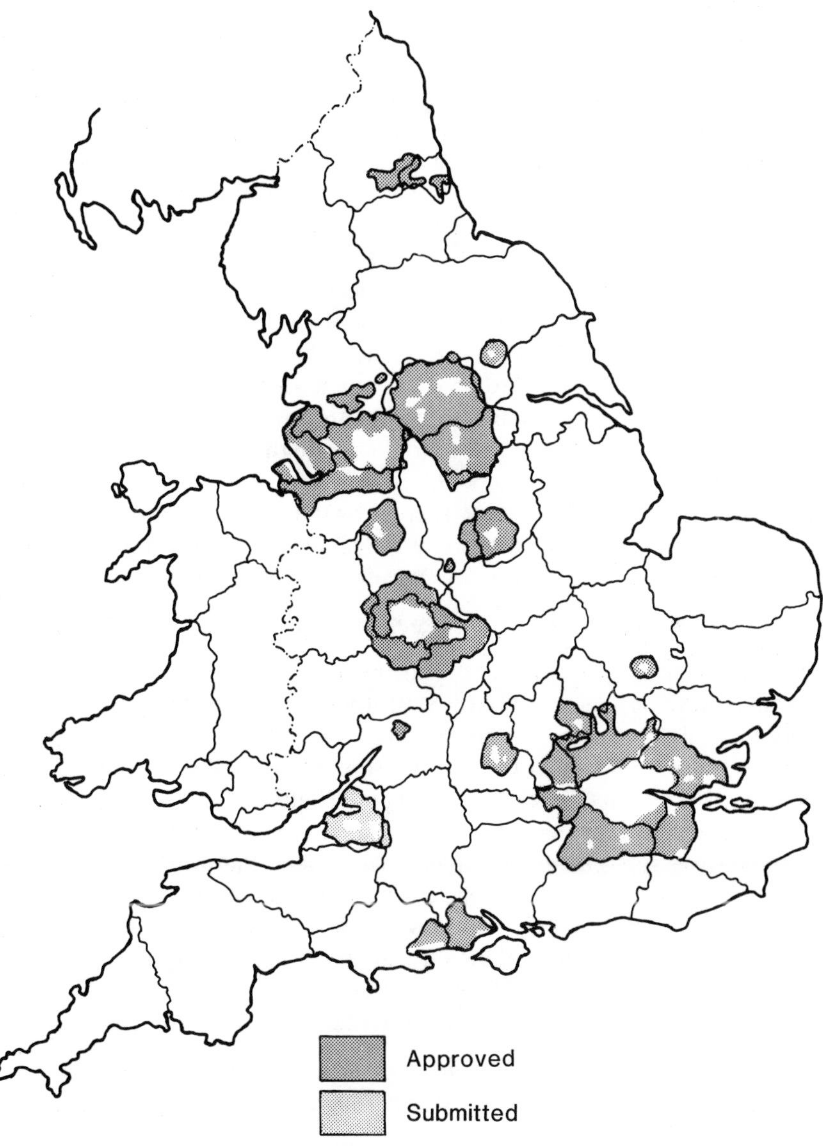

Figure 3.6 Green Belts Approved in Structure Plans 1984
Source: Adapted from House of Commons Environment Committee *Green Belt and Land for Housing*, HC 275-II (HMSO: London, 1984), between pp. 6 and 7.

servation and provision for expanding leisure demands. As a result the green belt was often put forward in structure plans as an all purpose policy. Faced with the alternative of a complicated priority zoning system for agricultural protection and selective recreation provision, this seemed the more intelligable solution. Thus, although counties such as South Yorkshire took the view '. . . in general terms to use the Green Belt as the main means of conserving environmental resources' this did not survive Government scrutiny.[41] In Buckinghamshire the Panel stated unequivocally, '. . . the reasons for establishing green belt are not related directly to the attractiveness of an area of countryside'.[42]

Where conservation and recreation objectives have been adduced, rulings have stressed that other policies are available. In Northumberland countryside management plans were suggested, in North Yorkshire Green Belts 'should not be used for controlling development where other administrative policies are already available for the purpose, for example, to protect agricultural land'.[43] The major contradiction to this theme appears to be the New Forest (Hampshire) where Green Belt status was approved to protect a natural resource under heavy recreational use. 'The New Forest is a significant area and it is appropriate to include the whole of it in the green belt *in the absence of any more suitable designation*' (Author's emphasis).[44]

2. *green belts can assist urban regeneration*

This has been accepted in all of the northern conurbations, as already noted. Around Stoke-on-Trent (North Staffordshire) the new 'tight green belt cordon' will not only resist the spread of the Potteries towns, but will also 'concentrate resources in the conurbation' with the active support of the conurbation District Councils.[45] Thus green belts now often receive support from the very authorities who opposed their creation in the 1950s, support derived from an argument which is the reverse of that which convinced the Government in 1955 that national coverage was desirable. The main contradiction here is in South Yorkshire where it was proposed to extend Green Belt coverage to the whole of the rural area to support a policy of inner urban Job Priority Areas. The EIP Panel offered the view that this was not an appropriate use of green belt policy and the Minister concurred.[46]

3. *green belts are not usually appropriate for preserving the character, or checking the sprawl of small towns and villages*

Thus in Tyne and Wear it was considered that Green Belt was not necessary to preserve the special character of any of the small towns in the County, though '. . . extension of the boundaries of Conservation Areas to preserve the open setting where this is of significance could be appropriate'.[47] In considering the proposed extension of the London Green Belt westwards in the Chilterns Area of Outstanding Natural Beauty (AONB) the Panel for Buckinghamshire stated '. . . we are sympathetic to the general aim of protecting as much of the AONB as possible from incongruous development, but we do not consider that the Green Belt is the appropriate planning instrument for this purpose'.[48] They considered that AONB and rural settlement policies were sufficiently strongly worded to perform the task.

4. *development pressures must be sufficiently strong, or the danger of coalescence sufficiently high, to make such a special policy necessary*

These highly subjective criteria have been liberally applied around the country. For example a proposal to extend the Cheltenham–Gloucester 'green barrier' south of Gloucester was adjudged unnecessary as there was considered no danger of coalescence with other settlements. Proposals in North Yorkshire were turned down on the basis that the Ministry was not convinced that there was sufficient pressure for housing and development 'to satisfy the national criteria for extending the Green Belt'.[49] However, in rather contradictory tone, Ministry officials accepted that national criteria did not apply to the green wedge between Burton upon Trent and Swadlincote. It was, nevertheless, approved as a Green Belt because it was the local authorities' intention to apply controls of green belt severity to the area.

5. *there are no technically-derivable formulae for green belt width or size*

Under this criterion the suggestion by Nottinghamshire that the width of the Green Belt around the City of Nottingham should be defined by reference to daily journey to work catchments was rejected. The 'twelve to fifteen miles' width for the London Green Belt is an administrative convenience. It would be difficult to claim that keeping open fields east of Haslemere in Surrey (32 kilometres from the Greater London boundary) is vital to stopping the unrestricted sprawl of Greater London, or of stopping coalescence.

6. *green belts should not be approved where the need for development can be foreseen*

As in the late 1950s, the Ministry has been keen to keep green belt out of areas where development may, at some foreseeable time, be contemplated. This well illustrates the idea of permanence, and rules out the use of green belt to concentrate development in particular locations during the course of development of a growth area, as suggested in 1970 in the Strategic Plan for the South East (see page 54). The Government view of this is well illustrated by Panel comments on the Central and East Berkshire Structure Plans. East Berkshire forms part of the London Green Belt and is an area of severe restraint, but Central Berkshire is part of one of the nominated growth areas in the Regional Strategy for the South East. Berkshire proposed Green Belt coverage in parts of the growth area not already allocated for development; this would allow them to limit new development to existing commitments in plans.[50] As these were used up, assessment of future land to be released would be made in the course of a review of the Structure Plan when '. . . sites within the Central Berkshire part of the Green Belt will be considered on an equal footing with sites further west'.[51] In rejecting this proposition the EIP Panel saw it as representing uncertainty and lack of permanence. They stated:

> . . . In our view permanence and certainty are necessary features of any green belt. A green belt subject to time limits or other qualifications . . . is not a true green belt in our understanding of the concept. By permanent we mean that at the time of . . . approval, there should not be in contemplation any substantial development in the foreseeable future inconsistent with designation.[52]

7. *green belts are not an all-embracing urban management device*

This argument can be explained most clearly with reference to Surrey. The County argued that the Green Belt was the cornerstone of the whole Structure Plan. It was the policy to which all others related. As the Panel states:

> . . . The Green Belt policy was to be drawn, initially, tightly up to existing urban areas and probably right across villages and smaller settlements, but these boundaries would then be retracted, albeit with reluctance, as circumstances dictated. As the County put it their Green Belt was to be used as their main management tool. What is really envisaged is a green belt *type* policy operating over the County.[53]

This method of use was seen as inappropriate by the Ministry as it would leave important areas subject to 'green belt policies' but not within fully approved Green Belt. In short the policy would be unclear. The release of land covered by 'green belt policies' would depend on the local authorities being satisfied that certain criteria of local need had been proven. As these involved narrow categories of the population (for example newly married couples who could not afford to own their own home at Surrey house prices), they amounted to a policy of access to housing supposedly managed by Green Belt controls. The policy was deleted and replaced by conventional provision for a quantum of development as defined by the predicted future number of households in the County within firm long-term Green Belt boundaries. Of course, a number of Home County Authorities *have* used green belt policy as a ubiquitous urban management device over the last ten to fifteen years, and intend to continue doing so. Again therefore, a distinction must be made between the justification for inclusion of the policy in a plan and its subsequent use in the making of decisions.

A Process of Mediation

The decisions made by Government to create the new pattern have been described as inconsistent.[54] This is because they have been analyzed as if the task of 'fitting' green belts was purely a technical exercise. No one would suggest that development pressures in areas not covered by Green Belt in West Sussex, Surrey or North Hertfordshire are lower than in South Tyneside or parts of West Yorkshire covered by the policy. To explain the decisions more accurately the nature of the roles of central Government in approving plans must be taken into account. Government has an *administrative* function in approving plans which are clear and defensible. It has, as Solesbury has described, a *policy agenda* which it is seeking to pursue in the national interest, consisting of a set of conflicting conservation and development aims.[55] Thirdly it is operating to *mediate between interests* in a political arena. The policy currency being handled – green belt – is important because it helps structure central–local power relationships. Large green belts, because of their strong inherent presumptive nature, accord high levels of local control over development. As such they strengthen the local authority against central Government. They offer insurance against changes in central policy direction thus narrowing the field of action of the executive. Both 'sides' are acutely aware that decisions on green belts can be seen as a quest for policy control, the centre seeking to keep discretion open, the periphery attempting to narrow it. Increasingly, however, Government has been called on as a mediator between counties and districts, and this has kept it in a strong position to dictate its own wishes. Many of the decisions on green belt size can be seen in these terms – decisions which give a little to each of two or more opposed parties, whether development or conservation interests, or different local authorities.

The interests which require reconciliation around a defined green belt may be divided into those broadly concerned with conservation and those promoting development. Structure plan preparation and submission involves a process whereby a resolution of interests can take place through consultation, public participation, and local council consideration of emerging proposals. This may be a genuine reconciliation in the sense that enduring decisions are made, as in the Northallerton–North Yorkshire case prior to the EIP. It may often only be a short-term 'resolution' in that certain interests or alliances resolve the argument in their favour only to have the decision overturned later. In Central Berkshire the Green Belt *proposals* in the submitted Structure Plan represented a resolution in favour of local environmental and broader local authority interests but the *final* decisions in the approved plan reasserted the national view and the views of residential developers.

After a plan is submitted the Ministry, through the EIP process, 'tests' the policy against a different weighting of interests than those expressed through public participation. EIP proceedings are geared to participation by Government and other national (corporate) agencies and interests. If the outcome of the EIP is at variance with submitted proposals the Circulars may be used to support the changes made, or the final form of a belt may reflect a Ministry judgement on the balance of opposed forces (including counties and districts) at the time. 'Realism', in the sense of the future ability to administer a green belt policy, suggests no county will secure approval for a green belt where all the districts who are likely to operate it through development control are opposed.

The roles of the various interests in this process – the general public, amenity, conservation and environmental groups, development interests, Government departments and local authorities – are relevant here.

The role of the *general public* has been strictly circumscribed. Where consultation has taken place on the desirability of new belts or the rentention of existing ones, strong support for the stance of the planning authorities has been found. The well-known phenomenon of local resident support for conservation of the *status quo*, and a tendency for certain types of people to participate, is evident here. There was strong public support for example for the extension of Green Belts across the north Cheshire plain, in south-east Northumberland, and in North Yorkshire. Where random sample surveys have been carried out to avoid the biases found in invited comments, majority support for green belts has also been evident. City residents remain attracted by the idea of open country and green fields 'out there'; and suburbanites, conservationists, and green belt residents' are concerned to keep new development out of their areas. At EIPs the unorganized public voice is rarely heard but it may already be incorporated in the policies proposed in plans through participation in local politics.

A higher profile has been seen from some *conservation groups*. Council for the Protection of Rural England County Branches have taken the lead in encouraging new extensions to existing green belts and in opposing land take from existing ones. The Chilterns Society, for example, proposed an extension of the area of approved London Green Belt in South Buckinghamshire westwards along the Chilterns, and the Buckinghamshire CPRE a new Green Belt around Milton Keynes. Other groups such as the Northumberland Society, the Lancashire CPRE, the Hertfordshire Society, and the Surrey Amenity Council have been active in their pursuit of achieving maximum green belt coverage. However such groups have had little success in altering broad areas of green belt. Even in Tyne and Wear where strong opposition to a strategic housing proposal on the edge of the high status residential area of Gosforth was mounted at the EIP, the desired deflection of development was not achieved.

Development interests such as the House Builders Federation did not become involved in disputes over the principles of green belt during the preparation and examination of the early structure plans, although they have had effects through their continual concern to free more land for private housebuilding. The Federation, with an enhanced regional presence since 1980, have attempted to re-open green belt issues at some of the EIPs into alterations to structure plans. Their tactic has been to challenge the principles of boundary definition, and to suggest an interpretation of the word 'long-term' in Circulars which leaves white land for a fifteen or twenty years' supply of housing before green belt boundaries are drawn. Large regionally-based builders have also challenged green belts in some areas on the basis that their speculative land banks should be allocated for development. These have been important in the North East around Tyneside, for example.

Regional offices of the Confederation of British Industry and other employers' organizations have made little contribution at EIP discussions on green belts. Where they contribute they tend to criticize the tenor of restraint policies generally, but not specific green belt issues. Individual large firms have been concerned to protect their room for manoeuvre in respect of sites for expansion, and some local chambers of commerce and similar bodies have been concerned about the level of restraint that green belt implies.

Some *Government Departments* with an interest in development, the Department of Industry for example, have been concerned about specific areas (like the Frodsham–Helsby Marshes in Cheshire, and South East Northumberland), and in this they have been supported by employers' organizations. Other Government Departments or organizations have seen green belt as giving general support to their own specific concerns and interests. MAFF have expressed concern where good quality agricultural land has not been included in green belt, and the National Farmers' Union have supported green belt proposals as a method of affording basic protection to agricultural land. MAFF have, on occasion, been concerned that development might leapfrog green belts and affect good quality agricultural land beyond. In this situation they prefer 'blighted' peripheral land to be taken for development. The Countryside Commission have supported green belts for the opportunity they give to promote informal countryside recreation near towns and as a basic measure of landscape protection. However all of these groups have maintained a low profile at EIPs and through written consultations.

Unresolved *county–district* and inter-county conflicts have resurfaced at EIPs. For example, Buckinghamshire objected to Hertfordshire's County-wide proposals on the basis that they would 'devalue the concept', but more importantly because it was felt that housing pressures would be greater in south and mid-Buckinghamshire as a result. Objections by Surrey and Berkshire to each other's plans had the same motives. In the case of Yeovil, Somerset objected to the Dorset proposal. Many districts have objected to green belts proposed within their areas; Uttlesford, in the Stansted Airport area of Essex, Gateshead and North Tyneside in Tyne and Wear, Derby and Mansfield in the Nottingham–Derby case, and the City of Manchester in Greater Manchester are some of those involved. Although these objections are in some cases tied to issues of the deflection of development pressures, many have objected because of the question of who defines green belts, in that County control of the process reduces their right to determine their own planning policies at local level (see Chapter 4). Green belt discussions at EIPs have been dominated by substantial unresolved conflicts between counties and districts and Ministry officials have used the forum as an information gathering exercise to explore the possibilities for compromise.

Concluding Remarks

Through its quasi-judicial and administrative actions central Government has carried out its aim of limiting the 'drift' of formal justifications for the policy, and thus its coverage, successfully. The limitation of expansion to less than 10 per cent by area in the decade to 1984 is testament to this. Concern for broad conformity with green belt Circulars has been complemented by insistence that a supply of marketable land for housing and other development requirements are allowed for in plans. The effect has been to lay the foundation for a rolling supply of land for housing. These decisions have thus gone against the wishes of those living in urban peripheries and green belt towns seeking to limit change. The Ministry has exerted what it interprets as the national interest (often under the guise of adherence to regional advisory plans) especially in the South East where it judges that the greatest national gains from allocating new development land are to be had. Where there has been intense county-district conflict, Ministry officials have been strongly influenced by district views, particularly since the 1980 *Local Government, Planning and Land Act* stripped the counties of much of their remaining participation in the detailed operation of green belt development control.

Ministry officials are in frequent contact with planning officers over the content and style of development plans. It might be expected therefore that the level of apparent misunderstanding between the 'bids' made in structure plans and what was realistically attainable is unnecessarily high. The culture of contacts between the two levels soon establishes what is likely to be acceptable to Ministry officials, but it is difficult for local authorities to omit a green belt proposal during the preparation of a Plan, particularly if it has obtained strong support through public participation. In this situation it is preferable to have a proposed green belt deleted 'in public' by the Minister, especially when there are many local votes to be had by being seen as vigilant in protecting local environments. Such factors suggest a delicately balanced set of negotiations between the centre and the locality. The lack of new advice on green belts in the eight years to 1982 certainly contributed to confusion among local authorities over how they should be incorporated in plans. New advice could however have made the tenor of central-local relations even more strained. The issues surrounding detailed boundary definition have if anything been the most contentious, and it is to these that I now turn.

4. Defining Green Belt Boundaries

The essential characteristic of Green Belts is their permanence and their protection must be maintained as far as can be seen ahead.

Green Belts, Circular 14/84

The two-tier planning system assumes a hierarchy of plans based on a rational model of initiation, information gathering and consideration, decision, implementation and review. In principle there is wide discretion at local level for policy-making and implementation subject only to the supervisory and reserve powers of the Ministry. In reality, as has been seen in Chapter 3, central Government has rewritten many green belt policies in structure plans in terms both of physical extent and statutory justification. At the local level disputes between counties and districts are magnified by being focused on specific tracts of land. This is because in order to be effective the broad areas of green belt approved in structure plans must be defined at field boundary level. The discretion available to local authorities to choose between *types* of local plan to achieve this end has led to disagreement over which tier of authority should have the final say in defining boundaries. In addition advice from Government has been unclear on how long green belts are intended to last. Words such as 'permanence' and 'long-term' appear contradictory. How then have such issues been resolved, and how far has the *process* of plan preparation led to the reconciliation of interests in the use of land which an approved plan implies?

Local Plans

Local plans were conceived as a general tool for the detailed guidance of development which could vary in their form and use according to local circumstances.[1] Plans may cover land use issues comprehensively for whole districts or parts of districts (district plans), may take specific issues such as minerals or green belt (subject plans), or may cover small areas of rapid change (action area plans). They may also be prepared and adopted by counties *or* districts (but curiously not by both), the priorities for preparation being agreed between the two tiers locally in a Development Plan Scheme. Government advice[2] stresses the function of local plans as:

1. applying the strategy of the structure plan – that is, proposals for green belt should *conform generally* to the broad areas previously agreed;
2. providing a detailed basis for development control – in this case clear and defensible green belt boundaries;
3. providing a basis for co-ordinating development – this involves securing the commitment of infrastructure agencies and builders to development on allocated sites thus making green belts more defensible, and
4. bringing local and detailed planning issues before the public – here, those mainly private interests affected by inclusion or exclusion from a green belt have the right to have their views tested at a public local inquiry (PLI).

Because of ambiguity in Government advice, the slowness of the statutory system, and overlap in the time scales of structure and local plan preparation, policy-making and policy implementation have tended to merge.[3] Often only vestiges of the hierarchical model exist in reality, with plans in preparation forming part of an interactive process between all the major interests. The work of planners is as much concerned with bargaining, mediation, and compromise as the 'technical' matters of whether bound-

Table 4.1 Local Plans Covering Green Belt Areas: 1984

Green Belt	*Adopted*	*On Deposit*	*In DP Scheme*	*Total*
London	16	21	49	86
West Midlands	10	7	14	31
GMC, Merseyside, Cheshire, C. Lancs.	19	9	34	62
Tyne and Wear[1]	0	5	2	7
Notts–Derby[1]	1	1	n.k.	2
York	0	0	6	6
South, West, North Yorkshire	6	9	42	57
Oxford	1	3	3	7
Bristol–Bath	1	1	11	13
Glos–Cheltenham	1	2	1	4
Stoke-on-Trent	4	1	7	12
Cambridge	0	1	1	2
Hants–Dorset	1	3	8	12
Lancaster–Morecambe	0	0	3	3
Total	60	63	181	304

1. Information incomplete.
n.k. Not known.

Source: Adapted from House of Commons Environment Committee *Green Belt and Land for Housing*, HC 275-II, (1984), pp. 14–18.

aries should follow streams, pylon lines, or the centres of roads.[4] This is carried on within a framework of formal and informal advice from central Government, and the need to be accountable to local populations.

Thus although green belt is considered by many to be an unusually clearly defined *concept*, the process of producing detailed boundaries has been lengthy. Perhaps the largest and most successful boundary definition exercise (in the Greater Manchester area) took six years ending only in 1984. In the South East, 86 local plans will have to be completed to define the London Green Belt. By January 1984 only 16 had been adopted (19 per cent) and only 21 more were on deposit (24 per cent).[5] For England and Wales as a whole (Table 4.1) only 60 out of more than 300 local plans containing areas of green belt had been completed by the beginning of 1984. Some nine of these were green belt subject plans (Table 4.2). This process of definition is unlikely to be completed before reviews of some of the early plans (already underway) alter detailed boundaries yet again. This slow rate of progress can partly be accounted for by conflict between districts and counties over the issue of *who* defines boundaries.

Table 4.2 Green Belt Local (Subject) Plans: Progress at December 1984

1977 :	1.	Solihull District
1980 :	2.	Warwickshire
	3.	Derbyshire (South and South East Green Belts)
1981 :	4.	South Cheshire
	5.	North Staffordshire
1982 :	6.	Sheffield District
1983 :	7.	West Wiltshire
	8.	Merseyside
1984 :	9.	Greater Manchester
On Deposit at 31.12.84:		
	10.	Berkshire
	11.	Cambridge
	12.	Derbyshire (North East Green Belt)
	13.	Nottinghamshire
	14.	Rotherham District
	15.	Tyne and Wear
	16.	Wharfedale

Source: DoE *Local Plan Progress*, Quarterly List (DoE: London, 1984).

Who Should Define Boundaries?

Counties and districts are unlikely to be in accord over the priorities to be given to development in specific areas. A county authority seeking a strategic housing location near a motorway, for example Avon County near the M4/M5 Motorways, may be in conflict with adjoining districts who would prefer a lower level of growth and impact in their locality. One district on the periphery of a conurbation may wish to see others adopt severe green belt restraint in order to enhance their own ability to attract new investment, and so on. These basic conflicts have surfaced as arguments about technical matters – who should draw up local plans for green belts, and who should adopt them. Room for these disputes is created by the discretionary nature of the local plan regulations which allow either tier, by agreement with the other, to adopt a plan. Counties can argue that speed, comprehensiveness, and the consistent definition of boundaries are best assured by the preparation of their own green belt subject plan. The Ministry's own *Development Plans Manual* (only withdrawn in 1983) instanced green belt as a suitable topic for a subject plan justified by the need for 'detailed controls before the preparation of local plans'.

The districts, on the other hand, see such a proposal as trespassing on their rights as local authorities to decide in detail the location of new development and of green belts. Detailed proposals should be a local planning matter discussed and determined by locally-elected members. Should a green belt local plan be prepared *and adopted* by a county then all proposals conflicting with the plan would be required to be notified to them and their comments invited. This would constitute a loss in many cases of newly-acquired district power to the counties. They also argue, using another part of the *Development Plans Manual*, that subject plans should not be prepared for topics which have more than 'limited interactions with other policies'.[6] Green belts, they claim, have close relationships with land allocations for housing, industry, and other uses and should be decided in the context of district local plans which look comprehensively at all competing uses for land.

It is clear that in terms of speed, the desirability for certainty, and clarity, the counties have a valid argument. The districts also have a valid case in terms of comprehensiveness of treatment and local accountability. Thus, overlying the traditional urban–rural dichotomy of view inherited from the past, there is now an often more vehement set of arguments reflecting the autonomy and relative power of authorities within the two-tier system.

A further complication is that of overlapping local plans. Under the regulations for local plans it is possible to have overlap between a comprehensive district local plan, a recreation subject plan for a river valley, and a green belt subject plan. These may also succeed each other in time. In this instance the green belt boundaries in the most recently approved local plan take precedence for development control. In order to retain their own power the counties (who predominated in the South East Standing Conference) suggested in 1976 that green belt subject plans should be prepared by them for parts of the London Green Belt *before* structure plans were approved.[7] As before 1980 a local plan for a green belt area could not be adopted in advance of a structure plan, these would have been informally-approved local plans. In Essex, Berkshire, Tyne and Wear, and Greater Manchester, work on green belt subject plans was advanced in parallel with the preparation of structure plans. In Tyne and Wear the County approved an informal green belt boundary in 1978 prior to final approval of the structure plan.[18] In Berkshire the draft Green Belt Subject Plan was superceded by Ministry amendments to the Structure Plan,[9] and in Essex the Ministry pursuaded the County that their Draft Green Belt Subject Plan was not needed in addition to existing planning guidance for the efficient conduct of development control.[10]

Although these issues had received much academic comment in 1978–9 informal Ministry advice on the responsibility for preparation of local plans containing green belts has varied through time and between regions.[11] Thus in the South East county-wide green belt subject plans have been resisted, but in Greater Manchester, Merseyside, Tyne and Wear, and the West Midlands they have gone ahead. Resolution of these conflicts has been pragmatic, contentious, and time consuming.[12] Ministry officials have sought to avoid making formal rulings although this has not always been achieved. Thus there have been challenges, in the form of objections to Development Plan Schemes, by a number of Districts in Greater Manchester, Tyne & Wear, and the West Midlands. These have challenged the rights of Counties to approve boundaries as well as the scope of policies for land uses within Green Belts.

In some Regions Ministry officials have encouraged the preparation of subject plans at county level and, more rarely, at district level. In others they have insisted that green belt boundaries are defined by districts, albeit with guidance and assistance from counties. As a result the range of methods being pursued is wide including:

1. county-prepared subject plans where green belt boundaries may be altered in minor ways in later district-prepared plans: examples include Greater Manchester, Merseyside, North Staffordshire, Derbyshire and Wiltshire. (This is the commonest arrangement);
2. county-prepared subject plans for *some* districts with boundaries in others decided in district-prepared district plans (Avon, Buckinghamshire);
3. green belt made up of boundaries in individually district-prepared whole or part-district plans (Hertfordshire, Surrey, West Yorkshire);
4. green belt defined by concurrently-prepared district plans with county-district officer level working (Cambridgeshire); and
5. definition by concurrently prepared district plans with a joint county-district committee; including elected members, to oversee preparation (Oxfordshire).[13]

Further variations on these themes include the treatment of boundaries in successive plans. For example a County plan may be prepared *after* districts have defined boundaries, as proposed in West Yorkshire, at which time minor amendments are introduced by the upper tier Authority to ensure consistency across areas.

The *content* of green belt subject plans has varied between Regions. A number of counties, following the logic that the definition of a new green belt can be a basic structuring device for positive open land policies, have proposed 'green belt – open land' or 'green belt – urban fringe' subject plans. These have also been challenged in terms of content by districts who argue that the detailed land use decisions they entail are most appropriately made at local level. In Tyne and Wear and Greater Manchester the Ministry has ruled that the plans should only define Green Belt and village inset boundaries and the general criteria for development control in the Belts.[13] However, in the West Midlands the County-prepared Green Belt Subject Plan has proceeded on the basis of defining the boundary *and* open land policies within the Belt.

The question of who defines green belt boundaries has proved a further test of the relative power of the three tiers of central and local government. Because of unforeseen problems it has involved Ministry officials in continued intervention at local level. Again, as in the questions of size and extent of green belt, the resolution of problems has reflected local political realities. Therefore it is not to be expected that an *ad hoc* 'fire fighting' exercise, such as that embarked on by the Ministry, would lead to consistency in the arrangements across the country for defining boundaries. The outcomes reflect the power of individual districts in the face of their county authorities. Where the Districts are small, have been newly formed since reorganization, and have similar policy priorities, the norm has been subject plans at County level with relatively little dispute (as in Wiltshire and Berkshire). Where the Districts were strong municipal power bases before reorganization, and where there is greater policy dispute, County plan content has been scaled down (as in Tyne and Wear, and Greater Manchester). Where Districts are at their strongest, as in West Yorkshire and Avon, no effective green belt subject plan has been possible despite the County's intentions. The major variations on these themes represent the individual interpretation of the regulations by Ministry officials at Regional Office level. For example the South East and Eastern Regional offices of the Ministry have prevailed over the wishes of two of the strongest green belt Counties, Surrey and Hertfordshire, to prepare subject plans. However even in these Regions there is little consistency, with Buckinghamshire and Kent defining some Green Belt boundaries in subject plans, for example the outer boundary of the London Green Belt but not those around inset towns and villages.

Long Term Green Belts and Permanence

How long are the new green belts intended to last? Where, given such a judgement, are the boundaries to be drawn? These questions have been hotly debated at EIPs and Local Plan Inquiries across the country. This has been necessary because the normal processes of consultation and discussion between planning authorities and the Ministry have not suggested ready solutions. The only advice prior to 1982 was the phrase in Circular 50/57 that the inner boundary of a green belt would 'mark a long-term boundary for development', and that any unallocated land left between a town and the green belt should be shown as white land.[14] In their structure plans most local authorities have equated the word long-term with the end of the plan period, normally ten or fifteen years. Thus many proposed that once the broad locations for development to 1991 or 1996 were fixed the green belt should be drawn at these limits. It could then be reassessed at reviews of the structure plan approximately every five years. In this way the green belt would retain local authorities' ability to manage the process of land release, at the same time securing contained urban form.

The Ministry has seen this as a misuse of the concept. Their rulings have suggested that a green belt once defined should remain fixed for a longer time period than the structure plan. This conflict can be illustrated by reference to the policy process in Hertfordshire. The County's proposal was to draw the Green Belt at a point where assessed local needs for development from 1976 to 1991 had been allowed for. The EIP Panel, reporting in 1977, considered this a proper approach stating, 'fifteen years seems to us to be a reasonably long period for the purpose of defining green belt boundaries'.[15] It was felt that retracting boundaries would make it difficult for the local authority to resist development in the white land 'gaps' created around settlements. Hertfordshire supported this view, and whilst agreeing that their proposal implied that boundaries might be moved after 1991 as later development needs arose, they argued this would be a more effective solution than that implied by central Government advice. In approving the Structure Plan, however, the Ministry considered that the degree of permanence implied by Hertfordshire's policies was not sufficient. Whilst agreeing that all planning policies are subject to review they felt that the inner boundaries of the Green Belt should have a degree of permanence beyond the period of the Structure Plan 'and it should be clear that the boundaries will not need to be revised in the foreseeable future. If this is not clear the concept of the Green Belt as a long-term constraint is, in the Departments' view, inevitably weakened'.[16]

This is principally a dispute about who is to exercise discretion over land release. Under the County's suggestion the local authorities merely refuse applications on land not allocated in the Plan, the major risk of losing appeals only occurring if the remaining land available falls below a five year supply. The 'long-term' concept accords greater discretion to Inspectors and the Minister to grant planning permissions for peripheral growth, without trespassing on approved Green Belt.

In 1982 decisions emerging from EIPs were formalized by central Government into the view that 'land should not be included within the Green Belt where it seems likely, looking well beyond the period of the structure plan, that further land may be needed'.[17] This policy has been written into nearly all structure plans, although it is not seen as realistic by some local authorities. The Ministry has also avoided putting any figure, in terms of numbers of years, to the term 'well beyond the period of the structure plan'. This keeps discretion to adjudicate on the timing of any necessary alteration to a green belt boundary in Ministry control. The concept of a long-term belt, they argue, is necessary to retain public confidence in the policy and to reduce the extent and severity of land speculation. A five-yearly reassessment of green belts in plans would only fuel such speculation.

As most local plans only look five or ten years ahead, local authorities face some difficulty in defining green belts at field boundary level. As local and structure plans for the same area may have different end dates, the situation created by the statutory system almost *invites* two-tier green belt proposals. But Ministerial speeches stress that only one category of green belt should be shown in plans.[18] Such historic distinctions as interim green belt are to be dispensed with. Also, the white land concept, it is suggested, has become obsolete. The land between the allocations in plans and the inner edge of the green belt should be protected by 'the normal process of development control'.[19] However there is no advice on what policies are appropriate. Local authorities would like to use phasing policies for land adjacent to urban areas, but not in green belt, but these were considered unrealistic by the Secretary of State in his comments to the House of Commons Select Committee in 1984.[20]

The need is to create through plans a degree of certainty such that the general public and landowners can be assured of the protected status of land, and builders and infrastructure providers can proceed with development and investment in allocated land with confidence. However the complexities of attempting to reconcile the need for a biennially topped up five year supply of building land as required in Circular 15/84, and the requirement for green belts to be long-term, have led to uncertainty and a number of white land-type proposals. For example around High Wycombe (a growing industrial centre embedded in the London Green Belt in Buckinghamshire) the County suggested areas of white land *within* the Green Belt. These would be treated as Green Belt until mechanisms could be found to control development for local needs only. The EIP Panel suggested that this practice would 'make uncertain the boundaries of the Green Belt'. The white land should be excluded from the Green Belt, and any development for housing should be promoted in a form which ensured that the resulting dwellings went for local needs.[21] Significantly, no advice was given as to how this was to be achieved.

Another, apparently permissible method is to have land for possible use beyond the local plan period shown as an 'Area of Special Restraint'. In Broxbourne, a District covering part of the Lea Valley and traversed by the M25 Motorway, settlements have been contained within the fully-approved

London Green Belt for 25 years. Wishing to allow for local needs for housing after 1986 (the end-date of the local plan) the District proposed leaving areas between the land allocated for housing and the Green Belt boundary. These would be Interim Green Belt. The Ministry objected claiming Interim Green Belt could only apply, according to Structure Plan Note 5/72, *until* a local plan was approved.[22] As a result Broxbourne have altered their plan notation to one of 'Area of Special Restraint' (see Figure 4.1) with a new policy wording:

> Until such time as the land . . . is shown to be needed for development in a development land availability statement or a review of (the) plan, there will be a presumption against development (other than would be allowed in the Green Belt)'.[23]

This appears no different to the notation, current between 1973–9 in the County, of white land where green belt policies apply.

Another method has been to prepare non-statutory green belt boundaries. Tyne and Wear County produced such a document in 1978 to provide 'an adequate basis for deciding on applications on specific sites'. It consisted of a line defining an Interim Green Belt and six 'insets' which 'cover areas where some land may be required for development or be held in reserve for possible future use' (Figure 4.2). Green belt policies would apply in the insets while detailed studies were carried out to define boundaries, and until replaced by an approved local plan.[24] However objections from landowners, developers, and residents' groups, uncertain of what the notation implied, led to its withdrawal.

In some counties the definition of boundaries has been a two-stage 'narrowing-down' process. In this situation the county prepares a minimum strategic green belt which the districts 'refine' by adding small areas of land in their own subsequent local plans. This method is found in Warwickshire where the County have defined a Green Belt which replaces the former regime of fully-approved and interim Green Belt with fully-approved Green Belt and 'Policy Boxes' around the main towns (Figure 4.3). The policy boxes are areas where Green Belt policies will apply until boundaries are defined in a district-prepared local plan.[25] Even at District level the narrowing down process is unlikely to achieve full clarity. On the northern boundary of Stratford Upon Avon the policy box has been narrowed in the draft Local Plan to two categories of land – Green Belt and an 'Area of Special Restriction' where existing uses are to remain undisturbed during the Plan period.[26]

However, this process of gradually 'drawing-in' the green belt boundary is not an immutable rule. In the case of the North Staffordshire Green Belt the approved Subject Plan defines a boundary which will subsequently be 'drawn back' in district-prepared local plans.[27] The Inspector

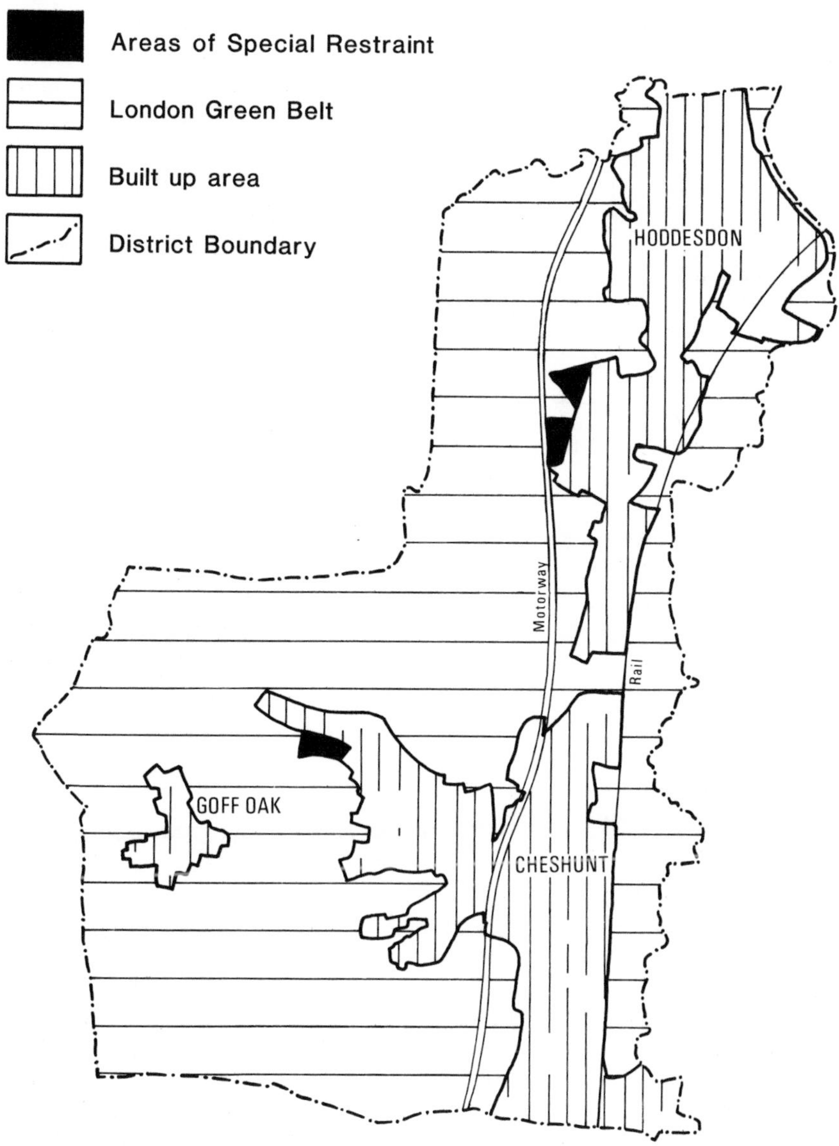

Figure 4.1 Areas of Special Restraint: Broxbourne District, Hertfordshire
Source: Adapted from Broxbourne District Council *Broxbourne District Plan* (BDC: Hoddesdon, 1981), map RE 1

Figure 4.2 Green Belt and Proposed Urban Fringe Insets: Tyne and Wear
Source: Adapted from Tyne and Wear County Council *Green Belt and Urban Fringe Subject Plan: Interim Policies* (TWCC: Newcastle, 1978), map 2.

at the PLI in 1982 argued (resurrecting the concept of white land at the same time):

> If pockets of white land are left around the urban areas this is bound to pre-empt some of the District Councils' options on how much and where land for development should be allocated in their District Plans . . . the white land pockets may not be the right size, shape or location.[28]

It has not proved possible to reconcile land for housing criteria and the Ministry idea of a long-term green belt without recourse to some form of interim status land. In practice if not in name, white land still exists around towns as a realistic response to an uncertain future and to give local flexibility. The major debate focuses on who has control over its release.

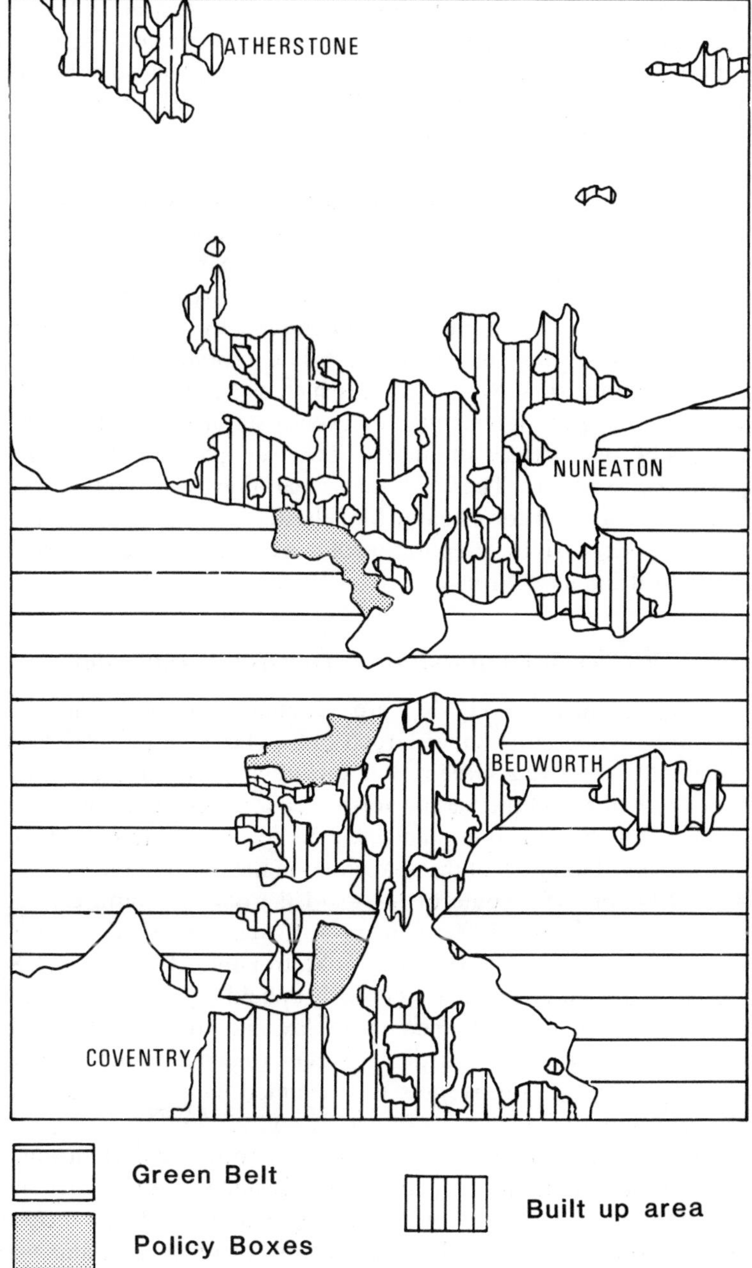

Figure 4.3 Policy Boxes in Warwickshire
Source: Adapted from Warwickshire County Council *Green Belt Local (Subject) Plan for Warwickshire* (WCC: Warwick, 1982), proposals map

Local authorities only have white land as a second best strategy because of the large amount of work generated by contentious appeals. Central Government are concerned that approved green belts in plans do not foreclose options to alter policies in the future. The result is a delicate and partially formed 'balance' with both sides having apparently logical arguments for their positions.

However the process of drawing boundaries, as opposed to the outcomes already described, is far more complex. Taking the broad 'public interest' ideology as a starting point, it is immediately apparent that in a two-tier system there will necessarily be different valid county *and* district views of the public interest. When this is compounded by the views of major consultees such as the House Builders Federation, CPRE, and local community groups, or sectoral agencies such as MAFF and the DoI, the process of arriving at 'agreement', or even a statutory conclusion to the process can become greatly attenuated. Two examples of policy-making in action are discussed here. The first is the preparation by a County of a Green Belt Subject Plan, that for Greater Manchester, an area with ten District Councils. The second is the preparation of two concurrent local plans for the City of Oxford and its environs.

County–District Accommodation: Greater Manchester

The Greater Manchester (GMC) area contained in 1974 some 52,245 hectares of land operating under Green Belt policies. Only 1,857 hectares were formally approved Green Belt including parts of Stockport and Oldham Boroughs, and the Saddleworth area formerly in the West Riding Green Belt. Of the remaining land, 35,750 hectares were Green Belt in submitted plans, but much of the remainder in the north of the County was provisional Green Belt, some of it excluded from the South Lancashire Green Belt in the early 1960s (Figure 4.4). The inherited pattern was fragmented and illogical when assessed at Metropolitan County level. Some of the old County authorities had rigorously upheld Green Belt policies, but most of the Boroughs had been more lax and 'some had ignored it altogether'. The County was particularly keen to avoid perpetuating white land, a policy whose effectiveness they claimed had been 'killed by the recommendations of Circulars 10/70, 102/72 and 122/73'.[29]

In order to confront the severe economic, social, and environmental problems of the County, the Structure Plan stressed measures for economic regeneration, the concentration of development near the Manchester–Salford conurbation core, and the protection of open land and natural resources.[30] More specifically the Plan suggested land for 88,000 new dwellings for the ten years to 1986, and sufficient choice of industrial land for any envisaged demand. Following the suggestions of the *Strategic Plan for the North West* the first proposal was for an omnibus open land policy. All

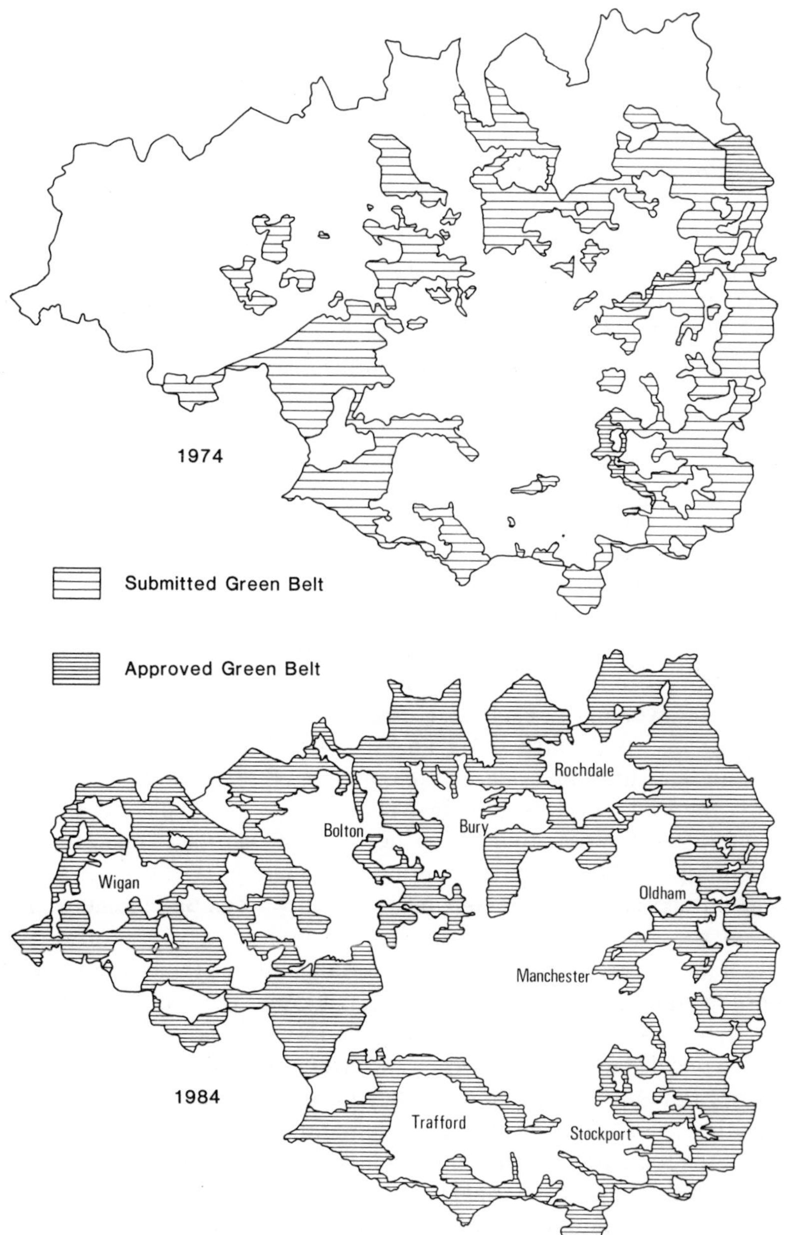

Figure 4.4 Green Belts in Greater Manchester: 1974 and 1984
Source: Adapted from Greater Manchester Council *Open Land and Physical Restraints on Development*, Structure Plan Report of Survey (GMC: Manchester, 1975); GMC *Green Belt Subject Plan* (GMC: Manchester, 1984)

open land (land not needed to 1986) would be Green Belt with complementary landscape, recreation, and agricultural policies, an approach considered unfeasible by the Ministry. The second idea was a two-tier policy – Green Belt and 'Other Protected Land'. In the 'Other Protected Land' category controls similar to those within green belt would apply, but demands of an unexpected nature (mainly for industry), or other post-1986 needs would be accommodated. Many consultees and the Ministry, considered this to be an approach which would create unnecessary uncertainty. Therefore the submitted Structure Plan proposed a conventional Circular 42/55 Green Belt, long-term and with no fixed end date. The early intention of the County had been to define a Green Belt boundary, and a comprehensive package of open land policies, in a *Green Belt–Open Land* Subject Plan which would come into force at the same time as the Structure Plan. Objections by Salford and Manchester Districts to the Subject Plan proposal occupied 1978 with a ruling by the Ministry only appearing at the end of the year.

The criteria applied in drawing boundaries were wide ranging.[31] The Green Belt would have to be long-term and defensible such that where district local plans were being prepared for the same area later they would normally add areas to the basic Green Belt. In addition the areas would have to 'conform generally' to the written description in the approved Structure Plan, and they would have to reflect the requirements for the construction of specified numbers of dwellings in each District. Also they would have to reflect the strategic themes of the Structure Plan, especially that of urban concentration, by discouraging the unnecessary development of greenfield sites remote from urban centres and services. Finally the boundaries should balance flexibility and commitment by not pre-empting the scope for Districts to select their own precise peripheral locations for housing and industry. Where Districts were concurrently preparing their own local plans the Green Belt might be drawn back and the 'gap' protected by an open land policy.

This daunting remit, involving co-operation between ten Districts and the County in a situation with no precedents, allowed the full play of County–District rivalries. At the heart of the Plan was the issue of who had the power to decide land allocations and the Green Belt boundary, and how far the upper-tier authority could reasonably constrain the actions of lower-tier authorities. At the technical level planning officers experienced little difficulty in agreeing recommended boundaries once the scale of development to be allowed for had been agreed.[32] At the political level a number of Districts were reluctant to be seen to be co-operating in narrowing their room for manoeuvre over land release in a situation where economic conditions were deteriorating. The County thus focused on the idea of a *strategic minimum* Green Belt as the way to progress the Plan. As the County Planning Officer stated in his report to the GMC Planning Committee in 1980:

> the . . . plan is not designed to be anything more than the best definition of the broad areas that seem to be feasible and sensible at the present time.[33]

This implies that a green belt may have areas of strategic significance and areas of local significance. Thus the gaps between the main towns may be strategic but some parts of the other peripheral areas less so. In Stockport for example, the County argued that nearly all of the remaining Green Belt was of strategic importance but that much of the open land in Wigan was less strategically important.

The question of permanence caused some difficulty. The County saw the Green Belt as not requiring review or significant reduction by other means 'for a considerable period of time'. This was later narrowed to the view that 'the Green Belt should retain its validity for some time after 1986', thus striking a balance between the desire for the Belt to last beyond the period of the plan and the requirements for development.[34] By the time of the LPI in 1981 the County had negotiated informal agreement with all the Districts that in total the housing needs of each area could be met without using proposed Green Belt. However there remained until 1983 some disputes over the location of housing development within Districts and here, if the Districts views were to prevail, some of the proposed Subject Plan Green Belt boundaries would need to be peeled back.

The process of plan preparation allowed considerable narrowing of disagreement between Districts and the County to take place. The publication of draft proposals led to formal responses from the Districts which identified the areas of doubt and remaining conflict. In response to the deposited Plan 2100 objections and representations were received, rising to 9100 if collective objections are taken into account. The majority, 70 per cent, were objections by property owners to non-inclusion in the Green Belt.[35] The pattern was one of well organized *objections to exclusion* in a relatively small number of areas where residents were willing to recruit assistance and take issue with the local authorities. Also there was well organized *support for retention* of proposed Green Belt in some areas previously threatened with development. A third, numerically smaller category, was made up of *objections to inclusion* from landowners seeking to maintain that their land was suitable for development.

By this stage disputes with the Districts had narrowed to a number of complex local situations. They included:

1. objections to the inclusion of possible large industrial sites near Motorways (Wigan, Bury, Rochdale, Salford);
2. objections where District-prepared local plans for the release of housing were under way (Bolton, Salford); and
3. objections to the inclusion of large moorland areas in the Green Belt (Rochdale).

As a result of negotiations with objectors the County resolved to make eighteen additions and twenty-four deletions from the deposited Plan before the PLI. Strong District opposition caused some retraction of boundaries. In this process the County were influenced by informal Ministry advice that in cases of disagreement with Districts the boundary should be drawn conservatively.

At the PLI the most significant attack on the principles of the Plan was mounted by the House Builders Federation (HBF). They argued that the Green Belt should be minimal and sacrosanct. It should, if it was to be long-term, be a line drawn after a fifteen year land supply for housing had been allowed for. Where there were areas of doubt the land should be omitted from the Belt. All sites subject to objection at the PLI (over 300) should be omitted from the Green Belt in the approved Plan. The County argued it was unrealistic to see so far ahead in terms of detailed land requirements, and that the HBF proposals would roll back the Green Belt so far as to render it a residual policy.

The major dispute therefore revolved around how the terms 'strategic minimum' and 'long-term' might be interpreted. Using Circular 50/57, the 1962 Ministry Booklet, and the comments of Henry Brooke when Minister of Housing, the Inquiry Inspector argued the Green Belt should be long-term:

> the Subject Plan should define a Green Belt which is limited in those parts of the County where . . . district plans are being prepared and generally, those locations which are listed as housing priority areas. However, having regard to the Regional Controllers' advice I consider that it is appropriate for the Green Belt as defined in the Subject Plan to be rather more than a minimum strategic Green Belt in those parts of the County where no district plan is either being prepared or is proposed.[36]

The Inspector also rebutted the HBF interpretation of 'long-term', suggesting that in some parts of the County, such as Stockport and Trafford in the south, the Belt should act in the short- to medium-term as a check on the outward spread of the urban areas. In other areas such as Bolton and Manchester it would act as a moderate restraint, but in Districts such as Wigan and Rochdale it would only be a restraint in the long-term. The Green Belt would therefore act to curb the spread of different parts of the Conurbation at different stages during the lifetime of the Plan.[37]

The CPRE, the Ramblers Association, and local amenity and residents' groups argued that housing construction rates were so low that all of the land releases implied by the Plan were not needed. The Green Belt could be drawn more tightly. The Inspector suggested that shortfalls in the take up of land could only benefit the Green Belt as they would allow land not required before 1986 to be used to meet housing needs after that date. He considered that the housing land allocations implied by the Green Belt boundary would probably last to the end of the 1980s, and in some Districts into the 1990s.

However, he noted that throughout the County there were 8,400 hectares of land not in the Green Belt, and not subject to major policy constraints. This land should be regarded as an 'area of search' which, with other land inside the urban areas, could be looked at for development as and when the need arose.[38]

The Green Belt approved in 1984 was 61,600 hectares. It is therefore 8,400 hectares larger than the old approved, interim and provisional Belts (Table 4.3). The Green Belt has been retracted from parts of the centre of the County where housing needs are greatest, but major additions have been made around the periphery. The largest additions are the Rochdale Moors and areas in Bolton where Green Belt policies had not previously applied. The largest reductions are in Salford where the City has sought to provide for its predicted housing requirements wholly within its boundaries.[39] Significant local pressures from residents' groups, articulated at the PLI and through District Councils, have provided tighter boundaries in the north of Bolton and Bury and around the Saddleworth villages in the foothills of the Pennines east of Oldham. In Stockport no Green Belt land has been deleted and some 'inset' towns such as Marple have tighter boundaries, adding 285 hectares to the Green Belt in the process.

How far will the Green Belt so far approved assist in implementing the Structure Plan? By protecting the major areas of open land between towns it should provide a basic insurance against coalescence. Considerable peripheral growth is, however, allowed for in areas cheap to service and close to facilities. The housing forecasts are ambitious and it is unlikely that the land released will be developed as speedily as intended. The most attractive land freed up in local plans is likely to be developed first, and relatively little new private housing will be 'directed' to the more difficult-to-develop inner areas. The County set out in 1975 to avoid white land, land

Table 4.3 Area of Green Belt in Greater Manchester 1974–81

		Hectares		*Net*	
District	*1974*	*Subtractions*	*Additions*	*Change*	*1981*
Wigan	10,334	564	2,046	(+) 1,481	11,815
Bolton	5,036	268	2,199	(+) 1,931	6,967
Bury	4,956	321	1,042	(+) 721	5,677
Rochdale	5,489	867	5,555	(+) 4,688	10,177
Salford	4,139	811	24	(−) 787	3,352
Manchester	593	58	1,044	(+) 986	1,579
Oldham	6,047	686	321	(−) 364	5,683
Trafford	4,648	499	161	(−) 338	4,310
Stockport	5,499	—	285	(+) 285	5,784
Tameside	5,504	474	293	(−) 181	5,323
Total	52,245	4,547	12,969	(+) 8,422	60,667

Source: GMC *Open Land Policy and Land Lost to Development 1974–80*, (GMC: Manchester, 1981) Figure 2. Data refer to the Deposited Plan.

subject in its own words to 'inevitable encroachment'. However there is now to be an 8,400 hectare area of search for future housing and industrial needs. White land by another name?

County–District Conflict[40]

Oxfordshire, a County with a population of 530,000 dominated by the City of Oxford as a service, academic, and industrial centre has faced a familiar mix of planning problems over the last 30 years. The land use policy discussion has centred on whether the propensity for growth shown by the City should be accommodated by peripheral growth, more widespread development in central Oxfordshire, or by the diversion of pressures further afield to the country towns. Early plans for Oxford, such as that of Thomas Sharp stressed containment by a green belt, dispersal, and maintenance of the heritage of the centre.[41] The 1958 Green Belt, a descendent of these ideas, was restrictive, penetrating well into the urban area along the main river valleys. At the local public inquiry into the proposal in 1961, a number of objections to inclusions in the Green Belt were substantiated and areas of land were omitted in draft amendments returned to the local authorities by the Minister.[42] The submitted Development Plan incorporating these amendments was to serve as the Oxford Green Belt for 14 years.

Following local government reorganization in 1974 the administrative area of the City was not enlarged – a victory for the County – but pressures for more development land remained. The Green Belt came under the jurisdiction of Oxford City, South Oxfordshire, Cherwell, and Vale of White Horse District Councils. In 1975 the Ministry confirmed the outer boundaries of the Green Belt but the inner part was left as interim, pending the outcome of structure and local plans (see Figure 4.5).

The County Structure Plan of 1976 proposed a policy of development restraint, in line with guidance in the *Strategic Plan for the South East*.[43] This involved limited provision for housing and employment in the City and environs, with consequent provision in selected country towns such as Bicester, Witney and Didcot. Retention of the Green Belt would be an instrument to this end. This strategy was opposed by the Labour-controlled City whose policy intentions included greater flexibility to accommodate employment growth, and a large programme of public sector housing. However Labour lost control of the City before the Examination in Public in 1977 and the incoming Conservative group, although keen to see City control over Green Belt and land allocation decisions, were less insistent in their opposition to the Structure Plan. By the time Labour had regained control of the City, decisions had been made in favour of low levels of housing development in and around Oxford. As a result of representations made on the Minister's draft modifications to the Structure Plan, the *form* in which the housing totals for central Oxfordshire were expressed was

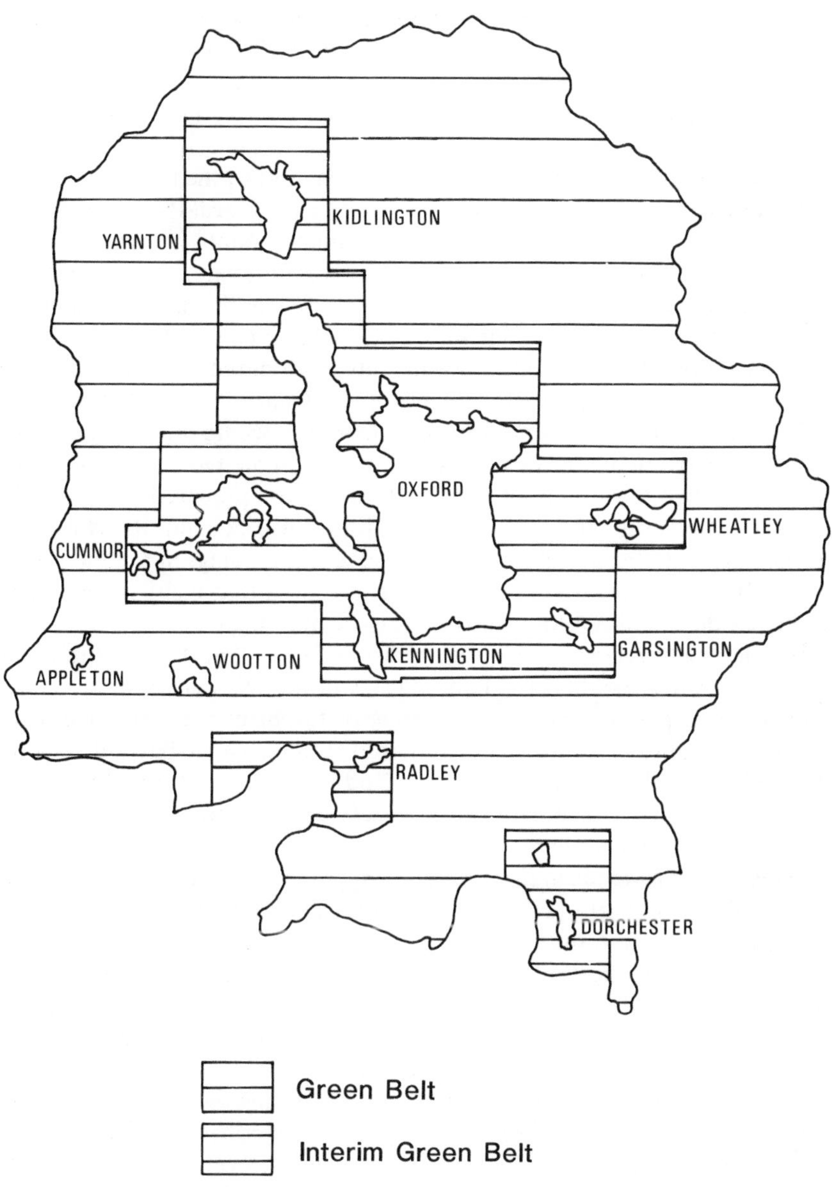

Figure 4.5 The Oxford Green Belt 1975
Source: Adapted from Scargill, I. *Oxford's Green Belt*, OP3 (Oxford Preservation Trust: Oxford, 1983)

changed. Instead of the housing totals constituting broad guidelines, the approval letter (1979) suggested that local plans should be prepared at an early date, and that they should include 'the *full provision* stated in the Plan'.[44]

In order to find sites in central Oxfordshire for 4,300 dwellings by 1991 – the strategic requirement – the County suggested two speedily-prepared local plans. A City (District) Plan, jointly prepared by the two Authorities, would be complemented by a single Oxford Fringe Local Plan prepared by the County. This would have given maximum County control over the placing and administration of the new Green Belt boundary. The Districts however wished to prepare and adopt the Local Plans themselves, maintaining it was not a County function to be involved in such detailed matters.

The compromise reached, following advice from the Ministry, involved the City preparing a District-wide local plan. Concurrent work, under the aegis of a Working Party of officers and members, would produce a plan for the Oxford fringe area. The results would be presented as a single plan, the Oxford Fringe Local Plan, made up of three parts prepared by Cherwell, South Oxfordshire, and Vale of White Horse District Councils. However, decisions made by the Working Party were not binding on the members' respective Councils. Subsequent events indicated that many of the 'decisions' made by the Working Party were to be overruled.

Marked differences in the pace and style of preparation of the plans emerged, reflecting the varied approaches of the Districts to local policy, public participation, and the provisions of the Structure Plan. The City argued for high proportions of the required housing land to be located in the fringe beyond their boundary, but on land in their ownership. The fringe Districts sought to avoid having to accommodate more than a locally politically-acceptable share of any development.

Most of 1981 was spent in searches for suitable sites and their assessment by the Working Party. The City looked for land within its boundary and produced what it termed a 'maximum list' of housing sites. This was important, as any shortfall would have to be made good by allocations in the Interim Green Belt area. The County and the fringe Districts disputed the totals, claiming there were other sites available in the City, that the assumed housing densities were too low, and there would be windfall sites which would come forward for planning permission during the Plan period. The Districts investigated existing settlements in the Interim Green Belt looking for sites with good drainage and accessibility, and in locations that would not compromise landscape objectives. Large areas of the fringe were ruled out on agricultural grounds following consultations with MAFF. Strong objection to village expansion emerged from parish councils representing settlements in the Interim Green Belt.

When the totals for the two Plan areas were added together, there was sufficient land (if parish protests were disregarded) for the 4,300 dwellings total in the Structure Plan, although each District had assessed the 'constraints' of drainage, agricultural land, and landscape quality differently. The Working Party, anticipating strong objections at draft plan stage from parish councils and the Oxford Preservation Trust, considered that land for a further 800 dwellings should be identified. The fringe Districts contended that no other land was 'available'.

As a result the County and the City embarked on further exercises to 'find' the extra land. A County appraisal suggested the release of land from Interim Green Belt around villages away from the immediate Oxford fringe (Yarnton, Wheatley and Garsington) but these proposals were turned down by the fringe Districts. The City then proposed a large peripheral site for housing and employment uses on the southern edge of the City (see Figure 4.6). The land, largely in City ownership, would be developed by a consortium of housebuilders together with a prestige industrial site.[45] Although the Working Party was not convinced of the suitability or acceptability of the site, the City and South Oxfordshire District then embarked on a joint feasibility study of this proposal which would be 'contained' to the south by a perimeter road. In a further round of informal consultation undertaken by South Oxfordshire (in whose area it was suggested most of the development would take place), two development alternatives were canvassed:

1. the dispersal of new land take around villages in the vicinity of Oxford, including a number of 'known' unacceptable sites; or
2. the development of the large site on the southern periphery of Oxford, together with the smaller 'acceptable' village sites.

The response suggested the first solution be adopted, but with the politically unacceptable sites left out. Thus the draft plans of 1981 contained a shortfall of around 1,000 dwellings out of the Structure Plan requirement. The proposed impact on the three fringe Council areas was also quite different, Cherwell proposing 36 dwellings, the Vale of White Horse 628, and South Oxfordshire 945. Only four hectares of new industrial land were allocated and the Green Belt boundary was shown coincident with these allocations. In the Oxford City Plan the Green Belt was extended inwards over new areas of open land to separate neighbourhoods within the City (Figure 4.6).

The Draft Plans evoked strong reactions.[46] The Ministry warned that it would object at plan deposit stage if *full provision* for housing was not made in the two Plan areas, and if the tight Green Belt boundaries were maintained. They felt land for the 1000 dwelling shortfall should be left between the land allocations and the Green Belt boundary. The House Builders Federation also objected to the shortfall as did West Oxfordshire District who were worried about development leapfrogging the Green Belt. Oxford City argued that many of the sites identified in their own Draft Plan were subject to constraints and therefore the fringe area must take its identified

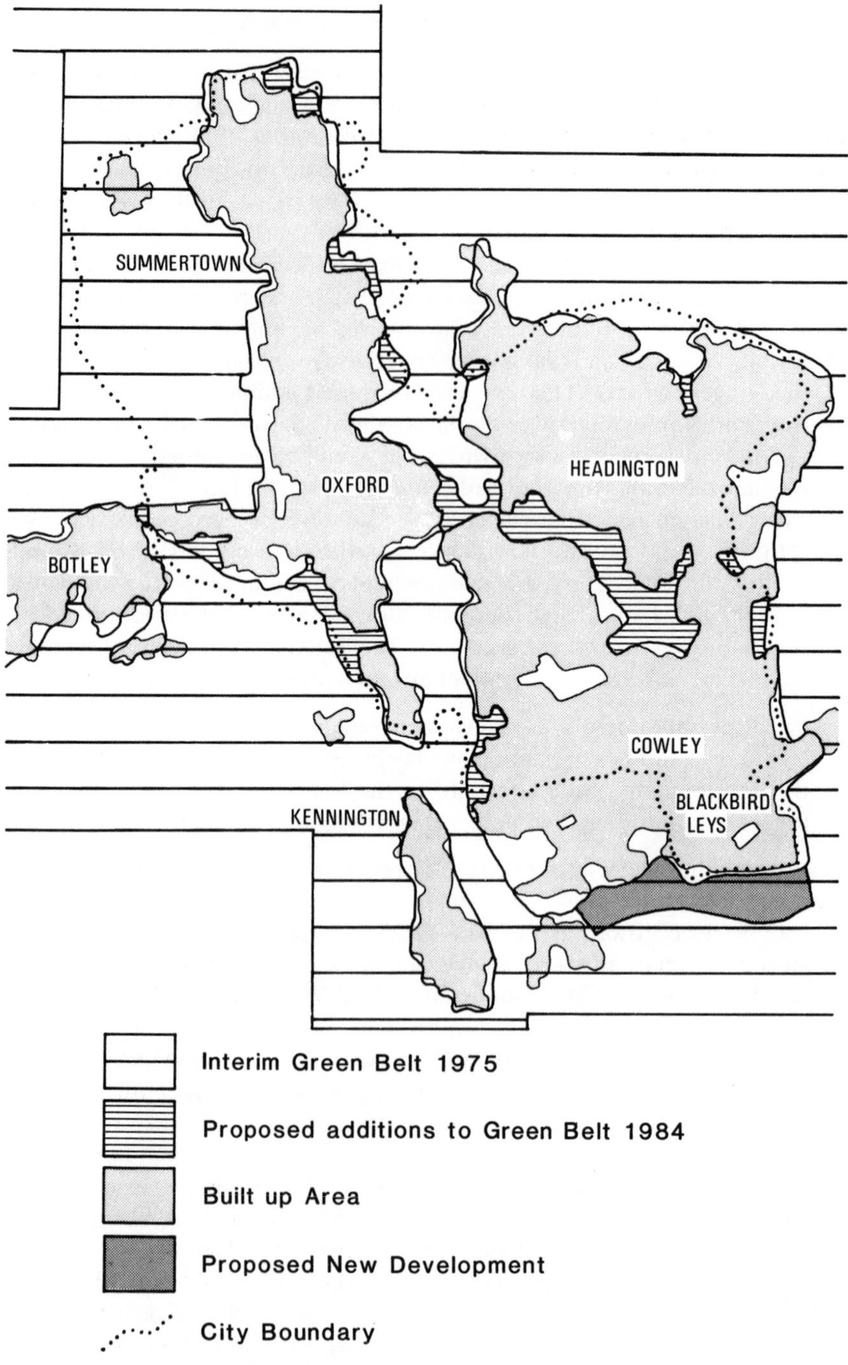

Figure 4.6 Proposed Changes to the Oxford Green Belt 1984
Source: Adapted from Oxford City Council *Oxford Local Plan*, Draft (Oxford City Council: Oxford, 1981)

share. The Department of Industry objected in strong terms claiming it was in both the County and the national interest to allow for more industrial development in the Oxford fringe. Thus a powerful grouping of interests emerged to challenge the restrictive nature of the plans.

After considering the representations Oxford and South Oxfordshire Districts resolved to go ahead with the suggestion of a large peripheral housing site south of the City. The joint feasibility study had shown, following negotiations, that the objections of MAFF and the Water Authority (whose land was encompassed by the proposals) could be overcome, and that land for 1200 dwellings and 13 hectares of employment-generating development could be released. This site would be the least undesirable location for development but would have many benefits. It would satisfy those objecting about the shortfall of housing and industrial land, and would avoid the need to take sites from the Interim Green Belt adjacent to villages further out in South Oxfordshire. Although outvoted at a meeting of the Working Party, South Oxfordshire District added the site to their proposals in the Fringe Plan in May 1982, deleting some more sensitive sites around the villages.[47] Subsequently the Oxford Preservation Trust decided not to oppose the southern fringe proposal and the other Districts agreed the South Oxfordshire proposal, due to its importance in demonstrating a five year supply of housing land in the area.

The Oxford area plans were refused a certificate of conformity by the County in July 1982. It was argued in the notice of refusal that the level of land release proposed, together with commitments, would be likely to fuel growth in central Oxfordshire contrary to the provisions of the approved Structure Plan. The County also contended that the proposed Green Belt had been drawn too far into Oxford City contrary to Circular 42/55 advice, and that optimum use had not been made of sites in Oxford for development prior to 1986. This attitude to the local plans arose from work being carried out by the County to review the Structure Plan.[48] It had become clear that the policy of deflection of growth to the country towns, due to the recession and other factors, had not worked on the scale required. The rate of housebuilding in central Oxfordshire was, meanwhile, continuing at rates above that envisaged in the Structure Plan. In response to this the County suggested reductions in the rate of development in central Oxfordshire, to give the 1976 strategy further time to work.

The disagreement over conformity was referred to the Ministry for determination. Although the latter sought to persuade the County to use the PLI into the deposited plans as a mechanism for expressing their opposition, the County demurred. Having made their decision on conformity, it was hardly likely that without any change in circumstances, they could then accept the local plans. The Ministry's proposed solution would remove any power to influence events from the County, leaving them dependent on Inspectors' recommendations to the City or South Oxfordshire. Even if these accorded with County views the Districts would not necessarily be bound to accept them.

After nearly 12 months of negotiation, and with no solution in sight, the Ministry used its reserve powers to issue a Certificate of Conformity in 1983. Plans have been deposited and at the PLI into the City Plan in 1984 the Ministry appeared as an objector to the policy which extends Green Belt within Oxford on the grounds that it did not allow for development beyond the local plan period. The fringe Districts and the Ministry agreed to defer a local inquiry into the fringe plans until after the inquiry into the Alterations to the Oxfordshire Structure Plan had been held. It would appear that Green Belt boundaries are unlikely to be approved before 1986. The boundaries in the deposited fringe plans are therefore being used on an interim basis.[49]

It is salutory to note that Oxford City has never had a fully approved inner boundary to its Green Belt. It shares this distinction with most large urban areas ostensibly surrounded by green belt in the UK. The basis for control of the spread of the City rests on a less than formally binding *concordat* between central Government and the local authorities. As the land under discussion in the local plans only provides for anticipated needs until 1991, the Ministry may yet request that a long-term reserve be inserted before confirming the Green Belt boundary. Although the Ministry is clearly reluctant to breach the Interim Green Belt, there is the possibility, under pressures generated by joint land availability studies with housebuilders, that the continued presence of an outdated statutory framework could result in some change of attitude. It was stated by the City Council in 1961 that the Green Belt would need early review; nearly twenty-five years later its boundary is virtually unchanged.

Assessment

These brief accounts hint at the complexity involved in drawing up green belt boundaries in the 1980s. They illustrate a technical process, the Circular 42/55 criteria, struggling to come to terms with the conflicting views and powers within the two-tier system. In the Greater Manchester case the *process* of producing the Plan assisted in reconciling the conflicts aided by central Government intervention at various points. It was important for the County to be able to show that all Districts supported the general concept of the Green Belt and this was achieved. For a new Authority set up in 1974 this was a considerable achievement.

The effect of the Plan has been to produce a 'bargained compromise' which narrows the area of uncertainty over land taken for peripheral development; too little in the view of the GMC, and too much for the House Builders Federation, other development interests and one or two Districts. The Green Belt is justified as long-term (lasting an unspecified time beyond the Plan period) particularly as the forecasts of land needs made in the

Structure Plan, dating from the mid 1970s, now seem very optimistic. This should leave room for development well beyond the 1980s. The PLI Inspector was keen to support the separation arguments of the 1955 Circular and was firm in cases where proposed development would, although strongly supported at District level, have led to a danger of coalescence. Significantly the close consideration of over 300 sites was carried out in physical planning terms, whether a land parcel was a 'natural break', 'barrier', 'buffer zone', or 'lung for urban areas', and so on. Administrative decisions in green belt planning are still physical planning *par excellence*.

Where the Districts held out against County wishes for room to decide their own land allocations in local plans these were upheld by both the Ministry and the Inspector. This has been the price to pay for District acquiescence in completing the Plan, but has retained uncertainty in many parts of the urban fringe and has loosened the Green Belt, possibly to the detriment of Structure Plan aims. The focus of conflict and negotiation has been between the two tiers of local government, a power struggle in which the Districts, where they have been clear on policy intentions, and willing to use their full powers, have prevailed. The House Builders Federation, who entered as a major challenger to the whole idea of the Plan only at the public inquiry stage, only succeeded in marginally loosening the Belt. Local objectors rarely succeeded in successfully challenging either County rulings on green belt or the outcomes of County–District accommodations.

In the Oxford case an apparently simpler situation has remained unresolved. This may be at least partly attributed to lack of clarity in drawing up the Structure Plan. In grouping housing, industry and Green Belt issues under one term 'central Oxfordshire' the Structure Plan left a number of quite different views of the public interest unresolved. These have been articulated anew and re-weighed at District level against a moving external environment. The mechanism of a non-executive Working Party appears to have been a relatively weak one for reconciling conflicts. In the 'place politics' sense the peripheral location which has emerged for major development is the least well defended area of the Oxford Interim Green Belt. Technical factors such as definitions of land liable to flood, agricultural land quality, and areas valued for their conservation interest, only narrowed down the options.

The roles played by non-local agencies have also been important. The Ministry has been involved at a variety of crucial stages including its problem in 1983 of making a decision on conformity with an increasingly out of date Structure Plan. The Circular 9/80 land availability exercise undertaken with the HBF in 1981–2, and Circular 22/80, concentrated the collective minds of the Districts and added urgency to the question of identification of new land. The intervention of the Ministry added weight to the post-1980 changes of attitude in the City towards a further loosening of restraints on new employment generating development. A loose-knit alliance of strong corporate interests is combining to weaken the Interim Green Belt in central Oxfordshire.

The definition of green belt boundaries is thus the outcome of a complex negotiative process. The statutory planning process partly structures a forum, or arena, in which the various parties attempt to assert their particular interests. The result is attenuation in time taken and policy complexity. White land, Areas of Special Restraint, and Policy Boxes are local manifestations of the asserted positions, as moderated through negotiation, of a mixture of local interests and of local and central Government. The green belt boundary represents a 'map' of the accommodations reached at a point in time. It is thus a reflection of local power structures and central–local relations rather than a determinant of them.

5. Urban Restraint and the Green Belt

A difficult balance has to be struck between, on the one hand, responding adequately to demands for land release for housing and other purposes and, on the other, maintaining sufficient control to preserve and enhance the environment and to achieve orderly, satisfactory and economic provision for development.

Secretary of State for the Environment 1980

Local need policies do not necessarily imply occupation by local people but rather are used as a means of deciding upon a politically acceptable level of growth and phasing its development.

South East Standing Conference 1979

Green belt, as a policy instrument, does not operate in isolation. It is deployed within a wider framework of *urban restraint policies* designed to protect local environments by securing physical containment, at the same time managing the quantity and rate of release of land, and controlling the types of new activity normally allowed. Whilst positive measures to provide recreation space, protect landscapes and manage open land within green belts have received most attention in the green belt literature (see chapters 8 and 9) urban restraint policies and mechanisms are less widely understood. It was a central concern of Circular 42/55 that green belts should be complemented by policies to: 'prevent any further building for industrial and commercial purposes' in towns enclosed by them. If allowed, such development would lead to a growth spiral made up of demands for more labour, which in turn would create demands for the development of additional land for housing.[1]

Although this advice remains in place it has been more liberally interpreted over time as many towns within green belts found themselves, by the early 1980s, short of jobs for the first time in 25 years. Restraint policies therefore do not imply no growth or land use change, they suggest *selectivity* between activities deemed beneficial to local economies and communities and those (often of a regional or 'footloose' nature) which may be diverted to areas where larger scale provision is made. Perhaps the best laboratory for analyzing such policies is the swathe of freestanding towns in the 20–100,000 population range embedded in the 4450 square kilometres of the London Green Belt. These settlements are of particular importance in the mid-1980s due to an inbuilt momentum for growth resulting from their favourable locations in respect of motorways, airports, and other major public investments. Such towns have been the subject of detailed research at the Department of Town Planning, Oxford Polytechnic, since 1978.[2] The focus of this Chapter is on the *forms* urban restraint policies have taken in such a green belt zone, the difficulties of their implementation by means of conventional development control, and changes since 1979 in the mix of restraint policies being operated.

The Restraint Policy Stance

Restraint developed as a package of planning policies in response to locally-expressed disquiet about the effects of rapid growth.[3] Originally a reaction to the planned decentralization of population from London in the 1940s and 50s, control was seen as necessary to protect the physical environment by containing the spread of settlements in danger of coalescence. Green belt, the primary expression of these intentions, was complemented from the mid-1950s by policies to restrict employment generating development to amounts suitable to provide jobs for the anticipated growth in the local population. Also growth was restricted to allow economy in the provision of services (by minimizing costs to the local authorities), and to protect the environments of villages and other small settlements. Throughout the 1960s and 70s this policy stance had firm local political support in areas covered by the London Green Belt; there was even support from locally-based industrialists for whom it acted to reduce competition for labour in sectors where skills were in short supply, by keeping out migrant firms.

In operating policies based on this local imperative authorities could instance support at regional and national levels. Approval of green belt policies was backed by the Industrial Development Certificate and Office Development Permit control systems. The *Strategic Plan for the South East* in 1970 stressed the importance of firm restraint in Green Belt areas in order to channel development to major growth areas such as Milton Keynes and Central Berkshire. In restraint areas it was suggested:

> . . . local authorities . . . will need to use planning controls with great discrimination to ensure that employment and population growth are kept in step with each other and that other local planning needs . . . are met.[4]

In 1976 regional planners, concerned at the low rate of development in the growth areas of the Region suggested *more* restrictive policies might be employed in restraint areas outside London.[5] The 1976 Plan[6] suggested that the level of restraint should be made contingent upon the rate of revival of the economy of London. Thus certain developments 'appropriate to local needs' might be allowed in restraint areas. The basic problem addressed in structure plans was therefore how to pursue urban restraint which minimized land take for new development, but also allowed for land use change for necessary industrial and commercial expansion, and provision for local community needs.

In translating these aspirations into a decision-making framework planners have utilized three concepts. First, the idea that a balance between population, housing, and employment will secure the containment aims of policy. Second, that physical controls such as green belt should be complemented by controls over the types of activity normally allowable in green belt zones. Third, that local needs could be effectively defined and operated as a proxy for a desired level of activity, and rate of change.

Perhaps the best example of this set of ideas in action is found in Hertfordshire.[7] The Structure Plan of 1976 sought to move towards a balance between jobs, housing, population, and the protection of the environment by 1991. The amount of growth to be provided for in each District was related to the assessed local needs of the resident population in each five year period. The technical task involved predicting the future population, making allowances for immigration. From this the number of jobs required by that population, allowing for daily out-commuting, and those not seeking jobs (the occupational pensioners) was calculated. When matched to predictions of labour demand from locally-based employers the number of new jobs to be allowed for within the policies of the plan (26–29,000 for 1976–91) was established. When industrial occupancy assumptions were applied to these figures it was found that pre-1976 plans had allocated sufficient land to 1981. No additional development land need be released.[8]

Having established the desired level of economic activity, housing provision was quantified by reference to the natural increase of the resident population, making allowances for the removal of sub-standard dwellings. The resulting figures, modified to take account of reductions in household size, and assumptions about the balance of migration in the future, constituted the 'five year supply' at Structure Plan rates for land availability purposes.[9] Translated into land requirements by the application of assumed densities, and making allowances for infill and unidentified sites in urban areas, it was suggested sufficient land had already been allocated in most areas of the County to 1981. Some new land might however have to be identified later in the Plan period.

The *policies* for employment related development in the submitted Structure Plan therefore suggested:

1. refusal of permission to industrial firms from outside the County;
2. restrictions on the creation of large new manufacturing activities by existing firms;
3. the use of local occupancy and named user conditions on developments permitted;
4. strong presumptions against new warehouses with larger than local catchments;
5. a strong presumption in favour of offices which only served local areas within the County; and
6. control of the office content of industrial permissions, normally to 10 per cent of total floor area, to reduce the number of job places that could be accommodated on allocated sites.

In addition, office and retail developments were to be restricted to the central areas of towns. Out of town greenfield developments would be firmly resisted.

For housing, apart from the control totals and land allocations, the policies consisted of:

1. extending Green Belt coverage to all areas outside the land allocated in plans;
2. resisting the loss of existing residential accommodation, by restricting changes of use to office and commercial uses near town centres; and
3. attaching conditions to residential permissions relating to the size and mix of dwelling sizes on sites to cater for local needs.

However, at County level each local needs policy developed in a different way.[10] This reflected different balances of interests at work, the varied attitudes of members and planners, and the different 'styles' of plan-making in authorities. In Hertfordshire the policies proposed for industry were more restrictive than in some other Home Counties, but all proposed significant controls on 'outsider' firms. In the case of housing, Buckinghamshire stated that land in the southern (Green Belt) part of the County 'should be used, as far as possible, for meeting local housing needs . . . the available land should be carefully husbanded and the rate of building should be no greater than the rate at which local need arises'.[11] In Surrey it was proposed that priority should go to 'meeting the needs of those experiencing greatest difficulty in obtaining adequate housing', although it appears that local demands could not be fully met by the provisions of the Plan. Land release for housing would depend on one-off negotiations between Districts and the County;

> If it can be demonstrated to the satisfaction of the County . . . that District(s) . . . , having investigated all other courses of action, are unable to meet the greatest priority housing needs, then limited additional land adjoining existing urban areas may be made available in local plans for residential development in areas subject to green belt policies.[12]

In a survey of 26 Districts in the Green Belt zone around London carried out in the summer of 1979 the main arguments for local needs policies emerged as in Table 5.1[13] They show a shift away from the motives of the Counties with maintenance of the local economy despite restraint being mentioned by well over half of those responding. The most common concern was to allow for the labour demands of local firms, particularly by providing housing for skilled workers. A majority of Districts also wished to support the establishment and development of small firms.[14] Of second importance was the traditional concern to restrain a buoyant local economy in order to reduce further land release for housing. The dilemma of how to avoid the adverse effects of such growth on the urban fringe countryside and good farmland, without at the same time stifling that growth, was a strong feature of the returns. Many interests wished to see a resolution to this conflict which satisfied both values. A good environment is a locational advantage to modern firms whose employees may also be strong conservationists. Nearly half of the Districts referred to this argument.

Table 5.1 Motives for Local Needs Policies in the Green Belt Zone Outside London

Argument	*Per cent stating the argument was 'important'*
maintenance of the local economy despite restraint	64
restraint of a buoyant economy	46
provision for those on lower incomes	38
conservation of the countryside	35
flexibility within restraint	31
maintaining a balanced age social structure	8
efficient use of limited public sector resources	4
no concern	12
(n = 26)	

1. Five Districts in Kent, 10 in Hertfordshire, 3 in East Berkshire, 5 in Surrey, and 3 in Buckinghamshire.

Source: Healey, P., Terry, S. and Evans, S., *The Implementation of Selective Restraint Policy*, WP 45, (Oxford Polytechnic, Department of Town Planning, 1979), p. 18.

The third argument, mentioned by 40 per cent of the respondents, was that provision should be made for the needs of those on lower incomes, either in the form of cheaper housing, or a wider range of job opportunities. Planners stressed this argument more than they thought their councillors would. There was little agreement on how such a motive could be realized, some stating it was entirely a matter for their housing departments. In addition around one third of Districts mentioned conservation of the countryside and the protection of existing communities from further intrusion by external (urban) influences, as a motive for the policy. The respondents (who were planning officers) claimed this motive was most often a political or councillor-held position. The final motive of importance, noted by one third of Districts, was the use that could be made of a local needs policy to allow any proposal for which an authority might like to see land released. Councillors were seen as favouring this position since it allowed them discretion in individual cases, a form of 'patronage' in decision-making. Some Districts reported that councillors supported specific local needs policy statements in plans but ignored them when it came to development control decisions. The need to maintain a balanced age or socio-economic structure, or to make more efficient use of public sector resources, did not gain much support as reasons for devising a local needs policy. Many such Districts had (and still have) the need to keep the rate levy low as a *sine qua non* of their administrative activities.

The above analysis suggests that 'local needs' is a convenient term describing a locally-politically acceptable but adjustable level of development.[15] By nature imprecise, it has the virtue of allowing local politicians to *select* what types of application or development pressure they will accept, and which they will deflect. As a safety valve policy it appeals to councillors' social consciences by its concern for the housing and job needs of local people, and it pacifies the business community by claiming their legitimate expansion needs will be catered for. The conservation lobby can be told that local needs will only generate limited development thus protecting valued landscapes, attractive town centres, agricultural land, and the green belt.

Restraint in Action – Employment

These policies, put forward when unemployment was less than three per cent in the localities concerned, suggested the erection of a set of hurdles which applicants must argue around to establish the principle of development. In practice this went some way to reversing the onus of proof which normally obtains in development control. Any significant employment proposal which would cause housing demand to rise, and which could not be accommodated within the boundaries of existing settlements, would be refused for these reasons. The policies were designed to exclude speculative development in that the planning case had to be argued in terms of the specific types of jobs the proposed industrial or warehousing activity would create. Without knowledge of an occupier's activities no assessment could be made. Accepting activities not essential to the functioning of the local community would use up land identified in plans too quickly, putting pressure on authorities for new land releases.

The style of policies is thus openly negotiative. Negotiation is invited from a set of presumptions against permission thus giving maximum strength to the local authorities in the process.[16] In order to conduct this negotiation applicants for *major* new development have, without exception, used agents.[17] The development agent is a specialist in the evolving planning policies of a particular area covering at most one or two counties, and may be engaged for this expertise by a nationally-known firm of agents operating from London who may have a national or multi-national client. Because local agents need to retain a successful working relationship with authorities they have generally accorded with restraint policies in the applications for new employment-generating development put forward. They act as an important pre-application filter ensuring that only developments with a reasonable prospect of permission come forward. This explains the apparently low figures for refusals in analyses of development control decisions in restraint areas. Data for Dacorum in West Hertfordshire for 1974–9 suggest that 18 per cent of new manufacturing and 22 per cent of new warehousing floorspace applied for was refused.[18] A higher rate (84 per cent) was found for new office floorspace but the amount of space applied for was low (Table 5.2). In the High Wycombe area the rate of refusal was 20 per

Table 5.2 Planning Decisions for Major Employment-Related Development in Dacorum, Hertfordshire: 1974–9

	Floorspace ('000 sq.m.)		
Use	*Applied for*	*Refused*	*Per cent refused*
Manufacturing			
new	43.7	8.1	18
redevelopment*	47.9	6.3	13
change of use	11.1	1.3	12
Warehousing			
new	78.7	17.3	22
redevelopment	56.3	12.0	21
change of use	3.2	0.4	12
Offices			
new	9.3	8.3	89
redevelopment	20.3	6.3	31
change of use	16.8	6.3	37

* includes extensions.

Source: Terry, S. and Elson, M. J. *Restraint and Employment*, Restraint Policies Project Paper No. 4, (Oxford Polytechnic, Department of Town Planning, 1981), p. 26.

cent for *all* forms of employment-related development, but 24 per cent for *new* employment related development (Table 5.3).[19] In the Dacorum area of Hertfordshire the land-take in approvals was 26 hectares over the five years to 1979. As three quarters of this land was already allocated in plans the containment aims of policy were secured. Research in Hertfordshire and Buckinghamshire suggests that the aim of restricting development by firms from outside the Counties was effective. Decisions by the origin of the firm suggest 'outsider' firms stood less chance of obtaining permission (Table 5.4) and in Hertfordshire over 90 per cent of new industrial and warehouse

Table 5.3 Planning Decisions for Major Employment-Related Development* in High Wycombe Area, Buckinghamshire 1974–81

	Floorspace ('000 sq.m.)	
Proposal	*Applied for*	*Per cent refused*
new development	50.8	24
redevelopment	119.5	33
extensions	85.2	6
change of use	84.1	15
Total	339.6	20

* includes manufacturing, offices, retail and warehousing uses.

Source: Wood, M. *High Wycombe: The Implementation of Strategic Planning Policy in a Restraint Area in the South East,* WP 67, (Oxford Polytechnic, Department of Town Planning, 1982), p. 29.

Table 5.4 Planning Decisions by Proposed Occupant: Major Employment-Related Development in Dacorum, Hertfordshire 1974–9

Occupant	*Applications*	*Number refused*	*Per cent*
Manufacturing			
already on site	55	7	
rest of County	21	3	13
rest of South East	4	3	
speculative	3	1	57
not known	15	4	
Warehousing			
already on site	24	5	
rest of County	15	6	28
rest of South East	—	—	
speculative	7	6	86
not known	14	6	
Offices			
already on site	48	11	
rest of County	55	26	36
rest of South East	7	3	
speculative	49	20	41
not known	41	15	

Source: Terry, S. and Elson, M. J. *Restraint and Employment*, Restraint Policies Project Paper No. 4, (Oxford Polytechnic, Department of Town Planning, 1981), p. 33.

approvals had named user and local occupier conditions attached in the period.[20]

The third policy, of limiting development to some expansion of existing firms that could justify a need to remain in a particular County, and which would not have significant employment effects, was not implemented. District councillors were not willing to hinder the extension of local firms on non-green belt land or to see them removed from the area. In any case in Hertfordshire, the Structure Plan was based on the view that policies would not be so severe as to harm the productivity and efficiency of existing firms. From detailed case studies of individual applications it is clear that the Districts were more inclined to take proposals 'on their merits' adhering to the more simple land-based guidelines in pre-reorganization plans. The County, on the other hand, sought to operate the policies using their activity-based criteria. The Districts did not use activity arguments in isolation as reasons for refusal, preferring to keep to land allocation, green belt, and other more familiar and tested planning reasons.

Effects of Employment Restraint

These examples suggest that in the late 1970s, restraint policies benefitted local employers and firms by allowing *in situ* expansion and relocation within Counties, and affording protection from the more severe labour competition that would have otherwise existed. 'Local' firms therefore kept a strong position in their local labour markets. Where physical expansion of firms was particularly rapid (for example in the electronics field) difficulties were experienced in finding *new* land. The result in some cases has been the fragmentation of enterprises among a large number of sites.

Policies have facilitated locally-based firms, not just those providing a local service. The plans of large multinational concerns have fallen within the definition of local needs and have been accommodated. Policies have also accommodated locational readjustments within Counties but have altered the intentions of employers if readjustment involved crossing a County boundary. As employment conditions in London deteriorated in the late 1970s this outcome was fully supported by the Greater London Council who wished to see even firmer restraint of employment in counties outside London.

Restraint and local user policies benefited private sector industrial developers who were in Hertfordshire and South Buckinghamshire and holding land allocated for employment uses before 1974. From 1974–80 the lack of new land allocations in plans retained the monopoly position of a small number of sub-regional industrial developers. Institutional funding as a backing for new development tended to be limited to town centre office and shopping redevelopments. The restrictions on new greenfield developments made the redevelopment and refurbishment of industrial premises within towns a feasible proposition, and this developed as the *main* opportunity for the pension funds and insurance companies wishing to invest in such environments.[21]

The major exceptions to policy have been based on national interest arguments. For example, a development involving 275 jobs in aerospace was permitted in Hemel Hempstead in 1976, based on international and national defence arguments. Later exceptions of greater magnitude have included arguments related to the importance of a particular firm to the export drive, and use of advanced technology, as 'justifications' provided by the Department of Industry. Indeed the Department of Industry will exert pressure for development on behalf of individual large applicants where they consider restraint policies are particularly harmful to industry. Although none of the cases involved, totalling nearly 2,000 jobs in Dacorum in the 1974–81 period, were on green belt sites, their potential contribution to new housing demands which could cause green belt land to be released is significant. These outcomes reflect how centrally-influenced sectoral decisions can cause local policies to appear illogical.

Thus with locally-based firms catered for, and with some large firms using national interest arguments successfully, those discriminated against by the policies were medium-sized, and some large 'mobile' firms who had no premises in the particular County, could adduce no particular reason, including the offer of planning gain, for a site in that County. Therefore, although policies sought to hold down the *level* of activity to that suited to local needs they have not been able, within the limits of planning powers, to control the *types* of activity generated to those serving local community needs only. The level of success has depended primarily on the deterrent effect of the policies (for example the widely held perception by firms that an area like Hertfordshire was a 'Green Belt' County), and the long history of relatively consistent policy application. There were few challenges on appeal during the 1974–9 period in the areas studied and no significant appeal decisions went against policies at this time.[22] Planning controls thus had a marginal effect on changes in local employment, 'controlling' only those elements of rationalization and intensification by firms which had physical implications for land use.[23]

In retrospect the mid-1970s were relatively favourable years for policy implementation. Industrialists' intentions for employment-related development could be bent away from preferred locations to other parts of the South East and other regions. Certainly in the early 1970s planners were most often dealing with owner occupiers seeking minor changes to premises consequent upon intensification, a problem of change which conformed relatively easily with the restraint philosophy.

Restraint in Action – Housing

In the case of housing the policies appear at first sight clear-cut and less negotiative. Development will be allowed in areas allocated in plans and will be refused in Green Belt. However most districts have categories of land with some form of intermediate, or indeterminate, status which allow greater discretion in decision-making. In both of the examples cited here, the High Wycombe and Dacorum areas, allocated land and London Green

Belt are complemented by areas of white land. In High Wycombe, following a study in 1969, the large (800 hectare) area of white land was divided into two categories; urban-related and rural-related. Development would be accepted on the former land subject to the removal of infrastructure restraints but not on the latter.[24] In Dacorum, green belt policies applied on land north of the London Green Belt pending approval of the structure and local plans.

In both areas fully approved Green Belt was upheld strongly in the decisions reached (Tables 5.5 and 5.6). Applications on Green Belt in both areas were less than one per cent of the total made. In neither case was the refusal rate 100 per cent, reflecting a trickle of 'conforming' development, made up of farm-related dwellings and minor infilling in some villages covered by green belt notation. The major conclusion is that white land acted as a significant safety valve in both areas. In High Wycombe over 700

Table 5.5 Planning Decisions for Residential Development by Policy Notation: High Wycombe area: 1974–81

		Dwellings	
Policy notation	*Permissions*	*Refusals*	*Per cent refused*
London Green Belt (LGB)	48	265	85
LGB/AONB	4	54	93
AONB/White Land	0	163	100
White Land[1]	724	764	51
Residential	1,019	665	39
Other	194	56	22
Total	1,989	1,967	50

1. 1,530 dwellings were also approved by the District Council as part of its public sector housing programme under the deemed consent procedure.
Note: Applications for one or more *new* dwellings only.

Source: Wood, M. *High Wycombe: The Implementation of Strategic Planning Policy in a Restraint Area in the South East*, WP 67, (Oxford Polytechnic, Department of Town Planning, 1982), p. 21.

Table 5.6 Planning Decisions for Residential Development by Policy Notation: Dacorum District 1974–9

Policy notation	*Permissions*	*Refusals*	*Per cent refused*
London Green Belt/AONB	39	85	69
White Land	2,084	2,446	54
Residential	4,370	1,380	24
Total	6,483	3,911	40

Note: Applications for one or more *new* dwellings only.

Source: McNamara, P. F. and Elson, M. J. *Restraint and Housing*, Restraint Policies Project Paper No. 3, (Oxford Polytechnic, Department of Town Planning, 1981), p. 28.

dwellings were approved on white land in the eight years after 1974 (2250 if public sector development is included). In Dacorum the same picture was found with much residential development permitted relating to the completion of the final neighbourhood of Hemel Hempstead New Town. In both cases white land acted as a reservoir for public sector initiatives in housing.

Planning authorities have found it difficult to *phase* land release at rates appropriate to local needs. In the Dacorum area over the years 1974–9 applications were received for over 11,000 dwellings.[25] If approved these would have represented development at four times the rate envisaged in the Structure Plan. Urban restraint and green belt policies led to the refusal of 40 per cent of the dwellings applied for. Over 15 per cent of dwellings refused were taken to appeal and 9 per cent of these were upheld, almost exclusively on white land. The result over the five year period was construction at over double the rate envisaged as necessary to cater for local needs. Given the importance to the builders themselves of husbanding allocated land, much higher densities than those assumed in plans have been achieved. More than 25 per cent of all dwellings approved have been infill, redevelopment, or intensification on urban sites on land not separately identified in plans. In High Wycombe permissions on white land (2250 dwellings) exceeded those on land allocated in approved plans (1020 dwellings). On appeal none of the 28 dwellings applied for within the Green Belt were approved, but 43 of the 100 dwellings taken to appeal on white land were approved.[26] Formally approved Green Belt was thus little affected during the period; development on white land was minimized, and the gaps between settlements were protected. The Green Belt policy was used as a reason for refusal (along with other reasons) in 30 per cent of all residential refusals (see Figure 5.1).

Attempts to negotiate with developers to secure particular dwelling types and sizes (small dwellings considered suited to local needs) have had little independent effect. Developers continue to argue market-based assessments of the potential of sites. If the site and area is attractive, high priced larger dwellings can be sold and will yield most profit to the builder. Analysis of specific cases around High Wycombe suggests little impact as a result of wider social need arguments on builders' intentions. In Dacorum and in North Hertfordshire a similar situation has prevailed.

In a test case in 1979 Hertfordshire County took on these arguments in an appeal against refusal of 110 dwellings on a four hectare site in Tring. The County argued that a particular mix of dwelling types, smaller than those proposed, should be approved and that due to the excessively high rate of development in the District the commencement of any development approved should be delayed for three years on grounds of prematurity. The Secretary of State upheld the appeal noting that the local needs policy should be 'flexible' and arguing that the proposed local needs amendments would constitute 'an unacceptable condition of consent'. The County's argument on prematurity was also dismissed.[27] This appears to follow the view that

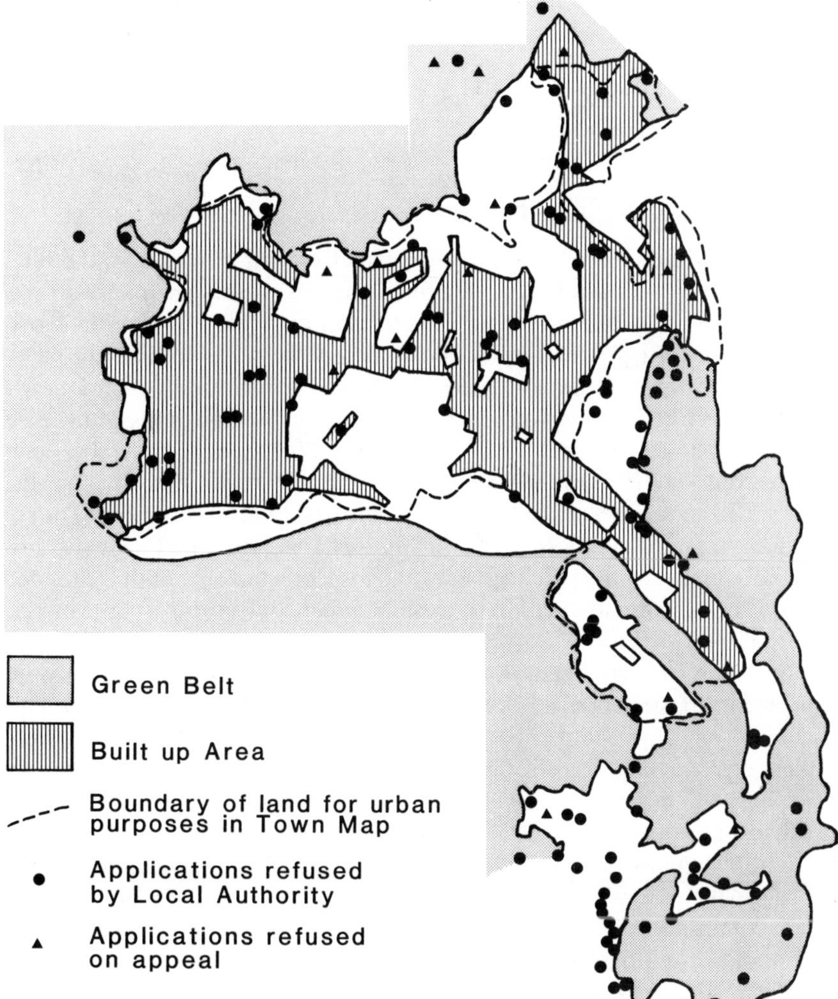

Figure 5.1 Policy Areas and Planning Decisions: High Wycombe 1974–81
Source: Wood, M. *The Implementation of Strategic Planning Policy in a Restraint Area in the South East*, WP 67 (Oxford Polytechnic, Department of Town Planning: Oxford, 1982), p. 25

conditions cannot be used to enforce local needs policies. The EIP Panel investigating the local needs policy in the submitted Hertfordshire Structure Plan put it this way:

> As we understand it, when land has been allocated for housing, planning permission could not properly be refused on the ground that the houses would become available to people other than those living locally. Conditions could be attached

> regarding design and densities, but could not be used to restrict occupation to local people.[28]

Planning can only use physical and amenity considerations to promote desired social ends.

Effects of Housing Restraint

These can be considered under two heads; effects on residents, and effects on the housebuilding industry. Detailed surveys of the occupants of new dwellings in Hertfordshire and other restraint areas suggest that new provision has not provided disproportionately for those in housing need. McNamara suggests that land prices have been forced up by restraint and that they have been passed on in turn to purchasers, although this is disputed by Ball at a more general level.[29] In Dacorum 30 per cent of new dwellings constructed from 1974 to 1981 were occupied by persons already living in the District. The majority of the 'outsiders' were first time buyers moving out of London to small dwellings, usually on large estates, which had relatively low purchase prices. As a result it appears that *local* first time buyers have tended to be pushed further afield to Bedfordshire, where one in six first time buyers are from Hertfordshire.[30]

Continued changes in employment demands, and labour turnover, were reflected in 20 per cent of all new dwellings being purchased by those moving as a result of a job change. Some 59 per cent of all house purchasers were either employers, managers, or professionals, many moving on the national job market. The policies provided for local need *if* this is interpreted as the need for key workers consequent on industrial change, but not if the definition includes those badly-housed, sharing, or on low incomes. Figure 5.2 suggests that an increased emphasis on smaller dwellings would draw out more commuters from the London area. An emphasis on large, four-bedroomed dwellings, favours local trading-up but also those moving to new jobs from outside the Region. Although complex processes are at work here this research suggests that, despite having socially-progressive objectives, the problem for planners is that the tools at their command (largely persuasion and negotiation), are insufficient to secure *any* predetermined result in terms of local housing needs.[31]

Restraint has different effects on the housebuilding industry depending on the size, financial resources, and operating area of the firm concerned. Local knowledge of opportunities, and good relations with agents, have helped the very small firms to secure a continued supply of infill developments on sites not identified in plans. A steady trickle of sites also emerges from decisions on appeal especially where green belt boundaries may be argued as illogical at field level, or where different Inspectors' attitudes to infill and intensification may release the occasional small site. Medium-sized

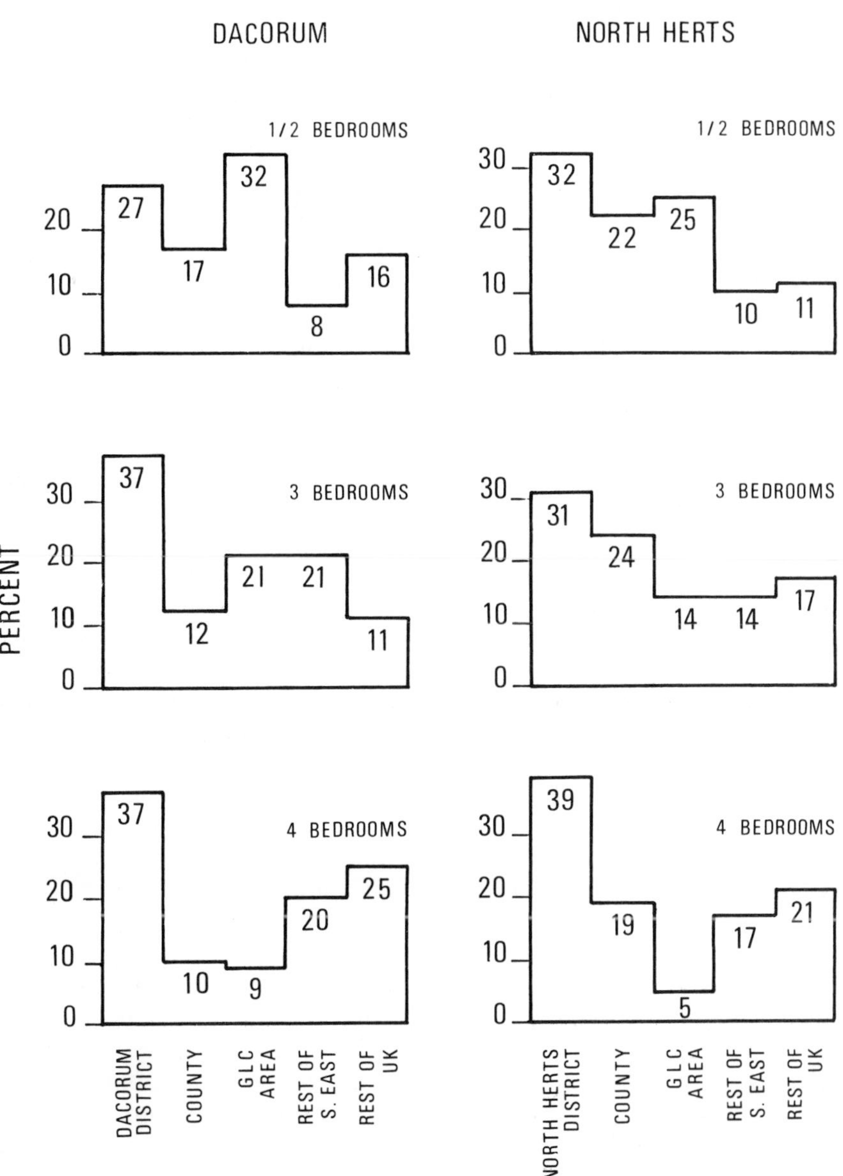

Figure 5.2 Origin of Purchaser by Size of Dwelling: Dacorum and North Hertfordshire
Source: Elson, M. J. and McNamara, P. F. *Local Needs and New Dwellings*, WP 62 (Oxford Polytechnic, Department of Town Planning: Oxford, 1981), p. 31

builders, operating in one or two Counties in the London Green Belt, benefited most from restraint in the 1970s. Historically they owned or had options on the land allocated in plans. They continued to work through their land banks at a pace suited to their individual business requirements during the decade. However few have had the resources to acquire new land ahead of requirements.

It is the volume builders, the top ten of whom build 35 per cent of all private housing in England and Wales, who have been most affected by restraint. The largest builders have most flexibility to insulate themselves against changing circumstances. They can acquire land during slump periods and hold it awaiting upturns, thus maximizing profits. In the early 1970s the largest firms were diversifying into non-housing areas such as office and industrial development, or taking up contracting opportunities in the Middle East, or those associated with North Sea Oil. However recesssion in the late 1970s, and the need to keep up the volume of their activities, has pushed the large builders into challenging the strong position of the sub-regionally based firms. The green belt restraint areas are the most attractive to exploit as speedy sale of completed houses is guaranteed, and profits are highest. To do this volume builders have had to first break into an established, localised pattern of land sales and development. They have been forced into greater contacts with local agents to find sites, to reduce the threshold size of sites they will consider (down to 25–30 plots from the 'desired' 100–150 plot size), and into buying land at unrealistically high prices to gain 'loss leader' entry into areas.[32] Also they have bought out sub-regionally based companies for their land banks, and have taken out options on land which they predict will be released in the near future, but which is not indicated in plans. Finally they have tried, with some success, to change the criteria of land availability in plans (Circulars 9/80 and 15/84 being the result of HBF lobbying), and to free up large new sites which, by definition, they have the financial power to obtain in the market. Thus a combination of general economic factors, restraint policies, and changes in Government advice, have brought volume builders and sub-regional builders into conflict.[33] These business pressures, of course, underlie the arguments in Chapter 4 regarding the definition of green belts in the new system, and the idea of setting back green belts to allow for long-term needs. This is to facilitate 'economic imperatives' within volume housebuilding. At the national level it brought forward the intense green belt and land for housing debate which preoccupied the 1983–4 period (see Chapter 10).

The likelihood is therefore that new housing land releases in green belt zones will increasingly be monopolized by volume builders. Sub-regional builders will continue to decline as part of the total picture, and the gradual rates of development they practised in their own interests are likely to be replaced by a far more rapid *rate* of development of allocated sites.[34] In such a situation local authorities would lose much of their control over the pace of housing development. Volume builders have far less commitment to a local area and its environment and are powerful negotiating agents compared to district councils. They are less likely to adjust their standardized developments to local needs. (Marketing pressures rather than negotiations with planners have created the move to single person dwellings.) This magnifies the importance of having a clearly-defined policy such as green belt to use in the face of such forces. It is thus a more 'desired' policy than ever at local level.

Other methods to secure control over the rate of land release and resist peripheral expansion have been emphasized since 1980. The most important is control by ownership by, for example, taking advantage of school closure programmes to allocate school sites and playing fields in towns for residential development. This process extends to hospital sites and other sites in public ownership. The land can then be developed at a rate consonant with local authority policies through building by licence, joint schemes to cut costs to first time buyers by discounting some of the real value of the land, and by agreements with developers to allow some measure of prior access to local people. Other methods include allowing the development of council-owned land by housing associations nominating local tenants, and by building public sector housing, although this latter activity is increasingly focused on 'special' categories such as sheltered housing for the elderly or accommodation for the severely disabled.[35] Some districts now specifically encourage infill on sites of up to 25–30 dwellings in towns inset in green belts at as high a density as possible subject only to the ability of developers to visually integrate schemes with surrounding development.

Attempts to create finer-grained controls than those implied in the land availability circulars have been frowned upon by the Ministry. East Hertfordshire District suggested that only a two year supply of housebuilding land should be released in any one year subject to a total of a six year supply every five years.[36] Any approvals beyond this would be refused. At the Public Local Inquiry the Inspector considered the policy too severe and it was deleted. It also would infringe private property rights in that applications would be dealt with on criteria other than 'planning-based' material considerations. The Ministry view is that the existence of a five year supply of available land is not a defensible reason for refusing an application which is acceptable on all grounds except the timing of its implementation. A 'pool of planning permissions' policy, whereby planning permissions would be 'banked' in order of approval by committee, the land only being released when completions reduced activity to a five-year supply, was proposed by North Hertfordshire District.[37] It did not survive early drafts of the local plan.

The logic of restraint suggests the need for local authorities to control the *rate* at which housing development proceeds. In large towns in the London Green Belt this is imperative if newly-approved Green Belt is not to be taken for housing in the future. The refusal of Government to countenance effective phasing policies must, in the absence of regional planning, lead to a conflict between green belt and land for housing criteria in a number of areas. Given the strength of the builders' lobby, and the economic imperatives of post-1979 Governments, a *gradual* process of 'statutory nibbling' of green belts must be expected.[38]

Policy Adjustment

A number of factors have combined to change attitudes to restraint and the form of policies. The wave of unemployment and closures of firms hit the South East outside London late, but has numerically been the largest of any Region in the Country. In the 16 months from May 1980 to September 1981 typical rates of registered unemployed in Green Belt restraint areas around London trebled from three to nine per cent. Although not high by the standards of the Northern Regions, such levels of joblessness are unknown in the lifetimes of many serving district councillors. Closures have created for the first time a considerable pool of vacated industrial premises and land, much of it not subject to user restrictions. In a situation where there are far lower levels of absolute demand for new industrial space, some difficulties have been experienced in securing speedy redevelopments. Such practical problems have weakened the resolve of local councils to apply full measures of restraint on redevelopment sites.

The early 1980s have seen the rise to dominance of an investment market in industrial property. This is fuelled by the growth of money available to institutional investors, the pension funds and insurance companies. In 1976 some £1000 million a year was being invested in industrial and commercial property. By 1981 this had reached £2000 million and it is generally agreed that only the shortage of supply of suitable propositions was then preventing further investment taking place.[39] As conservative bodies, financial institutions have focused on a narrow definition of what is a prime investment, including prime locational assets. The construction of the M25 is likely to reinforce the association of prime investment with proximity to motorways, such a location almost becoming a prerequisite for some types of investor.

Further, there have been rapid changes in levels of occupancy of industrial space, and the types of arrangement of space required by firms. Fothergill and his colleagues have estimated a decline of two per cent per annum over the last decade in the occupancy of industrial space, and have found that new estates built by the English Industrial Estates Corporation now have employee densities of 185 per hectare.[40] New high technology-based industries are not seeking well clad 'sheds' with six metre eaves heights but higher specification research and development, service, and manufacturing spaces with controlled conditions, interchangeability between office and manufacturing space, and prestigious settings. There have been some difficulties in obtaining institutional funding for some of this still unconventional space, particularly because of reletting problems.

Two further factors should briefly be recorded. First the success of containment has retained high quality countryside environments around London. In addition a large number of attractive medium sized towns, with carefully retained character and settings, are situated within this environment. Second, the effective devolution of power to district councils since the 1980 *Land and Planning Act* gives more scope for policy adjustment at local level. The firm tenor of restraint, operated by a structure of bargaining and control at County level, is giving way to a varied and more confused picture as differential adjustments to economic circumstances take place. Local planners and politicians remain in a position of assessing the veracity of claims of need to locate in particular areas, and on selected sites, and of influencing the terms under which new location and relocation will take place. They will have to assess whether claims for often spuriously-named science parks, 'business', 'high technology', or 'enterprise' parks constitute needs, or whether they are the inevitable demands of an investment machine over-supplied with money.

What has happened at the local level is a divergence among elements of the 'local need' political consensus arrived at in the mid-1970s. Some elected representatives now argue that the selective removal of restraints should take place to allow unemployment to be soaked up by incoming new development. In this they have now come into opposition with the local resident and environmental lobbies who see no need to release greenfield sites when there is much vacant land available within Greater London. In addition planners have pointed out that the skills demanded by likely incoming firms may do little to relieve the problems of the young, probably unqualified, school leavers who form a major part of the unemployment registers.[41]

The post-1980 period has thus seen a renegotiation of restraint, in some instances through the machinery of local plan preparation, but in others on a case-by-case basis through development control. This has gone on in parallel with exhortations from central Government to remove as many as possible of the controls on employment-generating development.[42] The process of local plan preparation has led to new allocations of land for employment-generating development in the London Green Belt zone. These have been allocated *before* detailed green belt boundaries have been drawn in new local plans. Therefore no green belt has been 'lost' but peripheral development will occur on land where 'green belt-type' policies previously operated.

The main change has been relaxations of local occupier and named user conditions. Local authorities themselves have done this. In 1981 Hertfordshire relaxed occupancy controls on small industrial units of under 235 square metres floor area. In 1982 policies were relaxed to allow 5000 manufacturing and 2000 non-local service jobs into the County. Also 'outsider' firms can locate on redevelopment sites in towns thus neatly allowing in new jobs and avoiding greenfield land being taken.[43] At the same time the Ministry has sought to weaken the effect of local occupancy conditions. They have done this by widening the catchments from which 'local firms' might be drawn from that of a particular town, a 15 kilometre radius, or a district area, to two or three districts or a whole county area. Also Inspectors at appeals have widened such catchments on *ad hoc* criteria with alacrity. The Ministry case is based on the need to protect private land and property owners. It is considered unduly onerous to have 'conditions which put a severe limitation in practice on the freedom of an owner to dispose of his (*sic.*) property . . .'

> An (occupancy condition), needs to be very carefully drafted. On the one hand, it needs to be sufficiently restrictive to perform its function, and discourage the abuse of permission. On the other hand, it should be no more onerous than is strictly necessary for its purpose . . . (It should) . . . cover a sufficiently large number of potential occupiers to prevent the restriction from being unduly burdensome on the developer and the future owners of the land . . . The area of the relevant county (or a group of districts of comparable extent) will normally be the minimum appropriate.[44]

Intervention by the Ministry in draft local plans where policy intentions were more restrictive has secured this outcome in the Dorking area in Mole Valley District[45] and in the South of the Downs area in Tandridge District,[46] both in Surrey. Within industrial buildings, as the need to keep employment levels down has lessened, far higher levels of office content have been allowed. By 1983 Hertfordshire were able to claim that employment policies were being operated mainly to exercise the exceptions to restraint which are available in periods of marked and prolonged unemployment.[47] In 1984 it was suggested that Hertfordshire was a 'County of Opportunity' for employment and that no proposal for a specific employment activity had been refused permission solely on *employment policy* grounds.[48] More jobs has become the new definition of local need. In 1984 demand for industrial premises by identified firms is low but pressure for speculative investment by development companies, backed by insurance and pension funds, is high. The pace of new building on redevelopment sites has thus increased and the green belt restraint areas may soon have a surplus of modern as well as older industrial space.

Central Government has moved away from regional scale physical planning strategies, relying more on sector-based industrial support. Where the land use planning system forms a block to such intentions in terms of specific proposals, the DoI may intervene to evoke the national interest. The DoI message is clear;[49] local authorities should take positive advantage of the construction of the M25 Motorway by freeing up industrial allocations in plans. Such a 'positive' attitude need not, it has been contended, significantly compromise the Green Belt. It is now seen to be in the national interest to develop more land for industry in the South East outside London.

This view implies overturning the criteria for development control already incorporated in development plans. At present local authorities are relaxing local need and similar policies with a view to soaking up local unemployment, after which it is intended to revert to the earlier policy stance. If criteria of local needs were to be replaced by those of national need as a basis for policy (as implied by DoI attitudes) it is difficult to see how the physical containment aims of many local authorities could still be effectively pursued. Such an outcome would also impose extra national costs. To the cost of existing infrastructure, land, and other assets lying idle or under-used in the Northern Regions, would be added the cost of developing incremental additions to existing fully-utilized infrastructure in the South East outside London.

The Primacy of Investment Criteria

Development controllers, operating at the interface between public interest and market views of 'acceptable' patterns of development, have more need than ever to understand the motives of investors in industrial and commercial space. The environment of the London Green Belt has essentially become an investment commodity. Institutionally acceptable development for industry comprises:

1. new freehold or long leasehold properties;
2. located in good quality physical environment with high quality access to motorways;
3. involving building designs and layouts of high quality and specification; and
4. that which can be let to tenants of unquestioned status on full-repairing and issuing leases that allow for frequent upward rent reviews.

The Henley Centre for Forecasting suggests that over the 1982–7 period the pension funds and insurance companies will invest £19.3 thousand million in industrial and commercial property. Half of this is likely to be in the South East Region. These large and concentrated sums of money have tended to intensify the 'natural' cycles of boom and slump in the economy, the delayed reaction of the development industry to demand for space creating large surpluses at just the point when firms' demands are slackening again. As a result there is some nervousness about both the level and security of industrial yields. This, in turn, is reflected in increasingly conservative definitions of what is prime, particularly in terms of location. Thus, at a time when developers' yield calculations seem increasingly out of tune with overall expectations of industrial growth, one attractive response is to attempt to break through existing planning restraint policies seeking ever more 'attractive' locations to secure an advantage in the increasingly competitive situation of a shortage of suitable tenants.

One area *par excellence*, has the ability to ease the property investors' dilemma, at least in the short-term. This is made up of the 'Western Arc' of the M25 corridor (see Figure 5.3) and the 'Western Triangle' stretching along the M4 to Reading.[50] Dudley Leigh of Goldstein Leigh Associates sees towns near to the M25 possessing all of the attributes sought by institutional financiers with, in addition, less commuting for executive staff,

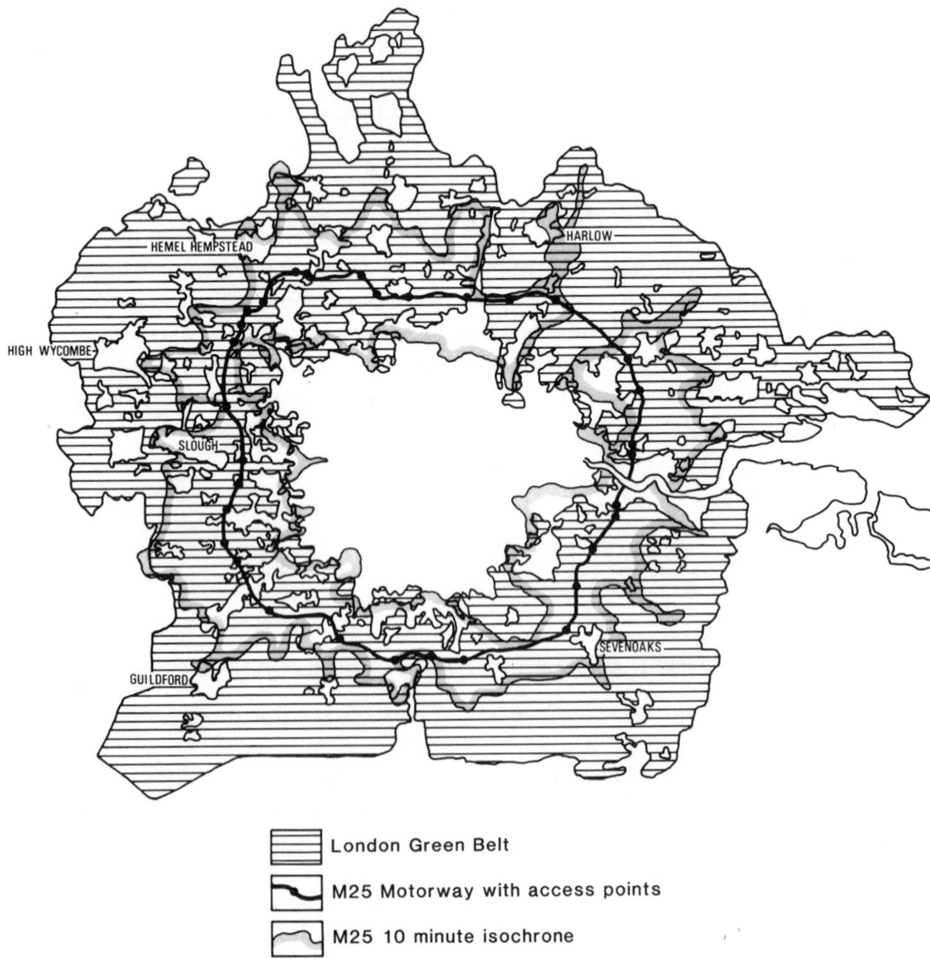

Figure 5.3 The M25 Motorway and the London Green Belt
Source: Adapted from SCLSERP *The Impact of the M25*, SC 1706 (Standing Conference: London, 1982), figures 3 and 9

good local housing, schools and shopping facilities, and high proportions of skilled staff in the vicinity by comparison with inner city areas.[51] One sector with high growth prospects, the electronic equipment and components sector, has been studied by the Department of Industry. Their study of 56 companies, virtually all located in the South East and started since 1970, showed considerable inertia in their locational choices. Three-fifths were located within 50 kilometres of Heathrow and Gatwick, with easy access for their skilled labour markets. Upon expansion, few were prepared to contemplate moves outside the South East, preferring to stay less than 160 kilometres from their original plant, usually along the M4 corridor, because of the importance of retaining their existing skilled workforces. Subsidiaries of American companies were located in the South East outside London as a base for sales and servicing facilities while European markets were being built up.[52]

Restraint has traditionally worked by restricting the range of types of site available. Assessing whether identified sites can provide for the needs of the new technology companies, and so avoid them setting up their European headquarters outside the UK, is now a serious problem. The stakes are higher than they were. The claims on land for investment in industrial space now cloud the issue of whether there is real demand for that space from entrepreneurs. The value of the land in question, frequently green belt, has been retained by public decisions prompted by the development control activities of local authorities for over thirty years. Government advice remains equivocal. There should be a positive response to the M25, but the presumption against taking Green Belt should remain the same.[53] Assumptions, such as those held by SERPLAN that development can be diverted from the western arc of the M25 to the east of the capital are illusory when, as the regional planning forum involved, they can list *no* ways in which this is to be achieved.[54] In such a situation it is likely that land will gradually be released at the insistence of the speculators, for activities which do not exist in sufficient quantity to utilize it. The economic pressures generated by ratecapping make the sale of local authority land, even if it involves ‘freeing’ the land from green belt controls through departures procedures, almost irresistible when 30 per cent of the proceeds can be spent in the year of disposal for local purposes.

The paradox revealed here is clear. Green belts, put in place to resist exceptionally strong development pressures, are far more difficult to sustain when those pressures weaken, and when district councils in the London Green Belt area are competing for new jobs.[55]

Concluding Remarks

Maintaining a balance between employment and housing in local areas appears the best way of securing containment. Green belts can be most effectively retained where there is a local consensus on the balance to be struck, and where national policies do not change. Although green belts imply a fixing of the physical extent of settlements they only affect development and change in a selective manner. There is little doubt that in the London Green Belt they have ensured the continued efficient use of land in towns by making redevelopment a viable proposition. At the same time, by rationing the supply of new land for housing they may, *in conjunction with other policies*, have had some effect on house prices. Just as restraint policies began to bite in the late 1970s, central Government changed the criteria for housing land availability, and loosened controls on employment uses to create new opportunities for investment in land and development. Thus both population and job growth continue in the London Green Belt zone at rates little slower than in the remainder of the South East outside London.

Planning controls on their own have proved ineffective in determining the rate of new development, and local needs policies for housing have proved illusory. External factors such as a depressed economy, high interest rates, and a resulting slowing down of the pace of migration of people and jobs have aided restraint as much as locally-derived policies. The main contribution of urban restraint has been as a physical deterrent and a shaping device, with local planners, although strongly in favour of local discrimination, unable to deliver any desired pattern of social and economic change.

Policies designed at local level have sought to retain local discretion to *choose* appropriate development. Central Government interventions have again had the effect of narrowing the scope of such local control. In this situation green belt has assumed greater importance because it is the policy which delivers the most stable set of central–local relations, and the greatest long-term commitment of Government to local policy aims.

Again, as noted in Chapters 3 and 4, the application of urban restraint must be seen as an interactive process rather than one of survey, plan, and implementation. Decisions are taken against a continually-developing background of policy, not all of which is published in plans. Local interests (residents and environmental groups), would like to hold local authorities to the policies in their plans, but powerful outside interests (such as housebuilders and industrial developers) wish to negotiate continuous incremental change. Local authorities are keen to negotiate with developers bringing jobs but are still resistant to the new influx of commuters that large land releases for housing would entail. It is difficult to see how districts can locate all the jobs they need without compromising the longer-standing environmental, containment, and green belt aims expressed in policy.

Part II. Land Uses Within Green Belts

6. Development Control and Rural Settlements

Outside the major urban areas embedded in green belts, local authorities pursue a variety of tasks in response to pressures for land use change. These include:

1. the management of *space-intensive* land uses, including demands for residential development in villages, and employment-related developments on greenfield sites and in country houses standing in large grounds;
2. the reconciliation of conflicts between *space-extensive* uses such as agriculture and mineral production;
3. the provision of land for a variety of leisure time uses, at the same time avoiding conflict with other users of open land; and
4. the safeguarding and enhancement of landscape, and areas of conservation value, *and* the assembly and development of resources for land renewal and the management of open land.

These four sets of activities involve managing conflicts between the expectations and values of a wide variety of individuals and groups with an interest in green belt environments. The methods used include manipulating rights in land (by the use of development control powers, or the conclusion of management agreements under the Countryside Acts, for example); acquiring rights in land by purchase; creating *ad hoc* structures to bring interests into a negotiative relationship to resolve differences; and the use of grant aid, publicity and persuasion. For each of the above tasks the mix of actions employed will vary according to the perceived strengths and shortcomings of existing powers and resources, the local priority attached to achieving particular outcomes, and the financial resources available.

The first of these tasks in green belts, managing change in the built environment, has been dominated by the use of development control. The advice on what are considered suitable uses within green belts has remained virtually unchanged since 1955. Governments have resisted elaboration, or *codification*, of such controls regarding the presumptions in Circulars as creating a suitable balance between the need for a firm stance in the face of development pressures, and the need to retain some scope for discretion to allow for local circumstances. What then is this advice? How has it been interpreted, and with what effects?

Acceptable Uses

As Chapter 1 has shown, the green belt was a formalization of a number of concepts relating to desirable urban form and the relationships between land uses. It bridged a number of ideas. The first, following the Scott Report, that a green belt would be 'an appreciable *rural* zone' surrounding a town wherein the predominant activity would be agriculture. The second, the more pragmatic Ministry conception, that the area should be predominantly *open*, and the third that there should be a clean-cut boundary on the ground between what were considered urban and 'rural' uses. The problem for the designers of the 1955 Circular was to allocate uses to the urban and rural categories. Looking at land near to cities the complexity of pre-existing land use suggested difficult decisions had to be made. Over 10 per cent of the original London Green Belt ring was by this time devoted to residential and commercial uses, and nearly five per cent to recreation. Ribbon development crossed many areas, and various institutional uses clustered in open land near to towns.[1] The prescription developed, combining these various considerations, stated:

> . . . approval should not be given, except in very special circumstances, for the construction of new buildings or for the change of use of existing buildings for purposes other than agriculture, sport, cemeteries, institutions standing in extensive grounds, or other uses appropriate to a rural area.[2]

In the 1957 Circular forestry was added to the acceptable uses, but the term 'building' was substituted for the phrase 'the construction of new buildings', making it clear the restriction was intended to be on the act of building, not merely the erection of new buildings.[3] The room for discretion, for local authorities and central Government, resided largely in the phrase 'other uses appropriate to a rural area'. Since 1957 almost every conceivable excluded use has attempted to gain entry to green belts but with little success.[4]

The Ministry suggested in the 1957 Circular, and again in 1982, that the basic wording on land use presumptions only was required in plans, applications for other uses being treated as exceptions and taken on their merits.[5] This would ensure that private property owners received consistent treatment across the country, at the same time according wide discretion to Inspectors and the Minister. However, pursuing their own policy concerns, and in order to close 'loopholes' that have appeared, local authorities have frequently elaborated and adapted the green belt instrument. The limits of discretion have been tested in local plans with Counties such as Cheshire proposing policy relaxations, but others operating tighter controls.

What has emerged is a distinction between *appropriate* green belt uses (for example development considered essential to agriculture, or open-air recreation uses), and those merely considered *acceptable* (such as the extraction of minerals, and the use of land for public utilities). In addition the special status of other departments of Government, such as the Department of Transport, has meant that the construction of commercial airport extensions and motorways has not been hindered by green belt designation. Changing demands have also led to *minor* readjustments of the formula. Therefore whilst new hotels appear unacceptable in green belts, being considered a commercial use,[6] Circular 28/77 suggests it may be necessary to accept the establishment of gypsy sites in green belts, particularly where the latter come close to urban fringes.[7] Works by statutory bodies such as gas and electricity boards are also normally acceptable if they cannot be located in urban areas. Recently waste disposal, in addition to mineral extraction, has been specifically listed as acceptable in policies in plans.

Green belts are thus *not* a blanket prohibition of development, but a highly selective one. Given the minor policy-wording changes that have gone on, and the discretion in the interpretation of policy allowed to development control planners and local councillors, no two authorities operate the green belt prescription in *precisely* the same way.[8] Cheshire have listed the uses that would normally be acceptable subject to environmental, traffic and other material considerations, and they are shown in Table 6.1, in comparison with those drafted for Staffordshire. Three criteria seem to be important; whether a use is essential to support a pre-existing green belt use (for example agriculture); whether it could reasonably be located in an urban area; and whether it is likely to infringe the predominantly open appearance of the countryside.

Table 6.1 Acceptable Uses Within the Green Belt

	Ministry Advice (1955 and 1957)	*Staffordshire (Proposed 1983)*
1.	for the purposes of agriculture and forestry	for the purposes of agriculture and forestry.
2.	for sport	the establishment of sport, recreational or leisure facilities which could not be expected to be located elsewhere, provided that such proposals will, in general be directed towards suitable parts of the green belt . . . unless they are to meet the needs of the local community.
3.	—	—
4.	institutions in large grounds	institutions or schools standing in large grounds.
5.	—	the mining and working of minerals.

Table 6.1 *Continued*

	Ministry Advice (1955 and 1957)	*Staffordshire (Proposed 1983)*
6.	—	the controlled tipping of waste.
7.	—	—
8.	other uses appropriate to a rural area	other uses appropriate to the character of a green belt.
Cheshire (Approved 1982)		
	Purpose	*Examples*[1]
1.	in connection with or meeting the requirements of *agriculture* and *forestry*	intensive food producing units (e.g. buildings for rearing animals and poultry, fish farms), commercial glass-houses, tower silos and grain stores.
2.	for outdoor *sport and recreation* where the use is appropriate to a rural area, or is associated with a natural resource and it is not possible for the use to take place elsewhere	playing fields, golf course, country park, marina and moorings on inland waterway, tourist facilities (e.g. transit picnic sites, sites for touring caravans).
3.	ancillary to *nature conservation*	information centre or viewing platform at a nature reserve.
4.	*institution* standing in large grounds	hospital, boarding school, convalescent or nursing home.
5.	*mineral extraction*	sand and gravel extraction, clay pits.
6.	*disposal of waste* by landfill	domestic refuse, industrial waste.
7.	*public utilities* and public works	roads, power lines, radio and telecommunications aerials, water, gas and sewerage pipe-lines and related structures, power stations, electricity sub-stations.
8.	—	—

1. Whilst such examples are of appropriate uses, they may not in specific cases, be considered acceptable. All development must also satisfy numerous other requirements of a general or specific nature.

Sources: MHLG *Green Belts*, Circular 50/57, (HMSO: London, 1957); DoE *Proposed Modifications to Staffordshire Structure Plan 1981*, (DoE: Birmingham, 1983); Cheshire County Council *South Cheshire Green Belt Local Plan, Written Statement* (CCC: Chester, 1982).

Residential Development

Circular 42/55 suggests the scale of physical development in settlements in the green belt should be highly circumscribed:

> . . . apart from a strictly limited amount of 'infilling' or 'rounding off' . . . existing towns and villages inside a Green Belt should not be allowed to expand further.[9]

This severe restraint is required to allow achievement of the basic aim of maintaining an open tract of land. The logic of stopping the coalescence of towns would be defeated if large-scale erosion of open land from within the green belt were allowed. Also, the land allocated for development in plans would be less likely to be used. Retaining compact villages largely at their existing limits will, it is argued, minimize public sector costs and retain agricultural land. However, complete prohibition of new development has never been locally acceptable and Circular 50/57 made distinctions between three situations. Where 'some limited measure of expansion' was intended, or where existing development was scattered and the intention was to close some gaps by infilling, an *inset* defining the limits of development should be prepared. Settlements where infilling but no physical extension was envisaged would be *listed* in the local area plan. In other parts of the green belt the presumption would be 'no new building at all'.

Settlement policies inside green belts reflect a trade-off between two objectives:

1. a wish to retain the predominantly open rural appearance and the separation and individual identity of settlements; and
2. a wish to accommodate locally-arising needs for houses, jobs and services.

What, however, are the needs of such settlements? Green belt villages are functionally part of the cities and large towns they surround. They have served this dormitory function for over 40 years.[10] Their residents are typically of high socio-economic status and income. The Martin and Voorhees study of rural settlement policy (which included Green Belt areas around Macclesfield (Cheshire) and in East Hertfordshire), shows that up to 70 per cent of economically active residents may commute out of an area daily, and 40 per cent may be in the professional and managerial groups (double the national average). The proportion of two-car households (nearly 30 per cent) may be three times the national average.[11] A combination of attractive 'rural' environments, the proximity of urban services to which access can be gained by car, and past restrictive policies, draw to such locations new generations of ex-urbanites seeking a small community atmosphere and able to afford the relatively high house prices demanded.[12]

A vestigial 'rural' community of agricultural and local service workers, and retirees remains. In social terms the phenomenon of the two class village, described by Pahl in the 1960s is still found.[13] More recent work in Cheshire distinguishes between the archetypes of the 'spiralist' ex-urbanite who has 'bought into' a green belt settlement, and the longstanding local resident who is dependent on local services and employment. For this last group the closure of schools and other facilities may pose considerable problems.[14] The effect of past policies of public sector dwelling provision in structuring this division has been noted by Connell in relation to the Surrey Green Belt.[15] More recently policies of the sale of council-owned dwellings have led to further gentrification and in-migration. The crucial distinctions focus around mobility and access. For example, the mobile use urban services and, as a result, rural public transport cannot survive on the level of patronage generated by non-car owners alone.

Inset and 'Recognized' Settlements

Two basic logics of settlement planning have developed in green belts. The first suggests that generalized local needs for housing and employment should be met *outside* the green belt, leaving only proposals that have a precise locational need to be considered. This is suggested in the 1982 draft Government advice where locally-arising needs in green belts are to be provided for in 'the appropriate locality', not in the village where they arise. This implies most rural settlements would be 'washed over', that is, retained *within* the green belt. The second suggests land for local needs should be allocated in the larger village settlements only, for reasons of economy and the retention of services, on the conventional logic of key settlement policy.[16] This implies a larger number of insets, (exclusions from the green belt), than if the first choice is taken.

A wide range of policies have been established at local level between these two positions. The former logic tends to apply around the major cities, particularly London, with the latter operating in the smaller Green Belts for example around Nottingham–Derby and the Potteries (North Staffordshire) (Figure 6.1). The technical process of defining insets stresses the importance of physical factors, following Government advice.[17] These include the landscape setting, or architectural and historic character of a village; the 'compactness' or otherwise of existing development (and thus its ability to visually 'absorb' new development); and the existence of local community facilities or spare infrastructure capacity. The Cheshire Structure Plan uses this process, stating that within the twenty-six Green Belt insets new dwellings would be allowed if they comprised limited infilling, small groups of up to six houses within defined areas in a local plan, or the restoration or conversion of non-residential accommodation. All development would also need to be 'well related to the existing form and scale of the village and not spoil its character', and 'of a scale and design appropriate to local needs'.[18]

Closer to metropolitan influence, most countryside settlements are designated as 'recognized' or 'listed' villages *within* the green belt. In Berkshire the Green Belt Local Plan includes all settlements with a 'village' rather than a 'town' character within the Green Belt terming them 'recognized settlements'. A recognized settlement is selected from all rural settlement not by whether it has some form of social or community facility but by its size, the

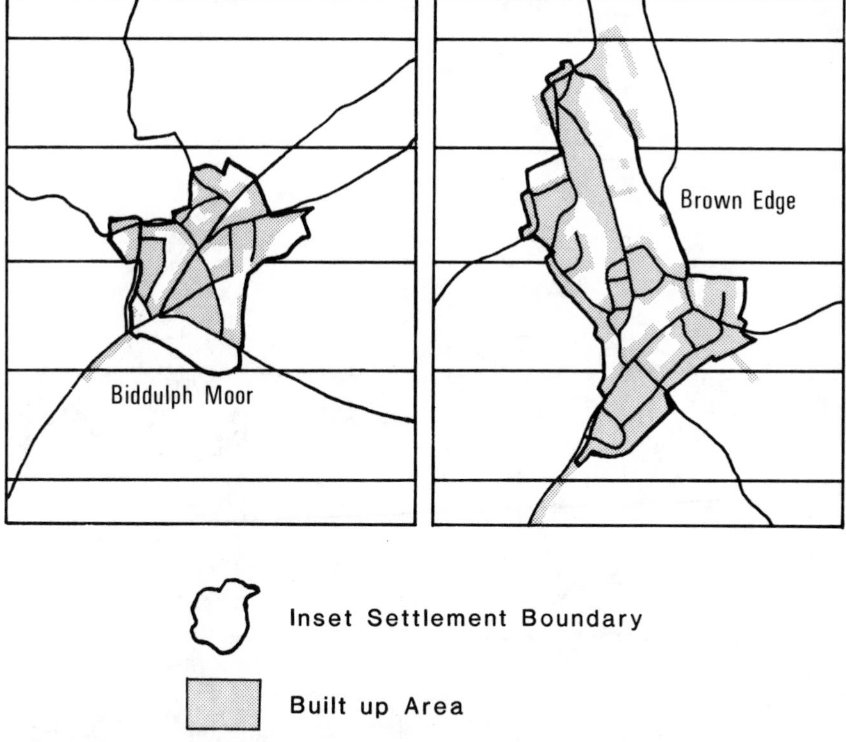

Figure 6.1 Inset Settlements Within the North Staffordshire Green Belt
Source: Adapted from Staffordshire County Council *North Staffordshire Green Belt Local Plan* (SCC: Stafford, 1983)

concentration of building within it, and the extent to which it dominates rather than is dominated by its rural surroundings. Inside recognized settlements only infilling will be allowed, within a defined line. The infill line does not encompass all development in the settlement but only that part which is most built-up, in order to protect 'the character of the locality'. This principle is shown for Littlewick Green (Berkshire) in Figure 6.2. Infilling is defined tightly here as:

> . . . the closing of an existing small gap in an otherwise built-up frontage . . . it must not harm the physical or visual character of the settlement or of the surrounding area. To be acceptable the plot should be of a size and shape comparable to the plots of the adjoining development, and must have an existing frontage to a suitable road.[19]

This definition, which excludes backland development, also suggests that proposals to erect two dwellings, or to develop sites whose present openness contributes to a settlement's physical or visual character, would not be

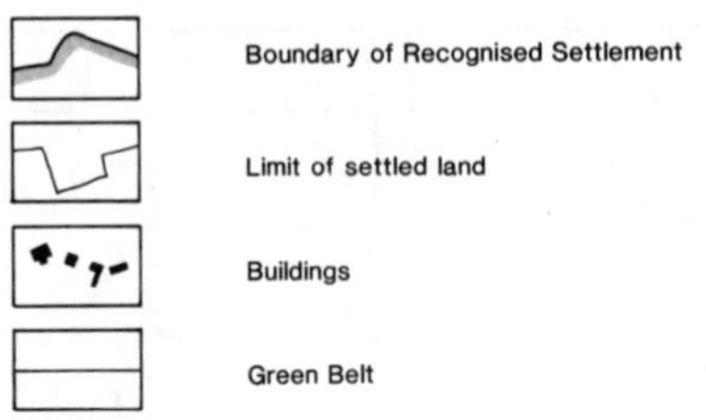

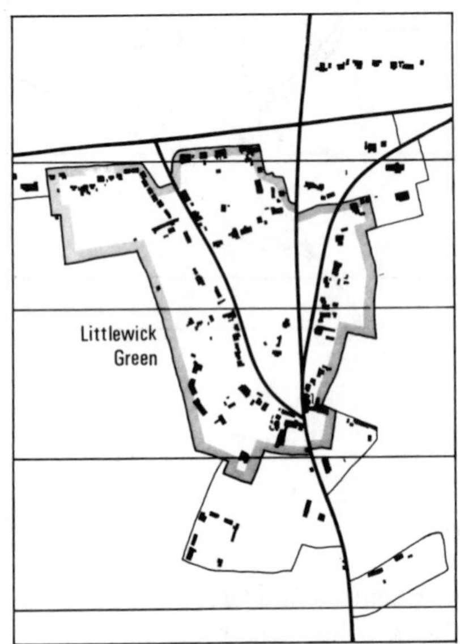

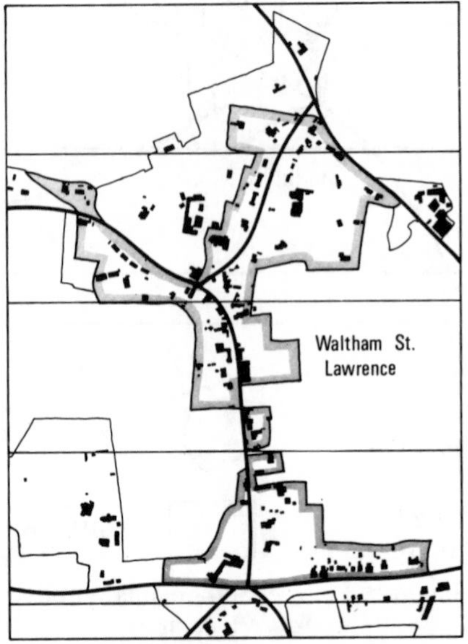

Figure 6.2 'Recognized' Settlements in the London Green Belt: Berkshire
Source: Adapted from Berkshire County Council *Green Belt Local Plan* (BCC: Reading, 1982), inset maps 16 and 21

acceptable. Infilling is not intended to result in solidly built-up villages. Gaps in a village street are part of its character and should be maintained, as the example of Waltham St. Lawrence demonstrates (Figure 6.2).

Policies have thus been *adapted to local circumstances* and pressures. In East Berkshire settlements of over 1000 persons are within the Green Belt, in North Staffordshire small hamlets of 20–30 houses have been taken out of the Green Belt as insets. The relatively generous scope for development in North Staffordshire Green Belt inset settlements has led to an increase of 6000 in the population of Green Belt parishes in the 1971–81 period, and some danger of coalescence of the most accessible settlements with the main Potteries urban area.[20] Green belt settlements have acted as reception areas for population in the depressed economic circumstances of the area.

Local village communities are well aware of the difference between inset and washed-over villages, and recognized and non-recognized settlements. In the process of renegotiation of settlement policy within green belts local groups have sought to demote their villages from inset status at the consultation stage, as around Nottingham, with some success.[21] In Berkshire, local groups have sought to remove their villages from 'recognized' status after the deposit of the Local Plan, but with less success. In some cases communities have sought more growth. In Horton, in the Colne Valley west of London and only eight kilometres from London Airport, the Parish Council complained of the loss of the local school and doctors' surgery, and the existence of only three buses a day out of the settlement. They contended more housing would 're-establish the community spirit' and maintain local services and voluntary activities. New housing allocations would allow negotiation with mineral companies for improved gravel pit restoration benefiting the local environment. The PLI Inspector did not regard these arguments as sufficiently strong to recommend an exception to Green Belt policy.[22]

Parish councils are closely involved in decisions on inset boundaries in local plans. Often representative of local property-owning interests, they seek to define tight boundaries to limit change. They may also challenge the general exceptions allowed in green belts. In both cases reliance is placed on the knowledge and advice of the federal green belt protection groups. Thus groups such as the *Green Belt Defenders* around Nottingham and Derby, the *Wirral Green Belt Council* around Merseyside, and County branches of the CPRE elsewhere, have co-ordinated local opposition to development proposals within green belts. Also, over time, some local authorities have changed the number of insets for other reasons. In Hertfordshire, Warwickshire, and Cheshire, villages close to major cities have been removed from inset status due to the likelihood of coalescence. In Surrey where insets, apart from those around large urban areas, had studiously been avoided, Ministry amendments to the Structure Plan have resulted in the definition of village insets in local area plans for the first time.[23]

Although there have been variations in green belt settlement policy across the country since 1955, within-county variation was minimal up to 1974. Since then districts have had more discretion to define local settlement policy. As a result variations within a green belt, in all aspects of development control, may now be emerging as a significant issue. Clarke has shown the 1984 position for 17 plans covering parts of the West Midlands Green Belt, indicating an apparently more severe stance in South Staffordshire than south of the Conurbation (Table 6.2). This evidence persuaded the House of Commons Select Committee to recommend the preparation of more detailed guidance to encourage uniformity of practice, but with no success.

Table 6.2 Green Belt policies in local plans in the West Midlands Green Belt

Plan	*Housing in the Green Belt*			*Industry in the Green Belt*	
	Replacements	*Infilling*	*Local Needs*	*Extensions*	*Local Needs*
West Midlands Subject	0	√	×	√	×
Solihull Green Belt	–	√	×	–	–
South Staffs. No. 1	×	×	×	√	×
South Staffs. No. 2	×	×	×	√	×
South Staffs. No. 3	×	×	×	√	×
Norton Canes District	–	×	×	0	×
Burntwood District	–	×	×	0	×
S. Area District	–	√	×	0	×
Tamworth District	–	×	×	×	×
Warwicks. Green Belt	–	√	√	√	√
Coleshill District	√	√	√	0	√
Bedworth Woodlands	–	–	–	–	–
Lapworth District	–	√	√	0	×
Hereford & Worc. G.B.	–	√	√	√	×
Wythall District	√	√	√	√	√
Bromsgrove Local	×	√	√	√	×
Redditch Local	–	√	√	–	√

Key: √ 'will be permitted' or 'presumption in favour'
0 considered 'on their merits'
× 'will not be permitted' or 'presumption against'
– not considered in the plan

Source: Clarke, S. R. *Green Belts and the Inner City Problem*, MSc in Public Sector Management, (University of Aston Management Centre, Birmingham, 1983), p. 59.

Development Control and Infill

Development control decisions are informed but not determined by policies in plans. In assessing the acceptability of proposals, Section 29 of the 1971 Planning Act states that local authorities 'shall have regard to the provisions of the development plan . . . and to any other material considerations'. This gives scope to take into account individual circumstances and make exceptions, although in green belts the fear of creating precedents tends to limit discretion. In assessing applications development control officers may use information from site visits, previous decisions, and discussions with applicants and other interested parties.[24] The principle tensions built into the development control process, such as the need to ensure fairness to local property owning interests in the face of outside development pressures, are well known.[25] Whilst existing residents are not entitled to expect complete protection at all costs from development, policies stress the protection of the character of green belt areas. There may be differences between councillors and planners, and property owners and developers, over the weight to be given to different factors affecting decisions. Also there are problems of interpreting what constitutes 'infill', 'rounding-off', or such terms as 'the confines of a settlement' in policies. Arriving at decisions is a negotiative process structured by the relative power of those involved (residents, planners, councillors and applicants) and only *informed* by policy.[26]

In this situation what has been the outcome of 'infill only' policies? Evidence from the Oxford Green Belt shows wide variations in interpretation by planning authorities and Inspectors of the term 'infill' (Table 6.3).[27] In Great Milton, a large rural settlement functioning as a minor service centre, the effect of Green Belt controls can be clearly seen (see Figure 6.3). In the ten years to 1961 twenty-seven new dwellings were permitted, but only two further infill plots were approved in the subsequent fifteen year period. Twenty-two dwellings were approved on local authority land in 1970 on local housing need grounds. One appeal was dismissed in 1973.

In the cases of Warborough and Shillingford controls curbed ribbon development upon their introduction in 1961, and reduced the *rate* of

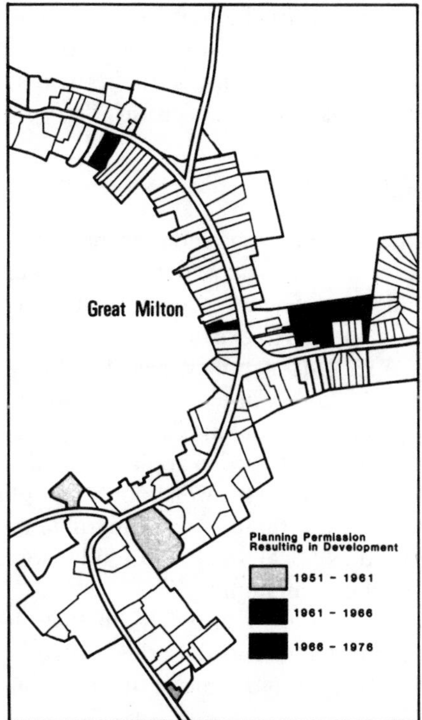

Figure 6.3 Development in Great Milton: Oxford Green Belt
Source: Adapted from Uzzell, P. *The Oxford Green Belt: Success or Failure?*, Part-time Diploma Special Study (Oxford Polytechnic, Department of Town Planning, 1977), map 8

Table 6.3 Development Control in Green Belt Settlements: Oxford Green Belt

Settlement	*Number of Permanent Dwellings Approved*		
	1951–61	*1961–6*	*1966–76*
Culham	13	18	9
Great Milton	27	1	23
Horspath	174	11	20
Stanton St. John	19	1	1
Warborough	30	17	12
Shillingford	22	6	15
Waterperry	9	5	1
Average per year	29	12	8

Source: Uzzell, P. *Oxford's Green Belt: Success or Failure?*, Part-Time Diploma Special Study, (Department of Town Planning, Oxford Polytechnic, 1977).

development after 1971. However a number of approvals not conforming with a strict definition of infill were approved and in only two of the approvals was essential operational need to be in the area established. Although Inspectors upheld the planning authority's case in 10 of the 12 appeals decided, 17 per cent of the *dwellings* contained in appeals were approved. This evidence, and case studies in Dorset and Hertfordshire suggest the predominance of physical criteria in the assessment of applications, and the element of discretion in decisions.[28,29]

Local and Personal Need

Realizing the attrition to green belt boundaries that would occur from a slow but continuous process of infill and rounding off, many authorities have suggested infill should be confined to specified categories of locally-arising need. This prescription appeals to existing local interests as a way out of the dilemmas faced by operating a policy based on physical criteria. The problem here is that such a policy implies taking account of certain personal characteristics of an applicant in making decisions. It is a long-held Ministry policy view that discrimination between applicants in this way is beyond the scope of the planning acts, despite the well known exception accorded to the agricultural industry. Further, there are considerable problems of defining who should be regarded as 'local' or, for example, someone providing an essential service to the local community.

The problem is as old as green belt policy. In 1959 the Counties around London formed a Committee to elucidate this problem. The County Planning Officer of Hertfordshire listed some of the questions:

> . . . who is a local person? Is birth in the parish of one of the partners in a marriage essential? Or is a period of residence in the district to suffice? . . . Would not local employment be a better criterion of need to live in a certain village than either birth or a housing list qualification?[30]

It was concluded that in Green Belt areas natural increase could only be accommodated by the compulsory purchase of land for housing. The policy introduced made distinctions in terms of employment in the immediate locality. Workers in agriculture and persons such as locally-employed doctors and school teachers would be allowed to build *if no suitable accommodation already existed*.[31] However, following a number of adverse appeal decisions policies were tightened and limited to physical criteria.

The argument has again been prominent since reorganization due to the passage of this level of policy-making to the local level, where it has been articulated again through the local political process. A local needs policy can operate at various levels of specificity. The most general level is demonstrated in the rural parts of Stratford District where the policy for non-key settlements states:

> . . . single dwellings or very small groups to meet particular local requirements may be permitted exceptionally . . . within the confines of an existing settlement where adequate social and public utility services exist.[32]

The phrase 'particular local requirements' is left to the discretion of decision-makers. In an analysis of 197 appeals covering 1975–82, O'Grady found that of the twenty-nine (15 per cent) which succeeded only eight had demonstrated a specific local need. Among the appeals upheld were agricultural workers' dwellings, those for the security of business premises and for widowed relatives, one which would 'add to the viability of the village', and another because it would be purchased by a local person. The main assertions made are categorized in Table 6.4. Inspectors were reluctant to interpret what a local requirement was and tended to favour physical arguments relating to the confines of settlements. They also tended to equate local need with agricultural need. What the applicants saw as local need, Inspectors treated as *personal* need. Local need, they regularly argued, is not a simile for personal convenience. Where one chooses to live is a matter of personal choice; to build a new dwelling for the sake of

Table 6.4 Categories of Asserted Local Housing Need in Appeal Cases in Stratford Upon Avon District 1975–82

Local need *Assertion*		*Per cent*
1. personal circumstances		
elderly relatives		9
other relatives		9
long association		9
house too big		6
medical		3
other		7
	total	43

Table 6.4 *Continued*

Local need *Assertion*		*Per cent*
2. employment-related		
agriculture		16
staff accommodation		10
security		5
other		5
	total	36
3. viability of village		
local resident		7
local service		5
cheap housing		2
other		7
	total	21

(n = 179)

Source: Adapted from O'Grady, P. *An Assessment of Planning Policies for Local Housing Needs With Particular Reference to Stratford-on-Avon District* (M. Phil., Department of Town Planning, Oxford Polytechnic), 1985.

convenience to accommodate that choice does not constitute a local need. Whilst Inspectors are sympathetic to personal need, (following Government advice), such factors rarely override physical planning considerations.

In Dacorum (West Hertfordshire) the Local Plan is more specific. In 'recognized' settlements small-scale infill is permitted within the defined core of a village if appropriate in scale, density, and design *and* if it constitutes:

> . . . a housing need of agriculture, forestry, leisure and local services in the rural part of the District and cannot practicably be located elsewhere, (or is for) the local facilities and service needs of individual rural settlements.[34]

A study by Hague has compared the operation of the policy by the local authority and Ministry Inspectors over the 1981–4 period.[35] Of 24 applications taken to appeal only 8 were allowed. In 14 of the cases the applicant pleaded a special need. There was little pattern to the appeals upheld although the majority were on sites with complex planning histories, or allowed for the 'rationalization' of land uses. Of the 24 approvals *by the planning authority* over the same period the majority were for agricultural dwellings or the improvement and rehabilitation of existing non-residential buildings. However four cases were approved where no special need had been argued, and three more were approved contrary to officers' recommendations.

The local needs argument has been taken farthest in the Wrekin District.[36] In an 'Area of Special Housing Control' around Telford New Town it is suggested that land within village 'infill lines' is to meet the needs of the local community only. Local needs are seen as:

1. the rehousing of a person who has lived in the community area for about 15 years or longer, and whose household circumstances have significantly changed;
2. the housing of a person who is employed in the rural area, provided the nature of that employment makes the erection of a new local residence essential; and
3. the rehousing of a person whose long-term residence is required to nurse or care for a permanently disabled relative.

Applicants are invited to submit supplementary evidence to allow the Council to arrive at consistent decisions including the names of intended occupants, their lengths of residence, and their place and nature of employment. In assessing the need, evidence of a *change of circumstances*, as opposed to a simple desire to move house, is considered important. This might include retirement out of tied accommodation, or the needs of young people brought up in the area who wish to set up home on getting married. This, in essence, elaborates the policy approach discussed and discarded in Hertfordshire in 1960. A study by Harding of appeals determined since the policy came into operation shows little difference in the ordering of presumptions to those in the Stratford area.[37] Where an application can be fitted into the physical fabric in the opinion of the Inspector it is allowed. Only in very rare marginal cases may a personal need argument tip the balance in favour of the applicant. The Ministry have objected to the Wrekin policy on the basis that planning permissions run with the land, and are restricted to considerations of land use and not the personal circumstances of individuals, and have requested a less specific policy wording.[38]

This area of policy appears in some disarray. It would be difficult to argue that policies are clear enough to ensure consistent treatment of applicants before the law across the country. The discretion allowed by the acts is used by councillors and planners to weigh presumptions in different ways in different areas reflecting the tension between political and judicial factors in development control. The land use planning system, as currently constituted, appears ill-suited to a selective policy at such a fine-grained scale. It could also be argued that the idea of 'self-contained' villages in green belts in social terms is an anachronism and therefore the whole notion is inappropriate.

Certainly the overall effect of these types of policy is to retain the local environments and property values of the small group currently living within green belts. However it is difficult to see how a relaxation of policy would allow for local needs given the presence of an open market in housing, and policies of council house sales. The types of ameliorative measure canvassed elsewhere, including development by housing associations, equity-sharing schemes on local authority land, and the use of Section 52 Agreements to control *first* occupancy, are all unrealistic in the financial and legal climate in which local authorities now find themselves.

Institutions in Large Grounds

Institutions in large grounds include hospitals, boarding schools, and convalescent and nursing homes. Some are in purpose-built premises dating from before green belt policies were operative, but others are new uses for old country houses. In principle these uses have been regarded as appropriate as they are not considered to infringe the open rural character criterion. Over recent years, however, economic pressures on the owners of large country houses have led to applications for changes of use to such activities as research and development, and for office use. A conflict therefore emerges between two policy aims: the conservation of the house (which is often a listed building in an attractive parkland setting), and the argument that only by change to some revenue earning use such as offices can both building and traditionally managed parkland be maintained. Country house locations are in demand as prestigious headquarters for large companies, affording also the opportunity to install staff training or leisure facilities. In seeking to operate policies local authorities are faced with two sets of Ministry advice. The wordings of Circulars 42/55 and 50/57 have not been further elaborated so it is a matter of interpretation as to what constitutes an 'institution', or 'large grounds'.[39] Circular 12/81 suggests that the adaption of listed buildings for new purposes is a useful way of retaining their character.[40] Thus local authorities are presented with an increasing flow of applications for changes of use to office, research and development, and similar activities which may be contrary to green belt policy.

This issue has been studied in the London Green Belt by the South East Standing Conference but the results have not been published. In the case of Hertfordshire, of over 220 country houses in the County less than half remained in *single* family residential use in 1978.[41] (Table 6.5). Nearly one in four had been adapted to traditional alternative uses such as old people's homes, nursing homes, schools, colleges and study centres, and one in eight had permission for office or research and development uses. This pressure was predominantly from firms moving out of London. Over the 1971–7 period fourteen applications for change of use involving research and development or office use were approved, ten of which were contrary to the policies for employment and offices in development plans. Together with twelve other change of use approvals these provided for over 600 jobs. Figure 6.4 shows the location of country houses by approved employment purpose indicating a concentration in the south of the County and along the M10 corridor.

Table 6.5 Use of Country Houses in Hertfordshire

Use	*Per Cent*
single residential	44
educational	13
office	8
research and development	6
hospitals and sanitoria	4
multiple residential	4
residential home	3
recreational	3
hotels and country clubs	3
training and conference centres	3
vacant	8
(n = 229)	

Source: Hertfordshire County Council *Change of Use of Country Houses in Hertfordshire* (HCC: Hertford, 1978), table 5.1.

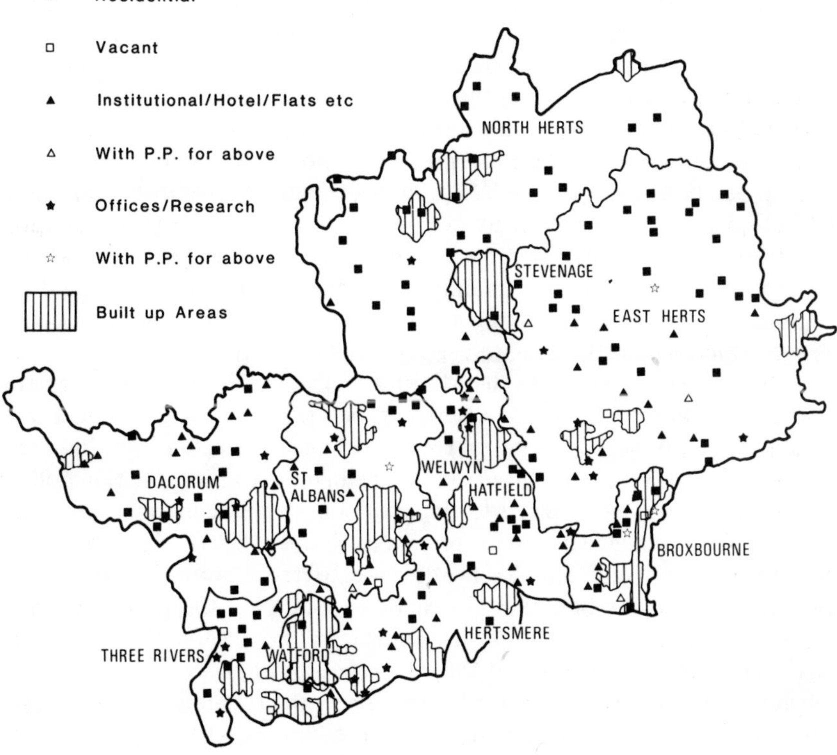

Figure 6.4 The Use of Country Houses in Hertfordshire
Source: Hertfordshire County Council *Change of Use of Country Houses in Hertfordshire* (HCC: Hertford, 1978), figure 1

The main results of negotiations with developers have been the use of conditions and agreements to lessen the visual impact of minor changes to the main and incidental buildings, to maintain parts of the gardens and paddocks, and to restrict activity to low traffic-generating uses. In some cases inability to conclude a Section 52 Agreement had led to the further deterioration of properties. The Hertfordshire case studies indicate the majority of country house applications have been accepted following negotiation. In some cases early insistence on occupation by a new user from within a District has been waived as the condition of a house has deteriorated. In others office use has been accepted as the only apparent way of retaining the property. There are other examples of public authorities, such as health authorities, obtaining permission for office use and then placing the property on the market. The County estimated that in 1978 there were twenty-eight country houses in research and development or office use employing over 3000 persons. Once established, the main trend was for the incremental growth of buildings in the grounds.

In the absence of an effective system of grants to maintain listed and other buildings of character authorities have had little choice but to permit commercial use. At the same time they have sought, by negotiation, to reduce the visual effects of such developments. Many of the approvals contravene green belt policy as they allow large sources of employment into green belts with attendant traffic movements, often along minor roads.

The sale of surplus institutional property is potentially a major challenge to the green belt concept. The DHSS owns over 20,000 hectares of land and 2000 hospitals and clinics nationwide.[42] A number of these in green belts are now regarded as surplus to requirements. They have argued that, where appropriate, redevelopment (mainly for commerce and industry) could be more in keeping with green belt objectives than the 'large hospital complexes' which they replace. If refused permission individual health authorities are advised to appeal to the Minister. This attitude to property assets was reflected at the PLI into the Berkshire Subject Plan, where the Oxford Regional Health Authority sought removal of all of its existing hospital sites from the Green Belt. It was argued that through their rationalization policy the Authority was committed to the provision of an economical medical service. This *required* sites to be removed from the Green Belt otherwise 'the provision of high quality health care to the community would be threatened'.[43] In the Sheffield Green Belt Local Plan the local authority suggested new hospitals should in principle be an acceptable green belt use.[44] The Inspector suggested they were not appropriate as new district hospitals had no need for, and therefore functional relationship with, large grounds.[45] In Berkshire the PLI Inspector recommended that development necessary to the continuation of existing hospitals should normally be allowed but, in principle, Green Belt coverage should not be removed.[46]

A new twist has been added to these arguments as a result of the recent growth in private medicine. Authorizations for private hospitals are given under the Health Services Act 1976 but the DHSS do not advise planning authorities on need. The appeals surveyed by Newcombe suggest a new private hospital in green belt would not necessarily constitute an institution in large grounds merely because an extensive area of land in the ownership of the applicant may surround the proposed buildings.[47] The 'large grounds' are not an integral part of the development as the hospital could still function without them. In other cases Inspectors have avoided the definition or discussion of what constitute large grounds and have taken as the determining factor the potential damage to the character of the countryside.

Experience of these pressures in Berkshire has resulted in a new policy which narrows the definition of an institution. The Local Plan suggests proposals must be unequivocally institutional, that is 'a more or less closed quasi-residential community'. The applicant must then demonstrate that an extensive open site or location in a rural area is essential, that the existing building will remain substantially unaltered, and that the use will not generate traffic or other movement to a degree which would harm the rural character of the locality. However if the building is listed, or is a large unlisted building which, together with its substantial grounds, makes a significant contribution to the open rural character of the Green Belt, it may be permitted to change in the last resort to office use.[48] This will only be done after the local authority is satisfied all other policy criteria have been met, and where 'genuine and strenuous efforts have been made, unsuccessfully, to find another alternative use for the building which is more in keeping with a rural or green belt location'.

The act of listing a building is an expression of a public interest in retaining its architectural character and setting. It thus appears to conflict with the criteria contained in Circular 42/55 to ensure the maintenance of green belt. However development plan policies are hedged with qualifying statements, the likelihood of permission depending on the applicant satisfying the authority that the *building* cannot be put to any other use which would retain its character. Therefore in the applicants' case it is an economic argument, but the planning authority are giving precedence to the built and natural environment arguments. Given the forces at work here a steady trickle of changes of use of country houses, from residential to a variety of employment uses, can be expected.

Industrial and Commercial Development

There is a general presumption against new industrial or commercial uses or buildings in green belts. Where settlements are 'inset' Circular 42/55 suggests that 'every effort should be made to prevent any further building'. This prescription was developed at a time when unemployment in green belt zones was negligible and, it was argued, the provision of new sources of employment would have led to local housing pressures. Therefore new land for industry and commerce is not normally located in such areas. Local authorities have dealt with proposals for extension, redevelopment and change of use on the basis of physical criteria; whether the *form* of the development or the *activity* generated would materially affect the character of the settlement or area.[49]

A number of factors are altering this position. Higher rates of unemployment have led to calls for a more relaxed view within green belts in order to meet locally-arising employment needs and demands for space. Opportunities for development exist in the form of disused farm buildings, vacant industrial premises, and in space-extensive areas such as airfields where existing use rights remain.[50] The *Council for Small Industries in Rural Areas* (COSIRA) have been active in promoting the needs of small-scale industry through loans, advice, and the support of individual planning applicants. Through their appearances at structure and local plan Examinations and Inquiries they have argued that a more relaxed view should be taken. In a recent study of the 'planning problems' of small industries in rural areas the 'rigid application' of green belt policies was cited as a major cause of difficulty in obtaining permission by COSIRA County Organisers.[51] Central Government has suggested a two-tier policy for small businesses arguing that many activities can be carried on in rural areas without unacceptable disturbance.[52] Where small-scale activities are proposed in existing buildings permission should be granted unless there are specific and convincing objections such as intrusion into open countryside, noise, smell, or excessive traffic generation. It is also stated, almost as an afterthought and realizing a likely conflict, that such advice does not contradict Circular 42/55, making clear the relaxed regime would not apply in green belts.

In Berkshire the basic green belt principles survive with little change. There is no provision in 'recognized' settlements for new employment-generating development. However, small-scale activities which will not harm the open or countryside character, once established, are normally acceptable. Such developments must generate minimal employment and new building, and have a minimal effect on the character of the area. The types of development possible appear to be those serving the local community (for example, a local village general store) small-scale cottage industries (such as a pottery attached to a private dwelling), or activities associated with a rural location (such as a small forge related to local crafts).[53]

In the North more pragmatic considerations of the need to retain and attract investment suggest a different set of criteria are being applied. The North Cheshire Green Belt is the location of this debate. As the County Planning Officer states '. . . if a firm in the Green Belt needs to expand to survive, certainly here in the North West it is allowed to do so'.[54] The County case is that with nearly six per cent of all manufacturing and service employment situated in the Green Belt a strict interpretation of the Circular would severely limit the scope for development of a significant number of Cheshire firms. A proposal suggesting new industrial and commercial developments up to 460 square metres floor area could be developed exceptionally, if they met the needs of those living in the locality, found no favour with the Ministry in 1977.[55] The proposal made in 1984 suggested the following would normally be allowed:

1. the extension and redevelopment of existing enterprises where it can be argued this is necessary for their continuance, and it can be established that they cannot be relocated on an allocated site; and
2. the change of use of an existing building of architectural or historic merit where its character can be retained.

This, it is suggested, is a positive policy in tune with the national economic situation and one which could *create* 1,500 jobs in the North Cheshire Green Belt in the next 10 years. Strict environmental safeguards will mean the essential features of green belt policy will be retained.[56]

However this set of arguments is countered by opposition from all of the Cheshire Districts, the adjoining Metropolitan Counties, and other rural interests. They argue that if implemented, the proposals would create a large pool of potential employment sites dispersed throughout the County, few *new* jobs would be created, and the result would be further decentralization from Merseyside and Greater Manchester. Sites allocated in towns would suffer slower take up, and pressures for scarce public investment in infrastructure on the many dispersed sites implied by the proposal would be created.[57] It is difficult to see how redistribution of economic activity to scattered rural locations in this way could be regarded as 'positive'.

A Ministry-commissioned Report on small industries reveals the most important reasons for refusal were *not* green belt (as perceived by COSIRA) but road safety, traffic and road access considerations. The rate of refusal for small industrial and commercial developments in the two 'Green Belt' Districts studied, Chester and Macclesfield, was not markedly different from the average (Figure 6.5). In Chester and Macclesfield Green Belt reasons were stated, among other reasons for refusal, in only 18 and 14 per cent of cases respectively. The other important finding was that of wide local discretion in action. The variations in interpretation of ostensibly the same Green Belt policies in the two Cheshire Districts were considerable:

> . . . proposed modifications to Green Belt policies incorporated within the Draft District Plan for the rural areas of Chester District represent a substantial relaxation of policies when compared with those applied elsewhere and those implied by Government guidelines. Officers in Macclesfield, where Green Belt policies have been applied less flexibly, expressed the view that different rural areas within the Green Belt required different policies to reflect variations in local circumstances.[58]

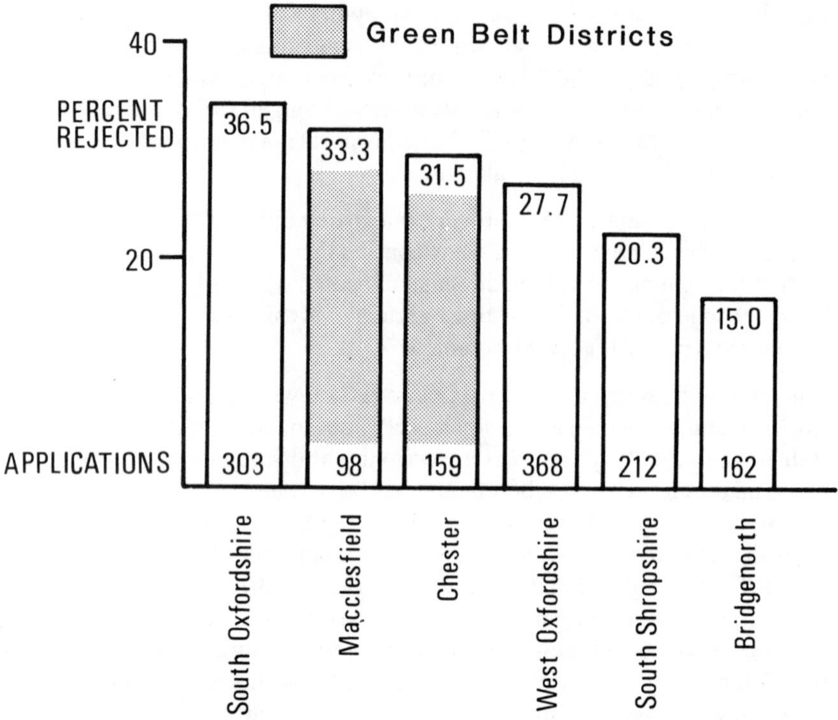

Figure 6.5 Rate of Refusal of Applications for Small-Scale Industrial and Commercial Developments in Green Belt and Non-Green Belt Rural Districts 1978–81
Source: Adapted from Joint Unit for Research in the Urban Environment *The Planning Problems of Small Firms in Rural Areas* (JURUE: Birmingham, 1983), p. 29

Where firms were refused permission in the Green Belt most found alternative premises in neighbouring towns. The main activities refused permission were those with high externality effects such as car repairers, car breakers, scrapyards, and haulage firms.

Fears of intensification and uncontrollable incremental growth have resulted in the extensive use of conditions. These most frequently limit the occupation of the premises to a specific user, or to a specified use. They may also seek landscaping or screening, and forbid or limit external storage. Problems of excessive growth and its effects on nearby residents and environments are occasionally addressed by the use of Section 52 Agreements. These may relate also to the number of lorries regularly used by a haulage contractor, or may constitute an agreement to move to a larger site allocated for the purpose in an urban or rural settlement on reaching a particular size. Despite this, it is concluded, 'the impacts of planning controls have not represented a severe constraint on the development of small businesses'.[59]

Many small firms commence activity without planning permission in domestic out-buildings or redundant agricultural buildings.[60] Where such businesses grow to an extent where significant local opposition is generated, enforcement action may be contemplated. However local authorities are reluctant to pursue this time-consuming and costly process and will often seek to control the use by granting retrospective or temporary permissions, or by seeking out more suitable sites on behalf of small firms. The available national evidence suggests appeals against the refusal of haulage businesses, car breakers yard, builders yards and vehicle storage areas are consistently dismissed by Inspectors. However, it does appear some relaxation has taken place over the re-use of existing buildings and the accommodation of 'rural' craft and similar activities within green belt settlements. Many authorities 'turn a blind eye' to some known developments, only taking action when prompted by local complaints. Also as the residential use value of disused farm buildings in green belts often outweighs that for industrial use, they are more likely to be bought by commuters. In addition the costs of converting farm buildings to Factory Act standards can be high for small firms, further limiting their scope for new employment use.[61]

There appears to be a need to clarify policy in this area. Do the Cheshire relaxations retain the *essential* features of green belt policy as is contended? Given the extra activity likely to be generated by the scale of relaxation proposed, almost certainly not. With such high levels of mobility among green belt residents it appears unlikely that jobs will be created on a significant scale for local people. Such an aim appears hardly a national priority in localities which are by definition very accessible to large urban areas. In most Regions, green belt zones represent the areas with the least unemployment. The long-term servicing costs of policy relaxations of this sort are likely to be significant, as are the effects of creating new areas with industrial and commercial user rights.

Large Firms

In a number of green belts the question of making specific exceptions for large-scale developments has arisen. Although Government advice suggests such proposals should be dealt with 'on their merits', local authorities have sought to define what an exception might be. Policies being developed reflect changing political attitudes to employment generation versus green belt. They also reflect central Government assertions that particular types of firm, notably those in the microelectronics and closely-affiliated sectors, are suited to greenfield locations.[62] The 'image' sought is of campus or 'technology park' developments, located in clean air among verdant surroundings and with a ratio of buildings to land as low as 10 per cent. Whilst all authorities wish to redevelop vacant urban land, and to direct development to allocated urban land, in the present situation of competition for economic activity outside the South East, most are suggesting that the opportunity to use green belt sites in this way should not be foreclosed.

In Merseyside the Green Belt Subject Plan, despite its *general* presumption against major development in the Green Belt suggests:

> . . . an exception may be made where . . . the enterprise is essential to the economic development of the area.

The justification for the policy states:

> . . . some industrial and commercial enterprises have special operational requirements which cannot be provided in the urban area while other enterprises may be attracted to sites in the Green Belt which possess good access to the regional motorway system or offer pleasant surroundings.[63]

The submitted Tyne and Wear Structure Plan suggested the development of offices and research establishments in parkland settings in the Green Belt should be encouraged 'in appropriate cases'.[64] Applicants would need to satisfy the Authority that employment could not be accommodated in the main urban and suburban office locations specified in the Plan. Although acknowledging the critical situation of the Tyneside economy the Ministry removed the proposal.

Local authorities therefore seem to be attempting to formalize the notion that major developments of benefit to regional economies would be acceptable in any location subject to normal site level constraints. This is despite the fact that green belts in these areas are conservatively drawn, and allow for all foreseen major new firm siting requirements. Although the Tyne and Wear EIP established that too much land had been allocated for industry, the question remains, particularly among politicians, whether more attractive and marketable sites *may* exist. In July 1983 Sunderland District negotiated the removal of a large site from the proposed Green Belt near Washington Airport. This was subsequently chosen for the new Nissan car plant. Other Counties had similar intentions. Four 'Nissan sites' were informally offered to the Company in the West Midlands, all partially or totally in existing Green Belt, and Merseyside County Council earmarked similar locations in its bid to Government. The only microchip manufacturing facility in the North West is on a Green Belt site in Neston (Wirral), and St. Helens and Stockport District have, in the 1982–4 period sought (the latter with some success) to release additional Green Belt for this type of development.

There are a steady number of 'exceptional' cases made which have been considered sufficiently strong to override the firm presumption against development constituted by green belt. The most famous, the National Exhibition Centre, in the Green Belt gap between Coventry and Birmingham, was resisted by Warwickshire and was called in by the Minister. The Inspector and the Minister regarded it as a 'unique' proposal which would not recur, and granted permission. At the same time he suggested it should in no way form a precedent for further development. Hall's prophetic view that this was hardly likely has been shown to be true as the 'High Technology' site next to the Centre, proposed in 1982, has shown.[65]

In the past firms who could establish an urban location was dangerous (for example chemicals companies) were, exceptionally, allowed to develop in green belts. Miller and Wood give an example of the negotiations involved in one case in Greater Manchester.[66] However this criterion is now being interpreted in a different way. If a large firm claims it is *uneconomic* to develop non-greenfield land, and threatens to locate in another area, then the local authority is in a no-choice situation. It is only the absence of new propositions of this sort which keeps the number of exceptions as low as they are, as Bolton's evidence to the House of Commons Select Committee suggests.[67]

Concluding Remarks

The idea that green belt policy provides an immutable prescription for land uses in the countryside and the development of villages is disproved by the discussion in this Chapter. Authorities have *adapted* green belts to local conditions some even operating policies of key village expansion. Both local and central Government attitudes to the expansion of existing employment concerns have become more lenient since 1979 despite the two-tier policy included in Circular 22/80. The central Government *policy* decision that land use policies cannot directly discriminate between local and non-local applicants in the housing market has been sustained. Local needs are dealt with at appeals as personal needs, and are factors which rarely overturn physical planning material considerations.

Since 1974, with a larger number of local authorities directly concerned, there has been a drift to greater variety in policy and development control practice within green belts. The Ministry has, through interventions in the statutory plan-making process, curtailed the extremes of divergent policies. However variety remains. How far this is a cause for concern is not clear. Given the discretion built into the planning decision-making system it seems unrealistic to expect central Government to issue a detailed and strictly defined listing of 'acceptable' uses. Such guidance would have little real effect and would act against their interests. Variety at local level is a function of the distribution of powers within the planning system, and appears accepted as a realistic response to uncertain conditions.

7. Agricultural and Mineral Production

In safeguarding open land by green belt controls near to urban areas local authorities have preserved an important and coveted resource. How should it be utilized? On what basis, and through which mechanisms, should decisions about the use and management of this open land be made? The conventional analysis of open land planning and management in green belts sees the issue as one of conflict between space extensive uses.[1] Conflicting demands, for mineral extraction or recreation on agricultural land for example, lead to the creation of externalities, or uncompensated effects of one activity upon another through physical disturbance and loss of revenue on the impacted use.[2] Mitigating such externality effects at the local level is the stock in trade of land use planning and management.

The scale and type of such demands in green belts are however the manifestations of wider social and economic processes and centrally determined priorities. Open land near towns is thus the scene of conflicts between the *production* and *consumption* aspirations of different sectors of the economy, and groups within the population.[3] Each interest, whether in favour of agricultural or mineral production, access for recreation, the conservation of the 'appreciative environment' (landscape), or ecological diversity and wildlife, has laid claim to the primacy of its view. These views represent, at a more fundamental level, adherence to different ideologies about the way natural resources should be utilized and managed. The 'need' to extract minerals at present rates until the 1990s is related to a set of beliefs held by most industrialists, politicians and economists that economic salvation depends on growth. There is, as the Nature Conservancy Council's Chief Scientist states, 'no forseeable reconciliation (of this belief) with the view of most conservationists that there have to be limits to growth because we exist within a finite (natural) system.'[4]

Each interest, either organized as a quasi-Government body such as the Countryside Commission or the Nature Conservancy Council, through employer organizations such as the National Farmers Union (NFU) and the Sand and Gravel Association (SAGA), or as a lay pressure group, is constantly seeking to assert its view by lobbying central Government (Table 7.1). Each has achieved a different accommodation with respect to the level

Table 7.1 Motives Towards the Use of Open Land in the Green Belt

Interest	*Motive*
Production interests	
Ministry of Agriculture	1. retain best quality soils 2. retain viable farm holdings
National Farmers Union	1. sustain productive agriculture up to urban fence 2. lessen restrictions on non-agricultural enterprises by farmers 3. contain and manage scale of access and recreation
National Coal Board – Opencast Executive	1. keep up rate of production, by type of coal, to meet market demand 2. avoid urban development sterilizing coal-bearing land
Sand and Gravel Association	1. maintain cheap supply of aggregates 2. retain freedom of location of extraction sites and associated plant 3. lower strength of presumptions against use of best quality agricultural land 4. resist 'onerous' restoration conditions
Consumption interests	
Countryside Commission	1. promote informal recreation in green belt 2. reduce loss of traditional landscape features 3. improve management of informal recreation facilities
Sports Council	1. promote use of green belt for sport, including associated buildings and indoor sport
Nature Conservancy Council	1. retain ecological diversity 2. retain landscape variety in pursuit of 1
Local Residents	1. retain openness 2. retain 'traditional' farming and associated landscape 3. deflect or reduce the impact of developments for mineral extraction and recreation

and type of public intervention deemed acceptable in making land use and management decisions.[5] It is this variety of policy tools – regulatory, fiscal, and persuasive – themselves constantly being revised, which constitute the basis for action of local authorities. In such a dynamic situation the place in the pecking order, and thus the power of each interest, is dependent on the ideology of the Government of the time. Some interests have achieved and retained incorporation at early stages in the local planning process, for example through strong presumptions in favour of good quality agricultural land, or the notification of 'mineral consultation areas'. Other interests, such as those concerned with landscape and recreation, have been left in a more defensive position but vehemently arguing for change.

There are no different powers available to influence changing land use within green belts compared to the general countryside. However the *stress* laid on the different functions of open land varies at national and local levels. Central Government advice, whilst suggesting the need to balance all interests, stresses the *requirement* to accommodate mineral and agricultural production, relegating recreation, conservation and landscape matters to a secondary level of priority. At local level policies aim to deflect mineral production and urban-related demands by elevating the importance of landscape, agricultural, and conservative factors as constraints. At district level the protection and improvement of landscape, and the maintenance of open land by the containment of urbanizing influences, are ranked higher than the promotion of recreation, as Munton's analysis around London shows (Table 7.2). The elected members of Metropolitan County authorities, and some county members representing urban areas, have a more promotional view towards recreation, emphasizing the complexity of operating within the two-tier system.[6]

Table 7.2 Local Objectives in the London Green Belt: 1978

Objective	*No. of mentions*
Containment of urban sprawl	25
Improvement and protection of rural landscape	21
Maintenance of 'openness'	21
Prohibition of coalescence of urban areas	15
Promotion of recreation	13
Protection of agricultural land and commercial farming	11
Preservation of the *status quo*	8
(n = 51)	

Source: Munton, R. J. C. *London's Green Belt: Containment in Practice* (Allen and Unwin: London, 1983), p. 35.

In balancing these objectives local planning authorities have a number of powers available; some obligatory, such as development control, others permissive, such as the compulsory purchase of land, the making of access agreements, and the serving of Tree Preservation Orders and Article Four Directions. Each aim for open land can only be pursued successfully using a mix of policy tools and mechanisms particularly where changes are not encompassed by development control. The forms of intervention used can be seen as either relatively *strong*; through ownership, regulation, and financial incentives; or relatively *weak* through agreements, pursuasion, advice and promotion. Because many of the relevant powers are permissive, there is wide variation across the country in the emphasis given by different local authorities to open land planning and management within green belts. Also the financial resources available vary. For example the presence of derelict land grants at 100 per cent in green belt areas in the Midlands and the North has encouraged a more 'interventionist' stance, the existence of these powers being a reflection of the degraded state of many urban fringe environments. The exercise of discretionary land management powers, such as those to conclude Access Agreements, represents the insertion of a 'public interest' view into the actions of individual land managers and constitutes a restriction of private rights. Some local authorities, albeit a decreasing number, regard intervention of this sort in open land as beyond the remit of public policy. In addition to ideological concern about the *basis for action* there is concern over the appropriateness of some forms of intervention (such as Management Agreements), and the costs involved. Many authorities are unwilling or unable to give priority and staff time to such activities given the other statutory duties placed upon them. Open land policies in green belts involve local authorities in co-ordinating the efforts of agents in the public, private, and voluntary sectors. Because of the weakness of many of the powers available a wide variety of *ad hoc* arrangements have grown up to move towards the implementation of objectives.[7]

Open Land and the Green Belt

Within this broad canvas of competing ideologies and resulting land use competition, green belt policy constitutes a number of ground rules and negotiating baselines for the various actors involved.[8] It is within the urban fringe, the area of mixed land use closest to towns, that competition is most severe and the externality effects of one use upon another are concentrated. The history of the green belt idea has mirrored changes in attitude to the compatibility and balance of production and consumption. The Scott Report prescription suggested that the primacy of agricultural production need not be severely compromised by the necessity for some measure of public access. The Abercrombie Plan for Greater London stressed the custodial role of farmers, but failed to foresee the extent to which a joint recreation function would require enhanced management powers in the absence of the continued acquisition of land for recreation purposes. The rise of recreation pressures in the 1960s led to the creation of the Countryside Commission charged with keeping under review matters relating to the conservation of the countryside and provision for recreation. However the powers to acquire areas of countryside for recreation, and negotiate Access Agreements over wide categories of countryside, were not widely used.

During the 1970s new agencies, such as the Sports Council and the English

Tourist Board, acquired powers to grant aid new developments within their respective remits. At the same time minerals interests created, with Government assistance, new structures to ensure that a ready supply of profitable coal and cheap aggregates would not be unduly compromised by other concerns. Despite reductions in land-take for agriculture, MAFF has retained, and even more strongly asserted, the need for firm presumptive policies against the loss of agricultural land. Over the 10 years to 1984 the Nature Conservancy Council has notified over 500 additional Sites of Special Scientific Interest to local authorities, requiring the latter to consult with the Council if development is proposed within their boundaries. In 1984 the steady groundswell of opinion that farmers and other owners are not the 'natural' custodians of the countryside landscape, which began with the CPREs publication of *Landscape: The Need for a Public Voice* in 1975, has given rise to the view that regulatory development control should extend to cover agricultural management changes which have importance for amenity.[9] Landscape, which is visually 'consumed' by the public should, it is argued, be the outcome of decisions made in a more publicly accountable manner.

Thus over time the conflicts between production and consumption interests have intensified as each has moved to sharpen and make more effective its method of intervening in decisions on land use and management. In 1981 the intention to insert a firm cultural emphasis into priorities for open land, by creating formal powers to introduce conservation criteria into agricultural decisions, was defeated during the passage of the Wildlife and Countryside Act.[10] This has reasserted the primacy of the proprietal ideology, and of market processes, for the time being. However green belt policy continues to stress the primacy of agricultural production and it is this function of local authority policy which will now be considered.

The Protection of Agriculture

The whole tenor of open land policy in green belts is one of retaining and supporting activities appropriate to the use of the land for agriculture and horticulture. Without the control over the worst elements of urban sprawl afforded by green belt, the oft-discussed problems of farming in urban fringes would extend to far wider areas. The green belts of the 1980s are not, however, agricultural preserves where the tenets of good husbandry hold uninterrupted sway. They have become, especially close to towns, a myriad of fragmented ownerships, each with differing abilities to adjust to the complex external environment of farm support, Government taxation policies on land, and planning controls. Ownership can be seen as a complex 'bundle of rights', including those for mineral extraction, access, the cultivation of land under tenancies, the grazing of animals, or the cutting of vegetation on commons. Superimposed on these are a set of land management units which differ in size and shape. The owners and managers of green belt farmland are thus a heterogeneous group each seeking to maximize their own view of profit in the short or long-term. This heterogeneity is suggested in information for the Tyne and Wear Green Belt (Figure 7.1) where 64 per cent of land is owned by public authorities such as the National Coal Board and local authorities, or by property interests such as housebuilders. In the inner parts of the London Green Belt the picture is similar, with 60 per cent of the land in the Hertfordshire part of the Herts–Barnet Green Belt Management area in public ownership.[11]

What then do agricultural interests around major urban areas want from the planning system? Their requirements fall under four headings.[12] First is *certainty*. This involves the planning system allocating land unambiguously between two discrete markets, an urban development market, and a protected rural land market in which farmers may invest with security. Second is

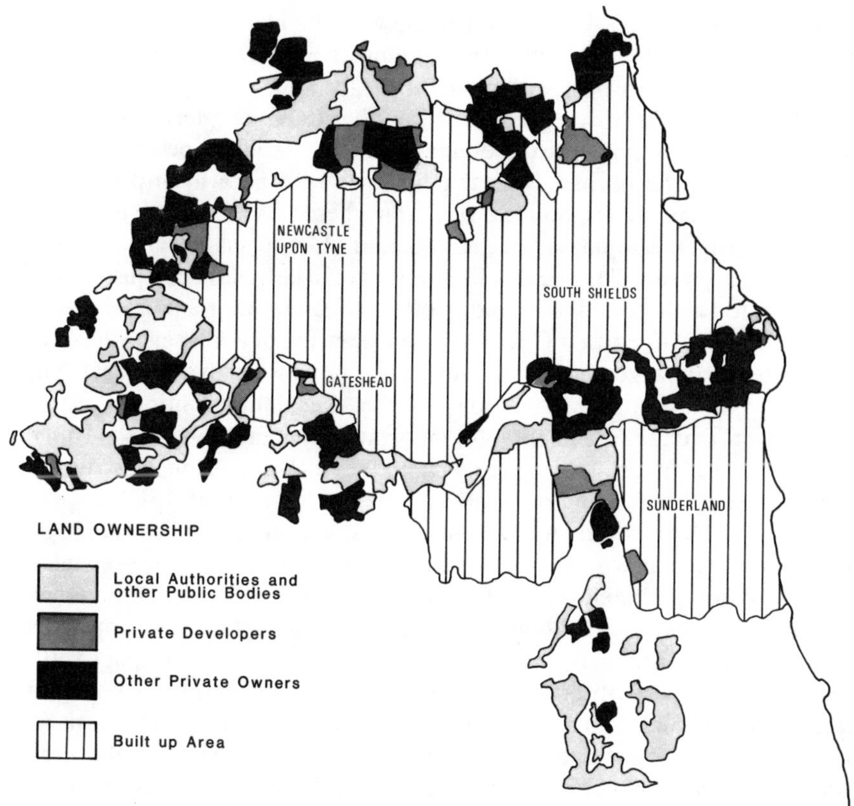

Figure 7.1 Land Ownership in the Tyne and Wear Green Belt
Source: Adapted from Tyne and Wear County Council *Tyne and Wear Green Belt and Urban Fringe Subject Plan*, Report of Survey (TWCC: Tyne and Wear, 1980), map 4

the conservation of the *best quality agricultural land*. Land varies in its productivity and in its flexibility for efficient food production. Effective planning would restrict necessary development to the poorer soils thus minimizing adverse effects on production. The third is *farmability*. Farming can become impossible if land is heavily fragmented or intruded upon by urban sprawl. The fourth is scope for *diversification* into activities not necessarily related to the use of land within a particular holding, but which may contribute to the financial return of the farm as an enterprise.

Certainty

Satisfaction of this first requirement would require green belts which are immutable. In this way much of the land speculation which typifies the urban fringe would be dampened down as the prospect of early windfall financial gains from planning permission would be eliminated. This concept, as pointed out in Chapter 4, is irreconcilable with the ideology of administrative discretion written into land use planning at all levels. Central Government officials and Inspectors have continually rejected the immutability doctrine, preferring to see green belt boundaries as long-term. Ministers have stressed the importance of boundaries lasting for an unspecified period beyond that of the normal 10-year period covered by a local plan. This appears to effectively respond to a situation where MAFF will not normally invest in Farm Development Schemes on land which is unlikely to stay open for less than 10 years. The ideal of long-term green belts has been justified as necessary to retain confidence among urban fringe farmers and land managers in the 1984 Green Belt Circular.[13] The doctrine of taking each application on its merits, together with the subjective process involved in green belt boundary definition, guarantees however that speculation continues.

This is particularly prevalent in the most marginal farmland in the fringe where potential investors frequently claim that lack of a viable agricultural use constitutes a *raison d'être* for development. However, MAFF are weak in this area. Their powers to dispossess owners or enter land to secure its proper management for agriculture, created during wartime, were repealed in 1958. Also the initiation of regular joint housebuilder–local authority land availability studies for housing, suggests that adjustments to approved green belt boundaries may be more frequent than in the past (see page 230). This could fuel speculation in green belts where the skill of the development agent is to predict which land will be released before any competitors therefore recouping the maximum financial difference between the agricultural and development value of the land. The creation of reservoirs of white land could concentrate speculative activity between the urban area and the inner green belt boundary and offer a more secure future for farmers in fully-approved green belt. However planning authorities have not generally been in favour of this solution because of the lack of control it gives in decisions on land release.[14] Farming interests would prefer plans to be unequivocal over green belt boundaries but this is precisely the assurance central Government will not give.

Protection of the Best Quality Soil

The protection of the best quality soil has been a preoccupation of MAFF Planning authorities are asked to ensure in assessing development needs, including those for mineral extraction and recreation:

> . . . that as far as possible, land of a higher agricultural quality is not taken for development where land of a lower quality is available, and that the amount taken is no greater than is reasonably required for carrying out the development in accordance with proper standards.[15]

Despite evidence that increases in agricultural production over the 1974–84 period have easily outstripped the loss from land transferred out of agricultural use, both the National Economic Development Office Report *Agriculture into the 1980s: Land Use*,[16] and the 1979 White Paper *Farming and the Nation*,[17] have stressed the need to place an even higher priority on the conservation and effective use of agricultural land.

The agricultural interest is protected during the process of allocating land in local plans, and in any development proposal involving the transfer of two hectares or more of farmland out of agricultural use, by a requirement placed on local authorities to consult MAFF. This process appears effective in limiting the quantity of good quality land taken, as Table 7.3 indicates. If land allocations in a local plan are judged by MAFF to be proposing the unnecessary release of agricultural land, and no resolution of the issue can be agreed, the power exists (created in 1980) for MAFF to instruct the Ministry to call in the plan.[18] This power has been little used but its existence is a powerful incentive for local authorities to negotiate with MAFF over land allocations at an early stage in plan preparation. It acts to considerably narrow the choice of local authorities in locating new development.

The stance of MAFF in relation to land use proposals is however regarded by farming interests as too defensive. MAFF will not formally challenge the *need* for land to be converted to urban uses but will restrict its comments to issues of land quality and farm structure. Land quality is broadly assessed, on maps at 1:63360 scale, into five grades. Objections are normally made to proposals to develop land in grades I and II. In order to bring more precision into the ubiquitous grade III (49 per cent of all agricultural land in England and Wales is in grade III) this category is being subdivided into grades IIIa to IIIc. Objections are also normally made to development proposals on land in the grade IIIa category. Where urban fringe land allocations and green belt boundaries are being decided in local plans, MAFF will carry out

Table 7.3 Agricultural Land: Outcome of Local Authority – MAFF Consultations: England and Wales 1977–80

Soil classification		Hectares: Approved and conditionally accepted	Hectares: Opposed	Per cent opposed
1977:	1	51	125	71
	2	383	1,227	76
	3	5,320	1,348	20
	4	1,531	273	15
	5	743	60	8
	total	8,028	3,033	27
1978:	1	13	229	95
	2	428	780	65
	3	3,953	1,459	27
	4	1,874	10	1
	5	568	33	5
	total	6,836	2,511	27
1979:	1	67	250	79
	2	497	796	62
	3	4,174	1,883	31
	4	1,770	126	7
	5	648	0	0
	total	7,156	3,055	30
1980:	1	75	196	72
	2	326	1,120	78
	3	6,497	1,918	23
	4	2,747	159	6
	5	1,151	17	2
	total	10,796	3,410	24

Source: Ministry of Agriculture.

detailed surveys of soil and farm structure and management, and make assessments of the likely impact of proposed development on the efficient management of holdings.[19] They do not normally make wider evaluative comments on the defensibility of proposed inner green belt boundaries in the long-term, but practice among MAFF regional offices is changing in this regard. This is in response to the criticism that over-reliance on agricultural land quality maps can lead to a myopic concern to retain good quality soil rather than efficient farm holdings. Certainly the land quality maps themselves are drawn at too broad a scale for reliable interpretation in many local situations and, it has been asserted, may not even represent a valid breakdown of land quality in MAFF's own terms.[20]

Farmability

Improving farmability, that is the ability of holdings to withstand the day-to-day effects of urban proximity, may take a number of forms. At the strategic level a number of planning authorities have sought to create *Agricultural Priority Areas*, as recommended in the Strutt Committee Report.[21] These comprise policy zones with a stronger than normal presumption against development which would conflict with agricultural use, such as mineral extraction, and any but the most small-scale informal recreation provision. Although priority areas have been approved for Bedfordshire and Hertfordshire, the farming industry fears it may lose more than it gains from the predilection of local authorities to turn the green belt countryside into a patchwork of special designations. NFU county branches have been in favour of such proposals in Hertfordshire but in Surrey and Derbyshire they have been opposed on the basis that agricultural land outside the identified areas would be given less consideration. In Surrey the priority areas were based on the MAFF Agricultural Land Classification. The NFU argued it would be unjust to penalise farmers outside the areas with extra development pressures or amenity controls merely because of assessments of soil characteristics which indicated little about farm productivity, and the economic interconnections between holdings within and outside the defined areas. Priority areas would make better sense if backed by MAFF grant aid at more generous levels for farm amalgamation and rationalization.

Farmers have discovered by experience that the shape of the urban edge can exacerbate the problems of farming in the inner green belt. Surveys in Hillingdon (West London) and in Tyne and Wear suggest *severe* interference is, however, limited to holdings within half a kilometre of urban development.[22] Recent work by MAFF and the County Council in South Yorkshire,[23] and in the Merseyside Operation Groundwork area, suggests individual *fields* may suffer penalties from an urban fringe location, but that urban effects are rarely evenly spread over farm units. There may be 'frontier fields', and in some cases 'frontier farms', where problems are concentrated. The 'field penalty assessment method' as it has become known, has been used in defining Green Belt boundaries around Sheffield. Although experimental, its use is likely to be extended.

A number of physical measures may be taken to reduce the incidence of trespass, damage and vandalism. In Greater Manchester and Merseyside policies to minimize the length of the boundary between farmland and urban development have been approved.[24] Others suggest that firm fenced boundaries, tree planting, or buffer uses should be negotiated with developers at the urban–open land interface.[25] Farming interests want a short, clear-cut edge to development which is defensible. They advise their members to avoid becoming isolated in a 'green wedge' or 'narrow finger' of green belt, albeit one designed to improve the setting of urban development or aid access to open land. Some protection can be afforded to farms as individual enterprises by personal negotiation and compromise, through co-operation with local authority countryside planners, or independent project officers employed for the purpose.[26] Work undertaken at little or no cost to the farmer might involve the creation and planting of buffer areas, the maintenance and re-routing of footpaths, or the clearance of fly tipping. *Management Agreements*, designed to reconcile the need for reasonable access with protection for agriculture normally involve payment, either in cash or kind, towards income foregone by the farmer.[27] Informal agreements are becoming more frequent but formal agreements, under the Countryside and Wildlife Act of 1981, appear less likely to be concluded for a number of reasons. On the local authority side these include cost and staff time in negotiation, despite support in principle for the results such agreements could bring. On the farming side there is an inbred streak of independence which cautions against formal arrangements or the taking out of commitments which stretch too far ahead. As the bodies providing grant aid for wardening (one of the major 'benefits' of such an agreement to the landowner) require relatively long security of tenure, then agreements become very unlikely indeed.

Of equal importance to farmability for the individual owner is the ability to attract and retain labour in a competitive situation near cities. This implies full provision for the housing needs of farmworkers in the green belt. Alternative housing in nearby towns and villages, given wage levels in farming, is too expensive, and the pool of available public sector dwellings is being depleted by the 'right to buy' legislation of 1980.[28] Ever since the *Fawcett v Buckinghamshire C.C.* case in 1960 established the principle, new dwellings for agricultural workers have been seen as appropriate within green belts, subject to occupancy conditions. In order to secure approval for a dwelling on agricultural land the applicant is required to show there is an agricultural need, and that such a need cannot be satisfied by erecting a house in a nearby built-up area. Local authorities will normally consult the Ministry of Agriculture Regional Surveyor, or their own Land Agent or County Surveyor, for a technical appraisal of agricultural need. This will cover the type of farming carried on, the relevance of the proposed development to the efficient operation of the holding, the number of people needed to work the farm, and whether any persons not housed on the land holding need to live on it. Should a need be proven for a new dwelling the applicant will normally also be required to show:

1. why there is no scope for the re-use or extension of an existing building on the holding, and
2. that the site chosen will not unnecessarily harm the open character of the area.

Permissions are normally subject to a condition limiting occupation to:

> a person solely or mainly employed or last employed in the locality in agriculture as defined in Section 290(1) of the *Town and Country Planning Act 1971* or in forestry (including any descendents of such person residing with him, or a widow (or widower) of such a person).[29]

This does not restrict occupation to a person working on any particular *holding*, as this is regarded as an unreasonable restriction on the right of an owner to dispose of property.

Where new farm holdings are created by subdivision the planning authority requires to be satisfied of the viability of the new holding before the erection of a dwelling will be contemplated. Where long-term viability is in doubt, Inspectors at appeals have looked for evidence of investment in farm buildings and contacts with Ministry of Agriculture Advisory Services as *bona fides* for a serious intention to farm the land. If these are forthcoming the normal result is to grant a time-limited permission for some form of mobile or temporary dwelling.

Increased efficiency and investment has led to large-scale shedding of labour in agriculture. Employment in agriculture has reduced by over 50 per cent since the introduction of green belts in 1955. Local authorities therefore receive a steady flow of applications for the removal of agricultural occupancy conditions. In such instances, which amount to granting a residential permission in circumstances that would not have been envisaged originally, planning authorities normally seek stringent evidence of lack of agricultural need before discharging the condition.

In a survey of all appeal cases reported in the *Journal of Planning and Environment Law* over the period 1966–82, Loughlin[30] suggests the following criteria are applied:

1. the applicant must demonstrate there is not a long-term need for dwellings for agricultural workers *in the locality* (including those retiring from agriculture);
2. the fact that the applicant's land holding is not capable of forming a viable agricultural unit is not a material consideration;
3. the fact that the dwelling is of a type not suitable for an agricultural worker (in terms of, say, size) is, of itself, no justification for removing the condition;
4. lack of demand for the dwelling will normally only be substantiated

where the dwelling has unsuccessfully been offered for public sale *with the occupancy condition* over a prolonged period; and
5. the price asked for the dwelling under criterion 4 must reflect the existence of the condition in dispute.

If these criteria are satisfied the condition will normally be discharged.

In order to reduce the scope for fragmentation a number of local authorities request applicants who are receiving permission for a new agricultural dwelling to enter into a Section 52 or similar Agreement tying the occupancy of the new dwelling to the whole of the farmland holding concerned. This Agreement assists in ensuring compliance enforcement, binding successors in title to the land, and avoiding the four year enforcement rule. No appeal to the Secretary of State is possible on a Section 52 Agreement.

Enforcement is a difficult issue, and the only systematic evidence available suggests the question of farm workers' dwellings is the subject of much abuse. A survey by Congleton District, covering part of the Potteries (North Staffordshire) Green Belt, reported by Loughlin suggests that in the period 1948–75 some 173 farm dwellings had been approved.[31] Although in each case the permission had been granted because the applicant had demonstrated a dwelling was *essential* to the efficient working of the holding, 19 per cent (33 dwellings) had never been built. Fifty-one per cent of those built did not comply with the standard agricultural condition by 1975. Over the whole period only one agricultural occupancy condition had been discharged.

The openness criterion and the requirements of farmability do, however, conflict. Local authorities are keen to blend new buildings into green belt landscape as unobtrusively as possible. One of the main features of day-to-day urban fringe farming is adjustment to a management system which allows constant visual supervision of animals and land. Buildings neatly tucked away in hollows, or masked by woodland, do not lend themselves to such inspection and supervision. The fringe farmer wants to be housed in a prominent and observable visual location in respect to the holding.

Other changes reflect investment in new methods as well as adjustments to constrained locations. The most visible elements are large farm buildings and intensive livestock units. Only farm buildings with a floor area of over 465 square metres, over 12 metres in height, or within 25 metres of a trunk road, require planning permission. This excludes virtually all farm buildings from control, certainly an anomaly if openness remains an important green belt criterion. In some areas voluntary notification agreements between farming interests and local authorities exist, and negotiation occurs over the siting, form, and aspect of buildings, and the use of materials.

Intensive livestock units may create externalities for nearby residents either directly through smell, or indirectly through slurry-spreading on surrounding land. As pig rearing, for example, may use foodstuffs predominantly or entirely imported from outside the holding some local authorities have argued such developments are not 'requisite for the use of the land for agriculture', and should be seen as an industrial uses subject to planning permission. Planning case law has become confused on this issue, which involves close interpretation of Class VI of the General Development Order (GDO). The position at the end of 1984 was that as long as intensive livestock units are on holdings of more than one hectare they remain beyond planning control.[32] In a draft Local Plan for Intensive Livestock Units in Humberside, buffer areas of 400 and 800 metres around small and large settlements have been negotiated.[33] MAFF used their call-in power to delay approval of the Plan by nearly three years lest this should become the norm. A draft set of alterations to the GDO,[34] recognizing these difficulties, suggests that all new buildings where *livestock* are to be housed within 100 metres of houses, schools or other residential institutions, should be subject to planning permission. This new proposal strikes a different balance between agricultural and local residential interests. In response to the Minister on the proposed changes the RTPI has proposed that *all* new agricultural buildings should be brought under planning control.[35]

Diversification

A green belt location may be exploited by the farmer and landowner by diversification into new enterprises. There is widespread evidence of the incidence of supplementary enterprises such as garden shops, farm gate sales, and pick-your-own schemes near to urban areas.[36] Planning policies seek to avoid such developments coming to dominate the farming enterprise and turning into large retail uses. Farm shops are normally acceptable in principle only where they sell mainly produce grown on that holding. Arguments at appeal suggest a small proportion of products brought in from outside a holding may be sold without infringing this criterion, although the 'imported' produce may be specified and limited by condition. Proposals to establish garden centres are normally resisted as these are considered a retail use and, because of a proliferation of sheds, greenhouses, sales offices and security fencing, likely to present a built-up appearance in the green belt. Farming interests suggest that Circular 22/80, which encourages small business in rural areas, has resulted in a more lenient view being taken on appeal of these types of proposal.[37]

Another obvious form of diversification is into leisure-related enterprises. One of the most popular, and rapidly growing, uses of green belt land is the grazing of horses – 'horsiculture'. In Surrey it was estimated in 1982 that 2,217 hectares of land were grazed in this way, the area involved having increased by 1,173 hectares in the 1976–82 period.[38] Nearly 800 hectares in the Herts–Barnet Green Belt Management area are devoted to this use, involving the stabling and grazing of nearly 3,000 horses (see Figure 7.2). Land for horsiculture fetches rents well in excess of those for arable

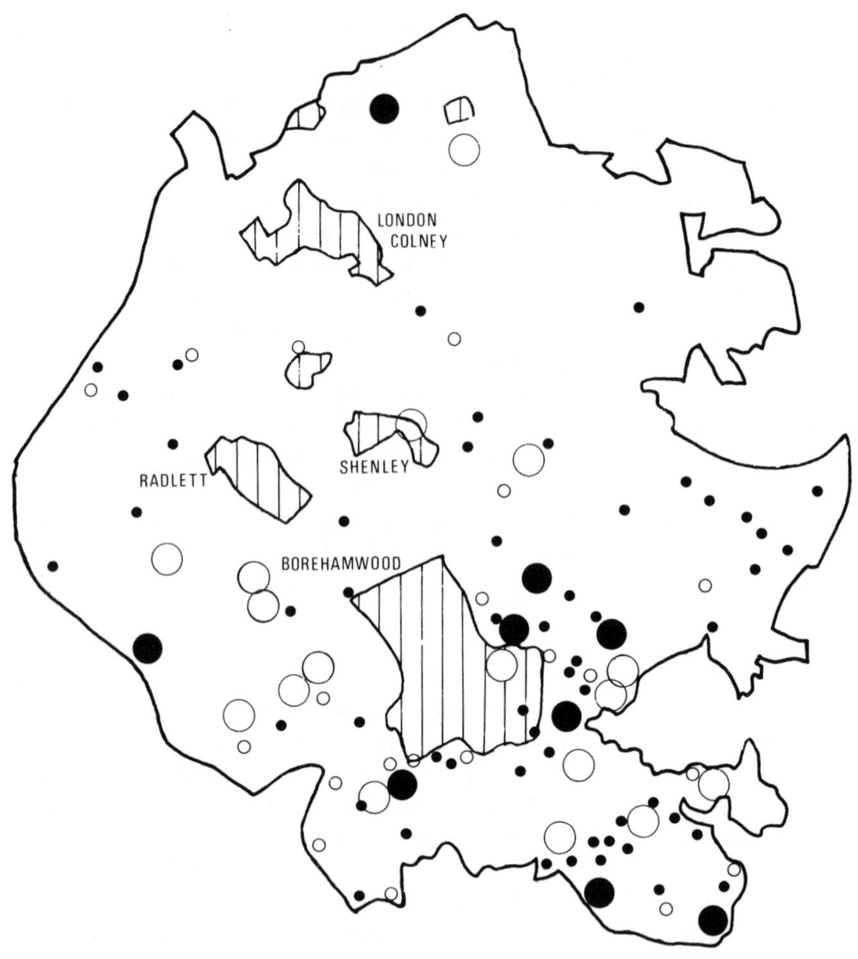

Figure 7.2 The Grazing and Stabling of Horses in the Herts–Barnet Area of the London Green Belt
Source: Adapted from Williams, H. *The Management of Publicly-Owned Land in the Hertfordshire–Barnet Experiment Area*, WP 17 (Countryside Commission: Cheltenham, 1979), appendix 2

production, and land prices paid, at £11,000 a hectare in 1980, are well above agricultural value. The trend looks likely to continue.[39] MAFF have no control over the transfer of land to such uses but are concerned at the large areas involved, and the apparent increase in the rate of transfer. The law in relation to the keeping of horses on agricultural land is complex. The arguments for and against the use in principle in a green belt are also finely balanced. In well-wooded heathland areas the visual effects of horse grazing, practice jumps and horse shelters may not be severe. On more valuable agricultural land, with low tree cover, they may create a considerable intrusion and their density and use may create conflict with pedestrians on the locally-accessible footpath network.

Under the 1971 Town and Country Planning Act agricultural grazing is exempt from planning control. A High Court decision in 1981 suggested that if the main purpose of keeping a horse in a field was grazing then no planning permission would be required.[40] If the grazing element of the occupation of a field was incidental, in that the horses were being fed wholly or primarily by other means, then the activity required planning permission. This suggests that where a paddock is too small to form the main source of food for a horse permission is required or enforcement action can be taken. It follows from the above judgement that the erection of structures designed for the protection of the animal is also subject to permission. Where a 'shelter' is applied for, local authorities again are faced with finely balanced decisions. The keeping of horses for recreation is, in principle, 'a use appropriate to a rural area' and as such should be appropriate to a green belt. The basic consideration is whether a proposal will cause material harm to the appearance of the countryside.

There are clearly different views on such a subjective criterion although a number of authorities in the London Green Belt, prompted by the concerns of their elected members, have produced supplementary planning guidance on the matter. Windsor and Maidenhead District have, since 1981, operated a policy that 'no more than two stables or field shelters for keeping of one horse shall be allowed on one acre, with no more than one structure on each acre thereafter.' Also the shelter shall be of a permanent nature and of an acceptable design.[41] In Rochford District a general guide of one horse and stable building per 0.5 hectare has been developed,[42] and in parts of Hertfordshire there is a presumption against the siting of stables (as shelters) in Agricultural Priority Areas where, in some cases, *Article Four Directions* are used to bring the activity within planning control.[43]

The County Councils Association lobbied to bring the category of horse grazing within planning control in 1977, by changing the definition of agriculture in the 1971 Planning Act, but no changes were made. In proposed revisions to the GDO in 1984 the Ministry suggested exemption for horse grazing up to a two hectare limit in any one instance, with planning permission being required for larger areas after consultation with MAFF.[44]

This threshold is widely regarded by local authorities under pressure as too high and there is reliable evidence of a number of landowners in Surrey, for example, preparing to 'lot' land for sale in parcels of just less than two hectares.[45]

Livery stables do require planning permission as they constitute a non-agricultural commercial enterprise. The main problems with such provision appear to be:

1. access, traffic generation and hazards to other road users;
2. physical damage to the countryside;
3. obtrusiveness within the environment and effect on the countryside, and
4. the extent and condition of the local bridleway network.

It appears from appeal decisions that applicants must demonstrate the need for provision in the locality, and that any increased use of roads or bridleways can be reasonably accommodated. Thus the Windsor and Maidenhead policy emphasizes the improvement and expansion of existing centres rather than the creation of new ones, the need not to take good agricultural land, the physical impact of any new buildings on the locality, and the availability of bridleways.[46]

Mineral Extraction

Demands for minerals of all kinds have grown significantly since 1955 and most of the profitable areas for extraction are located in green belts. The aim of central Government is to maintain an adequate and steady supply of material to industry at minimum social, economic and environmental cost. Few minerals can be regarded as truly ubiquitous in England and Wales but among the most widely found are aggregates including sand and gravel. Extraction is in the hands of a plethora of private companies and planning decisions on extraction are made by County Councils and the Greater London Council. The main questions addressed in policy and decision-making are:

1. how much material should be extracted (demand, some assessed 'requirement', or need)?;
2. what is an appropriate framework for the response of local planning authorities to demand; and
3. how are any resulting local conflicts resolved or mediated?

Demand and Need

The production of aggregates in Great Britain rose from 60 million tonnes in 1955 to 280 million tonnes in 1973, since when it has declined to around 210 million tonnes. It is estimated that production will remain at around this level to the end of the 1980s.[47] The demand for aggregates is dependent on the level of growth in the economy and associated construction (particularly housebuilding) requirements. Major projects, such as the M25 Motorway around London, create additional localized demands. In seeking to secure supplies, successive Governments have not been willing to deflect production from green belts and urban fringes due to the extra transport costs involved.[48] Despite the pre-eminence of cheapness of supply as a criterion for locating mineral extraction activities, there remain severe imbalances between demand and production. The South East Region only provides just over 60 per cent of its requirements from land-based pits, the shortfall being made up from marine dredging and imports from other Regions, notably the South West.

Maps produced by the British Geological Survey indicate the presence of mineral deposits by area, but are insufficiently precise to show whether the working of any particular site will be an economic proposition. The prospects of burgeoning demand, based on extrapolations made in the 1972–3 building 'boom', led to Ministry attempts to formalize the process of determining land requirements for aggregates. Regional Aggregates Working Parties, serviced by central Government, were set up and the Minerals and Construction Divisions of the Ministry devised formulae for forecasting demand. Although the validity of the methods used has been fundamentally questioned[49] regional guidelines have been produced in the form of a Circular to local authorities outlining requirements for aggregates production to 1991.[50] No county level totals have been specified making it difficult for local authorities to frame policies. Again, however, local authorities are required to balance market, environmental, and amenity arguments at local level. The minerals operators are seeking sites close to demand and thus green belt sites are under particular pressure. The Greater London Council area has an annual demand for 10 million tonnes of aggregates but only produces 2 million tonnes from pits within its boundary. Extensive extraction of sand and gravel, the most important sources of aggregates, has taken place along Thames river terraces east and west of the London built-up area, even where deposits are coincident with the main areas of grade I agricultural land in the Region[51] (See Figure 7.3.)

Central Government has continually stressed the need to accommodate any upsurges in demand should the level of construction rapidly accelerate.[52] At the same time it has provided some extra safeguards to assist the integration of extraction into the environment at local level. National guidance stresses the need for a 10-year land bank of planning permissions for sand and gravel at recent rates of production, and the need not to over-restrict the industry. The *Guidelines for Aggregates Provision in England and Wales* are intended to ensure that the demand assessments made will be provided for locally. The minerals industry has formed an appreciation of which Government policies can most profitably be influenced to

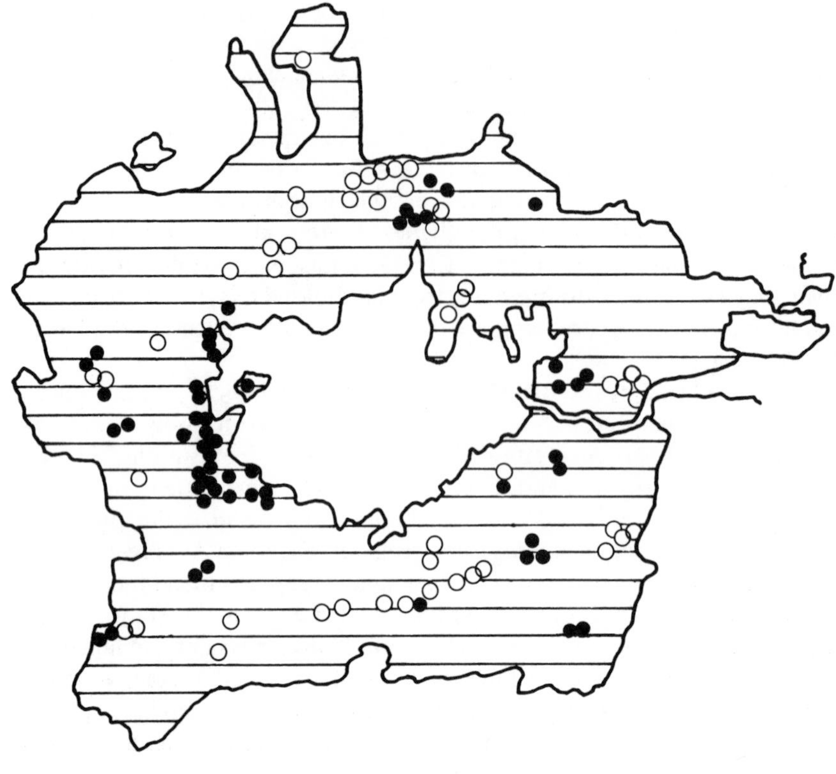

Figure 7.3 Sand and Gravel Extraction in the London Green Belt
Source: Adapted from SCLSERP *Restoration of Sand and Gravel Workings*, SC 1241R (SCLSERP: London, 1979)

bolster demands for its products. The interests of the industry are represented by the Sand and Gravel Association (SAGA), and the more recently formed British Association of Construction Materials Industries (BACMI). The influence of the minerals companies and their trade associations is exerted on Government through a complicated web of overlapping memberships among such organizations as the British Roads Federation, the

Freight Transport Association, the Society of Motor Manufacturers and Traders, and the Concrete Society. A vested interest in keeping up rates of construction is manifest in appeals to Government to encourage economic growth by increased expenditure on capital projects, rather than maintaining revenue expenditure, and by keeping open the *supply of land* for minerals. As one commentator has stated:

> . . . the current Government policy towards minerals supply is one of non-intervention in the market, with pressure groups trying their luck to alter demands to suit their interests. In these circumstances there is only one serious requirement placed upon the DoE demand forecasts by those whose interest is in promoting minerals extraction. This is for the forecasts to be high enough to ensure that mineral planning authorities and the Secretary of State continue to grant extensive planning permissions so as not to constrain the industry. Being on the safe side with land releases for future mineral working characterises the philosophy of the National Guidelines.[53]

Attempts to alter this philosophy have been conspicuously unsuccessful.

In the case of the South East Region problems of imbalance between supply and demand, and a conflict of view between planning authorities and central Government over the need to retain the contribution of land-won supplies at 60 per cent of total demand, led to the setting up of the Verney Committee.[54] Whilst local authorities felt that Government was doing too little to investigate alternative sources, such as marine dredging and 'manufactured' aggregates, the Committee recommended that land must continue to be made available over the period to 1991 'to meet, as far as possible, the Region's needs for aggregates.' The compromise reached was that Counties would 'top up' planning permissions to the six-year supply level present in 1974, but in areas which had been heavily worked local 'topping up' may not be justified. Circular 21/82 however suggested that local authorities should release land sufficient to maintain a stock of permissions for at least 10 years' extraction '*unless exceptional circumstances prevail*'.[55] A three per cent annual reduction has been approved in North West Surrey, the heaviest concentration of workings in the London Green Belt. However, Hertfordshire County attempted to introduce a policy to limit extraction at a ceiling of 3.1 million tonnes in alterations to their Structure Plan. This was to be achieved by controlling the number of processing plants. Above this figure, they argued, extraction would be proceeding at a pace beyond that acceptable to local people. SAGA and individual companies argued that they existed to meet *demand*, that major demands were likely to arise for construction of the M25 and a possible third London Airport at Stansted, and they should be left to decide when it was sensible to commence extraction subject only to local environmental considerations. The suggested policy was removed by the Secretary of State and one requiring a stock of land with permission 'adequate to enable an appropriate contribution to be made by the County over the next ten years to the Region's varying needs' suggested for inclusion.[56]

Local Issues

At the local level mineral policies in the five Local Plans covering green belt areas on deposit by the end of 1983 have relied on two principles. First, 'sieving out' all valued (good quality) resources, and applying presumptive policies that they would not normally be used for extraction; and second, avoiding the dispersal of extraction areas to minimize the extent of environmental damage. In *Berkshire* the Minerals Subject Plan divides open land, within and beyond the Green Belt, into 'Areas of Maximum Objection', 'Restricted Areas', 'Prospect Areas', and 'Preferred Areas', with a list of non-mappable constraints to be taken into account in negotiation at the development control stage. The Areas of Maximum Objection include AONBs, Areas of High Landscape Value, areas of historic designed landscapes and, (following the recommendation of the PLI Inspector), areas where mineral extraction applications have previously been refused.[57] In the *North West Surrey* Plan each of 39 'Mineral Working Areas' have been assessed according to agricultural land quality and farm structure, the need to protect land already used for recreation, nature conservation value, impact on the landscape, and likely disturbance to nearby urban areas. A three-fold classification of potential working sites is then derived. On 'category A' sites there are 'overriding' objections to extraction; 'category B' sites include valuable agricultural holdings which, it is suggested, should not be released for extraction unless satisfactory restoration to agriculture can be obtained, and unless working will not prejudice the security of agriculture in the locality. Category C (the least constrained sites) are subject to detailed non-statutory site by site guidelines which form a basis for negotiations with developers.[58] The policies in plans relating to the location of working are, however, only indicative. It is clear that preferred areas in Berkshire are merely those where the local authority *suggest* mineral operators concentrate their efforts with the greatest chance of obtaining planning permission. They do not preclude land outside preferred areas being granted permission if local constraints can be overcome.

The legacy of past aggregate extraction is, however, considerable. In the London Green Belt, areas of damaged and threatened landscape most often correspond with past mineral extraction, and local residents and district authorities are vocal in their dislike of new proposals which they feel threaten similar results. Minerals planning authorities are, in response, attempting to tighten controls over the phasing of working, its proximity to dwellings, the location of associated plant and buildings, traffic routing to and from pits, and the after-care of restored land. The *Town and Country Planning (Minerals) Act* of 1981 now allows for after-care conditions to be placed on land to be restored for agriculture, forestry or recreation use, and the renegotiation of previous restoration conditions (although some compensation payments may be involved). Local authorities are keen to implement the renegotiation measures, but there has been understandable delay in activating this part of the Act.[59] Central Government is attempting to produce guidelines for renegotiation which do not too seriously affect the commercial viability of minerals companies, but at the same time go some way to achieving better environmental results locally. Considerable bargaining has gone on. During the passage of the Minerals Bill through Parliament, Government suggested compensation on renegotiated minerals permissions would become payable by local authorities if the cost of works exceeded twenty per cent of annual value of the right to work the mineral, and that reviews could take place every five years. Following lobbying by the minerals industry these figures have been adjusted to ten per cent of the annual value, and reviews every ten years, thus downgrading the importance of local social and environmental factors when considering restoration.[60]

Local plan inquiries have proved the vehicle for storms of local protest against the effects of mineral extraction. The South Buckinghamshire Plan attracted 1,971 objections[61] and the North West Surrey Plan 1,500[62] the majority from local residents. Data for Kent and Berkshire are shown in Table 7.4. Parish councils have been prominent in their opposition, as have County CPRE branches and special issue-based alliances such as RAGE (Residents Against Gravel Extraction) in Berkshire, and SCRAM (Surrey Committee of Residents Against Minerals). The latter claims, through its affiliates, a membership of 16,000 persons. Local communities have sought to remove the likelihood that any nearby deposits might be favourably regarded by the local authorities. District councils have sought to deflect likely extraction to other areas, a practice that also occurs at county and regional levels.[63] Mineral companies have attempted to establish that extraction is not precluded from non-preferred areas in plans, that local authorities should take into account the willingness to sell of landowners as

Table 7.4 Interests Represented at Kent and Berkshire Minerals Subject Plan Public Local Inquiries

Interest	*Berkshire*	*Kent*
parish councils	21	16
individuals	18	62
amenity, conservation societies	16	11
district councils	12	3
mineral companies, SAGA	10	7
Government, statutory bodies, adjoining counties	15	1

Note: Includes appearances and unresolved written representations.

Sources: Analyses of DoE *Berkshire County Minerals Subject Plan: Report of the Inspector,* (DoE: Bristol, 1983); *Inquiry Into the Kent Minerals Subject Plan (Sand, Gravel and Ragstone), Report of the Inspector* (DoE: Bristol, 1983).

criteria in defining land availability, and to avoid complete restriction on the working of land of Grade I and Grade II agricultural quality. They have established that the extraction areas in plans are not exclusive and, in the case of the Buckinghamshire Minerals Plan have challenged the 'subjectivity' of the sieve factors suggested by the County, an issue which in 1984 was the subject of a County appeal to the High Court. Land ownership and willingness to sell have not been considered relevant planning matters by the local authorities or Inspectors. In Hertfordshire a suggested policy prohibiting the extraction of aggregates from Grade I and II agricultural land was amended by the Minister stating:

> . . . the maintenance of a steady supply of material is essential in the national interest, . . . and higher grade agricultural land may exceptionally have to be released for mineral extraction to maintain the County's contribution to supply.[64]

Thus the asserted national need to retain land of high quality can be overridden by the need to retain aggregate supply. Certainly evidence of land take in the only areas of Grade I and II land in the inner part of the London Green Belt confirms this.

The other main thrust of local plans is an attempt to *formalize* procedures and methods for protecting local communities and the environment. Protection may take a number of forms including the establishment of buffer zones around residential areas, or the control of traffic generation and lorry routing by the use of Section 52 Agreements. A policy for 100 metre buffer zones around major settlements in Berkshire was not supported by the Inspector at the PLI, who considered too many areas of mineral reserves could thus be sterilized. Buffer zones should be considered, if needed, on a case by case basis. Local communities use evidence of village character, landscape quality, and past refusals to make their case for no development. Existence of the green belt is also used and, where extraction is underway, arguments that settlements have 'taken their share' of nuisance and disturbance are made. The result has been one or two minor changes to preferred areas where historic landscapes or sites of particular nature conservation or archaeological importance have been 'discovered'. In Berkshire the Inspector suggested that areas of local landscape importance, resulting from further county or district (but significantly not parish) assessments, could be seen as constraints.[65] Section 52 Agreements have been used to control such matters as vehicle routing to and from sites, and the continued use of processing plant on otherwise restored sites. Gravel companies have been keen to establish that agreements can only be entered into voluntarily, and that they do not become a policy requirement.

Land Restoration

Restoration and after-care issues have focused around a number of questions:

1. can land be restored to its original agricultural quality, and can this be made a legitimate demand on operators?
2. can a fully detailed restoration scheme be incorporated in conditions on a permission?
3. what safeguards can reasonably be used to *ensure* restoration will occur?
4. can a contractor's previous performance over restoration be taken into account as a material consideration in weighing factors relevant to a new permission?

The problems of restoration have been vividly demonstrated by the work of Lowe in the London Green Belt in Havering. The basis of effective restoration to agriculture or woodland is the careful reinstatement of site soils to achieve proper texture, structure and drainage. Unless adequate soils are available, are stripped and stored properly, and are returned quickly and carefully to the site, and the land properly drained, future agricultural productivity will be severely inhibited. In the Havering area soil quality on restoration has rarely exceeded a level of two agricultural grades below its original state. A depressing treeless environment suitable only for light grazing, often by horses, typifies the area.

Circular 75/76 suggested land of grades I and II should only be used for mineral extraction where there is no reasonable alternative and where the land is capable of being restored to its *original quality*.[66] Joint MAFF–SAGA experiments at Bush Farm, Havering and Papercourt Farm, Upminster (under way for 10 years) and other schemes, such as that by Henry Streeter Ltd. in Hillingdon, have sought to test this proposition.[67] However MAFF will not yet accept that land of grades I and II can be restored to its original quality based on the evidence of the experiments, this being implicitly accepted in more recent advice which suggests land should only be restored to its original *form as far as is practicable*.[68] As land continues to be taken from grades I and II this suggests an enhancement of minerals over agriculture in the 'pecking order' of production interests in the green belt.

Until the 1981 Act came into force conditions on restoration schemes could not be concluded with a specific after-use in mind. This, it was argued, would be an unreasonable use of conditions. The new Act allows restoration and after-care schemes to be negotiated prior to planning permission with a particular end use in view. The land must be returned to a standard where it is fit for the use specified in the after-care condition. Again a balance between operator's costs and local benefits has been struck. In the case of amenity and recreation it suggests sites should be brought to a condition suitable for sustaining trees, shrubs and other plants:

> . . . if the land is to become a golf course it would be unreasonable to expect the after-care condition to be interpreted to require five years of green, fairway and bunker maintenance. Or again if the land is to become a public football pitch, all that can reasonably be required in an after-care condition is that the grass should be sustainable.[69]

Operators would prefer to only produce outline schemes for restoration prior to permission as detailed aspects of working may change during the lifetime of a pit. The Act allows for details to be negotiated subsequent to a permission, but local authorities seeking to create certainty for local communities are unhappy leaving such matters unresolved. The period prior to planning permission is the one when local authorities are in their strongest bargaining position and they are reluctant, because of past experience, to underplay their hand.

A number of factors have contributed to past environmental degradation. These include insufficiently precise planning conditions to ensure the retention of topsoil on site, poor tipping procedures, lack of management provisions to ensure restored land was returned to a productive state, and inadequate site inspection and enforcement. Less than 40 per cent of mineral land surveyed in Buckinghamshire in 1975 had been adequately restored and 40 per cent had not been restored at all.[70] As a result two procedures have been advanced by local authorities; *agreements* and *performance bonds*.

In Buckinghamshire the draft Minerals Plan proposes to enter into planning agreements with mineral operators under seal to ensure land will be restored quickly to a proper standard. These would include positive covenants to carry out works and would be binding even if the land changed hands; (they would be made under Section 126 of the Housing Act 1974).[71] These have been resisted by the industry as they contain no right of appeal to the Minister, although they are regularly used by a number of counties. Agreements are attractive to local authorities for the same reasons, and because they also avoid the complications of the normal planning enforcement regulations.

Bonding takes the form of an operator setting aside an inflation-proofed sum of money so that if for any reason the company is unable to comply with restoration conditions, the county can enter the land and complete the necessary work, using the money, at no cost to the ratepayer. These are not seen as a substitute for close working relationships between authorities and operators but as a last resort mechanism should negotiation fail. Clearly bonds are an economic burden on the industry although experience suggests they may, in the long-term, be necessary to secure standards of restoration acceptable to local communities. The same *principle* had been used within designated 'Ironstone Districts' in the ironstone industry since the 1951 *Mineral Working Act*, and for private opencast coal operators seeking extraction licenses from the NCB. Some authorities accept membership of the SAGA industry-wide default scheme as a surrogate for specific performance bonds. However, Ministry rulings have sought to avoid bonds becoming a policy requirement in plans. In Staffordshire bonds had become commonplace and they were proposed as a specific policy in the first alterations to the Structure Plan. The Ministry is suggesting removal of this *requirement* in amendments to the Plan.[72] Bonds are still firmly resisted by the industry.[73]

A number of authorities have policies which take account of an operator's previous performance in restoration as a material factor in assessing new applications. The Greater London Council[74] use this factor as a bargaining counter with operators and, in addition, there is the possibility of concluding Section 52 or similar Agreements on other land in the operator's ownership as part of a new permission. The Inspector at the Berkshire Local Plan PLI suggested the County 'could possibly be acting *ultra vires*' in attempting to operate such a policy.[75] Certainly the idea contradicts the principle of considering each proposal on its planning merits, although if approved in a plan it would need to be regarded as a material consideration. It is likely, on present evidence, that such policies will be removed from plans to free restraints on the industry, but they will remain a factor in negotiations at local level.

Concluding Remarks

The 'protection' offered to farmers by green belt controls is two-edged in commercial terms. Whilst the idea of a clean-cut boundary to urban areas is of benefit to agricultural operations, the narrow definition of activities essential to agriculture restricts scope for the diversification of farm enterprises. The openness criterion suits local politicians who appear to retain an image of a traditional pattern of small fields and farm buildings of the sort where recent investment has been minimal. A number of the 'exceptions' previously negotiated by farming interests, for workers' dwellings and farm buildings, either appear open to abuse or represent anomalies when compared to restrictions on other activities. In attempting to maximize protection for farmland, and minimize controls over the diversification of enterprises, lobbies such as the NFU have to tread a careful line. For example whilst *in principle* supporting the idea that horsiculture should be 'controlled' to retain good quality land in agricultural production, they are aware that their members' incomes will be enhanced if controls are not introduced.

Central Government has sought, with success, to keep open a steady flow of land for minerals. In the case of aggregates this has been achieved by setting up a regional level of assessment as a way of instructing local authorities about the rate of extraction to be accommodated. The minerals interest is therefore fully incorporated in the forecasting process at regional level. The Ministry is concerned that land use constraints are not made so severe as to deny a 'platform for investment' by the industry. The forecasts are intimately related to volumes and patterns of industrial use, and house and road building. They are thus required to underwrite industrial production and the drive to keep up construction rates and the pace of development, leaving the local authorities to deal as best they can with local externalities. Conservationists argue that to continue in this resource-extravagant manner will lead to the rapid exhaustion of non-renewable reserves, and the continued widespread loss of land of high agricultural quality. Different construction methods involving less aggregates may, it is argued, be a more responsible attitude to our total environment.

In the face of the predicted local effects of extraction, local authorities have attempted to restrict impacts to a few areas and to protect local residents. In making decisions on the admissibility and use of the various methods of control the Ministry is setting the commercial framework for the industry. The level of local intervention allowed continues to be low and in the local plans studied, amendments have on the whole been in the direction of keeping open opportunities for extraction. Indeed the minerals local plans appear to be little more than a formalization of presumptions previously applied to individual cases. They have not proved useful for checking the *rate* of mineral extraction, but act as a reassurance to local residents that their interests will be taken into account in future decisions.

Although there is a relaxed attitude to demand by Government the 1981 Act seeks to improve controls over restoration and after-care. Any improvements will be enforceable through planning conditions, a half-way-house to moving to mandatory bonds or other forms of legal agreement. These measures, together with the possibility of renegotiation of permissions (a provision yet to be activated), will require some years in use before their success can be judged. Extra pressure can be expected on local authority and MAFF staff resources to oversee after-care schemes. A new 'bargain' has been struck with the industry with the passage of the 1981 Act. However issues of need and demand appear beyond influence by individual local authorities. Fragmented local parish and environmental groups are little match for the corporate power of the minerals industries and their allies in the transport, housing and construction fields.

8. Access for Leisure

Green belts, leisure and recreation use, have always been positively associated in the public mind. The promise of accessible countryside near at hand has often been the basis of support for green belt creation, retention and expansion. The early London County Council Scheme, and those in other parts of the country, were based on the need to provide a supply of public open spaces and recreation areas. The Abercrombie Plan for London constituted an ambitious hierarchy of recreation provision linking the centre of the City to the deeper countryside.[1] It has frequently been remarked that access on the scale offered by these early proponents has not been fulfilled.[2] Insufficient *positive action* has been taken to encourage access for all sections of the urban population. It is further argued that attempts to increase provision are stifled by an unimaginative inheritance of negatively applied land use controls within green belts. Green belts are an excuse for inaction, operated by defensive district councils, whose elected representatives are seeking to minimize change.[3] In this they are supported by farming and other landowning interests keen to insulate themselves from 'urban' influences.

Certainly, as Chapters 1–3 have described, there has been a process of vacillation and reinterpretation of green belt objectives over the past 60 years. Evidence of changing demands for recreation can, in part, explain this. Prior to 1973 local authorities were facing a scenario of explosive growth. At its forefront was the increase in informal day-trips to the countryside. Fuelled by a growth of nine million in private car ownership between 1950 and 1970 a wave of 'gambolling humanity' had sought to use the countryside for walking and other forms of relaxation. Predictions in the mid-1960s were for a 19 million increase in population by the year 2000, and 26 million cars on the road by 1980.[4]

Demands for less defensive attitudes to leisure uses in green belts were put forward in a series of Government reports. The House of Lords Select Committee on Sport and Leisure in 1973 stated:

> . . . recreational facilities are a proper use of an existing green belt and can help to preserve it against other demands . . . a positive approach in recreational terms,

> making the green belt into a lung for the town, rather than the negative approach which sometimes threatens to convert the green belt into a demilitarized zone, should secure that the urban fringe is properly exploited.[5]

The last Government White Paper, *Sport and Recreation* (1975), also stressed the importance of increased recreation provision in the countryside near towns, especially for those without cars.[6] The Joint Committee of civil servants set up in 1974, the *Countryside Review Committee*, saw green belts as a 'key recreational resource', although admitting this view did not extend to 'highly organized sports which need extensive ancillary buildings, generate heavy traffic, and in particular give rise to heavy spectator followings'. They concluded an improved ability to meet leisure demands should have special priority in green belts, as it does in National Parks. Provision for recreation should be a positive *objective* of green belt policy,[7] an assertion repeated by the Countryside Commission to the House of Commons Environment Committee in 1984.[8]

These two strands of argument – the apparent suitability of the locale for leisure, and the presence of green belt as a deterrent to development – have come together at local authority level as an *area of policy attention*. The Countryside Commission and the Regional Councils for Sport and Recreation have promoted a number of arguments in support of the need to create an improved ability to meet recreation demands in green belts. Although the emphasis may vary in different geographical areas, the major themes are:

1. the likelihood of a continued growth in *leisure demand*, a large part of which could fall in green belt areas;
2. the *close proximity* of green belts to areas of high demand gives them greatest potential for countryside provision available to the whole population, including those without cars, living in inner cities, and with limited financial and other circumstances;
3. that recreation provision in green belts is, in the present economic climate, the only feasible method of *making good shortfalls in public open-space* and provision for open air sport and recreation found in many urban areas;
4. that recreation developments can provide a *positive identity* for areas of green belt which are derelict or under-used due to planning enforcement problems or the retreat of profitable agricultural enterprises, at the same time re-creating damaged landscapes;
5. *the basic 'infrastructure' for improved access and provision already exists* in networks of bridleways and footpaths, albeit poorly maintained and waymarked. Other linear elements such as 'remainder' canals (canals not fully maintained by the British Waterways Board), and the routes of disused railway lines, often remain as under-used networks of access;
6. green belts, as potentially the most accessible area of the countryside, are *a desirable location for environmental education and interpretation pro-*

jects designed to increase the knowledge and understanding of urban residents about processes in the natural environment; and

7. a combination of the public provision of specific attractors such as country parks, and wider countryside management, *can reduce the undesirable level of conflict which exists* between farming, conservation, visitor, and other interests in green belts.[9]

Over the 1974–84 period the weight attached to each of these arguments has varied. The main response to a scenario of a 10 per cent annual growth of informal recreation travel was the designation between 1970 and 80 of 156 country parks and 188 picnic sites, largely developed by local authorities and grant-aided by the Countryside Commission. These mono-use areas were particularly encouraged in accessible locations where large numbers of car-borne visitors could be accommodated, thus reducing conflicts in farmland and the deeper countryside. Higher levels of Countryside Commission grant were available from 1974 for green belt areas and 72 of the 130 country parks in England provided by the public sector are in green belts. Although these constitute 11,115 hectares many of the early parks were already in use for informal recreation and the existence of Countryside Commission grant aid acted mainly as a mechanism for improving management standards. Country parks represented a compromise between urban and countryside interests. Predictions of unending growth brought forth images of widespread physical erosion of natural surroundings, and large areas where farming would be made untenable. Rural residents would have to pay large sums for the creation and maintenance of recreation environments for urban visitors. Shoard suggests that early policies of *concentration* acted to deflect or decoy visitors from the so-called sensitive areas, persuading the leisure-seeker to remain in relatively undistinguished green belt environments near towns and cities.[10] There has been a trend since the mid 1970s towards the recognition of parks on land which was previously derelict and degraded, especially in the North West and Yorkshire, and to promoting other forms of access.

Evidence from the 1980 National Survey of the Countryside Commission suggests that informal recreation participation has reached a plateau under the influence of deteriorating economic circumstances. The volume of day trips to the countryside (101 million on an average summer month in 1977) was down to 81 million in 1980. Visits to ancient monuments have declined to the levels of 1972 and participation has begun to recede most severely among the semi-skilled and unskilled manual groups.[11] Around London the emphasis is shifting from new provision to improvement of the existing levels of management, and the capacity of sites. Elsewhere the minimal levels of provision inherited at local government reorganization have given urgency to major programmes to provide new opportunities in conjunction with large-scale environmental improvement and landscape reconstruction projects.

Although research and local authority action has centred on provision for informal recreation, not often contentious in terms of obtaining planning permission, this is only part of the picture. Green belts also attract pressures from formal or more organized activities such as team sports, golf, sailing and other water sports, commercial horse riding, and motor sports. They also generate commercial sector interest in providing zoos, theme parks, and country clubs, and tourist demands for hotels and caravan sites. In contrast to informal provision, growth in these sectors of leisure is continuing. Membership of the British Horse Society for example virtually trebled between 1970–80, and Pony Club membership rose from 30,000 to 50,000. The Chairmen's Policy Group paper *Leisure Policy for the Future* suggests outdoor sports 'which use open country, inland and coastal waters, footpaths and bridleways and other extensive and specialist resources' are at the forefront of this growth.[12] A number of these activities require corporate finance and rely on large accessible markets for their success, their proponents arguing the importance of green belt locations for commercial success.

Strategic Policies

Demands for access to green belt countryside form only part of a wider canvas of open land management and planning. The *Countryside Review Committee* have handed down the view that success lies in *consensus* – the bringing together of a wide plurality of interests.[13] Although the land use planning system is a weak vehicle for this, most of the relevant powers lying outside a strict definition of the planning acts, it remains the most important arena for identifying and weighing the demands of each interest at the strategic level. What then, have local authorities sought to achieve?

Open land policies at county level have, through zoning in green belts, attempted to:

1. reduce conflict with primary production interests;
2. allow a broader mix of recreation developments in the most accessible areas of green belt;
3. define and give emphasis to access by defining green wedges; and
4. identify areas for priority attention for landscape renewal, with extensive recreation after-use.

Comprehensive open land policies in green belts stress inter-relationships between uses and make judgements on likely compatibility and incompatibility. The major tasks of conserving high quality resources of agricultural land and landscape, renewing degraded environments, and providing for more access, have generated the use of *priority zonation* policies. These express the attitudes of an authority to the intensity and mix of recreation and leisure uses in farmland, and define areas where recreation is to be given priority in public expenditure. The basic thought process applied to arrive at

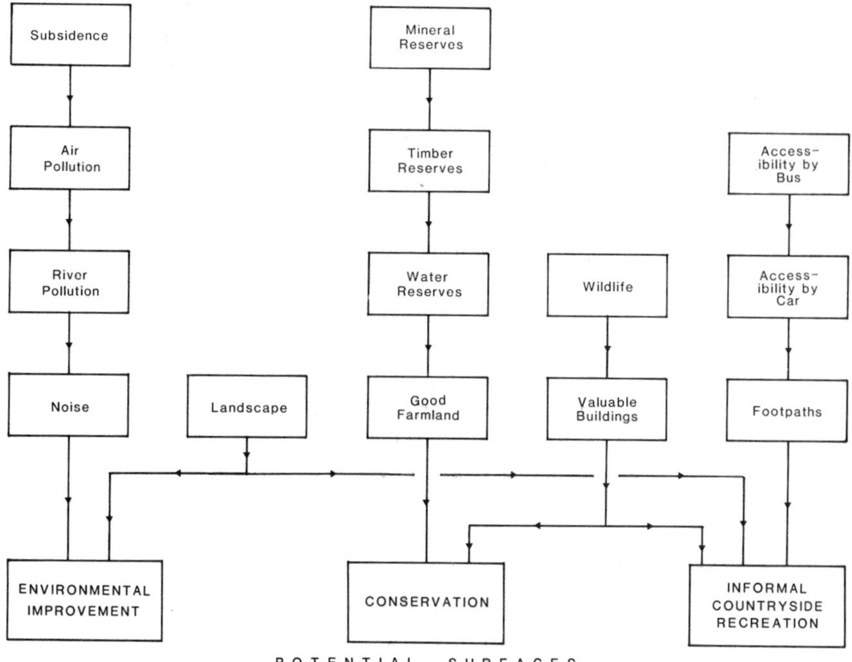

Figure 8.1 Open Land Priority Assessment in South Yorkshire
Source: Adapted from South Yorkshire County Council *County Environment Study* (SYCC: Barnsley, 1978), p. 19

priorities is shown in Figure 8.1 for South Yorkshire, where the definition of areas emerged from a Potential Surface Analysis of 14 interests in open land. The importance of each interest as an objective for public policy was weighed by councillors, planners, and the general public.[14] These decisions were used to establish priorities between projects in the environmental improvement and recreation budgets of the Metropolitan Council, the details of implementation being put forward in a non-statutory County Environment Study.[15]

Other counties have similar policies. In Hertfordshire open land is divided into *Agricultural Priority Areas* (APA) and *Amenity Corridors* (Figure 8.2). In APAs only countryside recreation 'of a quiet nature and low intensity' will be encouraged, recreation pressures being confined to a network of scenic drives, footpaths, and bridleways. In Amenity Corridors, (the transport corridors between the major towns), priority is to be given to leisure development and landscape improvement.[16] Leisure guidelines agreed with the Districts suggest 'medium intensity' activities should be located in urban fringes and low intensity activities between towns in the Corridors. The boundaries of Amenity Corridors have now been defined in ten local (District) plans for Hertfordshire. At the Public Local Inquiries, Inspectors

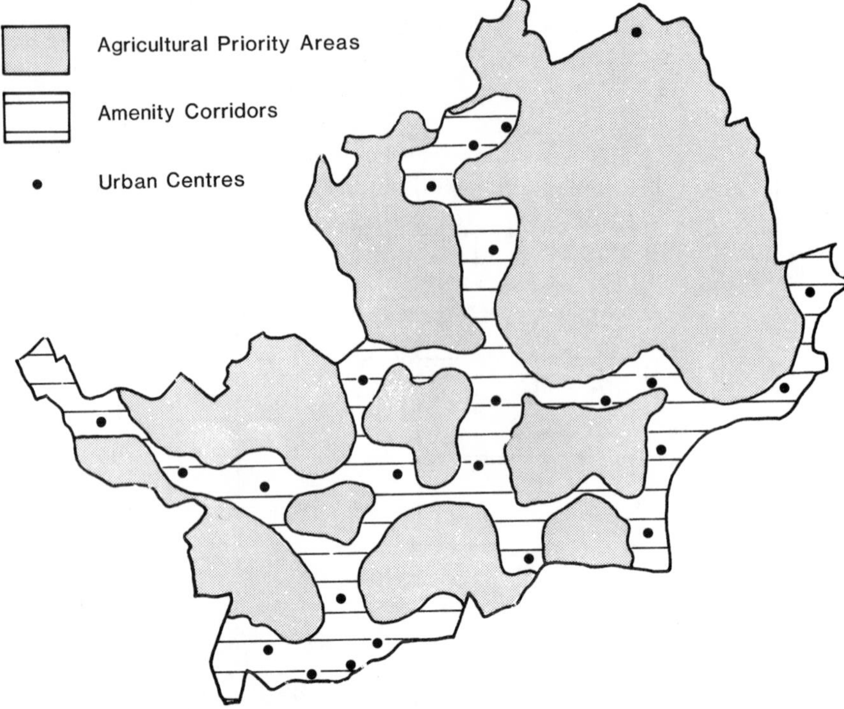

Figure 8.2 Green Belt Priority Zones in Hertfordshire
Source: Adapted from Hertfordshire County Council, *Structure Plan Written Statement* (HCC: Hertford, 1979) key diagram

dealt with a flow of objections from landowners seeking to be placed within Amenity Corridors, (thus potentially increasing the value of their land for alternative uses), and from local residents seeking to distance their properties from Amenity Corridors and the likelihood of future leisure development.

However progress in the delineation of priority areas has not always been straightforward, and there is growing evidence to suggest the Ministry are wary of creating 'categories' of green belt in this manner. In the West Yorkshire Green Belt the 'core area', (surrounded by the Leeds, Bradford, Halifax, Huddersfield and Wakefield urban areas), where open land has been severely fragmented by industry and mineral workings, forms a contrast with the outer girdle of Green Belt. The Draft Structure Plan argued that accessibility and opportunity in the core area dictated local variations in Green Belt policy to encourage major recreation investments. This idea was not accepted by the Ministry on the basis that such a measure would be too significant a departure from normal green belt controls.[17]

Although never spelt out in Circulars it is open to local authorities to justify more restrictive policies than those normally obtaining under the

Circular 42/55 prescription. However again these types of variation have been whittled away through the policy-making process. In the West Midlands in approving the six Conurbation Structure Plans the Ministry accepted the idea of *green wedges*, forming part of the Green Belt, and penetrating the conurbation area '. . . in recognition of the need for progressive policies in the Green Belt'.[18] The policies envisaged the highest proportions of land devoted to informal recreation use being achieved in green wedges, the extra need to retain their fragile open character being reflected in a stronger than normal presumption against the development of new institutional uses. Green wedges would act as visual relief for urban areas and, with their associated footpath links, would provide corridors for wildlife and access. In the draft Green Belt Subject Plan it was proposed that *Amenity Zones* be designated within the Green Belt as the areas most suitable for the provision of recreation facilities, taking into account accessibility and topography, and avoiding high quality agricultural land. Other Districts objected that such a policy might hinder recreation development in their sectors of the Green Belt. However, several petitions (with a total of around 8,000 signatures), and 150 individual letters of objection, were received from the public incensed at what they saw as the loss of Green Belt to recreation. The Amenity Zone proposals have now been withdrawn. The revised Local Plan does not distinguish between green wedges and the generality of the Green Belt.[19]

Recreation interests, such as the Regional Councils for Sport and Recreation, have generally welcomed the idea of priority areas believing they reflect positive intentions towards new provision. The Metropolitan Counties, reflecting the 'urban' view of green belts, have been most active in making such proposals. Around London SCLSERP have advised a higher profile for recreation, stating '. . . in certain areas and in certain circumstances recreation should have priority over other interests and activities', recommending that the *promotion* of recreation should be recognized as a *positive policy objective* by local authorities.[20] But Berkshire's Green Belt Local Plan makes it clear that any recreation permitted must not be of a form or type which would undermine the strategic and environmental aims of the Green Belt.[21] Recreation is basically *development*, bringing with it externalities of noise and traffic. Local attitudes are hostile. The Thorpe Water Park, a privately financed theme park attracting over half a million visitors a year, located in a prominent position in the London Green Belt in North-West Surrey, has attracted criticism for its 'devastating' effect on local residents.[22] A planning decision to extend Shipley Country Park in the Nottinghamshire–Derbyshire Green Belt has been taken to the High Court by objectors, and there are objections to the proposed extension of water areas around the Holme Pierrepoint National Water Sports Centre near Nottingham. The attitudes of the agricultural lobby are also resistant to recreation. The Sheffield Branch of the NFU has suggested that any development for recreation on agricultural land in the Green Belt around the City should be opposed.[23] The rulings at PLIs suggest the need to *balance* interests but there is reluctance in this and any other forum to suggest what the appropriate balance might be. With the Sports Councils and the Ramblers Association lobbying for more access, it is not surprising that a combative atmosphere prevails.

The policy-making process has thus tested the limits of discretion available to local authorities in defining priorities for recreation in green belts. Following a period in the mid-1970s when the scope of apparently permissible local variations was established, central Government has removed variety (not always consistently) through its interventions since 1980. Policy has reverted to the traditional interplay of presumptions regarding agricultural land quality, open rural character, and consultation over proposals affecting Sites of Special Scientific Interest. This action may be the result of a fear that local authorities would be more restrictive than Circular 42/55 criteria imply outside priority areas in green belts. If this was not the case the policy would have no meaning except as a signal to applicants seeking sites for commercial recreation ventures that their chances of obtaining permission might be higher in priority areas.

Although recreation demands and supply should clearly be looked at strategically given patterns of travel and the location of resources, this has not generally occurred in plans. In Greater Manchester the County intended to compile a green belt subject plan which also addressed issues of the priority to be accorded to recreation interests in green belt land. Following opposition from the Districts, in the form of an objection to the Development Plan Scheme, the recreation and other open land elements were removed from the intended plan on the basis that they infringed too closely on District discretion and responsibilities. This leaves open land policies in Greater Manchester to be operated by the ten Districts, presumably in different ways. In the case of Tyne and Wear a Green Belt Local Plan which also details open land policies *is* being produced following a contrary ruling on an objection by Districts to the Development Plan Scheme. The Tyne and Wear proposals are site-specific, listing locations for derelict land clearance, tree planting, recreation and access provision.[24] They partly derive from work carried out on a non-statutory *Leisure Plan*,[25] produced in co-operation with the Districts in 1977, and the continuing derelict land programme.

Local Approaches

Access to green belt resources is conditioned by historic factors. The basic pattern is largely of pre-war local authority land acquisitions for recreation, land owned by the National Trust, and historic houses open to the public. Important links include the historic footpath and bridleway network, 'green lanes', and disused railway lines or colliery waggonways. Superimposed on this basic infrastructure is a pattern of *de facto* and *de jure* rights of access along canal towpaths, and on common land. *Negotiated rights* are found on land subject to access, management, woodland dedication, and nature reserve agreements, some subject to time limits and involving payments by local authorities to owners. Many sports negotiate individual arrangements with land owners for the use of gravel pits for sailing or sailboarding, with the Forestry Commission for motor car stage rallies, the Ministry of Defence for trials riding, or individual farmers for motocross events.[26]

The attitudes and values of landowners and managers are thus an important restraint on access, and any green belt will contain a complex and often undocumented range of formal and informal arrangements.[27] Provision for recreation and sport is a *permissive* power at county and district level. No standard quantities of land or types of provision are required to be provided. In addition the complexities of predicting demand and matching it to available supply as a technically-derived basis of action have largely defeated recreation researchers.[28] Much of the demand for open-air recreation and sport emanating from cities falls in the territories of adjoining local authorities. These are reluctant to enter into commitments to acquire, manage and warden large areas at public expense for use by the ratepayers of other local authorities.

Although the *powers* exist to make provision, including by compulsory purchase, shire county authorities have not been able, even if willing, to secure the resources to maintain and promote access. Provision for recreation is a Cinderella of local authority spending, competing with other worthy areas of possible local authority intervention. Since reorganization, county authorities have tended to concentrate on providing and managing sites for *informal* countryside recreation, including some regional-scale sports facilities, leaving districts to provide for *formal* sports and urban parks.[29] At county level the commonest situation is one of a small recreation or countryside section within the planning department responsible for the whole field of countryside planning. In many cases responsibility for the management of different parts of the pattern of access falls to other departments, county land holdings often being under the control of the county Land Agent, and footpaths the responsibility of the Highway Authority. This fragmentation of duties, together with lack of priority in local authority budgets due to local political factors, has led to the emergence of a bewildering variety of *ad hoc* initiatives to improve access to green belts.

The *principles* of a policy for improved access are beguiling in their simplicity. Using a mixture of development control, negotiation, management, marketing, and promotion, they involve fitting recreation uses into the landscape such that primary land interests, and the interests of local residents, are not prejudiced. The main tasks that *local authorities* have been involved in are the following:

1. *negotiating* recreation after uses within the process of land renewal and recreation 'gains' from urban development projects;
2. *controlling* recreation development to that 'appropriate' to green belt areas;
3. *improving* the management of existing sites;
4. *enhancing* the quality of the recreation experience;
5. *maintaining*, improving, or creating access between town and country; and
6. *promoting* accessibility by public transport.

The Opportunistic Approach

Greater access for recreation has not, in practice, been secured by technical assessments of demand in plans leading to logically-placed provisions on the ground. The weakness of powers and a lack of resources have led to provision becoming an opportunistic process, seizing on situations where major land use change is occurring to insert a recreation interest through negotiation.

The main opportunities arise through decisions made on the after-use of derelict land and areas where minerals have been extracted (Table 8.1). Other significant opportunities occur where Motorway construction and road building is taking place and, in rare cases, where major development is permitted in green belt land. In seeking to avoid conflict with agricultural land, and being unable to fund new land purchases, green belt authorities outside the South East have turned to recreation as an output from derelict land and other reclamation programmes. Until 1982 derelict land could only be reclaimed following its transfer to local authorities. This was thus a ready

Table 8.1 Land Use Changes in the West Midlands Green Belt 1975–83

Development	*Hectares*	*Per cent of total*
Mineral extraction	1,438	51.9
Waste disposal	61	2.2
Combined mineral extraction and waste disposal	371	13.4
New highways	620	22.4
Other transport uses	87	3.1
Industry	180	6.5
Housing	13	0.5
Total	2,770	100.0

Source: Clarke, S. R. *Green Belts and the Inner City Problem*, MSc in Public Sector Management, (Birmingham, University of Aston Management Centre, 1983), p. 64.

'supply' of land for conversion to recreation use. Grants at 100 per cent of the costs incurred in reclamation have been available since 1972 in development areas where land was to be reclaimed to amenity use, its after-use value being assessed as zero.[30] The second source of land is from the NCB Opencast Executive's programmes of restoration. If after-use decisions can be made at an early stage, negotiations to restore land to recreation use can be successful. Examples such as the Rother Valley Regional Park near Sheffield, the Pennington Flash Country Park in Wigan, and the Pugneys Water Area in West Yorkshire, confirm this view.

Land renewal plans have been prepared for the South Cannock area of the West Midlands Green Belt, and an area west of Newcastle Under Lyme in the North Staffordshire Green Belt.[31] The recreation proposals for the Newcastle scheme (Figure 8.3) involve the creation of four major sites as the basis of a network of recreation spaces. 'Country paths' will link the major recreation areas to each other and to local recreation areas and settlements. Separate routes for cyclists and horse riders are also envisaged.

There are perhaps two major problems. The first is the unpredictability of reclamation programmes. The Opencast Executive, as with other mineral operators, are loth to hand over sites after working is complete, and there are sometimes severe problems in relocating coal dispersal points as working proceeds. In the case of the derelict land programme again, securing ownership is an unpredictable process and the Ministry system of only guaranteeing grants twelve months ahead can lead to uneven progress. Most significantly the introduction of priorities within the programme in 1982, preference being given to 'Category A' schemes (those with a 'productive' after-use such as housing or industry), has led to the demotion of schemes in Category B with recreation after-uses in green belts and has slowed progress. As the North Staffordshire Plan wryly states, 'opportunism is as important a feature of any reclamation programme as long-term planning'.[32]

The process of land renewal is complex involving continuous negotiation with non-local agencies such as Water Authorities, the Countryside Commission and the Sports Council, and with user groups. A good example of a successful scheme is the Rother Valley Regional Park, near Sheffield, previously an opencast coal site but now reclaimed to recreation with a parallel scheme by the Water Authority to improve the River Rother.[33] Negotiations led to an agreed scheme with the NCB to reclaim the site by creating contours in a form suitable for future after-uses. Once basic reclamation had been completed, tree planting, the creation of footpaths, and the design of particular areas was financed by the six local authorities involved with 50 per cent grants from the Countryside Commission. These types of projects thus run through a phase of engineering design (to create the basic land form), landscape design (to create a valid living environment), and recreation provision and management, in all lasting a decade or more.

Where the level of officially derelict land in the green belt is low, and

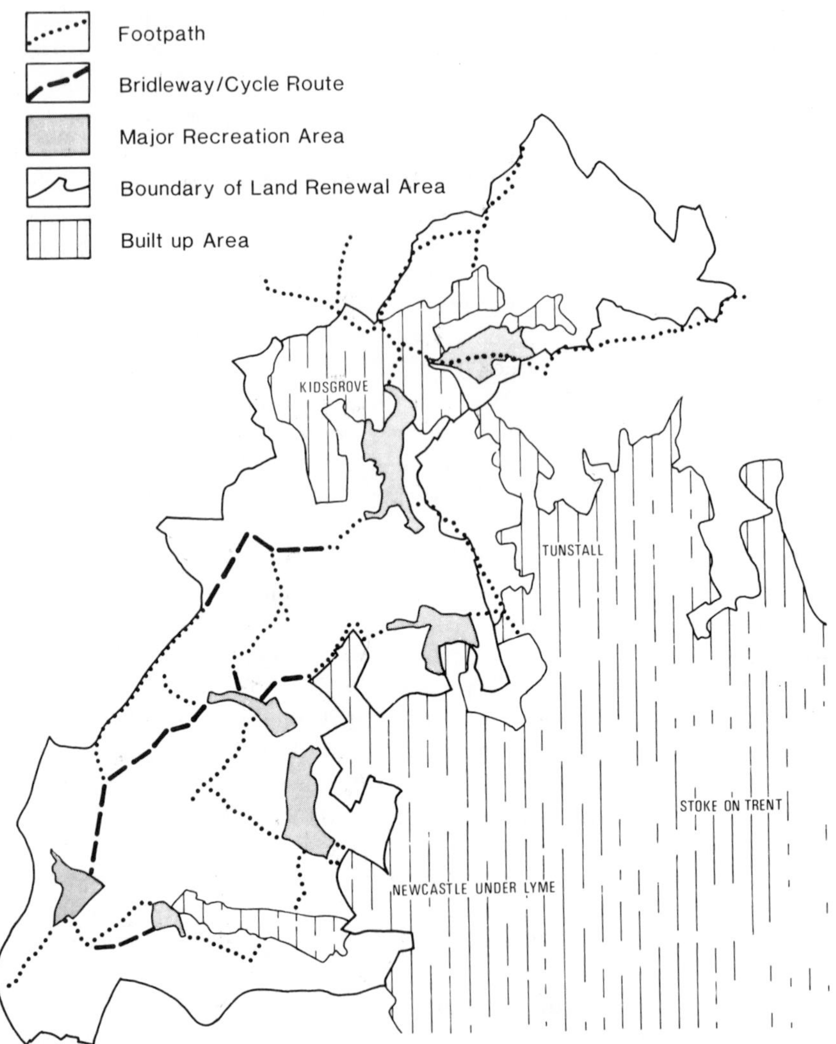

Figure 8.3 Recreation and Land Renewal: North Staffordshire Green Belt
Source: Adapted from Staffordshire County Council *North Staffordshire Land Renewal Plan* (SCC: Stafford, 1982), map 5

where derelict land grant is only payable at 50 per cent (as around London), the momentum of environmental improvement is slow. In the inner areas of the London Green Belt the Greater London Development Plan has identified 'Areas of Opportunity'.[34] Proposals in each area derive from its physical attributes (whether woodland, parkland, meadowland, or gravel pits), its position in relation to nearby facilities, and its location in respect of urban development. Opportunities to provide recreation and a wider landscaped 'matrix' are taken when major land use change is imminent. In the Roding Valley, on the northern edge of London, the building of the M11 Motorway allowed negotiation with the Department of Transport leading to improvement of the landscape by tree planting, and land shaping to provide an improved system of footpaths and bridleways. In the Beddington/ Mitcham and Dagenham Corridor areas, the freeing of land owned by the Water Authority (in each case an old sewage works) has allowed a mixed development–conservation package to be negotiated. In the Beddington/ Mitcham case, on the southern boundary of London, 5¾ million tonnes of sand and gravel will be extracted to create a major water-based recreation complex in the Wandle Valley. The lease for gravel extraction in 166 hectares of land will be negotiated with a consortium of gravel companies who will pay a royalty per tonne extracted. The land will be restored, following detailed planning permission, to a predetermined pattern to facilitate formal and informal use and access.[35] In the Dagenham Corridor (South of Romford) the Brettons Amenity Centre is being created with finance from the Sports Council, the Countryside Commission, two London Boroughs, the Greater London Council, and the Regional Water Authority. An inter-authority working party is managing the progress of the project.

Some open land and recreation schemes are pursued by negotiation with potential developers. Stockley Park, Hillingdon, on the western edge of the Greater London area and forming an island of approved Metropolitan Green Belt, is an area of 120 hectares of poorly reclaimed mineral land extracted under a pre-1947 permission. Here a Section 52 Agreement has been concluded which allows 30 hectares to be developed for a 'science and commercial park' together with the reclamation, at a cost of over £2 million, of the remaining 90 hectares for a golf course, district park, and canalside amenity area. This type of negotiative style typifies areas where mineral extraction is proposed. It should now be aided by the provisions of the *Town and Country Planning (Minerals) Act 1981* which allows conditions relating to after-care for a five year period to be negotiated with a particular after-use in mind (see Chapter 7). Provisions for the renegotiation of existing conditions may also assist. In the areas of greatest concentration of wet gravel workings around London however, local communities are resistant to increased recreation use. As the supply of appropriate filling material is low there is also a ready excuse for gravel companies to hold onto land with the hope of obtaining permission for more profitable uses. Eleven of the 39 areas of water in the Colne Valley west of London where water recreation takes place have unimplemented filling conditions from the original planning permission.[36]

Development Control

The interventions of the Ministry at policy level in plans reflect an intention to rely on taking applications for leisure development on their merits, having regard to the provisions of Circular 42/55. It is therefore important to form a view on what *is* considered appropriate if an assessment of the promise offered by present green belt designations is to be made. Circular 42/55 includes the term 'sport', in the list of uses acceptable in green belts. This was the result of debate between the Ministry and the Town and Country Planning Association's Green Belt Committee in 1956, the latter suggesting that 'sports fields' should not be incorporated in green belts, but the Minister demurring.[37] The 1962 MHLG Booklet stated:

> . . . the green belt conception implies no further building except where there is a positive argument for allowing it.
> . . . buildings for sport and recreation may be allowed . . . In such cases the decision is likely to turn on the need for the proposal as against any damage it will do to the rural appearance of the land.[38]

In 1977 the Countryside Review Committee further reinterpreted this issue:

> . . . Recreation in a general sense has always been associated with green belts. But not highly organized sports which need ancillary buildings, generate heavy traffic, and in particular give rise to large spectator followings.[39]

These themes have been reflected in a range of minor wording changes to the presumption in Circular 42/55 in approved development plans. Kent refer to 'open air' recreation, Warwickshire 'outdoor recreation' and Hertfordshire 'small-scale informal recreation' as appropriate uses.

The South East Standing Conference has provided further guidance in the form of an *acceptability matrix* of leisure uses by types of rural resource found in green belts (Figure 8.4). They consider that except on managed farmland, floodplains, water meadows, and marshlands, low intensity activities are acceptable in almost all land use or resource situations. Apart from locations on existing sports fields, disused airfields, and golf courses, high intensity uses are either unacceptable or only acceptable with careful siting, design, landscaping, and management. If high intensity uses are grouped together (as, for example, with motor sports on a disused airfield) the acceptability of the complex will then be judged in terms of the activity with the widest effects.[40] A major concern is the likely extent of ancillary buildings such as pavilions, refreshment rooms and storage areas, and their effect on the openness of the green belt. Attempts to further improve guidance by developing intensity measures for types of recreation activity have proved impractical due to the wide variations between proposals for the same use.

RECREATIONAL ACTIVITIES		RESOURCES AND LAND USE						
ACTIVITY GROUP	INTENSITY	MANAGED FARMLAND	WOODLAND	HEATH, CHALK DOWNLAND	WATER AREAS, RIVERS, LAKES, RESERVOIRS	DAMAGED LAND, DRY PITS, REFUSE TIPS	SPORTS FIELDS, AIRFIELDS, GOLF COURSES	ABANDONED PUBLIC UTILITY AND DEFENCE LAND
COUNTRYSIDE RECREATION	HIGH		○	○	○	○	○	○
	LOW	○	●	●	●	●	●	●
WATER SPORTS AND RECREATION	HIGH	/	/	/	○	/	/	/
	LOW	/	/	/	●	/	/	/
PLAYINGFIELD SPORTS	HIGH		/		/	○	●	○
	LOW		/	○	/	●	●	○
MOTOR AND AIR SPORTS	HIGH				/	○	●	○
	LOW		○	○	/	○	●	●

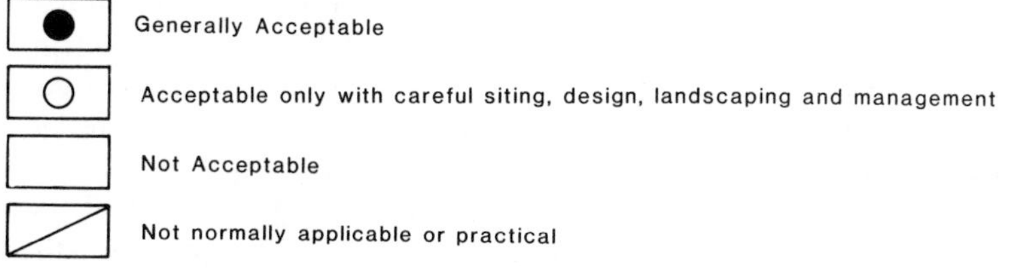

Figure 8.4 An Acceptability Matrix of Recreation Uses for the London Green Belt
Source: Adapted from SCLSERP *Policy Towards Provision for Recreation in London's Green Belt*, SC 1111R (SCLSERP: London, 1979), p. 6

It has not therefore proved possible to draw up policies which ensure that a given recreational use will always be acceptable in a green belt, or always unacceptable. Therefore planning authorities exercise wide discretion to evaluate each proposal against a number of material considerations. In Berkshire the Local Plan gives a comprehensive list of such criteria. To be considered suitable, a recreation proposal should be acceptable to its *specific green belt location* in terms of its nature, scale, and intensity. Uses likely to accord with these criteria would normally be:

1. passive countryside recreation;
2. recreation requiring specialized 'natural' resources, for example water sports on worked-out gravel pits;
3. activities requiring extensive areas of land (for example golf courses); and
4. open recreation uses serving local community needs (for example village playing fields).

In order to maintain the open rural character of the Green Belt the building content of proposals should be kept to a minimum. Negotiations will invariably take place with applicants to secure the most satisfactory siting and design of any necessary buildings. Recreation uses which alter the landscape, by removing trees or creating extensive hard surfaced areas are unlikely to be acceptable. A use of land for recreation which creates general disturbance by noise, or by placing heavy pressure on minor roads, is also likely to be resisted. Recreation taking agricultural land of grades I, II and IIIa will be resisted, as will proposals which because of their scale, nature, and intensity at the inner edge of the Green Belt, give the appearance of extending urban areas.[41]

The development control data available suggest that the above criteria are upheld. Gregory's study in the Seisdon area of the West Midlands Green Belt indicated that in the period 1957–66 some 95 hectares of land in planning applications were approved for recreation and sports use and 38 hectares were refused. Categories of use approved included sports pitches and riding stables on local and regional need grounds. A large recreation centre involving construction of a swimming pool, miniature golf course, bowling greens, and a car park was refused but the decision was not tested on appeal. Applications for golf driving ranges, and holiday and touring caravan sites, were also refused.[42]

An analysis of decisions made on applications for leisure use in the Hertfordshire area of the London Green Belt was carried out by the Author for the period April 1974 to April 1979.[43] (See Tables 8.2–8.4.) Of the 350 applications analyzed, 185 were for minor changes within existing curtilages already in leisure use, (including public houses and hotels), and 65 had new land take implications of less than 0.4 hectare. The total area of *land* in the applications covered by the study was 1,034 hectares, and 79 per cent of applications were approved. However the success rate of the *largest* applications by land area was low, resulting in only 31 per cent of the land area applied for being approved. Two-thirds by area of proposals involving the transfer of agricultural land were refused.

The applications which received most favourable consideration were playing fields and pitches. These were mainly local village facilities with, in addition, one or two approvals for college sports grounds and school playing

Table 8.2 Leisure Use Decisions in the Hertfordshire Green Belt 1974–79

Category	*Applications*	*Number Approved*	*Hectares in Approvals*	*Hectares in Refusals*
London Green Belt	180	146	199	327
Rural area*	170	136	117	391
Total	350	282	316	718

* Area where Green Belt policies applied

Table 8.3 Previous Use of Land on which Leisure Use Applications Made in the Hertfordshire Green Belt: 1974–79

Previous use	*Hectares in applications*	*Hectares in approvals*	*Hectares in refusals*
Agriculture	420	108	276
Leisure	261		
Transport	271		
Waste land, minerals		208	442
refuse disposal	69		
Others	13		
Total	1034	316	718

Table 8.4 Area of Land in Approvals by Leisure Use: Hertfordshire 1974–79

Leisure activity	*Hectares in approvals*	*Hectares in refusals*	*Total*
Golf	0	241	241
Motor Sports	50	135	185
Playing fields, local pitches	103	39	142
Riding	44	51	95
Water Sports	24	19	43
Indoor Sports	6	2	8
Camping, caravanning	0	8	8
Others	89	223	312
Total	316	718	1034

fields. Local pitches and playing fields are allowed for by policy, subject to siting and amenity criteria, as the legitimate special needs of individual rural settlements. They often involve facilities re-sited as a result of displacement by development from the centres of villages. The golf courses refused reflect the fact that South Hertfordshire was well provided with nine-hole golf courses at the time; and one major proposal was on land already open to general use which the local authority were unwilling to see lost to the public. The high motor sports figure reflects a permission for motor racing on a former airfield well away from the London fringe. Within the 'riding' category one permission was for the conversion of stables in the grounds of a large house set in 21 hectares of land; and one water sports approval on former mineral workings constituted 20 hectares. The 'others' category includes some large mixed leisure–retail–urban development proposals which were clearly speculative, and were refused. A number of extensions to country clubs and hotels in large grounds, and a number of changes of use, account for the majority of approvals here. Applications for two cinemas on waste ground in the London Green Belt were refused. As the areas of land involved in applications (the planning unit) are those put on the planning application forms by the applicant the resulting data greatly overestimate the impact of approvals on agricultural land.

If the results of the study are taken at face value the apparent transfer of agricultural land to leisure use was no more than 20 hectares per year. In practice the inclusion of large grounds, and the likelihood of unimplemented permissions, reduce the real rate of transfer to less than 10 hectares a year, a level supported by more recent monitoring evidence. These findings support the view that local needs are being provided for, that pressures for tourist use (caravanning and camping) are low, and that uses with a high ratio of buildings to site area or with high externality effects are normally resisted.

At appeals Inspectors ascertain whether there is any particular justification for a recreation use which might override green belt policy. In a study of twenty appeals in seven Districts in the London Green Belt, nine were allowed. Those involving large buildings, including a proposal for two squash courts in Broxbourne District, and indoor riding centres in Castle Point District and the London Borough of Bromley, were additions to existing approved developments. Schemes which involved the re-use of gravel pits received more favourable treatment, as did uses which can be argued as of local community benefit, as in the Hertfordshire study.[44]

Improved Site Management

Many of the green belt sites in local authority ownership have historically seen low inputs of land management resources. Some have been maintained by land agents using an 'urban' regime of management, or have been kept on a care and maintenance basis. The aim of Countryside Commission grants for country parks has been to upgrade management levels by the provision of improved car parking, toilet, visitor centre, and picnic facilities.[45] These, together with wardening, and the use of part-time volunteer wardens, have considerably improved management standards, at the same time improving the capacity of sites. This type of action has also occurred in common land in use by the public where conflicts between users require to be resolved. The separation of horse riders from pedestrians, the setting aside of valued areas as nature reserves, and the channelling of informal use may be achieved by measures agreed in a forum such as a Joint Management Committee set up to represent the main land and user groups concerned.[46]

Financial restraints, and a concern to improve management standards, have led to ideas of the *marketing* of informal recreation. A pilot study of Rufford Park, Nottinghamshire demonstrates the principles involved.[47] The aim was to ensure that the maintenance costs of what was a major capital investment programme would be substantially met by surplus income from trading activities. The scheme developed comprised craft workshops, demonstration areas, an art gallery, and shop and cafeteria, together with 'events' areas and additional facilities for children. Surveys of demand (by market segment) and of competing attractions led to the creation of specific management aims and the identification of market gaps in the area. (None but the most general of aims had existed before.) Studies of the market for different craft products, and of the attractiveness of particular 'live' craft displays, were made. The package assembled included a promotional strategy for mid-week and off-peak visitors, coach parties, organized groups, and foreign and UK tourists, involving such possibilities as publicity on cross-channel ferries. The preferred pricing option would reduce the cost to the public purse per admission from 66p per visitor before the scheme to 8p after. These principles have been promoted by the Countryside Commission to improve standards of 'service delivery' and to cut costs. For large new facilities the need to create revenue earning components has become a necessity. The balance sheet for the proposed Chasewater site in the South Cannock Regional Park in the West Midlands Green Belt,[48] suggests that profits from the sale of land with permission for hotel developments will be required to finance environmental improvement works, over and above those funded by derelict land grant, and by the NCB through opencast site restoration. The need to increase the viability of schemes is thus likely to conflict more frequently with a strict interpretation of green belt policy.

Enhancing the Recreation Experience

Another activity which has the potential to mediate conflicts is *countryside interpretation*. Aldridge describes interpretation as the art of explaining:

a) the past in relation to social conditions;
b) the character of a natural area through the inter-relationships of rocks, soils, plants and animals, including man; and
c) man and environment in more general terms.[49]

An interpreter is someone who devises a theme or themes, perhaps from the social history, landscape or economy of a countryside area, and uses it as a peg for an explanation of processes occurring in the natural environment. It is aimed at explaining the *significance* of a site or area by indicating what is worthy of conservation, or what is valuable about a particular configuration of human activity and landscape. Interpretation thus imparts conservation messages designed to educate an urban-based population about processes underway in the countryside and to develop understanding and sympathy between those living, working and seeking leisure in the two environments.

Various media may be used to 'interpret' the countryside including self-guided trails, listening posts, three-dimensional reconstructions, working demonstrations, or filmed material. Interpretation can be site or area-based as has been demonstrated by the Countryside Commission. For example, at Croxteth Country Park in the Merseyside Green Belt, a stately home with a range of static exhibits is complemented by a working farm managed by the County Council.[50] The Marsh Farm Country Park in Essex has a similar theme with the agricultural activities acting to recoup deficits involved in public provision.[51]

One of the most innovative examples of an area-based approach in a green belt situation is in Greater Manchester, co-ordinated by the North West Civic Trust.[52] This is suited to areas where environmental improvement has made significant progress, and where attention switches to increasing awareness of the resource created. The three-year Experimental Interpretation Project in the Tame Valley aimed:

1. to stimulate local interest by developing a sense of participation and involvement;
2. to establish channels of communication between local authorities, user groups, users, and interests concerned with the future of the Valley; and
3. to create a sense of identity for the Valley.

Information and interpretive material was addressed to non-participants who could potentially use the Valley for leisure, as well as to those who used it for specific sports and might be expected to widen their range of activities.

A large number of experimental initiatives were undertaken. These included:

1. *an audio visual presentation* of the Valley, a mobile information caravan and numerous leaflets on guided walks and trails;
2. specific *packs* for schoolchildren's nature and environmental studies, covering themes such as water pollution, nature conservation, geology and wildlife;
3. *an outdoor pursuits scheme* involving camping, canoeing, fishing and visits to working mills;
4. *farm interpretation* including farm open days; and
5. practical *conservation projects* for schools whereby children planted trees, performed other simple management tasks, or 'adopted' parts of the Valley.

The monitoring study suggested few new persons used the Valley, but visits by those who already used it had increased by 40 per cent as a result of the Experiment. Because of the large number of return visits it was noted that the interpretation 'message' could be more fully presented than in rural areas where an instant impact was required from the media used. Also the content of interpretive messages could be continually updated, stimulating curiosity and more visits.

Merging with the idea of interpretation is the wider theme of *environmental education*; a long-term attempt to reduce tensions between urban and rural interests. The wide-scale development of curricula in schools on environmental themes, backed by local authority provision of field centres, and programmes of farm visits encouraged by such agencies as the NFU, the Country Landowners Association and the Association of Agriculture, are some of its most widespread manifestations. Specific schemes include that of the GLC Land Agency Group which enables children from inner city areas to visit selected GLC-owned farms in the Green Belt. This is now formalized in new farm tenancies whereby clauses relating to limited access for school visits have been negotiated.[53] There is also a wide variety of such activity sponsored by BTCV, RSPB, local conservation corps and county trusts for nature conservation. Education by direct involvement in countryside conservation tasks is a fast growing activity with organizations such as WATCH and ACORN (the junior National Trust) particularly active.

Footpaths and Access

The inner parts of green belts are typified by fragmented footpath systems, over-use of paths, and poor maintenance. In such areas conflict between walkers and riders, and between both and agricultural interests is at its sharpest. The trends in agriculture towards larger field enclosures, and the clearance of vegetation, lead to paths being removed or otherwise severed. The most vocal of the access lobbies, the Ramblers Association, is pledged to oppose path closures and attempts to systematically 'walk' paths to assure their retention.[54] In this complex situation, where many footpaths are not waymarked, and maintenance is often non-existent, appropriate measures focus on 'problem' areas to:

1. ensure paths linking town and country are retained;
2. reconnect fragmented path systems to form 'routes' which traverse parts of the inner green belt;
3. negotiate diversions, or 'permissive' paths where conflict with agriculture is excessive, or where a diversion would be more logical; and
4. improve maintenance by repairing surfaces where heavy use occurs, and by waymarking.[55]

Paths may be linked by utilizing prominent linear features such as disused railway routes, canal towpaths, or by negotiating paths as part of mineral restoration schemes. Schemes, such as the *Leeds Country Way*, or the *Greensand Way* in Surrey, involve lengthy negotiation and consistent planning. Attempts to resolve day-to-day conflicts are often made at county level by joint committees made up of farming, local authority, and user interests. The Ramblers Association have suggested that the establishment of comprehensive access committees should become a norm in green belt pressure areas.

The situation of the footpath system in the urban fringe must, however, be seen as unsatisfactory. The resources devoted to maintenance by the majority of local authorities are minimal, with little prospect of improvement. The use of volunteer or MSC labour is frequently only a short-term solution. Proper vigilance would require the employment of full-time staff.

There is the potential to link footpath use to the provision of incidental picnic or recreation areas along such routes. Management agreements provide a device to achieve this although finance and wardening costs may be the price of any agreement.[56] Access agreements can be concluded on land which is mountain, moor, heath, down, cliff, foreshore, woodland or river bank, but *not* on improved farmland.[57] Few access agreements have been concluded in green belts although Surrey have such agreements over 1390 hectares of downland, heathland and woodland.[58] In this case the land is managed by the County and supervised by wardens employed by them. Far more use could be made of this mechanism to solve twin problems of access and management. It is significant, in such a politically-charged conflict, that Conservative Governments have taken a more restricted attitude to access. A general review of access to the countryside, announced in 1966, was rescinded in 1970 by the incoming Conservative Government. It will thus be of interest to trace the success of the Countryside Commission Sports Council initiative on access in the future.

Public Transport – The Equity Argument

Surveys at green belt recreation attractions suggest that 95 per cent of visitors travel by car, and high proportions are in the managerial and supervisory socio-economic groups. Access is not available equally, and the groups for which the green belt offers the 'promise' of peace and fresh air in attractive surroundings are just those without the means to benefit from the opportunities that exist. This problem is most notable around London where travel times and distances to the Green Belt are greatest, and costs highest.[59] At the same time the frequency of public transport services at suitable times has reduced greatly since the mid-1970s. Whilst some local authorities promote recreational public transport schemes to national parks, examples in the urban fringe are more rare.[60]

Many experiments to promote increases in the use of public transport for recreation have been carried out over the last 10 years. Early schemes involved the co-ordination of timetables so that visitors could link to scheduled services by walks across country, and some have combined rail and bus travel.[61] Where marketing studies have been carried out to gauge the demand for travel prior to provision, the results have been disappointing. Those who suggested they would use public transport did not do so when the service was provided.[62] The most successful scheme – the Wayfarer scheme – in the West Yorkshire and Greater Manchester areas relies on a heavy marketing input for its success.[63] One-price Rover tickets, extensive advertising, and television promotion, have yielded results which suggest the extra use generated is an important supplementary source of revenue to operators. Such schemes however require the skills of public transport planners, and the resources of Passenger Transport Executives, to be effective. Given the scale of the problem it is difficult to see even such schemes as these having more than a marginal impact on the latent demands of the non-mobile.

Concluding Remarks

Priority area proposals in structure plans, as a means of structuring the arena for conflict mediation, have generally not been acceptable to central Government. Comprehensive open land policies worked out at strategic level have survived in a number of areas but the abolition of the Metropolitan Counties is likely to render the progress made nugatory. There is a preference for *not* grouping recreation facilities together but keeping the general Circular 42/55 presumptions in place.

It is difficult to judge whether great progress has been made in improving access to the green belts. Compared with the situation in 1974, there have been many schemes implemented in the North, mainly through their attachment to derelict land clearance programmes. On the whole provision has been in *opportunistic* high-cost schemes which are not always well-related to urban areas for access. The large number of agencies involved in provision present formidable co-ordination problems for local authorities. Many schemes have not been implemented as a result. In the case of smaller-scale interest mediation, shortages of funds have assumed greater importance than any lack of knowledge of what should be done. In the area of access to farmland a combative situation prevails and again lack of practical on-the-ground commitment has limited progress. Indeed the decline of public transport, combined with the effect of agricultural improvements, may have led to a deterioration of the situation. The private proprietal interest still dominates in green belts backed by local resistance, articulated at district level, to new development.

Progress in most of the areas related to recreation and access is crucially dependent on *negotiation* to achieve mediation between interests and to create a climate where compromises can be reached. It is therefore important to look at the ways of concerting action that have emerged in order to implement wider open land policies, including those for recreation and access.

9. Green Belt Management

The third major interest in green belts is an amalgam of two concerns; those of landscape appreciation and nature conservation. Concern over the first stems from a realization that farmers, propelled by MAFF and EEC grant and guaranteed price incentives, have achieved greater productivity only at the expense of a 'landscape' denuded of valued features.[1] Hedgerows have been lost at a rate of over one per cent per annum since the last War, lowland historic broad-leaved woodlands have been reduced by 50 per cent, and the number of individual trees in lowland landscapes has declined by an average of over 70 per cent in the last 20 years.[2] Such losses are considered 'unacceptable to the general public',[3] and a survey carried out by the Countryside Commission suggests that an attractive countryside is rated only second to safe city streets as a desirable environmental aim.[4]

Concern over nature conservation stems from observation of the destruction of wildlife habitats, as well as the publicizing of broader logics such as that of *resource sustainability*. This latter suggests that resources (soil, water, vegetation and wildlife) should only be exploited at a rate which allows natural regeneration and the retention of existing levels of diversity of flora and fauna. The link between the removal of landscape features and reductions in the diversity of habitats was demonstrated in 1977 by the Nature Conservancy Council (NCC).[5] Such losses of habitat lead to reductions in genetic diversity, also reducing stability in the environment. As much scientific progress, for example in biotechnology, depends on retaining naturally-occurring genetic diversity, future pathways to sustainable economic progress may well be lost. However away from the level of principle, what practical measures have been taken to safeguard landscapes and conserve natural habitats?

Countryside Conservation

Perhaps surprisingly the conservation interest has always been lowest in the countryside 'pecking-order'. Few controls exist over the loss of valued features in the general lowland countryside (covering most green belts), a side-effect of the exclusion of most agricultural operations from the purview of land use planning in 1947. In attempting to shift the balance between private and public interests, organizations such as the Countryside Commission and the NCC are starting from a weak base of powers and resources. Dependent on central Government for finance, they are opposed to the trend of support for agricultural production – currently running at £3.35 thousand million annually (£13,000 per farm holding) – yet require the voluntary co-operation of farmers if a wider conservation ethic is to be brought to fruition.[6] The powers available are weak, and have grown in an *ad hoc* way. They are largely ineffective.

Historically the nature conservation interest has been expressed through the purchase of National Nature Reserves and the designation of Sites of Special Scientific Interest (SSSI). However this has not led, in the case of SSSIs, to eradication of the loss of habitats of scientific importance and economic potential. The 1981 *Countryside and Wildlife Act* includes a system of *voluntary* controls over SSSIs (which cover 6.3 per cent of England and Wales) but the cost of concluding management agreements, should the wish of a farmer or a landowner to remove valued features be resisted, is prohibitive. No protection exists for land outside SSSIs and National Nature Reserves, the only other successful method employed until recently being the purchase of land by county conservation trusts and similar bodies.

Landscape areas may be *designated* as Areas of Outstanding Natural Beauty (a number already cover parts of approved green belts) but they confer no additional public rights over the land management decisions of owners.[8] Private woodland can be effectively maintained through *agreements* made with the Forestry Commission (now under the Small Woods Scheme) whereby grants of up to £600 per hectare are payable for tree planting and fencing.[9] However evidence for green belt areas in the Metropolitan Counties suggests less than one third of small woodlands are included in such arrangements.[10] A wide range of grants exist to aid the retention and replacement of landscape features, but again the only systematic evidence available suggests they may be little used in the critical urban-fringe parts of green belts.[11] In the absence of stronger powers *advice* regarding conservation matters is now heaped upon farmers and landowners. Certainly much of this is needed. The Countryside Commission's *Second Look* at the state of lowland landscapes in 1984 pointed out the lack of knowledge and expertise possessed by many farmers on conservation matters.[12] Demonstration Farms, designed to show how modern farming and new agricultural landscapes can co-exist, have been established throughout the country.[13] Farming and Wildlife Advisory Groups are the agricultural industry's response, and they exist in each County in England and Wales.[14] They provide advice on conservation matters to farmers on request. The Farming and Wildlife Trust now sponsors the employment of county-wide farm conservation advisers grant-aided by the Countryside Commission, in an attempt to move onto a more promotional footing.

Local authorities vary in their level of involvement with detailed landscape and nature conservation matters. Most are directly involved in managing the recreation land they own (see Chapter 8) but many are reluctant to extend the public interest principle to the general green belt countryside. Munton's survey around London suggested elected members were not unduly alarmed about the appearance of the Green Belt, preferring a 'farmed' landscape to the alternatives of mineral extraction or recreation development.[15] The range of management work being undertaken in the general countryside of the London Green Belt in 1978 was insignificant, and little further progress had been made by 1983.[16] However many have become aware of the day-to-day conflicts between different users of open land near towns, and the inability of development control to affect many (though not all) issues at this level. Local authorities have focused their attention on areas of landscape devastation, attempting to create new landforms and landscapes from those scarred by mineral extraction. There are signs that some now realize complementary measures must also be taken to retain and manage existing valued features.

Because of the weakness of available powers local authorities must work largely by persuasion and example. A number of Counties have been noted for their initiatives in *aspects* of countryside management. Essex, for example, has operated extensive programmes of promotion and assistance for tree planting, covering the County by area over a number of years. Others operate agency agreements for tree planting which are funded by the Countryside Commission, and a few offer a free design service for farmers and landowners. Oxfordshire has a footpath officer operating within and beyond the Oxford Green Belt to resolve access conflicts. Avon County has employed staff under the Community Programme of the Manpower Services Commission on footpath clearance and resurfacing work.

However analyses of the extent of management problems in green belts has suggested a need to *focus attention*, and *concert action* in defined areas. These may be areas of threatened landscape, or areas where after-uses of mineral land have to be secured and managed, or where conflicts (for example between recreation and agriculture) are particularly severe. Attention has thus centred on how best to bring to bear the disparate powers and resources available operating in a persuasive-negotiative way. Five special mechanisms, each relating to *multiple use objectives* in open land in green belts are discussed here. They are: standing conferences, *ad hoc* authorities, formal county-district working, the use of intermediaries, and environmental trusts.

The Standing Conference Mechanism

The *Colne Valley Standing Conference* is a mechanism for focusing attention on the recreation potential of a 100 square kilometre area on the inner edge of the Green Belt west of Greater London. The area has a number of major physical planning problems. It is severed by major communication routes (the M4, M40 and M3 Motorways) and much of its southern part is dominated by sand and gravel extraction. It is also subject to some of the most severe pressures for industrial, commercial and other urban-related developments in Britain. In 1982–3 an Inquiry took place into the possibility of a fifth terminal for Heathrow (London) Airport, and construction of the M25 London orbital Motorway will dissect the area from north to south. Much land is owned by local authorities and statutory undertakers, other land is covenanted under the 1938 Green Belt Act, and large tracts are in the ownership of private gravel companies. In 1967 the GLC and adjoining local authorities produced a study of the recreation potential of the area, and an agreed policy. The aim was to develop a facility of regional importance which would also act as a green lung for Central and West London.

The Park has as its overriding aim the preservation of rural character, and within this, provision of recreation accessible to large urban populations.[17] As a result informal recreation was planned to be confined to 'activity centres' grouped around foci such as a water sports centre, or an historic house. In other areas low intensity free-ranging activities such as walking, horse riding, or cycle touring would be the norm. Substantial areas were to be retained in agricultural use as a green background or for nature conservation. The Regional Park idea constitutes an acceptable planning compromise between the differing attitudes to open land of the local authorities involved. Currently the Standing Conference has 11 members, including four County and six District Councils, and the GLC. The GLC wishes to see a lung for West London, and the shire Counties consider that urban fringe provision will soak up pressures which would otherwise penetrate into the Chilterns AONB or other Green Belt areas. The project has no separate Act of Parliament and until recently had no specific project teams. It works as a loose-knit Standing Committee of the Local Authorities served by an Officers' Working Party dedicated to pursuing the aims of the Park Plan as they apply to their own administrative areas.

In the absence of adequate implementing mechanisms, progress on new recreation provision has been slow, although two country parks and a farm centre have been established. Similarly the after-use of wet gravel pits has been secured for water-based recreation activities, although there is concern that too high a proportion of such use is for private clubs only. The landscape of the area has deteriorated severely over the 10 years to 1984 and the condition of woodland has been a particular cause for concern. In response to this situation a Countryside Commission-sponsored Countryside Management Project was established in 1978.[18] Employing three persons, the Project is charged with negotiating improvements to landscape and access with landowners, which are then carried out using volunteer labour. The Colne Valley Park Volunteers plant trees, clear and fence footpaths, and assist in publicity. The Project has also had some success in building up a picture of land ownership and use in the Valley, as well as carrying out surveys of the condition and use of woodlands.

In 1983 the strategy and objectives of the Park were updated.[19] A revised list of major recreation and conservation projects was developed and 'lead agencies' identified. Lead agencies are preparing detailed reports for schemes in their areas. A broader environmental management rationale has developed including policies for wildlife conservation, and improved visitor enjoyment through the provision of information and interpretation (Figure 9.1).

In 1982 the GLC suggested a programme of initiatives to more closely match the scale of the problems in the area. They sought the contribution of greater funds by other authorities, as well as new ways of involving the private and voluntary sectors. The proposals included:

1. the development of a centre for the Park having educational, interpretive, marketing and publicity roles, and the provision of space for countryside conservation studies;
2. the creation of a project implementation fund – the Colne Valley Park Green Belt Fund – £250,000 initially – for proposals which would cover more than one local authority area, and involve the acquisition of land;
3. the creation of a Projects Fund of £300,000 for two years, for a programme of environmental improvement; and
4. the creation of a Colne Valley Park Trust to attract funds from the private and voluntary sectors.[20]

These suggestions have yet to secure the necessary political commitment from the other authorities involved. There remain tensions between the concept of the *development* of the area as a significant recreation attraction, and the more defensive approach of the peripheral Green Belt authorities. The preoccupations of the latter are demonstrated in the revised policy where existing Country Parks managed by Berkshire are seen as 'nature conservation sites', and emphasis is laid on avoiding any development for recreation that would affect local residents. The Countryside Management Project has been used as a catalyst in this difficult situation in an attempt to rekindle interest in the Park.

The Regional Park is thus an example of a mismatch between ideas and action. The necessary impetus to implement the scheme could only occur if powers and resources were given to a new body charged with realizing the concept. The formula as currently operated suits the peripheral local authorities, allowing local interests to resist GLC pressure to utilize the area more fully for recreation. It is also significant that central Government has not stepped in to match intention to action through new implementation mechanisms. The Park proposals are used to assist in defending the area

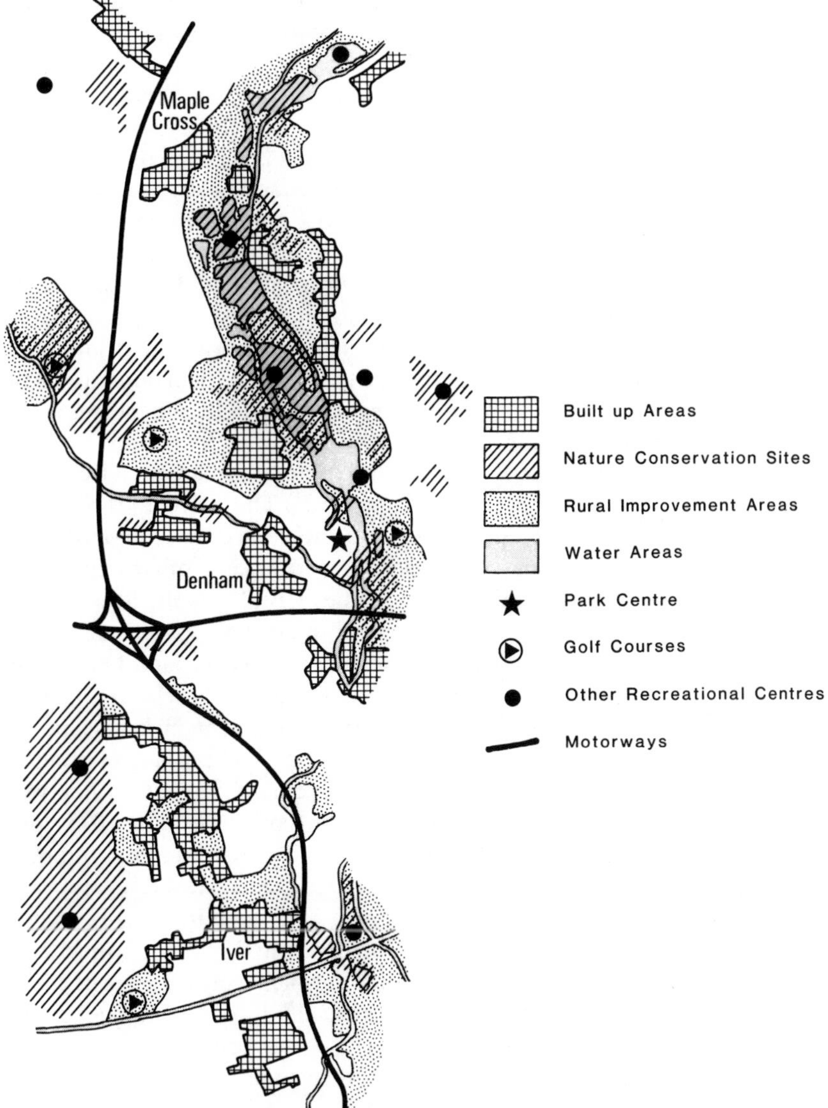

Figure 9.1 Colne Valley Regional Park: Proposals in the Northern Area
Source: Adapted from Colne Valley Standing Conference *Draft Proposals for the Regional Park* (CVSC: Hillingdon, 1983)

through development control and act to reinforce Green Belt policy. The lack of positive progress is reflected in the GLC view that:

> . . . there will be difficulty in sustaining confidence in the Colne Valley Park so long as its achievements are mainly small scale and unco-ordinated, the identity of

the Colne Valley Park is not firmly established in the area and there is insufficient public awareness of what the Standing Conference is trying to achieve. . . .[21]

County–District Joint Working

A more effective method of concerting action has been proven in the Greater Manchester area. This involves Counties and Districts working on a regular and more formal basis through Joint Committees covering geographical areas of Green Belt close to the urban boundary. In 1974 it was estimated that less than 400 hectares of non-urban parkland accessible to the general public existed in the new Metropolitan County. Large areas were scarred by past industrial and extractive activity and levels of landscape maintenance were low. This situation gave the local political impetus for the development of a conurbation-wide system of open land enhancement and informal recreation provision.

A major element of the programme is the creation of six Green Belt River Valley management schemes.[22] (See Figure 9.2.) These provide, potentially, a system of 'greenways' penetrating to the centre of the conurbation incorporating a wide range of landscapes and leisure environments. A number of the Valleys, including the Tame, Croal–Irwell, Mersey, and Medlock, had been envisaged as peripheral open space by urban districts before 1974, and large amounts of Government derelict land finance had been used to reclaim areas within them. Greater Manchester Council (GMC) have progressively increased their involvement in landscape improvement, recreation, and leisure after-use in the Valleys, augmenting the rolling programme of environmental improvement already under way. Important in securing this outcome was the conclusion (in 1975) of a County–District Agreement relating to strategic environmental improvement.[23]

Emphasis has been placed on establishing *landscape frameworks* within which appropriate recreation activities can be located.[24] Each project has a rolling programme of reclamation schemes to which a programme of capital works for tree planting and minor works is attached. As new land is brought into effective open land and recreation use, agricultural tenancies and grazing licences have been used as cost-effective methods of land management. Information and interpretation centres have been created in each Valley and issues relating to the effective conservation of wildlife are tackled through a Wildlife Working Group whose members include the local Trusts for Nature Conservation, the Nature Conservancy Council, and the RSPB.

The role of statutory local plans is interesting here. Although much major work had been done *in advance* of their preparation, plans have acted as a device to formally present the technical backing to the improvement proposals, to focus public interest on the work and to gain support for it, and to provide a framework within which private interests in the Valleys can work.

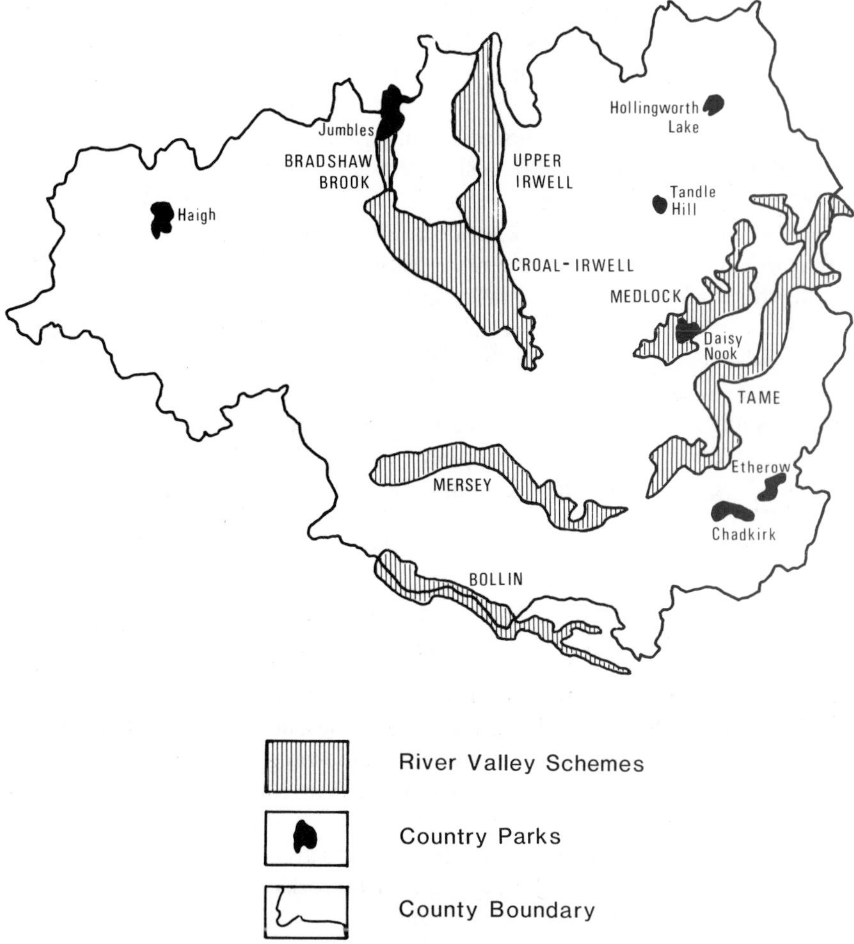

Figure 9.2 The Greater Manchester River Valleys Scheme
Source: Adapted from Webster, P. 'Local Authority Action in the Urban Fringe', *Countryside Recreation Review* (1976), vol. 1, p. 15

The plans include surveys of land use, landscape and ecology, geology, land ownership, the quality and management of agricultural land, and other factors leading to the definition of 'identity areas'. These areas, basically of differing landscape character, form the basis for types of recreation considered appropriate. GMC have identified a need for urban recreation in terms of children's play, walking, playing fields, and the use of allotments; and a need for 'countryside' recreation including walking, picnicking, visits to information centres, and the use of nature trails and features of historic interest.

The most important feature of the schemes is the arrangements for implementation. Although each covers parts of three or four local authority areas management decisions are made by a *Joint Management Committee* (JMC). These are made up of County and District representatives and the Regional Water Authority who have voting rights. It also has co-opted members such as the Countryside Commission and the British Waterways Board. The JMC is advised by a similarly-constituted team of officers. All authorities within a management area make land within their ownership available to the JMC and small-scale land management, tree planting, and other informal schemes are the responsibility of the warden in charge of a team who work specifically on tasks within one Valley. Major schemes such as Country Parks or water recreation areas involve design work by engineers and landscape architects which is then put out to contract. The Joint Committees now manage over 800 hectares of land, thirty-eight reclamation schemes have been completed or commenced, and thirty-five tips restored. Over six million trees have been planted since 1974. The six River Valley schemes together with eight Country Park projects have a capital budget which has grown five-fold since 1975 and is now £1.3 million a year (Figure 9.3). Revenue expenditure for the same projects was over £1.2 million in 1982–3.

The GMC schemes have had remarkable success compared to similar efforts on the fringe of London. This appears to be due to:

1. agreement at County and District level on the severity of environmental problems in the Green Belt, including problems of derelict land, river pollution and tipping, and the need for wide-ranging action;
2. pre-existing derelict land schemes, funded at 100 per cent rate, giving early impetus;
3. a willingness to pool knowledge, finance and land; and local political and resident support, as evidenced by the early work of the Civic Trust for the North West in the Tame Valley;[25] and
4. a willingness by the Metropolitan County to carry most of the financial burden.

The commitment of local authorities and others to the improvement of open land has been reflected in the creation of an effective *framework for action*. One of the major concerns has been the increasing revenue expenditure implications of success. Large areas now require management and at a time when rate capping is being introduced central Government appears little concerned to secure the progress made for the future. The impetus of the programme has already slowed since 1982 and the implications of abolition of the Metropolitan Counties for this initiative will be little short of disastrous.[26]

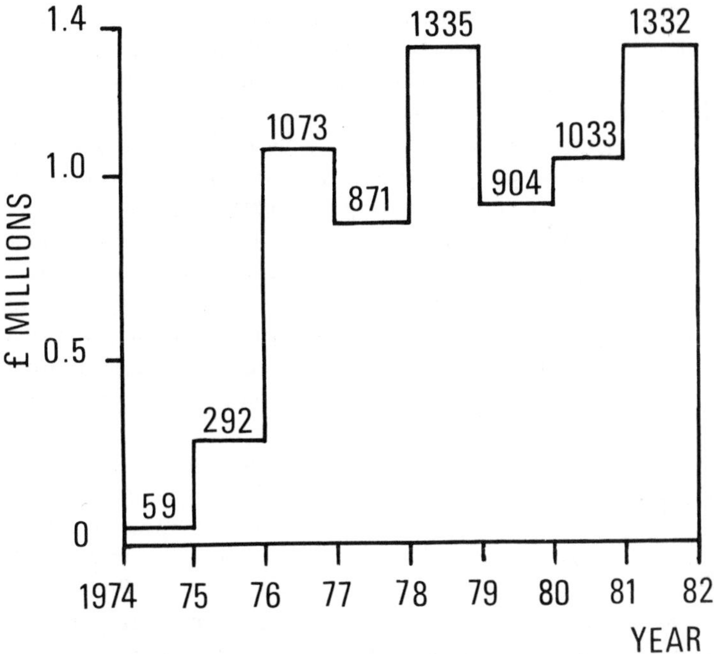

Figure 9.3 Expenditure on River Valleys and Country Parks: Greater Manchester
Source: Adapted from Maund, R. 'The Greater Manchester Adventure: An Exercise in Strategic Environmental Improvement', *Environmental Education and Information*, (1982), vol. 2, p. 92.

A Purpose-Designed Authority

Unlike other countries, Britain has not produced general legislation giving strong powers for unified park authorities in green belts. Although not as ambitious as the Huron–Clinton Metropolitan Authority in Greater Detroit, USA[27] or the Ruhrkohlenziberk in the Ruhr in West Germany,[28] the *Lea Valley Regional Park Authority* stands out as a unique product of its time.

The Park is an area of 4,000 hectares, running for 37 kilometres from the east end of London to Ware in Hertfordshire. Connecting town and country, its northern half is within the London Green Belt. In its upper reaches intensive market gardening is in decline; further in towards the City gravel extraction, sewage works, reservoirs for water supply, and derelict industrial areas predominate. The impetus for the Park arose from a strongly politically-articulated need in East London to clean up the river, remove flooding and dereliction, and provide an area for recreation, sport, entertainment and leisure. Early plans by the Civic Trust, a voluntary body, suggested that sixteen areas could be identified, each with scope for a park with its own distinctive character. These would be 'linked' by the unifying features of the canal and river in a north–south direction.[29]

The Government accepted arguments that in order to untie the complicated web of central and local machinery surrounding such a project, an *ad hoc* authority should be created. In 1967 the *Lea Valley Regional Park Act* came into operation, creating an agency with powers to acquire land, and erect and manage facilities. The Regional Park is run by a Committee on which representatives of twelve local authorities, whose land impinges on the Park, are represented. It employs a planning, architectural, engineering and management staff of around 250 persons. Park finances are met by a precept on the rates of surrounding authorities up to the product of a half penny rate. In 1981–2 the Authority precepted £4 million for its operations. However, it has no direct power over development control in its area acting only as a consultee on planning applications.

Over the last fifteen years considerable progress has been made, although the ten-year time horizon specified by the Civic Trust in 1964 has proved hopelessly ambitious. The Authority has acquired 880 hectares of land and has pursued a policy of intensive provision in the southern part of its area, with more low-key provision in the northern (Green Belt) area. Major provisions include leisure and sports centres, horse riding facilities, a cycle racing track, and a caravan park. Over the period 1967–83 some 31 per cent of capital expenditure was devoted to land acquisition, 41 per cent to major built development, and 28 per cent to smaller developments and landscape improvement. This is basically an environmental improvement and recreation project which has acquired land opportunistically rather than compulsorily. The major actions have been to provide for formal sports but there have been problems in creating a consistent Park identity, and improving access to and within the area. The Authority has restricted itself to landscaping and managing land under its control and no coherent area-wide landscape strategy has been implemented. There have been considerable problems in obtaining land for Park use from statutory undertakers, Government and other public bodies.

A review of Park aims was instituted in 1981 and the result has been to re-cast the 1969 objectives.[30] More emphasis will be placed on Park-wide landscape improvement and management, measures to improve access, and the protection and management of areas of nature conservation importance. More work will be done using the resources of the voluntary sector. The upper part of the Valley in the London Green Belt is likely to see greater attention given to small-scale environmental improvements and measures to reconcile farming, access, and recreation. A concern for *creating* environments for recreation is now to be supplemented by one to more effectively *manage* natural environments. A *piecemeal* basis of action is now to be more overtly an *area-based* approach.

This method of concerting action has not produced widespread acclaim.

Central Government has decided on various occasions, notably in views expressed in the Countryside Review Committee in 1977, that new *ad hoc* authorities are not, in normal circumstances, required.[31] The Park Authority does seem to have pursued its activities largely unheralded. Surrounding local authorities have naturally resented its powers, particularly that to precept money at a time of financial stringency. Consultation during the Review revealed considerable criticism of Park aims and the projects undertaken. The Park Plan remained unaltered for twelve years from 1969 to 1981, although the Act gave no guidelines on how it was to be reviewed. In retrospect, perhaps a wider framework of accountability, and more incorporation of relevant interests in day-to-day decisions and management, should have been provided for in the Act at the outset. Its 'master plan' method of guidance contrasts starkly with the flexible approaches now common in other areas in the 1980s.

Intermediaries: The Persuasive Approach

The shortcomings of statutory approaches to land management problems have long been recognized. In 1967 Hookway recognized the need for new ways of bringing together public and private interests in the management of open land.[32] His judgement that the introduction of formal powers to conclude agreements might be counter-productive suggested the need to employ informal methods to achieve the same ends. The method piloted and promoted by the Countryside Commission has involved the employment of intermediaries (project officers) operating in defined areas of green belt, and has become known as *area management*. The method is seen as complementary to the use of land use planning powers, operating in an opportunistic and responsive way.[33] Although each area management project has different emphases, the following aims are broadly discernible:

1. conservation and enhancement of the green belt and its landscape character;
2. improvement of the quality of access and provision for informal recreation;
3. conservation of wildlife, habitats and natural resources;
4. support for and protection of agriculture and forestry from urban and urban-related pressures;
5. enhancement of public understanding and respect for the countryside and its activities; and, increasingly
6. the encouragement of voluntary action through community-based enhancement projects under 1–4 (above).[34]

The *project officer* is concerned with reaching practical compromises between private interests and wider public pressures. For example footpaths may be cleared and surfaced, and new permissive routes for walkers and

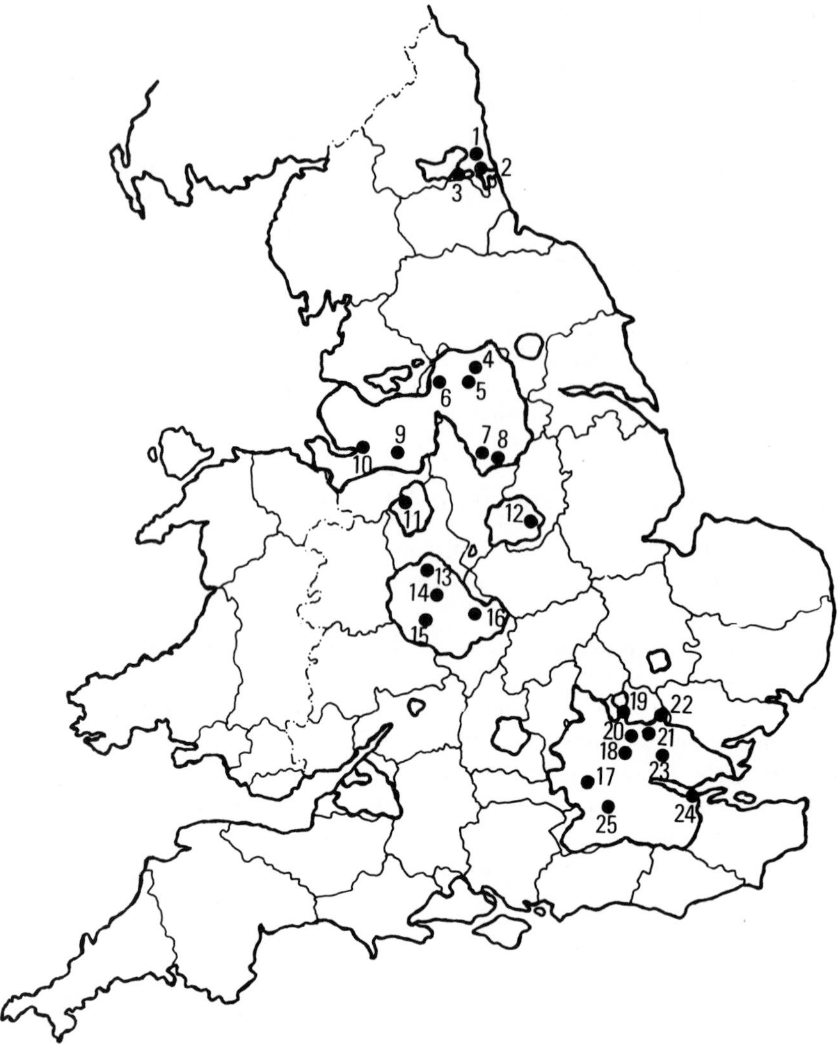

Figure 9.4 Countryside Management Areas in Green Belts

Green Belt	*Commenced*
Tyneside	
1. North Tyneside	1982
2, Boldon Corridor, Sunderland	1982
3. South of Gateshead	1982
West/South Yorkshire	
4. Kirkstall Valley	1983
5. Tong-Cockersdale	1973
6. Colne Valley	1984
7. Sheffield River Valleys	1982
8. Moss Valley	1984

Figure 9.4 – Continued

Merseyside/Manchester	
9. Bollin Valley	1973
10. Mersey Valleys	1980
North Staffordshire	
11. Newcastle Countryside	1981
Nottingham/Derby	
12. Nottinghamshire Countryside	1983
West Midlands	
13. Operation South Cannock	1980
14. Beacon Regional Park	1983
15. North Worcestershire	1980
16. Coventry Countryside	1983
London	
17. Colne Valley	1978
18. South Herts/Barnet	1975
19. Mid-Herts Valleys	1982
20. Broxbourne Woods	1976
21. Upper Lea Valley	1976
22. East Herts Bridleways	1981
23. Havering	1976
24. North West Kent	1984
25. Lower Mole Valley	1983

Note: Compiled with the assistance of the Countryside Commission

riders negotiated. Help may be given for small-scale tree planting, and with aspects of woodland management. Facilities in picnic areas and on informal recreation sites in a variety of ownerships may be improved. Local goodwill and interest may be harnessed to carry out voluntary tasks, or arrangements made with voluntary groups such as the British Trust for Conservation Volunteers to harness work to project objectives.

It was realized early that the project officer would be most effective if seen as accessible and helpful, able to build bridges between owners and land managers and what is often seen as the remote machinery of local government. Qualities required of the project officer include abilities to select feasible management tasks within the resources available, to gain the confidence of farmers and landowners, and an element of leadership to awaken the imagination and interest of all groups concerned, including sometimes sceptical local elected representatives. Project officers therefore need to operate informally, and require the ability to respond quickly to negotiated opportunities.

This form of conflict mediation and resolution is seen as particularly appropriate in green belt areas. By early 1984 there were twenty-five area management projects in different Green Belts in England (Figure 9.4), with the likelihood of more being negotiated in the future. Half of the projects have commenced since January 1982 suggesting an upsurge in local acceptability of this form of action. Some are district-wide schemes, but others cover

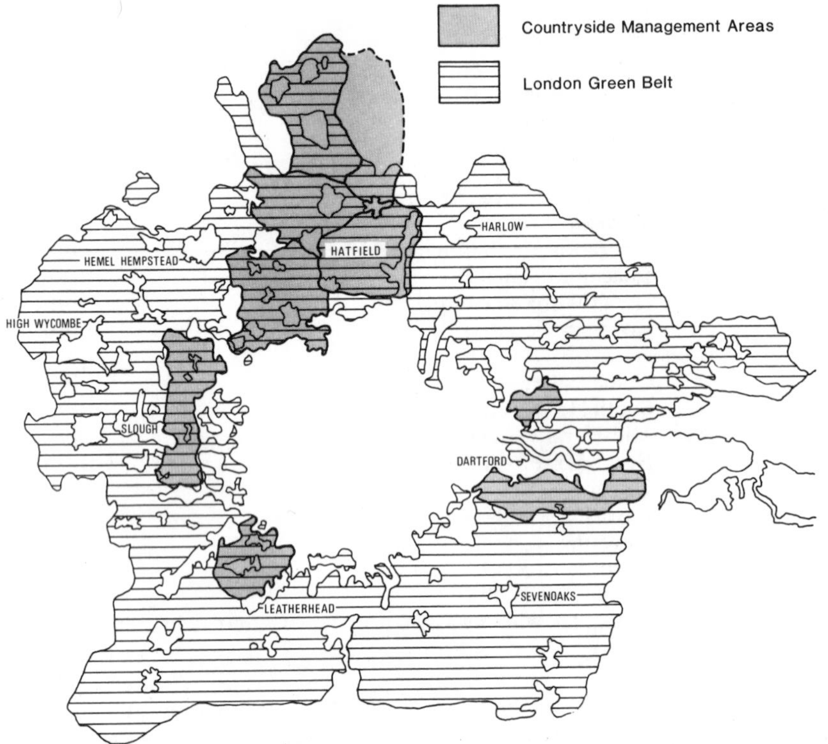

Figure 9.5 Countryside Management Areas in the London Green Belt
Source: Information from Kent, Surrey and Hertfordshire County Councils

'problem' areas spanning district and county boundaries such as recent projects in the Moss Valley (South Yorkshire–Derbyshire) and North-West Kent (GLC and Kent). Over 15 per cent of the London Green Belt (Figure 9.5) and most of the Tyne and Wear Green Belt are covered by such schemes. The early *experiments* (in the Bollin Valley on the southern fringe of Manchester, and in South Hertfordshire–Barnet on the northern edge of London), did not start from a predetermined plan.[35] The project officer, working to a general brief, began by getting to know the area, and the individuals and organizations involved. During this stage particular site specific conflicts were identified and the feasibility of cost-effective solutions assessed. A series of relatively small-scale tasks to produce immediate and visible results, and geared to project objectives, were then carried out. This work gained the confidence of landowners and showed elected representatives the cost effectiveness of solutions (Figure 9.6).

As the experiments continued information from which to assess priorities more closely has been gathered in a more structured way. For example, in

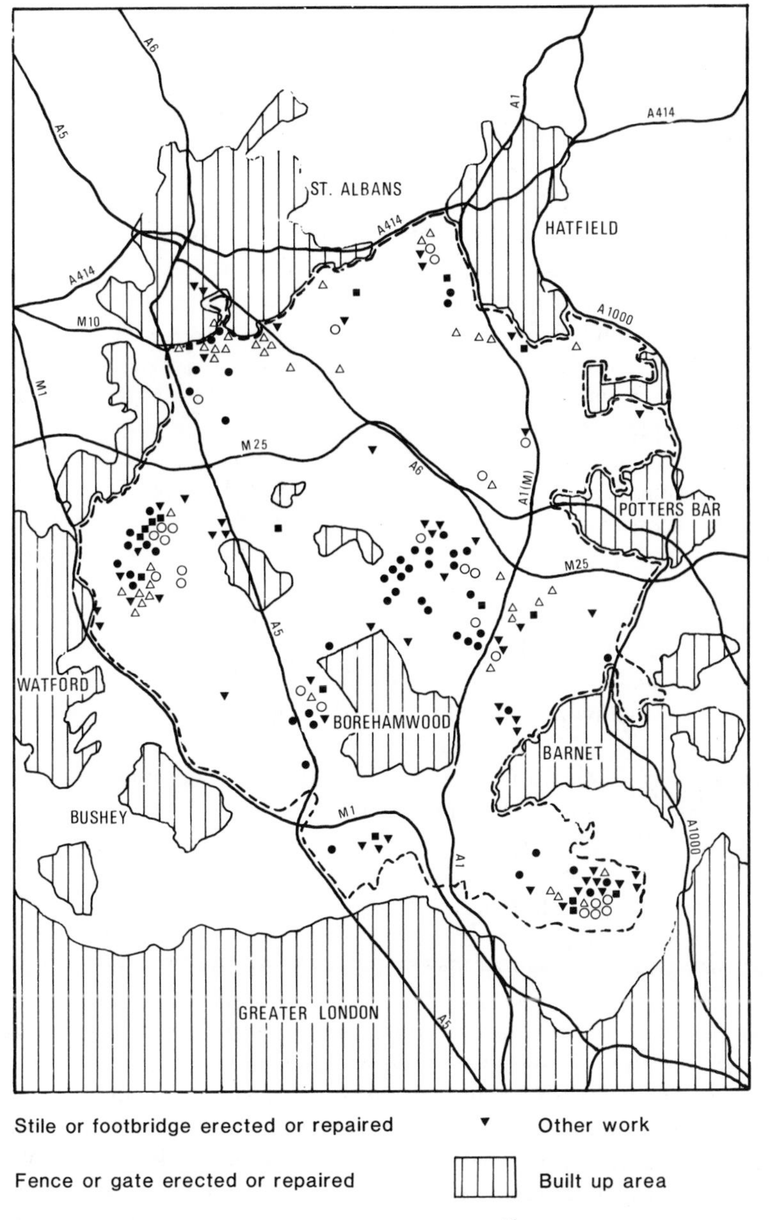

Figure 9.6 Project Work in the Herts–Barnet Area
Source: Adapted from Countryside Commission, *Countryside Management in the Urban Fringe*, CCP 136, (Countryside Commission, Cheltenham, 1981), Figure 6.

the Herts–Barnet area information on the distribution of horse riding establishments and horsiculture, and on land ownership, and the condition of woodland has been assembled.[36] As the projects have gained impetus a wide range of possible tasks has been uncovered and there have been changes in emphasis in the work carried out. At the conclusion of the three-year experiment in the Herts–Barnet area in 1979, a further experiment was funded by the Countryside Commission to explore the problems of management of publicly-owned land, and the long-term future of countryside management. A five-year Management Plan was produced in 1982 linked to the second aim.[37] Work during the second experimental phase has included larger schemes involving more complex negotiations, the increased use of volunteers, and more community involvement.[38]

The approach is now applied in a variety of situations. In the Hertfordshire cases emphasis is placed on resolving conflicts between farming and the need for access and recreation, and on landscape maintenance. In Tyne and Wear the three projects place greater emphasis on environmental improvement and the creation of a more varied landscape with large-scale tree planting in the bare eastern part of the Green Belt. In the South Cannock and Newcastle Under Lyme areas the major environmental problem is mineral extraction. Landscape renewal using volunteers and environmental education is the main theme. The projects in green belts in the North have tended to employ MSC-financed labour whereas the southern ones have made less use of this source.[39] Although the early London area schemes were 'project officer centred', most schemes have become more community conscious in the early 1980s.

The juxtaposition of practical work with the production of planning and management plans has also varied. The less-publicized Tong–Cockersdale management scheme between Leeds and Bradford in West Yorkshire, was working to a Management Plan in 1975.[40] Some of the more recent projects are working to aims and programmes derived in statutory local plans. The *Operation South Cannock* and *Newcastle Countryside* projects have used programmes of work derived from statutory local plan proposals as a starting point for recent project officer appointments.[41] Although such plans are not strictly *land use* plans, according to narrow Ministry definitions, they have been allowed to proceed towards adoption because of the likelihood of their provisions being at least partly implemented, and because of their links with active derelict land programmes. The new Beacon Regional Park management area is also based on work in the Barr Beacon–Sandwell Wedge Subject Plan produced by West Midlands County Council.[42] The work will continue to operate using a variety of quasi-inductive processes, but there is increasing awareness that this form of action can implement a number of the proposals emerging in local plans for the resolution of conflicts within green belt open land.

At a time of economic stringency one of the most appealing features of the method is its low cost. Here a delicate balance has been struck by the Countryside Commission in the level of funding accorded to schemes. The early experiments, to publicize and prove the method, were 100 per cent grant aided by the Commission. Many of the schemes had their early impetus in officer persuasion of elected representatives. The early Hertfordshire schemes were not enthusiastically received initially, but their output has convinced local elected representatives to finance an expansion of activity at later stages. The second phase of the Herts–Barnet Experiment received tapered Commission financial support with grants at 75 per cent, 66.6 per cent, and 50 per cent over the three years to 1981. Currently the smallest management project may have a basic budget of around £20,000 per annum with 50 per cent contributed by the Countryside Commission and the remainder shared among the county and district authorities involved. Twenty five per cent of the cost of Operation South Cannock, for example, is paid by Staffordshire County Council, with the two participating Districts each paying 12.5 per cent. This is a good bargain for a district which may see the benefits of small-scale improvements locally at a fraction of their 'real' cost.

The differential take up of the area-based countryside management approach is accounted for by many factors. In relatively 'rich' Counties such as Surrey, Berkshire, and Buckinghamshire there may be ideological opposition to 'intervention' which goes beyond normal land use planning powers. Also existing arrangements may be seen as adequate,[43] or there may be no tradition of environmental improvement on the scale pertaining outside the South East. The Midland and Northern Conurbations were early into this field and have devised their own arrangements, working through environment committees, and across the two-tier system. In such cases the acceptance of a countryside management project may help reduce revenue costs in that grants are available for wardening. However the Countryside Commission is keen to see local authorities assuming more responsibility for ongoing costs.

In Hertfordshire the initial experiment in the south of the County has been augmented by four further area-based schemes, including one with a focus on bridleways in East Hertfordshire. In 1983 these schemes were converted into a 'countryside management service' with the aim of covering the whole County in due course. This has caused some organizational changes. Previously the project officer worked to a Project Steering Group made up of the various interests and meeting quarterly, with an annual Review Group meeting chaired by a Countryside Commissioner. It is now a *service* guided by a Project Working Group which reports to the Countryside Sub-Committee of the County Council, and to other District and County Committees.[44] The County operates a support team of full-time officers collecting survey material, and collating policy, leaving the countryside managers to focus on practical tasks. This change risks losing some of the attributes of the Countryside Commission idea. The schemes may no longer be seen as quasi-independent, thus compromising the 'intermediary' status of the project officers.

Environmental Trusts

Countryside management projects appear successful in resolving small-scale conflicts. If pursued consistently in the long-term, a point often stressed by the National Farmers Union,[45] they have the potential to become an indispensible part of public action in green belts. However more difficulty has been experienced in tackling the larger-scale environmental and land use problems of the type discovered in the Havering London Green Belt Experiment. Here over 20 per cent of the initial project area had been the subject of gravel extraction over a fifteen-year period.[46] Evaluation work has noted the dangers of only pursuing a low-key approach; 'there is even a danger that the resulting improvements, by obscuring the real nature of the problems, might be counter-productive'.[47] One lesson of this Experiment was that some way of incorporating the major interests spending money in the area (the DoE and local authorities through derelict land grant, the MAFF, NCC and Forestry Commission, and private interests), was required. The aim should be to 'bend' their investment programmes to some wider common purpose. However intensive negotiations at the conclusion of the Havering Experiment failed to secure the necessary commitment, a good example of the continuing strength of sectoral interests.

The response has been to develop the mechanism of an *environmental trust*. This involves setting up a limited company which then obtains charitable status for its expressed purposes. A committee of trustees are then appointed from public and private interests in an area. They can then employ a project director, a number of countryside managers, landscape designers, and wildlife managers. The charitable trust mechanism can act as a focus for commitment, and financial and manpower resources, in a community-based effort to improve the urban fringe environment. In this way it is hoped the various interests will 'fuse together' for common purposes.

One project, *Operation Groundwork*, was established in 1981 in the Green Belt around St Helens, Merseyside. The use of a mechanism to 'lever' finance from the private sector was a prerequisite laid down by the 1979 Conservative Government for support of the project. In 1983 a regional programme – *Groundwork North West* – was also set up, and five schemes, (chosen from the fifteen bids made), covering Wigan, Macclesfield (Cheshire), Rochdale–Oldham, Rossendale (Lancashire), and Salford–Trafford, are under way.[48] (See Figure 9.7.)

Groundwork projects aim to reach out into the local community to involve a wide range of organizations and individuals. The intention is to act as an

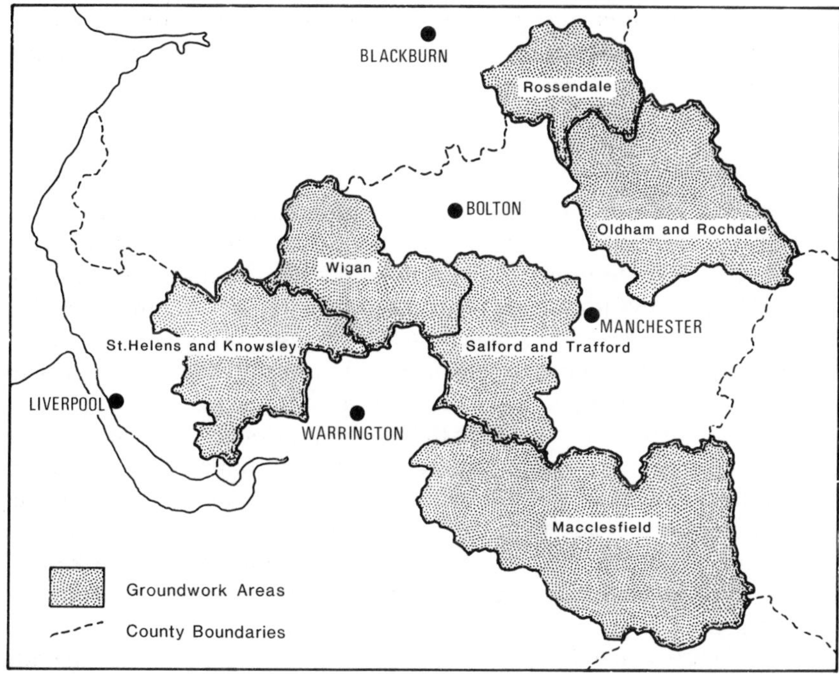

Figure 9.7 'Groundwork' Areas: 1984
Source: Groundwork North West Unit *Groundwork News*, no. 2 (GNWU: Manchester, 1983)

umbrella for efforts to clear dereliction, find productive uses for waste land, bring countryside closer to the homes of townspeople, and create conditions that allow farming and forestry to prosper.[49] In seeking to harness the resources of public bodies, and the knowledge of local people and industry, it is argued, they will be 'fundamentally different' from traditional publicly-funded improvement projects'.[50] In addition to Trustees and the full-time staff, Operation Groundwork has a group of patrons – 'Friends of Operation Groundwork' – made up of local bodies, companies and individuals, prepared to assist the Trust as volunteers or sponsors. A task force of unemployed people is carrying out countryside improvements funded under the Community Enterprise Programme of the Manpower Services Commission.

It was accepted that early impetus could be given to the schemes by earmarking funds for extra derelict land clearance in the project areas. As a result £3 million was made available for accepted schemes within the five Groundwork Trust areas during 1983–4, although priority on this scale was not guaranteed for future years. The Countryside Commission were also allocated additional funds of £825,000 in 1983–4 to assist with the costs of setting up the Trusts. This funding will be tapered covering 75 per cent of costs in the first year, 50 per cent in the second, and one third in the third year. The Trusts are expected to generate 15 per cent of their funds externally (including revenue from donations) in the first year, rising to 30 per cent in the second. It is hoped they will be independent of Countryside Commission revenue support within five years.[51]

The Trusts are assisted by staff seconded from MAFF, who are concentrating effort on achieving co-operation with the farming community and landowners. In October 1983 a Groundwork Nature Conservation Advisory Service was set up to provide advice to local authorities, the Groundwork Trusts, the Agricultural Development and Advisor Service, and others on ways of maintaining and enhancing wildlife interest on Groundwork sites.[52] One of the problems will be to convince local authorities that the new Trusts complement, rather than duplicate, existing arrangements. Many local authorities have been torn between bidding for the derelict land carrot which the scheme promised, and concern over loss of control of priorities in derelict land reclamation and environmental improvement which may result. Authorities outside the Groundwork areas in the North West have complained about loss of derelict land grant especially as the 'earmarked' £3 million seems to have been found by readjustments, rather than additions, to the regional budget.

Groundwork schemes are becoming wider community-based projects covering town as well as country.[53] As such they are slipping beyond the strict remit of the Countryside Commission. This has been recognized by Government acceptance of a proposal to establish a Groundwork Foundation in 1985 to promote the idea nationally. It is likely that this method of concerting action will extend beyond the North West in 1986 with the approval of schemes in other conurbation peripheries. However no monitoring information had been published by September 1984 and it must be accepted that these are not *yet* a proven mechanism; in some areas there remain considerable tensions with local authorities.

The trusts are being established at a difficult time. The potential sponsors, local authorities and industry, are not often able to guarantee support for the initiative due to the insecurities of local government finance. In many of the Groundwork areas industry is in a parlous state with many closures and much contraction of activity; its priorities are more likely to be survival than environmental improvement.

Concluding Remarks

The five sets of arrangements discussed above constitute attempts to fit together a range of external resources in geographical areas. The Greater Manchester example showed that where there is willingness to cede *some* power from conventional local authority committee structures to an area-based management committee, significant benefits can accrue. The other examples suggest an unwillingness by local authorities to set up separate 'power centres' for open land issues. This is the surest test that such problems are ranked low in their order of priorities. Jealousy of the autonomy of the Lea Valley Regional Park authority among London Boroughs is paralleled by distrust of the new Groundwork Trusts by Greater Manchester Council. It was these types of local authority pressure which saw the demise of other area-based ventures such as Rural Development Boards in 1970, and the downgrading of the independence of the National Parks designated after 1954.

The more conventional management tasks are bedevilled by lack of any significant powers to intervene on private land. The need to intervene in the *use* of land in the public interest was the *raison d'etre* of the planning system. In that sense land management powers are in a pre-1947 condition. The Countryside Commission area management projects must be seen as a response to the failure by central Government to accord sufficient weight to management arguments changing the *powers* available. It is not surprising that green belt management should be regarded by some as a cosmetic exercise, a partial treatment of the symptoms of declining vegetation cover and poor levels of land maintenance. In the present climate of farm support many of the landscape features 'valued' by the general public have no apparent utility to farmers. They are removed, not as a provocative act against urban dwellers, but as a functional response to farm management conditions. In this situation the best method of retaining features is to stress their economic (income-generating) value, such as the revenue to be earned from coppicing small woodlands.[54]

The idea that the persuasive approach will deliver a change in the attitude of farmers and owners is implausible. There are few signs of large numbers of owners carrying out countryside management work of their own volition, despite efforts to suggest the contrary by the Country Landowners Association. In such a situation local authorities are perhaps deluding themselves if they consider present prescriptions for green belt management will do more than 'solve' a number of superficial problems. *Major changes in the balance of private rights and public powers are required.* While the NCC and the Countryside Commission remain peripheralized, and the 'conservation voice' diffuse and fragmented, anything more than marginal change can be resisted.

The logic of the arguments of the landscape and natural resource conservationists is that public ownership (and resources for acquisition) of the most valued features must be assured, and a procedure akin to development control instigated for other important changes. The problems of designing such a system are no greater than those which faced the inventors of the original land use planning system. The ability to negotiate anything approaching such powers will depend on conservation interests demonstrating unequivocally that large numbers of the *general public* are alarmed by landscape change and conservation issues, and that it is in the long-term national interest to secure rapid change to existing arrangements. Discussion restricted to a narrow coterie of 'informed' insiders is insufficient to secure change.

Part III. Green Belts and the Future

10. The Politics of the 1984 Circular

Green belts, like motherhood, are beyond reproach in our culture. Unlike motherhood they are a very recent invention and the fact they have achieved their current status is a remarkable tribute to the marketing skills of the planners egged-on and even led in some areas by the anti-development lobby.

Roger Humber 1982

We believe green belts should be sacrosanct

House of Commons Environment Committee 1984

The explosion of interest in green belts in the 1983–4 period is often typified as a conflict between two lobbies; private housebuilders, essentially speculators on the market for new housing; and the CPRE, the oldest champions of countryside protection. During the year following September 1983 however, the politicization of the debate by its elevation to the corridors of Westminster also revealed the symbolic status of the green belt. The concept became little less than the symbol of Government's commitment to land use planning as a legitimate public sector activity. During the battle surrounding the 1983 and 1984 Draft Circulars two parts of the Conservative party in Parliament were set against one another; those representing active investment in land and property for development, and those reflecting their constituents' traditional concerns for countryside protection and resistance to rapid change. Interwoven with these themes have been concerns about the increasing centralization of Government decision-making, the perceived threat to local democracy from the proposed introduction of 'rate capping' and proposals for 'streamlining' the cities by abolition of the Metropolitan Counties.[1] All of these issues, cutting across the traditional 'countryside versus houses' set piece debate, were to surface as the arguments over green belt developed. Where then were the seeds sown for the apparently ill-fated attempt to formally change the balance between green belt and development in August 1983?

The Seeds of Conflict

These are to be found in the complex relationships between the public and private sectors which produce the built environment. With reductions since the mid-1970s in public sector investment in development Governments have had to accept the economic logic of the private developers' need to create profit at site level in order to sustain development. For employment and housing uses, profits are best realized (and sites are most marketable) in urban peripheral locations. Thus a policy of dependence on the private sector runs increasingly counter to policies for containment and checking sprawl, and their main manifestation, green belt.[2]

This contradiction has been heightened by the strident pursuit of free market and monetarist philosophies by the post-1979 Thatcher Governments. The main planks of Government policy are to allow restructuring and regeneration of the economy by removing restrictions on the use of private capital. This is to be achieved by controlling public expenditure, drawing back the boundaries of state intervention, and promoting self-reliance and the virtues of private ownership.[3] Particular attention has been paid to 'privatising' housebuilding as part of a drive to increase home ownership. Funds for public housing have been cut by over 50 per cent in the 1979–84 period. The need to avoid any public sector activity, including land use planning, becoming a hindrance to investment, and particularly the satisfaction of housing demand 'in places where people want to live', have been stressed. Of major significance to local authorities with green belts, whose status depends on the central–local concordat reached through the approval of formal plans, have been attempts to downgrade the importance of plans. These have included advice to cut public participation in local plans to one period of six weeks, to reduce the number of plans being prepared, to limit their scope (removing social matters and countryside management policies for example), and to waive their provisions if industrialists particularly want sites not allocated in plans.[4]

This package of measures represents the most significant readjustment of the frontiers of local authority intervention in land use since the early 1950s. Post-1979 Governments have, paradoxically, found that in order to 'free' land for the use of production interests such as housebuilders they have been forced to take a more interventionist stance with local authorities. Policy-making has become more overtly centralist as witnessed in the rewriting of the provisions of many structure plans (see Chapter 3). Tensions between central and local government have steadily increased. Mistrust of each others' intentions, and barely concealed hostility, now typify central–local relations over many land use planning matters.

Land for Housebuilding

The 1970s had seen the introduction of stronger measures by different Governments to ensure a continued *supply* of developable land for housing in areas of development pressure.[5] This was posited on two arguments; that there was a shortage of land in relation to housing need (particularly in the early years of the decade); and that the planning system was an independe source of *delay* in bringing forward land for development. The acceptance by Government, following the boom–bust period of 1972–4, that provision was adequate in terms of a five year supply of building land identified in plans, led to concerted efforts by the housebuilding industry to alter plan-based definitions of availability. The House Builders' Federation set out, from the mid-1970s, to challenge structure plan provisions for housing. Their first Land and Planning Officer was appointed in 1975 and five regionally-based Officers had been recruited by 1984. They have been employed to challenge local authorities on the assumptions underlying housing projections and significant concessions have been won from sympathetic Governments, who have used their powers to modify housing totals in development plans. In addition, the Volume Housebuilder's Study Group (VHSG), a breakaway group of the ten largest builders, angered by what they saw as the ineffectiveness of the HBF in representing their *particular* interests, was formed in 1975. It set out to 'fundamentally alter the complexion of planning in favour of private housebuilders'.[6]

In 1978 the housebuilding lobby obtained scope for incorporation of their commercial criteria for housing land availability into the local decision-making process. Circular 44/78, issued by a Labour Government, suggested co-operation between local authorities and builders to arrive at 'realistic local appraisals' of availability.[7] The Conservative Government introduced the *requirement* for joint land availability studies to be carried out in 1980, and formally included in guidance issued the criterion of *marketability* (commercial assessment) of land as a relevant factor in defining availability.[8] Housebuilders were able to persuade Ministers that land was not 'available' if houses could not be built and sold in a five year period. They also persuaded Government that a ready supply of land in high, medium, and low market categories was also needed at local level, thus implying more land in high quality environments should be identified for development by local authorities. This philosophy is well expressed in Circular 9/80 where to be generally available sites were to be 'free, or easily freed, from planning, physical and ownership constraints', and 'in areas where potential house buyers are prepared to live, and be suitable for the wide range of housing types which the market now demands'. Protests from consultees had secured a concession, before the Circular was finalized, to the effect that the amount and type of land required 'should be derived from the housing policies and proposals in approved plans' and not from past building rates.[9] However this built into the Circular the conflict between the wider 'public interest' view of need, and the narrower private interest criterion of marketability.

Therefore the locational strategies of local authorities have been under attack. A higher proportion of the new development for housing, it is implied, would be in greenfield locations reflecting the commercial judgements of builders, which would be incorporated from the outset of the plan-making process. Frequently prepared land availability studies would gradually overtake policies in development plans and would, by definition, conflict with defined green belts.[10]

The Misuse of Green Belts?

Until the early 1980s housebuilders had largely steered clear of the *specific* green belt issue, as Chapter 3 has discussed. The onset of Local Public Inquiries for the Greater Manchester, Sheffield, and Merseyside Green Belt Local Plans generated a new line of attack. Green belts were criticized as 'extinction by conservation' by the President of the HBF in 1982. Local authorities were accused of misapplying the green belt concept. By rushing to prepare green belt subject plans they were guilty of 'an attempt to pre-empt decisions about the implementation of Structure Plan dwelling provisions, prior to the detailed consideration of housing land requirements'.[11]

The HBF thus challenged the *principles* of green belt definition in Greater Manchester and Merseyside, but Inspectors refuted their arguments and upheld the basic approaches of the two planning authorities (Chapter 4). These reverses led the builders to call, as many have done before with less success, for a review of green belt policy:

> Having re-examined the history from scratch, we are convinced that guidelines for green belt policies are being misapplied and that, in any event, they are so out-of-date as to require restatement in the context of current legislation and social pressures.[12]

The appeal to social pressures was to develop as a major tactic suggesting relaxation of green belts would provide houses that would not otherwise be built for young people, and simultaneously playing down other probable financial consequences of relaxation, such as the enhancement of builders' profits from the holding of larger land banks with planning permission. Other suggestions were the reintroduction of the 'enormously important' category of white land in plans, and the idea that blighted and unkempt sites in green belt (many, of course, held by their members) would 'benefit enormously' from development.

The Need for Change?

During 1982–3 the HBF developed their arguments on a number of fronts. Firstly an attempt was made to establish again that an *insufficient total area of land was available in plans*. The Government, since 1979, had consistently refused to predict future housing requirements, preferring to hand down forecasts of population, migration, and household formation to local authorities, leaving them to balance conservation and development factors at local level.[13] To circumvent this the HBF joined with the Housing Research Foundation (HRF) and the RTPI to create the Joint Land Requirements Committee. The primacy of the housebuilding interest in this forum is reflected in its remit 'to provide a framework which will help to ensure that overall land supply does not act as a constraint on housebuilding'. Their first paper concluded that 250,000 new dwellings a year were required in *Great Britain* in the decade after 1982 (allowing for a desirable 'marginal over supply' of land) if housebuilding 'was not to be restrained by lack of land'.[14] When the allocations in approved structure plans were totalled, dispute reached such proportions that Sir Wilfred Burns (a retired Ministry Chief Planner) was called in by the HRF to mediate. The first round of structure plans suggested dwelling provisions of 220,000 per annum in *England and Wales*, a figure in accord with the estimates of requirements, but one which the housebuilders would not agree as it depended on a flow of small sites coming forward that were not specifically indicated in plans.[15] The outcome was a confusing impasse with statements being made that as housebuilders in 1982 were holding land banks for much shorter periods than previously, (an assertion not backed by evidence), local authorities should plan for unexpected as well as predicted land requirements.[16] The creation of land forums, tripartite groups with housebuilders, local authorities and the DoE, to pre-empt the local plan-making process was also proposed.

The second line of argument was to suggest that *insufficient land could be made available in cities* to make any impact on the scale of peripheral land allocations ('new land') required. In 1980 and 1982 the Government had introduced Land Registers whereby unused and underused sites in public ownership of 0.4 hectares or over should be listed with a view to disposal. Conducting their own studies of these lists the HBF asserted that only 11 per cent of the 40,450 hectares listed was immediately developable for housing, representing three per cent of annual output. Ninety-seven per cent would have to be on new land. Other interests have countered with higher figures,[17] but again the 'yield' of urban land remains the subject of bitter dispute between the HBF and the Ministry, with the former accusing authorities such as the City of Manchester of being 'politically motivated' in the slow release of City-owned land for private housebuilding.

The third part of the strategy was developed by *a survey of 66 sites located on the inner edge of the London Green Belt* listed as vacant or under-used in land registers. The HBF concluded that 21 sites were performing 'no useful function whatsoever' and that the Minister should use his powers to *direct* local authorities to dispose of them for development. The study, it claimed, 'provides evidence in support of HBF's call for a review of green belt policies, particularly where housing land is in short supply'. The release of the sites, it was claimed, would not set a precedent.[18]

The fourth set of actions involved proposing *new forms of development*.

Housebuilders have always been particularly keen to free land from constraints in the profitable South East outside London. Although joint HBF/SCLSERP studies in 1981, and a SCLSERP study in 1983,[19] had suggested sufficient land was available for expected new household formation, migration, and the eradication of need, the HBF have mounted a campaign convinced that their case is incontrovertible. The VHSG argued that a shortfall of 60–80,000 housing plots existed outside London for the period 1982–91. Through a subsidiary company, Consortium Developments Ltd., they proposed fifteen sites (some in green belts) where new 'villages' (in reality new towns of 15–17,000 population) should be built. This was linked with the social exclusivity argument:

> To keep expanding existing settlements, you're going to get political outcry because the 'haves' are going to object to the green fields going. It is better to have one big row and solve it by dropping it in an area surrounded by cows, because moos don't vote.[20]

The 1983 Draft Circulars

This sequence of events placed Government on the defensive. Despite a limited propaganda victory for the CPRE over the issue of a rise in the volume of local authority–MAFF consultations over the release of agricultural land,[21] and the publication of *Planning – Friend or Foe?*, a powerful polemic documenting the whittling away of local powers in the face of strong development interests, the green belt case had not been fully articulated.[22] Indeed the production for the first time since 1957, of guidance on the drawing of green belts in development plans in November 1982, evinced little reaction.[23] The advice stressed that the 'broad areas' of green belts already approved in structure plans would only be altered exceptionally. Considerable stress was laid on the need for boundaries to be long-term. In defining green belts in local plans, 'land should not be included within the green belt where it *seems likely*, looking *well beyond* the period of the structure plan, that further land *may* be needed' (Author's emphasis). HBF noted with some pleasure what they interpreted as a more 'flexible' attitude of the Government to green belts in order, they suggested 'to phase land release'.[24] Other consultees, such as the Association of District Councils (ADC), noted the link between this advice and the view that 'phasing will only be justified in exceptional circumstances' later in the same document. This would leave large areas of white land for which no policy advice was given, and thus no secure way of husbanding the release of scarce building land could be devised.[25] This alerted local authority and conservation interests to what the Government had in mind.

The first draft Circulars, issued in August 1983, should be considered together. The *Green Belt* Circular[26] stressed that:

1. where detailed green belt boundaries were being drawn in local plans, local authorities should satisfy themselves that adequate provision is made for long-term development needs, so as to ensure that the boundaries would not need to be altered in the foreseeable future;
2. authorities should specify policies to be adopted on land not required during the plan period but not within the green belt; and
3. authorities should consider omitting green belt notation from 'relatively small detached areas of land among existing development'; if the green belt was to be modified in this way local authorities should consider incorporating other land into the green belt to compensate for the adjustment.

It concluded by stressing the need to draw the inner boundaries of the green belts carefully so as not to include land 'unnecessary to keep open for the purpose of the green belt'. This appeared an invitation to local authorities to set back green belt boundaries stemming from the Minister's admission at the Select Committee in 1984 that he had 'evidence', on coming into office in June 1983, that the planning system had become too restrictive.[27]

The Draft *Land for Housing* Circular took matters further.[28] Without any mention of green belt as a restraint on development it set out to enhance the importance of land availability studies against the approved policies in development plans. In this it accepted most of the arguments that had been put forward by builders over the previous two years. Plans were to provide sufficient new land for housing to meet demand. This would imply that most new housing would be on new land and could even involve new settlements (the Consortium Developments proposal). The idea that planning policies could direct population growth by means of land allocations in any significant way (a central tenet of urban policy including green belts) would need to be reassessed. In this way the point of compromise between private and public interests would be adjusted. Plans should take account of current trends in the market demand for housing, and allow flexibility in the rate at which land was made available subject only to the need to relate provision to new infrastructure. Plans should provide a seven year supply of housing land. To be regarded as available land should be:

1. serviced and have planning permission, or an early prospect of obtaining it;
2. have 'a reasonable prospect of a willing sale for development'; and
3. be capable of taking the range of house types for which there is demand as assessed by housebuilders.

Housebuilders would be able to offer formal views on the timing of alterations to structure plans every two years, and give views on local authorities' priorities in preparing plans. This would have given the industry a status in advance even of nationalized industries in the planning process, and could have resulted in one corporate group having an undue influence over the pace and priorities within the system.

The HBF, clearly feeling the door was open, and that flexible green belts had arrived, sought even greater changes. These would relegate green belt to its desired status – a residual policy. In order to 'strengthen' the Green Belt Circular they suggested sufficient land should be left for a twenty-year programme of building in structure plans before green belt boundaries were drawn; the Minister should call in any plan which did not provide such land.[29] They considered plans should identify a nine year supply of available land, and ways should be found of allowing housebuilding to go ahead in excess of planned rates in structure plans. Detailed proposed amendments would remove any reference to housing needs, obtain a Ministerial statement that there was insufficient land for private housebuilding nationally, and would exclude any land likely to be subject to a Section 52 Agreement from land considered 'available'. In the event of a local plan being found inadequate on the builders' marketing criteria the Minister should call in the plan, direct that new land availability surveys be carried out, use Special Development Orders to bypass the local authority system altogether, or grant permissions on appeal.[30]

The Public Reaction

The first Green Belt Draft, and the accompanying press release, were interpreted as an intention to set back green belts. Indeed the tone of the accompanying press release, with its stress on the reconsideration of whether certain existing green belt areas should be retained, implied this view even for those in newly-approved local plans.[31] A prescient article by John Carvel in the Guardian, '*How they came to unbuckle Britain's green belt policy*', suggested this would be *the* issue on which 'the planners' would be able to reassert themselves with some prospect of popular support. Conservative party members in the shire counties would 'rise up as one' against any effort to erode green belt boundaries. It concluded 'there are more votes in conserving green fields than in swelling housebuilders' land banks'. Despite the views of a Sunday Times leader, '*Green Belts: A Neat Adjustment*', that the Minister had a stronger case than he had effectively deployed, and that the Circular was a realistic attempt to shift the balance between conservation and development, the initiative moved from central Government.

The CPRE launched a national campaign to seize upon the disquiet being expressed across a wide spectrum of opinion. The issue even united labour and conservative members of the GLC and George Nicholson (Chairman of GLCs Planning Committee) took members on a tour of 'threatened' green belt areas, only to be lambasted by a vitriolic press release from the Minister accusing him of waste of public money.[32] There were five themes within the

CPRE argument. They linked the specific issues of green belt to wider trends. Underlying the draft Circulars, they contended, was a wish by the Government to *circumscribe local control* over new development in a way which 'strikes at the roots' of the planning system. Second, the Circulars were against the *public interest*; they would give undue freedom to the wishes of the development industry against those of the local authorities who were working for the *whole community*. Third, the planning system should not have to conform to the commercial preferences and *marketing tastes* of the building industry. Fourth, the effects of freeing up green fields would be as disturbing for the economies of the *cities* as for the countryside; and finally, such policies would damage public confidence in the *fairness* of the planning system.[33] Setting out to mobilize Conservative back-bench opinion a fringe meeting was held at the Party's Annual Conference in Blackpool, and the Tory back-bench Environment Committee was addressed in the House of Commons in the early autumn. Action packs were sent to the forty-three CPRE branches with sample press releases to exercise the skills of local newspaper sub-editors. A deluge of letters descended on MPs, and individual lobbying of selected members representing green belt areas was also carried out. An essential thrust of the CPRE case was that the two Circulars were *linked*. Their political success was to be that of persuading MPs of the link thus sustaining pressure on the Government for the withdrawal of both.[34]

On 1st November 1983 Julian Critchley MP, in whose constituency two of the new towns of Consortium Developments were proposed, put down an Early Day Motion (drafted with the assistance of CPRE) calling on the Government to withdraw both Circulars. Within four weeks nearly a hundred MPs, including ten Social Democrat, Liberal and Labour Members, had signed. Despite attempts to backtrack by the Minister, who later claimed that no change in green belt policies was implied, and that some groups had deliberately misinterpreted Government intentions, suspicions remained high.[35] If no change was intended, suggested MPs, why was there a necessity to produce new advice in the first place? Questions in Parliament asked the Minister to declare which sites or areas of green belt were being contemplated for building, and to assert that approved structure plans would be respected in decisions on planning applications. The opposition Environment Spokesman declared, 'A great many people on both sides of the House feel there are some things which are more important than mere speculators' profits.' The Minister had narrowed down his intentions by this stage:

> . . . there is no suggestion that this Circular is proposing anything other than the most modest changes for particular difficulties that have arisen in the past and where we have to make sense of green belt policy.[36]

The decisive point came at the end of November. An adjournment debate in the House of Commons, opened by Roger Sims (Member for Chislehurst, Kent), sought answers to the many questions posed. Suspicion was the dominant theme, the MP stating, 'I have no reason to doubt the genuineness of his (the Secretary of States') assurances, but many people are very suspicious . . . and I want to establish beyond doubt what is the Government's policy on the green belt'.[37] The carefully phrased Government reply stressed 'the proper use' of green belt, and the idea that in defining boundaries in local plans authorities must consider them over a longer time-scale than contained in approved structure plans. The new advice was needed because of the large number of local plans containing green belts which were being prepared. The statement concluded 'As a result of the views that I have received, changes will be made'.[38]

On 21 November CPRE held a press conference at which five organizations (the ACC, ADC, AMA, NFU, and Civic Trust) joined with CPRE to condemn the Circulars. Most were also there for other reasons in addition to the main green belt argument; (the AMA because of their proposed abolition, and the ADC and ACC because of concern over loss of local autonomy and the emerging rate capping controversy). The Circulars, they argued, were part of the general attack on local democracy. Despite strenuous attempts by Conservative Central Office staff to reassure MPs that no problem existed, the bulging constituency postbags belied this view. The volume of questions in the House, the political capital being made by opposition parties, an incipient back-bench revolt, and united local authority opposition, caused the Government to state on 23 November that a revised Circular would be issued. The *Land for Housing* Circular was withdrawn one week later (see Table 10.1).[39]

Table 10.1 Drafting Circular 14/84: Timetable of Significant Events

Date	Event
3 August 1983	First Draft Circulars on Green Belt and Land for Housing issued.
1 November 1983	Early-Day Motion put down by Julian Critchley MP.
18 November 1983	House of Commons Adjournment Debate on Green Belt.
23 November 1983	First Draft of Green Belt Circular withdrawn for revision.
2 December 1983	Land for Housing Circular withdrawn.
9 February 1984	Second Draft Circulars on Green Belt and Land for Housing issued.
15 February–28 March 1984	Oral evidence taken by House of Commons Select Committee.
20 June 1984	Select Committee Report published.
4 July 1984	Final Circulars issued.

The 1984 Draft Circulars

Before revised Circulars could be issued, the House of Commons Environment Select Committee announced its intention to take, as its first topic for the 1983–4 session, the issues of Green Belt and Land for Housing. They set out specifically to investigate the content of advice in the Circulars and to suggest to Ministers how it might be revised to create a better balance between housing land requirements and the green belt.[40] For the first time since its inception, therefore, the initiative for advice on green belts shifted briefly from the administrative to the legislative arm of Government. Those responsible for the writing of the Circulars would be closely cross-questioned by a small Committee of 11 MPs drawn from the three main political parties.

In order to clarify the situation, and to re-draw the ground rules of the debate, the Ministry put out revised draft Circulars on green belts and land for housing five days before the first public meeting of the Select Committee. The 1984 Draft Circular on Green Belts was a partial retraction and clarification of the 1983 Draft.[41] It made clear that green belts, once approved as part of a structure plan, would only be altered in 'exceptional circumstances', and that green belt boundaries defined in adopted local plans would be 'altered only exceptionally'. It also asserted that green belts, if effectively maintained, would assist in the process of inner city renewal and the bringing back into use of areas of derelict and degraded land. In a new departure the Circular also stressed the need to develop and maintain a positive approach to land use management in run-down areas of green belt.

In December 1983 the Minister had accepted that over the country as a whole there was no immediate shortage of housebuilding land available for development[42] and the 1984 Land for Housing Draft Circular reflected this.[43] Land availability was redefined as a five year supply at structure plan rates, and emphasis was placed on any consideration of 'new settlements' (the Consortium Development proposals) only in the context of comprehensive plans. However the Circular still stressed the requirement to provide sufficient land for the *demand* for housing and it was this particular concept which the majority of local authority consultees saw as irreconcilable with green belt policy. In seeking views on the new draft, the Secretary of State suggested of consultees:

> We need their views on this broad issue . . . (whether . . . the new versions reflect a sensible and practical approach to the needs of development and the interests of conservation) . . . rather than a further round of detailed textual amendments. It is impossible to find precise words which will satisfy everyone's particular interest.[44]

The need to create some common ground, even at the risk of vagueness or contradiction, had come to dominate almost anything else. This was curious not least because the quasi-judicial forum of the planning appeal inquiry pays most careful attention to the precise form of words in Circulars, and the consultees knew it. Also, if the Minister could not produce a set of words satisfactory to all parties, what likelihood was there of local authorities being able to successfully balance such interests at local level?

Alarmed and annoyed by the successful linkage of the green belt and land for housing issues by opponents of the Circulars, the tactics of the HBF were clear. They involved avoidance of a direct clash over the issue and principles of green belt. These were seen as too politically sensitive. General expressions of support for the proper use of green belt, (that is long-term belts well set back from urban areas to allow peripheral building to proceed), were to be complemented initially by two tactics. The first, the result of hurried production of the third report of JLRC,[45] was to suggest that less than one per cent of the *total* land (not of agricultural land) in England and Wales need be taken for housing development to the turn of the century to make Britain the best housed nation in Europe. The second was to utilize the Select Committee hearings to convince Government of the problems of speedily bringing forward marketable supplies of land in large cities.

The Select Committee

The Committee took evidence over 12 days. The urban land issue dominated HBF evidence where out of the total 20 pages, less than one is devoted specifically to green belts, much of this reiterating the charge of misuse of the concept by Greater Manchester and other Councils.[46] If it could be established that the potential of the cities to provide recycled land was very limited, especially in the Greater London Council area, then further approaches could be made to the Minister armed with the results of the House of Commons inquiry to alter presumptions again in favour of development in future Circulars.

The CPRE evidence stressed the need to secure the character and variety of England's countryside for future generations to enjoy. It stressed the legitimacy of the green belt instrument put in place in the 'compelling public interest' of restraining development pressures.[47] It challenged the HBF assertion that the green belt concept had been misused in local plans, and it argued (as did the RTPI) that the prime importance of green belt was its location and not the condition of land within it. On housing the CPRE disagreed, as did most other witnesses, with the view that providing land 'to meet market demand' could be reconciled with the traditionally wider remit of planning authorities of providing for the housing needs of the population as a whole. Pointing out the narrowness of the green belt-housing land debate conducted by the HBF they stressed the importance of a wider view including consideration of problems of repair, renewal, and management of the existing housing stock in cities.[48]

The recommendations of the Environment Committee in June 1984 represented a strong reassertion of green belt philosophy.[49] Green belts once defined should be *sacrosanct*. Pressures for new development, it was argued, could *only* be controlled or redirected effectively by the constraints imposed by green belts. Green belts should protect rural land by promoting the efficient use of land within urban areas. The 1984 Circular should be revised to make clear that green belts have a broad and positive planning role to 'better shape urban areas, particularly on a regional scale'.

Reviewing the purposes of green belt set out in Circular 42/55 they found the separating and character preservation functions easy to support. But there was more difficulty in deciding at what point further physical expansion of an urban area should be constrained. They concluded that urban growth became urban sprawl when a town is 'over-stretched' and development on peripheral sites is creating inefficient use of urban land. Large amounts of derelict urban land would be a symptom of over-stretching. Reflecting the need to make efficient use of this land (and what had already happened around the country – see Chapter 3) the Committee recommended a fourth objective, that of assisting urban regeneration, should be added to the Circular.

The issue of green belt *longevity* clearly caused problems. The Committee agreed with all witnesses who had expressed a view that green belt was not permanent or immutable, but that developers should be placed in the clear presumptive position that a green belt, once defined, could not be challenged in the foreseeable future. They considered the phrase, much admired by consultees, that 'the essential characteristic of green belts is their permanence and their protection should be long-term' in the Draft Circular, to be self-contradictory. (In practice this means that the *idea* of having a green belt in a particular area is considered by the Ministry to be permanent, but the *detailed boundaries* can alter if justified by changing circumstances). They recommended that green belts should create a presumption which is indefinite; the words 'as far as can be seen ahead' should define the longevity of green belts.

The Committee appeared to endorse the Ministry definition of long-term. In order to make green belts defensible local authorities should ensure that their boundaries do not need to be altered at the end of the structure plan period. This may imply that peripheral white land is indicated in plans, but this would depend on the amount of developable land available in urban areas. White land would be 'land left for possible development in the indeterminate future'. It was recommended that in drawing boundaries no account should be taken of the *condition* of land and, once fixed, boundaries should not be moved to release land which had become derelict. Strong support was given to the protection of separate pockets of green belt land, particularly where they performed the function of separating district communities. Taking pieces of derelict land from along a 'thin green pencil' of land separating urban areas would also 'wreck the function' of the green belt. Where land in green belts was in 'pocket handkerchiefs' its function should be *least likely* to be reviewed. This should be made clear in the Circular. The Committee also recommended greater emphasis on countryside enhancement in green belts; the concept of countryside management should be built into the Circular, and 'Groundwork-type' initiatives (see Chapter 9) should be promoted in all green belts with additional public funds, if this would generate private and voluntary sector funds and resources.

The housing recommendations were less full and provided scant support for the HBF case. Although the Committee stated, 'the planning system has to attempt to reconcile the two sides . . . (demand for housing and conservation) . . . by protecting agricultural land, controlling urban sprawl, yet bringing forward sufficient land to match demand', it made no pronouncements on what the total demand to be satisfied should be. Further it recorded that Government, housebuilders and others accepted that *demand*, interpreted as 'where housebuilders are prepared to live' in the 1984 Draft Circular, *was subject to green belt policy and other constraints*. Crucially they failed to pronounce on the central thrust of the HBF case, the amount and proportion of land which was likely to become available in urban areas, stating it was a balance to be struck county by county, and decided at local level.

The Final Circulars

Following the recommendations of the Select Committee in June 1984 Ministry officials moved speedily to publish, in less than ten working days, the final Circulars. This was to avoid any re-opening of the debate, and to forestall further controversy. In a *Memorandum* sent to the Select Committee, the Ministry listed the amendments made to the second Draft Circular as a result of the Committees' recommendations.[50] The amendments accepted were largely inconsequential. Urban regeneration was added as an objective of green belt, reflecting existing practice, but there was no change as a result to the criteria for drawing boundaries. A positive statement that where land has been allowed to become derelict this would not constitute a reason for removing land from the green belt only formalized the position in case law emerging from appeals and PLIs. However if the normal Ministry definition of derelict land only is taken this will not extend the presumption to land which the lay-person most often considers as derelict, that is most of the degraded and neglected land found in green belts.

Of more significance were the recommendations *not taken up*. No mention was made of the shaping or regional roles of the green belt; and no reference was included to the need to maintain small pockets of green belt land *within* conurbations where they separate district communities. Also the view that where countryside enhancement measures are required their existence would be material factors in development control, (presumably leading to some minor relaxations), was not included.

Of greater significance was the selection by the Ministry, from the forty-seven paragraphs discussing housing land, of comments (which did not reach the status of a recommendation) related to phasing. The Committee found that phasing 'is a means by which planning authorities attempt to control or direct the development market'. Despite almost universal support for phasing among those giving evidence the Minister suggested 'If the land is suitable for immediate development, we do not think it should be withheld simply because of some arbitrary rationing process'. Agreeing with the Minister the Committee suggested 'phasing is *not* an end in itself, and local authorities should be more responsive to market demand'.[51] Seizing upon this the Ministry amended the *Land for Housing* Circular to this effect before publication.

Thus Ministers have *incorporated* a number of words from the Select Committee's recommendations into the new Circular but with no resulting alteration to the essence of the 1984 Draft. As with the earlier Abercrombie and Sandys prescriptions, and this time prompted by Ministers, officials have moved to selectively 'accept' the recommendations. On the whole significant elaborations to the concept with a meaning for urban planning have been avoided. The main effect has been to remove the specific suggestion that approved green belt might not be retained in certain circumstances and the phrase referring to 'modification' of the green belt in the first Draft Circular. New statements relating to making full use of land in urban areas, and to countryside enhancement, alter little. The obvious conflict at local level between allocating enough land for market demand for housing, and the need for long-term green belts, has not been faced.

Concluding Remarks

The Recommendations of the Select Committee represented a reassertion of the Conservative party back-bench interest in retaining approved green belts. The wider importance of the recommendations is thus in the *support they give to the activity of town and country planning*. The stress on the regional and urban regeneration roles of green belts will, in the longer term, be difficult for the Government to shrug off. The stress on the *positive* aspects of the policy has provided a counterbalance to the housebuilding (and other development) lobbies who have consistently failed to credit public intervention with anything more than a strictly preservationist ethic.

The Government can perhaps be charged with insensitivity and lack of foresight in putting out the 1983 Circulars. Previous Administrations had resisted issuing new guidance for twenty-six years and in retrospect they were proved wise. Although the first Draft Circular on green belts only stated what was already going on around the country, (for example, the reassessment of small detached areas of green belt and the selective rolling back of interim green belt boundaries), the formalization of these notions in a Circular alarmed those who (erroneously) see the green belt as a fixed physical concept. The alternative view would suggest that the Government was trapped by its own honesty, and its belief in the efficacy of using large numbers of Circulars to alter the parameters of the system at local level. During 1983–4 more draft Circulars suggesting alterations to major aspects of the planning system were circulating than at any time in the working lives of most planners in practice.

In many senses therefore the *status quo* over green belts has been maintained. The 1984 Circulars *reflect* current planning practice rather than signalling a change to what is going on around the country. The Ministry had spent the 1982–4 period objecting to a series of green belt boundaries drawn in local plans on the basis that they did not allow for the long-term development needs of urban areas.[52] Because most of the inner belt boundaries around towns, with the exception of those in the London Green Belt, had never been fixed in plans, what is going on in the 1980s is the logical consequence of the process interrupted in 1962 (see page 30). To this extent Government advice has been consistent through time and the Select Committee's recommendations do not signal alteration of the methods for drawing green belt boundaries.

By contrast the CPRE claim to have 'won' the 1984 argument. Its press release announcing the 'victory' seizes on the idea of sacrosanct green belts.[53] Although it has conducted an impressive one-off campaign, for which those who seek a counterbalance within the conservation–development argument should be grateful, its difficulty will be to retain the impetus of its campaign with small resources. Despite good contacts in Parliament, and an improving ability to project issues, it remains an outsider organization. No member of CPRE has been seconded as a Special Advisor to a Minister in recent years, if ever. Yet one of the leading members of the HBF acted as special advisor to Michael Heseltine, then Minister responsible for planning, in the months prior to the issue of the 1980 Circular on housing land. This, and the constant rhythm of meetings between the HBF, Ministers, and officials, suggests the different status accorded to production as opposed to consumption interests in Government policy-making.

In tactical terms, the main error of the HBF was to attack the green belt concept head on in the 1982–3 period. The symbols evoked, that green belts were an expression of the antipathy of the 'haves' for the 'have nots', that they were 'extinction by conservation' and linkage of the debate with their own interests in the marginal activity of new housebuilding (marginal in terms of national custodianship of the *total* of our housing stock), evoked little sympathy among Conservative back-benchers or in other parties. The strong suggestion of behind-closed-doors collusion between Ministers and such groups as Consortium Developments mentioned by Mercer,[54] helped to alert and concert opposition.

Although the builders may not like it, green belt has wide public and party-political support. It symbolizes deeply held cultural views: *manageability*, the idea that despite social and economic tensions created by the pace of de-industrialisation, land and property issues can be balanced through a publicly-accountable system of decision making for the general public good. Secondly, there is the idea of *protection of the countryside*, part of a strong environmentalist ideology which has grown in strength in the 1970s, and is argued by some to be a significant vote winner. Thirdly, the idea of *continuity*, that there are ways of handing on a 'civilised' heritage of town and countryside to future generations. Finally, the idea of *fairness*, that one sectoral group should not achieve a level of influence out of all balance with other interests in the formulation of planning policy. Many of these attributes, some almost mystical, were 'captured' in the CPRE case.

The HBF continues, as do all good lobbies, undaunted by such reversals. The bland side of the approach, put by the Chairman of Consortium Developments in an interview with CPRE in 1984, suggests:

> . . . If the CPRE would accept there is a need for increased release of green field sites until the end of the century, and worked with housebuilders to ensure that all the new houses went in places that did least harm to the environment, then together I think we could form an extremely powerful lobby.[55]

The 'reasonable' middle-of-the-road strategy is to attempt to separate green belt from more general housing and land use policy considerations. This involves building the argument that green belt is an out-of-date concept suited only for relegation to the dusty bookshelves along with Abercrombie's plans. The green belt issue, in this scenario, has been 'exaggerated out of all proportion'; 'this exaggeration has been particularly irritating and unhelpful to any sensible debate about land use planning'.[56] The green belt debate, it is argued, has involved the misuse of a planning instrument which has a specific and defined purpose as a paradigm for a wider and often politically-motivated opposition to development; 'green belt is extended and defended as an end in itself and is not related to broader questions.'

The hard-line rhetoric threatens concerted attack on conservationists. Pursuing the argument that *the* problem of private housebuilding is a shortage of land (despite evidence of slackening demand consequent upon economic recession, a reducing rate of new household formation, and the near saturation levels of private home ownership) the call to builders by mid-1984[57] was to raise a £0.5 million fighting fund to confront the self-interested opposition:

> If we get into a war we have got a lot more financial muscle than the CPRE . . . if we put our considerable resources behind publicity and media campaigns, we could be a lot more effective than perhaps you think . . .' 'The Environment Secretary has been blackmailed by a minority of Shire County MPs . . . He's just accepted the easy way out. The rate capping and met. counties (*sic.*) will go through and then he'll be compelled to take them on – unless he's prepared to abandon the Government's housing policies . . . so it's only a postponement.[58]

What the 1983–4 period has taught Ministers is that if further adjustments are to be made, it would be unwise to use the method of issuing a new green belt circular.

11. What Future for the Green Belt?

The green belt should be regarded as part of the urban and regional structure of the area, evolving with this and not dictating it.

Chairman of EIP into West Midlands
Structure Plan Alterations, 1983

With the approval in 1985 of the last Structure Plan in England and Wales the *broad areas* of green belt will have been formally approved around all of the major conurbations for the first time (see Figure 11.1).[1] Although this appears to have reaffirmed the basic pattern of urban development for the long-term over 80 per cent of the local plans, which are intended to define the new boundaries in detail, have yet to be completed. Green belts, an apparently simple and uniform concept, have been deployed in a wide variety of situations, and their current forms and status are the product of a variety of central and local influences. Superficially they are similar, but on close investigation each is tailored to local circumstances. As an instrument to achieve the wider policy ends of local authorities their most important functions have been:

1. to manage urban fringe land release;
2. to assist in structuring the complex pattern of central–local relations; and
3. to help in structuring relationships between local authorities, development interests, and the wider public

The implementation of containment using green belts is also believed to have a number of effects, or outcomes. The balance sheet cannot be precisely weighed but the benefits of contained development include economy in the provision of new development, the retention of agricultural land and attractive countryside, and conservation of the character and separate identity of many towns and villages. These outcomes *may* have been bought at the cost of larger and more expensive daily commuting, some increase in land and house prices, and increased social segregation within regions due to the selective nature of outwards migration.

Following the recommendations of the House of Commons Environment

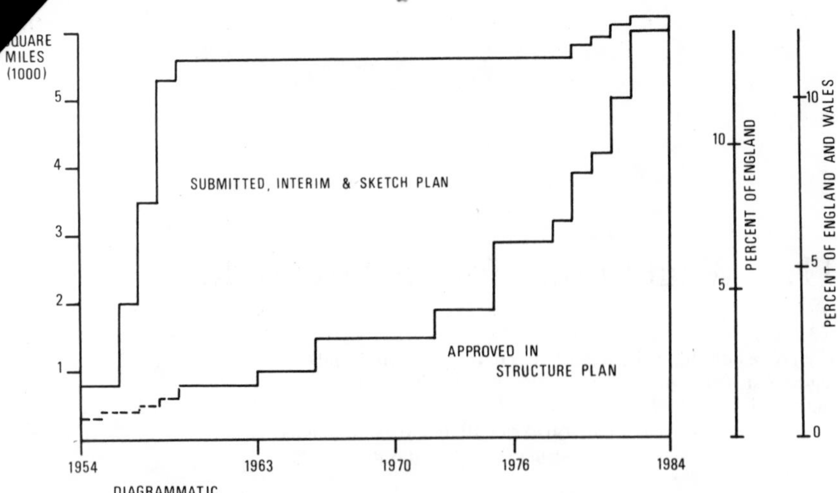

Figure 11.1 Area of Approved and Interim Green Belts 1954–84

Select Committee in May 1984,[2] the Government moved speedily to publish Circular 14/84.[3] Ministers and officials, chastened by the experience of producing the Circular, are unlikely to alter the advice again in the foreseeable future. However, as a *product* of economic, social, and administrative processes green belts will continue to be challenged by corporate groups such as housebuilders, employers' organizations and, in controversies over individual projects, by other arms of Government such as the Department of Industry and the DHSS. Changes to the established pattern of central–local relations, such as the introduction of rate capping and the abolition of the Metropolitan Counties, will also have short and long-term repercussions. In the longer-term changes in economic prosperity, the ability of local labour markets to adjust to new technology, and the acceptance of new attitudes to work and leisure, will be important. The probability of continued high unemployment appears likely to be matched by a higher and more fully-articulated environmental consciousness from those in work.[4] Is the green belt instrument suited to these other challenges that lie ahead?

Green Belts in Operation

Green belt was conceived as part of a consensus package of post-war measures to physically rearrange the pattern of town and country. It was however never used in quite this way. Ministry officials from 1955 tailored the concept to fit the administrative and quasi-judicial roles of central Government. Green belt has survived because it 'delivers' decisions, a major preoccupation of central Government. Local authorities are not merely *agents* of central Government in planning matters otherwise there would be no variation in the application of green belt policies across the country.[5] They are however increasingly unequal partners in a relationship where the centre is prepared to actively use its discretion to alter policies through the use of reserve powers.

The interests of the centre and the locality are, by definition, different. Central Government seeks policy *clarity* so that decisions can refer to unambiguous criteria, and to ensure that landowners in different green belts are treated consistently. These attributes assist in assuring that policy can continue to be *administered* in as trouble-free a manner as possible. Local authorities are, naturally, keen that they should retain *control* over major policy-decisions of importance to their areas. This is best done from a position of strength in the bargaining which goes on. They may also wish to retain discretion to make decisions which act counter to established policies. Thus both the centre and the locality are seeking to balance commitment and flexibility, each wishing to maximize its own flexibility and the other's commitment. It is therefore not surprising that central–local relations are complex and, at times, ambiguous.[6] The inclusion of a green belt policy in a development plan places severe limits on the future discretion of both local and central Government. Its stark, clear-cut nature narrows and makes more manageable the debate over which land should be developed and which retained in its present use. Each side knows that the other will only depart from its presumptions in exceptional circumstances, and that the arrangement is intended to be long-term.

The history of the green belt also demonstrates *a strong continuity in the form of central–local relationships*. Since the early 1950s Governments have been closely concerned with the detail of green belts. An unforeseen consequence of two-tier local government was the break-up of the hegemony of county councils, with a potential loss of power by the centre to influence local decisions. The outcome of interest mediation at local level (local planning) has been green belt boundaries which were more restrictive than *all* post-war Governments would have liked. Governments have used a wide variety of tactics to adjust the ground rules for green belts, including sponsoring one-off departures in 1963 and 1973, and more recently altering definitions of land availability. These culminated in a formal attempt to alter the advice by Circular in 1983. The 1963 and 1973 exercises were ineffective in achieving their immediate intentions because of resistance to the idea at local level. Most of the land in the '2000 acres' exercise of 1973–4 remained undeveloped by 1979 partly due to the scope for delay exercised by local authorities – a good example of local discretion in action. In the 1980s the methods used have included use of the results of joint-land availability studies as material considerations in development control and insistence that local authorities provide for demand in their areas. Advice from Government avoids detailed guidelines on how resulting conflicts with green belt are to be resolved. If local disputes arise because pre-existing green belt boundaries have been reached, central Government can then intervene to set them back or arrive at some other solution. Moving slowly to approve boundaries in local plans, or finding other ways to keep the local situation fluid, can be seen as among the only manoeuvres open to local authorities to protect their interests when under the severest development pressure. Suggestions that further clarity be introduced to 'solve' such problems are perhaps naive as 'clarity' would reduce the power of central Government to influence local events.[7]

This analysis suggests 'the green belt' has not only never been fixed but is never likely to be. The green belt concordat is, by definition, not fully binding. The principle of taking each application 'on its merits' still pertains, and in formal terms decisions need only *take account* of the provisions in development plans. The need to respond to changing priorities in the future is written into all circulars, and Circular 14/84 is no exception. Permanence is an intention of the policy, but only as far as can be seen ahead. A green belt is long-term, and although this represents a period longer than that of a structure or local plan, has no specified time limit. This allows central–local discussions to be reopened at any time in what may be judged 'changed circumstances', with central Government being the arbiter of what changed circumstances are. It also avoids the problem of running up against fully-approved green belt boundaries, by definition, in the foreseeable future. This makes green belt a very desirable policy as its implications never have to be worked through in the tenure of any one Parliament or Minister.

Does the green belt concept therefore imply urban areas have, at some stage, an appropriate limit to their physical spread?[8] Over time a gradually increasing number of settlements embedded in green belts will reach their long-term limits of development. Taken literally it is difficult to see how the optimum size of a town could be arrived at, and economists suggest there is no such thing.[9] In any case such an argument would need an assessment of the efficiency of the working of urban areas of various sizes and not, as suggested by the Ministry evidence to the Select Committee, a concern for really good physical boundaries.[10] The situation has not been reached where all towns in a district have reached their long-term limits of development as defined in new local plans. Government interventions have, over a 25-year period, ensured this does not happen. Even should this occur, say in the London Green Belt, leeway exists in the *Land for Housing* Circular to allow for housing demand to be assessed for more than one district together.[11] Where districts do not voluntarily pursue this course, (which would involve a district not fully covered by green belt accepting part of the housing demands of another), structure plans could be altered to make this happen. It is more realistic to suggest that the green belt marks *a* long-term boundary to development, (as stated in Circular 50/57), not *the* long-term boundary as some of the Select Committee discussion implied.

All of these factors, inherent in the planning system, suggest that green *belt has acted as a land release device*, and will continue to do so. Measures such as interim and provisional green belt have performed this function outwith the 1959 London Green Belt Ring for many years. There seems no likelihood of change. The price paid for the sophistry contained in Government advice is perhaps twofold. The general public believe the green belt is fixed, as do articulate local residents and pressure groups. This is reflected in virtually all national press coverage of the issue. The concept is used in attempts to maintain a locally politically desired size to a town, (starting from a position of retaining its existing size), and to minimize external pressures. When boundaries are changed, even those of interim green belts, local residents lose confidence in the land use planning system. As green belts can only in the long-run survive through broadly-expressed public support this situation carries with it the clearest dangers to the continued use of the concept. It could thus be argued that the concept suits central Government *because* it has not been tested to its logical conclusion, and local authorities because it is widely misunderstood by local people.

The local policy-making and development control process offers a forum in which the interests of private developers can be adjusted through negotiation to some wider view of the community interest. It is a mistake to imply, following Humber, that local authorities are pursuing conurbation-wide physical prescriptions to the exclusion of all other concerns.[12] Authorities are making incremental decisions in an attempt to lessen the impact of specific proposals on local environments and ratepayers' pockets. After all, as local interests suggest, what kind of a 'deal' is it which would fill the local view with houses, increase the local rates, and produce new pressures for schools and other services? The Housebuilders accuse others of self-interest whilst seeking to conceal their own. The positive role for planners in such situations is to reach accommodations which have an element of local community benefit in physical, financial, and socio-economic terms.

Developers do not relish lack of guidance over the location of new development. Housebuilders' organizations would like green belts set back to give leeway to purchase developable land, at times of their choice, in attractive settings.[13] Individual builders already possessing land in such locations would like the green belt tight to keep out competition. (This is why a corporate group such as the HBF do not challenge the allocation of individual sites in local plans but keep to wider issues of the scale and rate of development.) The green belt prescription which now emphasizes 'containing' and 'shaping' development, and not the first aim in Circular 42/55 of 'checking' urban sprawl,[14] provides a formula which has proved a very useful *mediation device* between housebuilders' views and local desires for almost total restriction.

As a crude form of basic management of investment, green belts have positive functions in limiting the geographical extent of intense land speculation, thus reducing the number of abortive planning applications, and keeping down costs by reducing the need for more planners and planning inspectors. An element of restriction also appears to enhance the level of appreciation in the value of land on development which benefits those companies who own developable land in restraint areas. Such restriction creates conflict *between* housebuilders with the rapidly-expanding volume builders seeking a stronger position in green belt zones.[15] Thus their recourse to planning, to ease constraints and lessen the internal conflicts which constantly threaten to fragment their lobbying efforts. The discretionary nature of planning however acts to retain some land speculation and makes it difficult for a large number of one-off relaxations of the policy to occur without creating confused market conditions. The prescription of green belts as 'long-term' is the loophole which housebuilders can exploit, and it is no surprise that they should have pressed to see a figure of fifteen years included in the earliest versions of the Draft Circular of 1983.

It should be stressed that the planning system *responds* to structural processes determined outwith green belt localities. Its main attribute is to facilitate development; indeed the technical procedures written into the production of plans dictate this. By helping to structure central–local and other inter-group negotiations, green belts *reduce* the level of futile discussion but keep the main actors engaged and involved. It is not the name that matters, it is the strength of the presumption, and the policy control it affords, which are important.[16]

Some Effects

It follows from this explanation of green belts in use that planning authorities are using the green belt increasingly in an *ad hoc* instrumental way. Emphasis has shifted to its role in conflict mediation at local level. As a result any wider assessment of social and economic effects has barely figured in debates and decision-making, which is by nature highly-localized and specific in nature. The outcomes of green belt policy are difficult to isolate from those of other land use policies, and wider economic factors such as changes in Government fiscal policy, and the structure of economic activities.[17] Any discussion is further complicated by the realization, from the studies in this volume, that green belts have been drawn in different ways around each major conurbation. Most assertions about the effects of green belt policy are simplified overstatements of a complex reality, usually made in the context of special pleading by a sectoral interest.[18] What, however, may be listed as likely outcomes of green belt policy?

1. *Green belts have 'managed' the process of decentralization into specific physical forms*

This appears a plausible outcome given the extensive evidence which suggests that, *once formally approved*, the rate of attrition of open land in designated green belts can be reduced below 0.1 per cent by area per annum. Green belt controls have avoided the worst excesses of scattered development by restricting growth to contained additions to existing towns and villages. The renegotiation of green belts has selectively set back boundaries (many not formally approved) to allow this to happen. What green belts have not done is greatly affect the pace and rate of decentralization. Local authorities have *sought to use* green belt as a way of slowing the pace of decentralization to a level generally acceptable to the populations of receiving areas. Whenever such an outcome appeared likely, however, Governments have intervened to keep up supplies of developable land.

Decentralization policies in the 1960s and early 1970s assumed that deflection of economic activities and housing could be achieved over relatively long distances. Since the mid-1970s there is little evidence that this has occurred, even in the South East. The rate of development in the London Green Belt Ring has continued to keep pace with other parts of the Region. The Green Belt Ring now has a population of 1.75 million, some 1.3 million greater than in 1939.[19] The marked reduction in the pace of decentralization since 1970 is attributable to lower population increases, the large decline in manufacturing employment, and lower levels of investment nationally. Indeed, the effective removal of policies to phase development suggests that 'management' of decentralization may be too grandiose a term to describe any effect of green belts in this context. The historically low level of dispersed decentralization that characterizes the 1980s has been *shaped* in local areas into contained settlements by the policy. The green belt may merely have assisted in giving the comforting appearance of managing decentralization.

2. *Green belts have contained patterns of new development in the interests of economy and access to existing services*

This assertion has not been tested, not least because neither of the alternatives (urban sprawl, linear patterns of development, or new settlements) have been fully costed either. Apart from work in the 1970s by Stone and the South East Joint Planning Team little is known about whether peripheral development is cheaper than other *forms* of development.[20] If cost is taken in the narrow sense of incrementally-borne public sector expenditure it appears that in situations of relatively small-scale change which now dominate planning decisions, peripheral development is most cost-effective. Good access to services may be best achieved at the urban periphery, particularly as most conurbations already have motorway routes through green belts.

In practice containment effected by peripheral additions to urban areas is seen by local authorities as an economic imperative if development, particularly for housing, is to proceed. In many areas a prime determinant of planning is to arrange new development so that slack in existing services is taken up, and no new facilities (for example schools) need be provided.

Local authorities lose money as a result of Rate Support Grant adjustments if they accept large-scale housing development, as evidence by Wokingham District to the House of Commons Environment Committee has shown.[21]

3. *Green belts have maintained separation between towns, thus retaining their much-valued individual identities*

This is an important, though unquantifiable, effect of green belts rivalling the comforting image wherein large swathes of green ink on maps imply that local authorities are managing the development process. Physical separation, and links between this and local community identity, are strong local urges. In economic terms there are penalties to coalescence in higher road building costs to relieve congestion, and the disruptive process of remoulding town centres.

Perhaps more important are the *side effects* of retaining separation. For example opposition to the disturbance likely from building any of the London 'Inner Ring' motorways was bypassed by constructing the Capital's orbital route through the gaps jealously maintained by 40 years of Green Belt development control. Thus modernization of the Region's transport system, and the creation of new patterns of land values that could be exploited by development investors, was secured. Although the propaganda of the development industry sees the green belt as an out-of-date concept slowing the process of regional renewal, rather paradoxically it has proved a boon.[22] The M25 Motorway will have four service areas. The English Tourist Board (sensing a development opportunity) want hotels, large coach parks, picnic areas and caravan and camping sites in 'environmentally attractive' locations.[23] British Rail has plans, for the first time since Beeching, to open vast parkway stations in Green Belts at Iver, Buckinghamshire and Hinksey near Oxford.[24] These would link Inter-City trains to the Motorway system in South East England. In drawing the new green belts, significant amounts of land have been left near Ringway Airport, Manchester, at Washington Airport in Tyne and Wear, and along Motorway corridors such as the M62 in South and West Yorkshire. Along the M4 corridor nearly 20,000 high technology jobs have found locations in the last ten years, and there is competition to find tenants for new property from the Winnersh Triangle in Berkshire to Stockley Park in Hillingdon. This hardly represents a rigid denial of industrialists needs. Indeed brief reflection suggests the London and other Green Belts have *helped create* the conditions whereby profitable new investment can take place. By denying development in one era they have acted to boost the capital gains of the present generation of investors and speculators in development.

4. *Green belts have retained valuable agricultural land and other space-extensive uses*

The idea of a clear-cut boundary between town and country suits agriculture. But agricultural land policies are probably equally important in retaining land of good quality. They are an important predeterminant of detailed green belt boundaries, the development control package then being used to keep out (most) small and medium-sized intrusive elements. However road construction and mineral extraction cause severe conflicts as, to a lesser extent, do localized urban boundary problems. No powers exist to retain open land in agricultural use, therefore whilst two thirds of all green belt land is nominally agricultural, not all is effectively farmed. The effects of ownership are as important as urban proximity in this. Green belt controls have done much for mineral producers, keeping land open for aggregate extraction near to major sources of demand. Pressures exerted by the minerals industries have effectively negated any restriction on their activities from the independent effect of green belt controls. In an area such as the South East around London this must have had significant economic benefits, though they are unquantifiable as no knowledge exists of what type of land release policy would have been in place had green belts not been invented.

5. *Green belts have retained accessible land in pleasant surroundings nearer to people in inner cities than would otherwise have been the case.*

Provision of recreation space has not been quantified for all green belts, but around London informal recreation appears well provided for. In the North much progress has been made in opening up new countryside areas near the main cities as part of wider environmental improvement programmes, as Chapter 9 has shown. In the Greater London case, distance and the cost of travel mean that inner city residents rarely use peripheral open spaces, but in areas around Greater Manchester, Tyneside, and Merseyside the relative proximity of Green Belts has led to a wider cross-section of use. Provision for recreation has been limited for many reasons. It is not a mandatory duty on local authorities, it has low financial commitment, responsibilities are fragmented, and there is opposition from local residents, which is articulated through district councils. Successive Governments have failed to accord sufficient priority to recreation provision in green belts.

6. *Green belts can be used to assist urban regeneration*

This assertion has managed to unite two previously opposed forces in support for the policy; shire counties who wish to resist housing pressures; and urban authorities such as the GLC who feel that firmly-held green belt boundaries are a prerequisite to successful urban regeneration.[25] The effectiveness of using green belts for urban regeneration is based on two premises. First, that large areas of land are not available immediately beyond the green belt, or adjacent to towns within it, which will attract economic activity and populations to areas outside city jurisdictions. And second that inner city or other land within built up areas will prove attractive enough to investors deterred adjacent to green belts. Both appear implausible in current economic conditions. The only detailed study addressing this question, that by Clarke for the Green Belt around the National Exhibition Centre in the West Midlands, suggests that most applications refused permission for ostensibly employment-related development were speculative.[26] These would, if built, have drawn more economic activity out of the inner parts of the City.

At the same time as major cities have been keener to retain economic activity, districts within and beyond green belts are taking a more relaxed view of the growth of existing firms and the relocation of new ones. Thus local authorities are in competition *across* green belts to attract investment. While the City of Birmingham for example wishes to develop prime areas of Green Belt next to its boundary it does not wish towns in Warwickshire and Staffordshire to do the same. The City vehemently complains of the 'massive amounts of land' (over 2,000 hectares) which have been made available in the surrounding shire Counties.[27] In seeking land which is 'competitive in quality *and quantity*' with that available elsewhere, they are attempting to cream off an imagined supply of footloose industry which would otherwise obtain sites in the South East outside London. In short the City are *marketing* their Green Belt (Figure 11.2). A bucolic image will be fostered by marketing factories as 'village clusters'. The result will be the attraction of *some* firms using high technology, (and many others not in this category), and further additions to the stock of 40 million square metres of vacant industrial space in the West Midlands Conurbation.

In the South East the same argument is being played out. The Ministry suggest advantage can be taken of the M25 to redress the imbalance between the economic fortunes of the western and eastern sides of the Metropolis.[28] Local self-interest suggests that no district around Heathrow or along the 'western arc' of the M25 will voluntarily forego jobs to benefit the residents of Chatham or the East End of London. Furthermore Government policy ensures this could not occur with assertions to free more land for industry in Circulars.[29] The 1984 monitoring evidence suggests the highest levels of planning permissions for industry in the process of being implemented are 'in a broad arc to the West of London, from West Hertfordshire through Buckinghamshire and Berkshire into North Hampshire', with further 'pockets' in areas such as North Surrey – predominantly the western sector of the London Green Belt.[30] Knight, Frank and Rutley have noted an eight year supply of outstanding office permissions in the north-western sector of the M25 Corridor (sixteen years if 'development proposals' are included) at

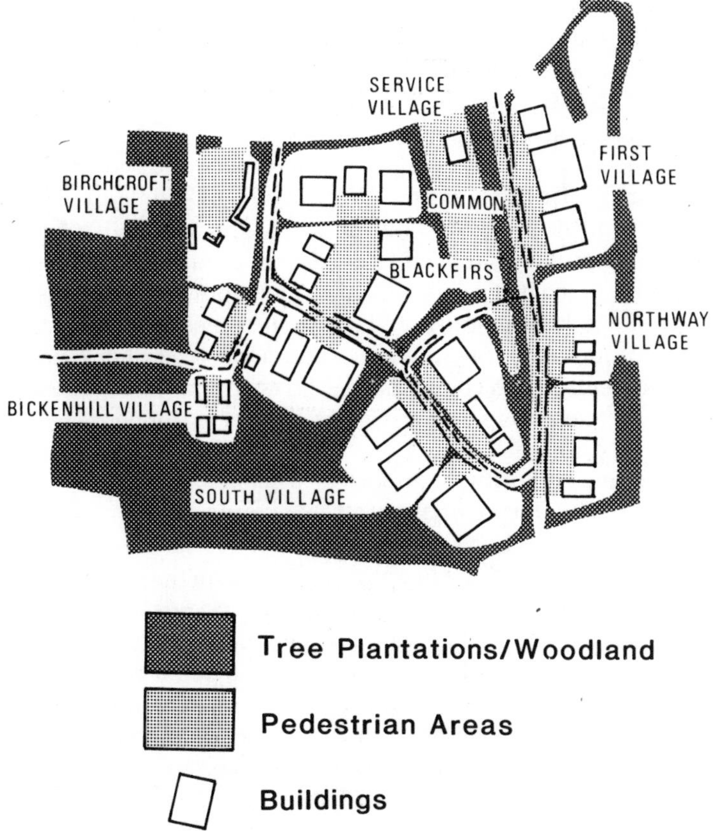

Figure 11.2 A 'High Tech' Country Park in the West Midlands Green Belt?

The image to be sold must come wholly from the site and its immediate area. . . . The key is the sheer scale of the site. This large scale must be exploited in terms of a powerful and prestigious image.

The detailed design concept is thus a Country Park – an extensive area of natural and variable countryside which encompasses the positive images of copses and trees, ponds and streams, hedgerows and wildlife and varying slopes. . . . In this scene industrial buildings will be grouped into 'villages', each with its own name, identity and separate sense of place.

Source: West Midlands County Council *Bickenhill Marston Green Local Plan: Business Park Design Brief* (WMCC: Birmingham, 1984), pp. 14 and 17

1983 rates of take-up. These figures, as they suggest, 'throw a glaring light on the limited effect of planning constraints'.[31]

A decentralized planning system cannot deliver adherence to the guidance about tight green belts in this situation. This makes a clear case for some form of accountable strategic planning. The same thought process resulted in the creation of regional planning by a Conservative administration in 1962 (see page 30). In the absence of a realistic urban policy to make use of unused land and property in cities, land release will continue to represent the softest option to answer critics of the Nation's inability to address structural employment problems. Although indicating that *some* relaxation of green belts *could* ease the problems of firms with little expansion space, the Fothergill and Gudgin study concluded that land use planning policies have been relatively unimportant, one way or another, to the problems of British industry.[32] A study by Middlesex Polytechnic suggests *none* of the 500 firms in a survey in Greater London had experienced planning problems related to expansion needs.[33] Releasing land for employment in green belt zones will redistribute jobs to the detriment of city economies. Land is being released because it is the *easiest lever to pull.* It suggests a concern for local economies but masks the political problem of how Governments are to communicate the news that full employment, as traditionally defined, has gone forever and how then to organize rewards in a post-industrial society.

Local planning authorities in a depressed economic climate will not cling to fixed green belts. Furthermore central Government will not allow them to. Thus suggestions by Lawless that 'partial abandonment' of the green belt would allow industry to locate in optimal positions in the city region,[34] or by Gregory that green belts should *reflect* future lifestyles and preferences,[35] are *already taken account of* in the way green belts are being redrawn. The *process* described in this volume shows that local authorities *have* assessed industrial and housing requirements generously. Where any doubts remain central Government has stepped in to ensure wide choices of site are provided either through altering plans or on appeal. If green belts are becoming tighter this is belied by the facts which show that housebuilders managed to construct more new dwellings in 1983 than at any time in the previous ten years.

Furthermore green belts represent a different balance of existing and 'new' land around each conurbation. In Tyne and Wear 1,400 hectares not required in any envisaged set of development options is neither within the Green Belt or the generous land allocations in plans. As a result planning applications over the period April 1981–April 1982 were submitted on only 90 hectares of land designated as Green Belt. Some 23 hectares of this obtained permission, 10 hectares for mineral development and 11 hectares for various types of residential infill.[36] These data suggest the Tyneside Green Belt is already a residual policy. In Greater Manchester 8,000 hectares exist between land allocations in plans and the inner boundary of the Green Belt. Housing land calculations in Greater Manchester take *no account* of any contribution from 'infill', a figure which may be 30 per cent of all housing land in shire Counties around London, and 80 per cent in some Outer London Boroughs.

It must be concluded that it is unrealistic to talk of a static designation – 'the green belt' – to be 'defended', 'given away' or otherwise. It follows that great care must be taken in making assertions about its effects. Green belts in use (of whatever category) no longer resemble the grand designs of the Abercrombie era. They are far more pragmatically used than that. They have the dual capacity of retaining the confidence of the public as an image (their mystical quality), whilst allowing central Government and the local authorities to continually adapt them to different situations. They are almost always *used* in conjunction with other policies. It appears that green belts have been used in the South East around London, in parts of the West Midlands, and south of Manchester, to *check* sprawl and concentrate development in certain locations. In all of our Conurbations they have acted to retain the separation of settlements. In the Conurbations north of Birmingham they appear to have been used as a *shaping* device with little significant deflection of activity (especially economic activity).

The Future

The period 1984–90 is likely to be taken up with approval of the bulk of detailed green belt boundaries in over 300 local plans. The need to reconcile the large number of interests actively involved will, despite attempts to speed up local planning, result in this process being overtaken by alterations to structure plans. Experience suggests that county-prepared local plans have proved timely and cost effective for defining boundaries at local level and recourse to these, following rapidly upon structure plan reviews, would give greater clarity to the situation for developers and local populations in many areas. The danger for local interests is that if the statutory planning process becomes attenuated by conflict and acrimony ways will be found of circumventing the resultant confusion.

The *Land for Housing* Circular now suggests land availability studies should be carried out every two years, and the persistent campaign to force the hands of districts in land release by the use of non-elected regional land panels, continues.[37] Once boundaries have been defined the process of review should be more speedily accomplished. As *all* approved local plans, (and if not local plans the Green Belt Circular), give scope for the amendment of green belt boundaries, it is likely that in the most pressured areas numerous minor revisions – 'statutory nibbling' – will continue to occur. This will be occasioned by the strength of the economic arguments where employment-related development is involved, as well as the need to provide for the 'demand' for private housebuilding where it arises, which will dictate a more even and dispersed pattern of new development. The influence of corporate power by housebuilders at the centre of decision-making will continue to outweigh any minor 'victories' obtained by the plurality of 'outsider' environmental interests.

A number of other factors will lead to the renegotiation of green belts. The effect of rate capping is forcing many authorities to reappraise existing attitudes to their land and property holdings. Many authorities are taking the opportunity, (some reluctantly, others less so), to realize the development value of such land and to use the proceeds to support public sector housing or other services. The effect of the 1984 *Planning Act* will be to allow health authorities to seek planning permission to enhance the value of land and property assets prior to disposal.[38] Surveys in the property press have already noted these 'weaknesses' in the planning system.[39] As planning is basically reactive, *incorporating* such influences, local plans will in time come to reflect these patterns of land ownership. Chapter 4 demonstrates this effect south of Oxford, but Essex, Hertfordshire, and Buckinghamshire among many have been involved in the sale of surplus educational and other institutional land, some of it in areas indicated as green belt at various stages of the local planning process. Publicly-owned sites are already one of the main sources of new development land within towns embedded in the London Green Belt, allowing scope for greater numbers of jobs and population to be accommodated well into the 1990s.

Other influences external to green belt policy will also be important. The demise of the GLC requires the 10,240 hectares of 1938 Act 'Green Belt Land' in which they have a full or contributing interest, to be re-allocated among the districts or counties in which it is located. Various alternatives canvassed in a Government consultation document, included:

1. transfer of the GLC interest to one authority, the City of London, with a new advisory committee to oversee policy, or
2. the transfer of land outside the GLC boundary as in 1 (above), but with land inside the boundary transferred to the individual boroughs, or
3. the transfer of land inside the GLC boundary to the individual boroughs and that outside to the relevant county if there is a joint interest with that county or to the district if there is a sole GLC interest.[40]

There was almost universal condemnation, apart from in some 'receiving' authorities, of these proposals. A comprehensive view would be lost, long-established land management abilities dissipated, and a strong temptation to dispose of such land for development put in the way of peripheral boroughs.[41] The NFU feared that land management would be impoverished over large areas of the Green Belt and tenants evicted.[42] Certainly the situation is unique, as no organization with the size and skills of even the pre-1966 London County Council appears likely to remain to manage the land. The best alternatives canvassed by consultees included transfer to the National Trust, together with some financial assistance, or the passage of legislation requiring the local authorities to hold the land in trust for the benefit of the people of London. Few had faith in the existing 1938 Act arrangements whereby the original covenants made with owners may be waived by the Minister on application, as has occurred to facilitate development of the M25. Fragmentation under alternative 3 (above) has been chosen.[43]

Apart from *land ownership* issues the abolition of the Metropolitan Counties will fragment the political control of green belts to the detriment of the aims and objectives of effective urban policy. Freed of the mediating and moderating influences of the Counties individual districts will sponsor major incursions into previously approved green belts. The price to be paid in the West Midlands may be six or seven major employment-related land releases with, in the long-run, much of the space unused, undeveloped, or quickly vacated due to demand volatility or lack of demand. Alternatively excursions into fully approved green belt to allocate housing land in non-statutory plans, as instanced by the case of Dudley, may occur more frequently.[44] The only control over this process appears to be provisions for the joint consideration of the new unitary borough plans at EIP. The Ministry may be ineffectual here having a poor track record of meshing proposals across counties in structure plans. (Internal vetting of plans is normally carried out on a county rather than a region-wide subject basis.)

Guidance at higher than district level will be written by civil servants.[45] Although subject to 'comment' by major interests and others, this form of instruction (within which the draft guidelines already suggest primacy should be accorded to housing and industry) is likely to harm the credibility of planning as an accountable process of decision-making. Whilst the problems of unbridled local authority self-interest were not invented in 1983 it is likely that intense and wasteful competition between authorities to 'attract' development will intensify with adverse consequences for agricultural land, access to recreation, and the regeneration of inner cities.

The 'Streamlining' proposals[46] are likely to have many adverse consequences in the area of conflict management in green belt open land, and in environmental improvement. The painfully created pools of expertise in local authorities related to minerals, a necessary response to the strictures of the Verney Report, will be dissipated among districts or the tasks taken over by private consultants. Either solution will make problems of the management of a ready supply of minerals more difficult as SAGA and BACMI have acknowledged in their arguments to Government. Major programmes of *strategic* environmental improvement and recreation provision have been a success story for a number of Metropolitan Counties. Only they appear able to create the necessary impetus, and retain the expertise necessary, to make significant inroads into the massive legacy of dereliction and neglect. Painstakingly negotiated schemes involving complex accommodations between districts, and across the two tiers of local government, are likely to be forfeited by abolition. The same problems of the transfer of land (much of it reclaimed derelict land on the inner edge of green belts) again recur, but in the northern conurbations a lower proportion of the land is good quality farmland and therefore the net maintenance and management costs to the districts are likely to be higher. No details of the financial arrangements to be made on abolition for such matters have yet been released.

Thus whilst a gradual readjustment of green belts to accommodate 'justified' development requirements will continue, actions of the Government in other related spheres of decision-making are likely to have the most profound influences on green belts in the short and medium term. Given the need to draw up new regional guidance and unitary plans, and even taking into account the nugatory level of public participation allowed, experience of introducing new planning systems suggests that the 1986–90 period is likely to be one of great uncertainty in planning for metropolitan areas.

The agricultural interest has benefited considerably over the last forty years from the dual protection of the agricultural land quality presumption *and* green belt policy in plans. Analyses of agriculture at national level suggest that self sufficiency in temperate produce has advanced from under 50 to over 75 per cent in the last 25 years. Rapid productivity increases, aided by generous intervention pricing from the EEC, and a vast input of grants for modernization and rationalization, have led to over-production. Body notes that the surplus of wheat was 5 million tonnes in 1982 and 1983, a figure certainly exceeded in since.[47] Milk quotas were introduced in 1984 and some reduction in support for cereals was introduced in 1985. Cereal quotas may be on the way. Munton has suggested, following an exhaustive farm survey in the *inner* London Green Belt, that 'there is a case for preserving farmland at the urban fringe, albeit not a very strong one'.[48] Despite such hints of changing priorities, and emerging discussions about 'set aside' policies, MAFF continue to adhere to the basic formula for protecting agricultural land established in the Circulars of the early 1950s. In the absence of any innovations from MAFF, the agricultural industry would be well advised to develop new arguments, based on wider and more fully-developed criteria, if it wishes to sustain the strength of its interest in the future.

The problem of the appearance of the green belt (its landscape) is likely to continue to cause heated controversy over the next 5 years. It is the contention of the Countryside Commission that the speed of landscape change is unacceptably high to the general public. Ministers have accepted that new conservation measures must be built into the mechanisms of farm support, and that grants to agricultural production should give more weight to conservation interests. New powers to shift the balance are likely, and a special project team has been set up in MAFF to produce policy innovations. The main debate is likely to be about *modes of action* not the need for action. The most strident voices, such as Friends of the Earth, have followed CPRE in seeking planning controls[49] over landscape features as the most *publicly accountable* way of setting a new balance between landscape conservation and agriculture. Even the Countryside Commission, following their survey of lowland landscape change, have not ruled out some form of planning controls (as they have already advocated in parts of the uplands).[50] The issue is not *whether* the primacy accorded to agriculture will change but *how* it will change. Examples from Denmark of a flourishing agricultural industry *with* planning controls over landscape features, contributed to MAFF 'losing the argument', as Lord Melchett has asserted.[51] Agriculturalists, however, have always responded to financial inducements and it is likely that a package of financial measures to promote conservation will be canvassed as a first alternative. MAFF and the NFU will conduct a very long and well-orchestrated campaign, on the successful 1980–1 model, should any form of planning control be seriously suggested. Without some legislative change area management, as promoted by the Countryside Commission, will remain a cosmetic and partial solution, even in those schemes which survive the demise of the Metropolitan Counties.

Green Belt Survival?

Any assessment of the prospects for survival of green belt will not emerge from accounts of its socio-economic effects. A more fruitful investigation would weigh those real interests in society that support it, and those opposed, and attempt to predict their influence on Governments in the future. In this hazardous exercise two trends are perhaps discernible. The first is the rapid growth in the number of organized and active interest groups, from those representing major sectors of production down to the smallest green belt village. The second is the impact of recession. As each production sector – housing, minerals, retailing – has come under pressure so it has resorted to energetic lobbying of central Government to change the planning system in its favour. Significant headway has been made by housing and mineral interests, with a move towards a corporate style of decision-making. Given the dispersal of planning powers around many hundreds of districts, such interests do not have the resources to challenge planning policies locally; a better tactic is to direct efforts at the centre. Therefore, contrary to the views of at least one green belt researcher,[52] the focus of future action will not be at local level, but will remain at the *national level.* Local disputes are but a function of loosely-articulated national priorities. The 'point of reconciliation' between interests can be most easily moved by altering circulars or, more fundamentally, by setting up new structures for making decisions. The danger in this process is that local land use planning will become peripheralized.[53] The strength of the green belt will then decline due to the relegation of planning as an important local government function, not by erosion of its physical extent.

The two most active green belt lobbyists are the House Builders Federation and the CPRE (The lack of contribution to the debate by the TCPA except in calls for a broader retreat to localism is in marked contrast to the situation in 1955.)[54] The HBF and its offshoot, Consortium Developments, can be expected to continue on a wide-ranging front in their attempts to alter public opinion. In reality they would be quite pleased just to change the opinions of Ministers but the events of 1983–4 disproved such a thesis. During the summer recess following the issue of the Circulars, HBF representatives met Ministers to obtain delivery on the words of Circular 15/84 which suggest that 'demand' should be met where it occurs. Research studies of land availability in the Outer South East will continue the search for chinks in the defensive armour of planning authorities. Solicited newspaper articles will appear in the national press and attempts will be made to maximize regional press coverage. Wider attempts to contact 'friendly' MPs will be made and 'briefings' will be held. Pressure to gain a place at the table, writing the sub-regional guidance for development in the metropolitan areas will be kept up, and the possibility of purchasing the services of professional publicists pursued.[55]

On the CPRE side an extensive membership drive is being mounted funded partly by the Countryside Commission. A large-scale survey of public attitudes to green belts is being carried out. The importance of a strong Central Group within the organization is being stressed, and wider use of professional advisers on a voluntary basis will be made.[56] In addition the usual methods, briefings and literature, will be used to garner to the cause MPs and Members of the House of Lords who can either feed written questions through the system or make contact with Ministers.

Consortium Developments Ltd applied in May 1985 for permission to construct a new village settlement at Tillingham Hall, in the London Green Belt near Thurrock in Essex. The scheme involved accommodating approximately 14,000 persons on 400 hectares of land, with 60 hectares being devoted to industrial and commercial uses. The decision on this highly publicised appeal, which commenced in March 1986, will be seen by many as the most important indicator of central Government's attitudes to settlement policy and the London Green Belt since the 1984 Green Belt Circular was issued.

The adjustment of the balance between market and non-market interests will not be through green belt circulars but through *other advice* which will have implications for green belts. Manoeuvring, compromise, and readjustment will continue to typify policy-making. Green belt will survive because of its symbolic status; like tax relief on mortgages it is immune to removal. But like tax relief on mortgages it may be subject to some attrition. Even in the present harsh and strident forum of political, economic, and social debate, it carries with it more advantages than disadvantages.[57] It acts to foster rather than hinder the material and non-material interests of most groups involved in the planning process, although it may be to the short-term tactical advantage of some not to recognize the fact. To *central Government* it assists in the essential tasks of interest mediation and compromise which planning policy-making represents. It also gives, in their view, sufficient clarity to allow development investment to proceed and a defensible measure of local accountability and discretion. To *local Government* it delivers a desirable mix of policy control with discretion. To *local residents* of the outer city it remains their best form of protection against rapid change. To the *inner city local authority* it offers at least the promise of retaining some economic activities that would otherwise leave the area; and to the *inner city resident* it offers the prospect, as well as often the reality, of countryside recreation and relaxation. To the *agriculturalist* it offers a basic form of protection against urban influences, and for the *minerals industry* it retains accessible, cheap, and exploitable natural resources. *Industrial developers* and *housebuilders* complain bitterly about the rate at which land is fed into the development pipeline, yet at the same time are dependent on planning to provide a degree of certainty and support for profitable investment.

The issues of organizing and co-ordinating development, protecting agricultural land, retaining valued scenic resources, and providing for leisure use *simultaneously* within a locally publicly-accountable framework will not go away. Planning may be 'an attempt to reconcile the irreconcilable' but green belt is one of the most successful all-purpose tools invented with which to try.

Notes and References

The common abbreviation op. cit. has been used where work by an author is referred to more than once. Where many publications of similar dates are referred to (as in the case of the Department of the Environment) the convention is only used where the work is referred to more than once within a chapter.

INTRODUCTION: POLICY SURVIVAL AND ADJUSTMENT

1. HOUSE OF COMMONS ENVIRONMENT COMMITTEE (HCEC) *Green Belt and Land for Housing, Report together with the Proceedings of the Committee relating to the Report, First Report from the Environment Committee, Session 1983–84*, HC 275-I, (HMSO, London, 1984a), p. xxxv.
2. This term is used throughout the book to refer to the Ministry of Housing and Local Government (MHLG) and its successor the Department of the Environment (DoE).
3. MHLG *Green Belts*, Circular 42/55 (HMSO: London, 1955); MHLG *Green Belts, Circular 50/57* (HMSO: London, 1957).
4. Department of the Environment (DoE) *Green Belts*, Circular 14/84 (HMSO: London, 1984).
5. GRANT, M. *Urban Planning Law* (Sweet and Maxwell: London, 1982), pp. 37–8 and 59–60.
6. SOLESBURY, W. 'Defining and Defending the National Interest in Land Use', paper given at Conference *Land Policy: Problems and Alternatives*, Oxford Polytechnic, Oxford, March 1983.
7. BLOWERS, A. *The Limits of Power: The Politics of Planning Policy* (Pergamon: Oxford, 1980), ch. 1 and 2.
8. UNDERWOOD, J. 'Land Use Planning and the Scope for Discretion', paper given at Conference *Land Policy: Problems and Alternatives* (Oxford Polytechnic, Oxford, March 1983).
9. HEALEY, P. *Local Plans in British Land Use Planning* (Pergamon: Oxford, 1983).
10. ELSON, M. J. *Land Release and Development in Areas of Restraint*, End of Grant Report to Social Science Research Council, 1982.
11. HCEC (1984b) *Green Belt and Land for Housing, Minutes of Evidence and Appendices, First Report from the Environment Committee, Session 1983–84*, HC 275-II, p. 79; HCEC (1984c) *Green Belt and Land for Housing, Appendices, First Report from the Environment Committee, Session 1983–84*, HC 275-III, p. 543.

12. MANDELKER, D. R. *Green Belts and Urban Growth: English Town and Country Planning in Action* (University of Wisconsin Press: Madison, 1962).
13. HALL, P., GRACEY, H., DREWETT, R. and THOMAS, R. *The Containment of Urban England* (George Allen and Unwin: London, 1973).
14. THOMAS, D. *London's Green Belt* (Faber and Faber: London, 1970); MUNTON, R. J. C. *London's Green Belt: Containment in Practice* (Allen and Unwin: London, 1983).
15. *See* JOYCE, F. E. (ed.) *Metropolitan Development and Change: The West Midlands: A Policy Review* (Teakfield: Farnborough, 1977).
16. The only comprehensive assessment of green belt *bids* is found in GAULT, I. *Green Belts in Development Plans* WP 41, (Department of Town Planning, Oxford Polytechnic, 1981).
17. MUNTON, R. J. C. (1983) op. cit., p. 3.
18. SIMMIE, J. M. *Power, Property and Corporatism* (Macmillan: London, 1981).
19. Housing Research Foundation (HRF) *Is There Sufficient Land for the 1980s?, Paper II: How Many Houses Have We Planned For: Is There a Problem?* (HRF: London, 1983).
20. LOWE, P. and GOYDER, J. *Environmental Groups in Politics* (Allen and Unwin: London, 1983).
21. DoE *Memorandum on Structure and Local Plans* Draft for Consultation, (DoE: London, 1982).
22. DoE *Memorandum on Structure and Local Plans and Green Belt*, Draft for Consultation, (DoE: London, 1983).
23. See HEBBERT, M. and GAULT, I. *Green Belt Issues in Local Plan Preparation*, WP 34 (Department of Town Planning, Oxford Polytechnic, 1978).
24. Standing Conference on London and South East Regional Planning (SCLSERP) *The Philosophy and Implementation of Restraint Policies*, SC 1107 (SCLSERP: London, 1979a).
25. BODDY, M. and FUDGE C. (eds.) *The Local State: Theory and Practice*, WP 20 (School for Advanced Urban Studies, University of Bristol, 1981).
26. CLOKE, P. J. *An Introduction to Rural Settlement Planning* (Methuen: London, 1983), ch. 3.
27. HERINGTON, J. *The Outer City* (Harper and Row: London, 1984).
28. MHLG *The Green Belts* (HMSO: London, 1962).
29. McAUSLAN, P. *The Ideologies of Planning Law* (Pergamon: Oxford, 1980).
30. Advisory Council for Agriculture and Horticulture *Agriculture and the Countryside* (HMSO: London, 1978); Agriculture Economic Development Council *Agriculture into the 1980s: Land Use* (NEDO: London, 1977).
31. BLOWERS, A. *Something in the Air: Corporate Power and the Environment* (Harper and Row: London, 1984).
32. Greater London Regional Planning Committee *Interim Report on Open Spaces* (London, 1931).
33. TRAVIS, A. S. and VEAL, A. J. (eds.) *Recreation and the Urban Fringe* (Sports Council and Countryside Commission: London, 1976).
34. ELSON, M. J. *The Leisure Use of Green Belts and Urban Fringes* (Sports Council and SSRC: London, 1980).
35. Department of Education and Science *Report of the Land Use Study Group: Forestry, Agriculture and the Multiple Use of Rural Land* (HMSO: London,

1966); Programme Organizing Committee of the Conservation and Development Programme for the UK *The Conservation and Development Programme for the UK* (Kogan Page: London, 1983); Nature Conservancy Council (NCC) *Nature Conservation in Great Britain* (NCC: Shrewsbury, 1984); Peak District Planning Board *A Tale of Two Villages: The Story of the Integrated Rural Development Experiment in the Peak District 1981–1984* (PDPB: Bakewell, 1984).

36. WARD, C. 'Breaking the Girdle', *New Society*, 1983, vol. 65, p. 481.

CHAPTER I: CITY SPRAWL AND THE EARLY RESPONSE

1. OSBORN, F. J. 'The Green Belt Principle: A Note on its Historical Origins', *Town and Country Planning*, 1956, vol. 24, pp. 288–94.
2. Anon. 'Ye Olde Englishe Green Belt', *J. Town Plann. Inst.*, 1955, vol. 42, p. 68.
3. GINSBERG, L. 'Green Belts in the Bible', *J. Town Plann. Inst.*, 1955, vol. 42, p. 165.
4. HOWARD, E. *Tomorrow: A Peaceful Path to Real Reform* (Swan Sonnenschein: London, 1898).
5. See BULL, W. J. 'A Green Girdle Around London', *The Sphere*, 1901, No. 5; MEATH, Lord 'The Green Girdle Around London', *The Sphere*, 1901, No. 6; and PEPLER, G. *A Belt of Green Around London*, (Garden Cities and Town Planning: London, 1911).
6. Greater London Regional Planning Committee (1931) op. cit.
7. Ministry of Works and Planning *Report of the Committee on Land Utilisation in Rural Areas* Cmnd. 6378 (HMSO: London, 1943), p. 71.
8. ABERCROMBIE, Sir P. *Greater London Plan: 1944* (HMSO: London, 1945).
9. THOMAS, D. (1970) op. cit.
10. FOLEY, D. *Controlling London's Growth: Planning the Great Wen: 1940–1960* (California University Press: Berkeley, 1963).
11. WATSON, H. M. 'The West Midlands Green Belt', *J. Town Plann. Inst.*, 1960, vol. 56, pp. 58–61.
12. London County Council *Green Belt Around London* (LCC: London, 1956), p. 2.
13. SHEAIL, J. *Rural Conservation in Inter-War Britain* (Clarendon Press: Oxford, 1981), p. 12.
14. See LAMB, P. and EVANS, M. *The Law and Practice of Town and Country Planning* (Staples: London, 1951), pp. 605–619.
15. This figure had reached 24,000 hectares by the early 1980s.
16. CADBURY, P. *The Expansion of Birmingham into the Green Belt Area* (Cadbury Brothers Ltd: Birmingham, 1968).
17. Council for the Preservation of Rural England (CPRE) *Sheffield's Green Belt* (CPRE Sheffield and Peak District Branch: Sheffield, 1945); HAYTHORNTHWAITE, G. *The Sheffield Green Belt* (CPRE Sheffield and Peak District Branch: Sheffield, 1984).
18. Oxford Preservation Trust *Twenty-Ninth Report to 9 June 1960* (Oxford Preservation Trust: Oxford, 1960); SCARGILL, I. *Oxford's Green Belt* OP 3, (Oxford Preservation Trust: Oxford, 1983).

19. CULLINGWORTH, J. B. *Town and Country Planning in Britain* (8th Edition, Allen and Unwin: London, 1982).
20. NEWHOUSE, J. 'Defending the Green Belt', *Town and Country Planning*, 1955, vol. 23, pp. 273–5.
21. HAYTHORNTHWAITE, G. 'A New Sheffield', *Town and Country Planning*, 1955, vol. 23, pp. 311–17.
22. CPRE (1945) op. cit., p. 6.
23. Town and Country Planning Association (TCPA) 'Dispersal: A Call for Action', *Town and Country Planning*, 1955, vol. 23, pp. 263–8.
24. LAWS, P. 'Ribbon Development: Present Trends', *Town and Country Planning*, 1955, vol. 23, pp. 167–9.
25. NAIRN, I. *Outrage* (Architectural Review: London, 1955).
26. MHLG *Report of the Ministry of Housing and Local Government for the Year 1955*, Cmnd. 9876 (HMSO: London, 1956).
27. WATSON, H. M. (1960) op. cit., p. 59.
28. MHLG (1956) op. cit., p. 55.
29. See 'Commentary', *Town and Country Planning*, vol. 23, p. 277.
30. MHLG *Green Belts*, Circular 42/55 (HMSO: London, 1955).
31. HEAP, D. 'Presidential Address', *J. Town Plann. Inst.*, vol. 42, pp. 5–6.
32. MANDELKER, D. R. (1962) op. cit., p. 30.
33. HEAP, D. (1955) op. cit., pp. 8–9.
34. SILKIN, L. 'Green Belt Policy', *Municipal Journal*, 1955, vol. 43, pp. 2334–5.
35. TCPA 'Implications of Green Belt Policy', *Town and Country Planning*, 1955, vol. 23, pp. 401–2.
36. DOUBLEDAY, E. *Green Belts – The Operation of Effective Control*, 31st Annual Spring Meeting (Town Planning Institute: London, 1957).
37. COLLINS, B. J. 'A Talk on Green Belts', *Town Plann. Rev.*, 1957, vol. 27, p. 221.
38. BURNS, W. 'What is a Green Belt', *The Surveyor*, 1956, vol. 115, p. 1033.
39. TCPA *Green Belts: Their Establishment and Safeguarding: A Memorandum by the Executive Prepared at the Request of the Minister of Housing and Local Government* (TCPA: London, 1956), 8 pp.
40. CHORLEY, Lord *Green Belts* (TCPA: London, 1956) 8 pp.
41. MHLG *Green Belts*, Circular 50/57 (HMSO: London, 1957).
42. ibid, para. 6.
43. ibid, appendix, paras. c and d.
44. MHLG *Report for the Year 1956*, Cmnd. 193 (HMSO: London, 1957), p. 43.
45. Much of this section is constructed from MHLG Annual Reports 1957–61 (Cmnd. 419, 737, 1027 and 1435).
46. Wycombe Urban District Council were unwilling to see any Green Belt within their administrative boundaries.
47. See HEAP, D. 'Green Belts and Open Spaces: The English Scene Today', *J. Plann. and Property Law*, January 1961, p. 18.
48. BATES, A. 'Green Belts in the West Riding', *J. Inst. of Municipal Engineers*, 1957, vol. 84, pp. 127–30.
49. MHLG *The Green Belts* (HMSO: London, 1962).
50. MHLG *Objections to Proposed Modifications to Alteration 7 to Buckinghamshire County Development Plan* (MHLG: London, 1961).

CHAPTER 2: GREEN BELTS AND REGIONAL PLANNING

1. For example MHLG *County of Surrey Development Plan: Proposed Extension of the Metropolitan Green Belt; Local Public Inquiry Proceedings* (MHLG: London, 1960).
2. MHLG *The Green Belts* (HMSO: London, 1962), p. 25.
3. JAMES, J. R. 'City Regions', *TCPSS, Proceedings of Town and Country Planning Summer School* (Town Planning Institute: London, 1962), pp. 11–24.
4. MHLG *The Review of Development Plans*, Circular 37/60 (HMSO: London, 1960).
5. CULLINGWORTH, J. B. *Environmental Planning: Vol. IV; Land Values, Compensation and Betterment* (HMSO: London, 1980), p. 235.
6. MHLG *London: Employment, Housing, Land*, Cmnd. 1952 (HMSO: London, 1963).
7. THOMAS, D. (1970) op. cit., pp. 93–4.
8. South East Joint Planning Team *The Metropolitan Green Belt and the Green Belt Concept, Report of Studies No. 2* (HMSO: London, 1971), p. 176.
9. HALL, P. et al. (1973) op. cit., pp. 514–20.
10. See LONG, J. R. (ed.) *The Wythall Inquiry: A Test Case* (Estates Gazette: London, 1962), particularly the account by Self of the deficiencies of regional policy.
11. MHLG *Statement on Green Belts*, Press Release, 14 January (MHLG: London, 1965).
12. MHLG *The South East Study 1961–81* (HMSO: London, 1964).
13. ibid., pp. 88–95.
14. ASH, M. *The Human Cloud* (TCPA: London, 1963); WATES, N. 'Building in Britain: The Challenge to Central Government, Local Government and the Building Industry', *J. Town Plann. Inst.*, 1963, vol. 49, pp. 201–5.
15. South East Economic Planning Council *A Strategy for the South East* (HMSO: London, 1967).
16. See discussion in McNAMARA, P. F. and ELSON, M. J. *The Evolution of Restraint Policies in Hertfordshire*, Restraint Policies Project Paper No. 2 (Department of Town Planning, Oxford Polytechnic: 1981).
17. THOMAS, D. (1970) op. cit.
18. West Midlands Economic Planning Council *The West Midlands: Patterns of Growth* (HMSO: London, 1967).
19. HALL, P. et al. (1973) op. cit., refer to this.
20. HALL, P. 'Underspill in the West Midlands', *Town and Country Planning*, 1971, vol. 31, pp. 244–6.
21. CADBURY, P. *The Expansion of Birmingham into the Green Belt Area* (Cadbury Bros. Ltd: Birmingham, 1968).
22. SUTCLIFFE, A. and SMITH, R. *History of Birmingham: Vol. 3: Birmingham 1939–70* (Oxford University Press: Oxford, 1974) have a lively account of this period.
23. GREGORY, D. 'Green Belt Policy and the Conurbation', in JOYCE, F. (ed.) (1977) op. cit., pp. 231–52.
24. SAUNDERS, D. L. 'The Changing Planning Framework' in JOYCE, F. (ed.) (1977) op. cit., pp. 37–49.

25. HALL, P. *The World Cities* (Weidenfeld and Nicholson: London, 1966), p. 49.
26. ALLISON, J. R. 'Green Belts and Urban Growth', in *TCPSS*, *Report of the Town and Country Planning Summer School* (Town Planning Institute: London, 1966), pp. 55–69.
27. SMART, G. 'Green Belts: Is the Concept Out of Date?' *Town and Country Planning*, 1965, vol. 33, pp. 374–8; WALLIS, H. F. 'Is the Green Belt Concept Outdated?', *Housing and Planning Review*, 1965, vol. 21, pp. 4–5.
28. JACKSON, J. N. *The Urban Future* (Allen and Unwin: London, 1972) p. 100.
29. SHARP, E. *The Ministry of Housing and Local Government* (Allen and Unwin: London, 1969).
30. LEE, J. M. *Social Leaders and Public Persons* (Clarendon Press: Oxford, 1963).
31. See DUNLEAVEY, P. *The Politics of Mass Housing in Britain; 1945–75* (Clarendon Press: Oxford, 1981) for an account of the policies of Bristol City Council during the period.
32. GOLDSMITH, J. *Politics, Planning and the City* (Hutchinson: London, 1980), p. 93.
33. ALEXANDER, D. 'What are Green Belts for?', *Town and Country Planning*, 1971, vol. 31, pp. 386–90.
34. South East Joint Planning Team *Strategic Plan for the South East* (HMSO: London, 1970).
35. Coventry City Council, Solihull County Borough, and Warwickshire County Council *Coventry–Solihull–Warwickshire: A Strategy for a Sub-Region* (Coventry City Council: Coventry, 1971).
36. BALL, M. *Housing and Economic Power* (Methuen: London, 1983), ch. 3.
37. DoE *Land for Housing*, Circular 10/70 (HMSO: London, 1970).
38. DoE *Widening the Choice: The Next Steps in Housing*, Cmnd. 5280 (HMSO: London, 1973).
39. DoE *Land Availability for Housing*, Circular 122/73 (HMSO: London, 1973), paras. 9 and 10.
40. Hansard, vol. 867, cols. 107–8, 16 January 1974.
41. Hansard, vol. 893, cols. 184–5, 11 June 1975.
42. DoE Letter to County Councils Association, 14 March 1974.
43. Department of Economic Affairs *The North West* (HMSO: London, 1965), p. 90.
44. Hansard, vol. 871, p. 1254, 3 April 1974.
45. HALL, P. et al. (1973) op. cit.
46. See RUGMAN, A. J. and GREEN, M. D. 'Demographic and Social Change' in JOYCE, F. (ed.) (1977) op. cit., pp. 50–74.

CHAPTER 3: CENTRAL GOVERNMENT AND THE NEW PATTERN

1. MASSEY, D. and MEEGAN, R. *The Anatomy of Job Loss: The How, Why and Where of Employment Decline* (Methuen: London, 1980), ch. 10; MASSEY, D. *Spatial Divisions of Labour: Social Structures and the Geography of Production* (Macmillan, London, 1984).
2. GODDARD, J. B. and CHAMPION, A. G. (eds.) *The Urban and Regional Transformation of Britain* (Methuen: London, 1983).

3. FOTHERGILL, S. and GUDGIN, G. *Unequal Growth: Urban and Regional Employment Change in the U.K.* (Heinemann: London, 1982), ch. 5.
4. See for example HERRING, SON and DAW *Property and Technology – The Needs of Modern Industry* (Herring, Son and Daw: London, 1982); Association of District Councils (ADC) *High Technology Development* (ADC: London, 1983).
5. NEWBY, H. *Green and Pleasant Land?: Social Change in Rural England* (Penguin: London, 1979) p. 14.
6. ELSON, M. J. 'Development Control, Employment Policies and Requirements for New Industrial Development', in BREAKELL, M. and ELSON, M. J. (eds.) *Development Control and Industry*, WP 73 (Department of Town Planning: Oxford Polytechnic, 1983), pp. 3–13.
7. HEALEY, P., McNAMARA, P. F., DOAK, A. J. and ELSON, M. J. *The Implementation of Planning Policies and the Role of Development Plans*, A Report to the Department of the Environment (Department of Town Planning, Oxford Polytechnic, 1986).
8. But see the discussion on private sector 'new towns' proposed by Consortium Developments Ltd. on pp. 233–4.
9. DAVIDSON, J. and MacEWAN, A. 'Enough Theory: More Practice', *Town and Country Planning*, 1983, vol. 52, pp. 216–8.
10. HRF *Housing and Land 1984–1991: 1992–2000: How Many Houses Will We Build? What Will be the Effect on our Countryside?* (HRF: London, 1984).
11. See MOSS, G. *Britain's Wasting Acres* (Architectural Press: London, 1981); NORTON-TAYLOR, R. *Whose Land Is It Anyway?* (Turnstone Press: Wellingborough, 1982) for polemical accounts; BEST, R. H. *Land Use and Living Space* (Methuen: London, 1981) gives a contrasting view.
12. TRAVIS, A. S. and VEAL, A. J. (eds.) (1976) op. cit.
13. Planning Advisory Group *The Future of Development Plans* (HMSO: London, 1965), pp. 5–8.
14. HEALEY, P. (1983) op. cit., ch. 3 contains a critique of the structure plan process. See also SOLESBURY, W. 'Structure Plans: Underlying Intentions and Overriding Influences', in CROSS, D. T. and BRISTOW, M. R. (eds.) *English Structure Planning: A Commentary on Procedure and Practice in the Seventies* (Pion: London, 1983), pp. 1–27.
15. Yorkshire and Humberside Regional Economic Planning Council (YHREPC) *Joint Green Belt Study* (YHREPC: Leeds, 1974).
16. North West Joint Planning Team *Strategic Plan for the North West* (HMSO: London, 1973).
17. South East Joint Planning Team *Strategic Plan for the South East: The Metropolitan Green Belt and the Green Belt Concept* (HMSO: London, 1971), vol. 2, ch. 11.
18. LAYFIELD, F. H. B. W. 'The Need for Practical Green Belt Policies', in College of Estate Management, *The Future of the Green Belt*, Occ. Papers in Estate Management No. 5 (College of Estate Management: Reading, 1974), pp. 25–32.
19. YHREPC (1974) op. cit., p. 8.
20. The DoE estimated the area of Green Belts in approved structure plans as 7184 square miles (18,390 sq. kms.) in 1984; however this figure *includes* the

urban areas enclosed by the Belts in all cases except the London Green Belt.

21. See GAULT, I. (1980) op. cit., and ELSON, M. J. 'Structure Plan Policies in Pressured Rural Areas', in GILG, A. (ed.) *Countryside Planning Yearbook*, vol. 2 (Geo Books: Norwich, 1981), pp. 49–70.
22. Tyne and Wear County Council (TWCC) *Tyne and Wear Green Belt and Urban Fringe Subject Plan: Draft Proposals* (TWCC: Newcastle, 1980), pp. 9–10.
23. TWCC *Structure Plan: Written Statement* (TWCC: Newcastle, 1979), pp. 95–6.
24. DoE *Notice of Approval: Tyne and Wear Structure Plan* (DoE: Newcastle, 1981a), paras 7.3–7.6.
25. DoE *Northumberland County Structure Plan: Report of the Panel* (DoE: Newcastle, 1980a), p. 45; DoE *Secretary of State's Proposed Modifications to Northumberland Structure Plan* (DoE: Newcastle, 1980b), para. 5.5.
26. See KAISERMAN, D. *Green Belts – A Review of Current Practice*, Seminar Paper, Town and Country Planning Summer School (RTPI: London, 1982), p. 3 for this and a national summary of other rulings.
27. DoE *North Yorkshire Structure Plan: Examination in Public: Report of the Panel* (DoE: Leeds, 1980c), pp. 19–20.
28. Merseyside County Council *Structure Plan: Written Statement* (MCC: Liverpool, 1980), para. 60.
29. DoE *Notice of Approval for the Birmingham Structure Plan* (DoE: Birmingham, 1973), paras 22.1–22.5.
30. Hereford and Worcester County Council *Green Belt Subject Plan: Draft Written Statement* (HWCC: Worcester, 1982).
31. House of Commons Standing Committee on Regional Affairs *The 1976 Review of the Strategic Plan for the South East* (HMSO: London, 1978), proceedings of 12 July 1978; DoE. *Strategic Plan for the South East Review: Government Statement* (HMSO: London, 1978a), pp. 13–14.
32. DoE *Cambridgeshire County Structure Plan: Statement of Proposed Modifications* (DoE: London, 1980d), p. 6.
33. DoE *Essex County Structure Plan: Statement Relating to Proposed Modifications* (DoE: London, 1981b), pp. 10–11.
34. Excluding the 161 square kilometres of the Cambridge Green Belt.
35. DoE *Green Belts*, Circular 14/84 (HMSO: London, 1984).
36. LAMBERT, C. and UNDERWOOD, J. *Local Planning in Practice (1): East Hertfordshire, South Staffordshire, Restormel*, WP 30 (School for Advanced Urban Studies, University of Bristol, 1983), pp. 30–89.
37. See HCEC (1984c), pp. 613–20.
38. Hertfordshire County Council *Structure Plan* (HCC: Hertford, 1979), key diagram.
39. DoE *Hertfordshire County Structure Plan: First Alteration: Examination in Public: Report of the Panel* (DoE: London, 1983).
40. DoE *Hertfordshire County Structure Plan: First Alteration: Statement Relating to Proposed Modifications* (DoE: London, 1983), pp. 8–9.
41. South Yorkshire County Council *Green Belt Policy: Technical Report TV3* (SYCC: Barnsley, 1975), p. 7.
42. DoE (1978b) op. cit., p. 37.
43. DoE (1980c) op. cit., p. 20.
44. KAISERMAN, D. (1982) op. cit., p. 2.

45. loc. cit.
46. DoE *South Yorkshire County Structure Plan: Examination in Public, Report of the Panel* (DoE: Leeds, 1978c), p. 16.
47. DoE *Tyne and Wear Structure Plan: EIP Panel Report* (DoE: Newcastle, 1980c), p. 77.
48. DoE (1978b) op. cit., p. 37.
49. DoE (1980c) op. cit., p. 20.
50. Berkshire County Council *Green Belt Subject Plan: Draft for Public Comment* (BCC: Reading, 1979), p. 15.
51. DoE *Central and East Berkshire Structure Plans; EIP: Report of Panel* (DoE: London, 1979), p. 37.
52. ibid., p. 40.
53. DoE *Surrey County Structure Plan: Report of EIP Panel* (DoE: London, 1979), p. 8.
54. See KAISERMAN, D. 'Green Belts – A Review of Current Practice' in *Report of Town Planning Summer School* (RTPI: London, 1983), p. 37.
55. SOLESBURY, W. (1983) op. cit.

CHAPTER 4: DEFINING GREEN BELT BOUNDARIES

1. HEALEY, P. (1983) op. cit., ch. 4–8.
2. DoE *Memorandum on Structure and Local Plans*, Circular 4/79 (HMSO: London, 1979a).
3. BARRETT, S. and FUDGE, C. (eds.) *Policy in Action: Essays on the Implementation of Public Policy* (Methuen: London, 1981), parts 1 and 3.
4. HEALEY, P., WOOD, M., DAVIS, J. and ELSON, M. J. *The Implementation of Development Plans, A Report to the Department of the Environment* (Department of Town Planning, Oxford Polytechnic: 1982); FUDGE, C., LAMBERT, C., UNDERWOOD, J., and HEALEY, P. *Speed, Economy and Effectiveness in Local Plan Preparation and Adoption*, OP 11 (School for Advanced Urban Studies, University of Bristol, 1983), ch. 2.
5. The London and South East Regional Planning Conference (SERPLAN) *Progress in the Definition of Inner Green Belt Boundaries in Local Plans*, SC 2004R (SERPLAN: London, 1984).
6. D.o.E. *Development Plans: A Manual of Form and Content* (HMSO: London, 1970).
7. SCLSERP *The Improvement of London's Green Belt*, SC 620 (SCLSERP: London, 1976).
8. Tyne and Wear County Council *Green Belt and Urban Fringe Subject Plan: Interim Policies* (TWCC: Newcastle, 1978).
9. Berkshire County Council *Green Belt Local Plan for Berkshire* (Reading, BCC: 1982), p. 1.
10. See 'Green Belt Plan is Shelved', *Planning*, 359, 2 May 1980, p. 4.
11. HEBBERT, M. and GAULT, I. op. cit. (1978); ELSON, M. J. Green Belts: Towards Consistency or Confusion?, *Housing and Planning Review*, Winter 1979, pp. 5–7; ELSON, M. J. What Future for the Green Belt?, *Architects Journal*, 9 May 1980, pp. 711–14.
12. See 'Green Belt Threat: Is It Strategic?', *Planning*, 480, 6 August 1983, pp.

12–13 for the dispute between Hereford and Worcester County and Bromsgrove District Councils; and 'Mansfield Says "No" to Belt', *Planning*, 503, 28 January 1983, p. 4 for the dispute between the District and Nottinghamshire County.

13. See KAISERMAN, D. (1982) op. cit.
14. MHLG *Green Belts*, Circular 50/57, (HMSO: London, 1957), para. 3.
15. DoE *Hertfordshire Structure Plan; Examination in Public: Report of the Panel* (DoE: London, 1977), p. 45.
16. DoE *Hertfordshire County Structure Plan: Notice of Approval* (DoE: London, 1979b), p. 4.
17. DoE *Memorandum on Structure and Local Plans, Draft for Consultation* (DoE: London, 1982), para. 4.00.
18. In a speech to the AGM of the Planning Inspectorate on 24 October 1980, Michael Heseltine stated 'one of the benefits of speeding up the structure plan process is that an approved plan establishes the boundaries to a particular Green Belt. The provisional notations of "interim" and "submitted" Green Belt in old development plans are thus removed'.
19. DoE *Green Belts*, Circular 14/84 (HMSO: London, 1984), para. 4.
20. HCEC (1984b) op. cit., p. 398; see also DoE (1979a) op. cit., para. 4.16.
21. DoE *Buckinghamshire County Structure Plan: Examination in Public, Report of the Panel* (DoE: London, 1978c), p. 47.
22. DoE *Green Belts*, Structure Plans Note 5/72 (DoE: London, 1972).
23. Broxbourne District Council *Broxbourne District Plan: Written Statement* (BDC: Hoddesdon, 1981), p. 18.
24. Tyne and Wear County Council, (1978), op. cit. p. 3.
25. Warwickshire County Council *Green Belt Local (Subject) Plan for Warwickshire* (WCC: Warwick, 1982), p. 7; DoE *The Green Belt Local (Subject) Plan for Warwickshire: Report of Public Local Inquiry into Objections* (DoE: Bristol, 1982).
26. Stratford District Council *Stratford-upon-Avon Local Plan* Draft Written Statement (SDC: Stratford, 1984), p. 52.
27. Staffordshire County Council *North Staffordshire Green Belt Local Plan; Written Statement of Policies and Proposals* (SCC: Stafford, 1983), para. 2.22.
28. DoE *North Staffordshire Green Belt Subject Plan: Report on the Objections to the Plan Made at a Public Local Inquiry* (DoE: Bristol, 1981), para. 0.9.
29. Greater Manchester Council (GMC) *The Evolution of Greater Manchester Open Land Policies* (GMC: Manchester, 1980).
30. GMC *Greater Manchester Structure Plan: Written Statement* (GMC: Manchester, 1981a).
31. GMC *The Greater Manchester Green Belt Subject Plan*, Proof of Evidence for GMC delivered by D. Kaiserman (GMC: Manchester, 1981b), pp. 3–20.
32. Interview with GMC staff.
33. GMC *The New Green Belt*, Report of County Planning Officer, (GMC: Manchester, 21 January 1980), p. 87.
34. GMC op. cit. (1981b).
35. GMC *Objections and Other Representations Based on the Deposited Plans*, Report to GMC County Planning Committee (GMC: Manchester, 28 July 1981c), p. 1.
36. DoE *The Greater Manchester Structure Plan, Report on Objections and Repre-*

sentations to the Plan, Including Those Made at a Public Local Inquiry (DoE: Bristol, 1982), p. 6.
37. ibid., p. 7.
38. ibid., pp. 9 and 22.
39. GMC *Open Land Policy and Land Lost to Development 1974–80, Policy Background Paper 81/3* (GMC: Manchester, 1981d), figure 2.
40. This brief account is based on detailed work carried out by Liz Hill at Oxford Polytechnic. Her permission to use the material is gratefully acknowledged. See HILL, E. (forthcoming) *Statutory Local Plans: An Examination of Aspects of the Relations Between County Councils and District Councils*, for Ph.D, Department of Town Planning, Oxford Polytechnic; and HILL, E. A. and NADIN, V. (eds.) *Responding to Economic Change: Development Plans in Oxfordshire*, WP 82 (Department of Town Planning, Oxford Polytechnic: 1984).
41. SHARP, T. *A Plan for Oxford* (Oxford, 1947).
42. UZELL, P. *Oxford's Green Belt: Success or Failure?* BA Special Study (Department of Town Planning; Oxford Polytechnic: 1977).
43. Oxfordshire County Council (OCC) *Structure Plan: Written Statement* (OCC: Oxford, 1976).
44. DoE *Letter of Approval of the Oxfordshire Structure Plan* (DoE: London, 1979d), p. 10.
45. Oxford City Council *Consultation on Possible Development: South of Blackbird Leys and Littlemore* (Oxford City Council: Oxford, undated).
46. Oxford City Council *Oxford Local Plan: Draft* (OCC: Oxford, 1981); Vale of White Horse, South Oxfordshire and Cherwell District Councils *Oxford Fringe District Plan: Draft*, Parts One to Four, (VWHDC, SODC and CDC, Abingdon, Wallingford, Banbury, 1981).
47. South Oxfordshire District Council *Oxford Fringe District Plan: Draft*, Part Three (SODC: Wallingford, 1982).
48. Oxfordshire County Council *First Review of the Structure Plan: Draft for Consultation* (OCC: Oxford, 1982).
49. See ELSON, M. J. 'Containing Settlements', in BLUNDEN, J. and CURRY, N. (eds.) *The Changing Countryside of England and Wales* (Croom Helm and The Open University: London, 1985), pp. 84–113.

CHAPTER 5: URBAN RESTRAINT AND THE GREEN BELT

1. MHLG *Green Belts*, Circular 42/55 (1955) para. 6.
2. ELSON, M. J. (1982) op. cit.; WOOD, M. *High Wycombe: The Implementation of Strategic Planning Policy in a Restraint Area in the South East*, WP 67 (Oxford Polytechnic: Department of Town Planning, 1982); HEALEY, P., WOOD, M., DAVIS, J. and ELSON, M. J. (1982) op. cit.
3. McNAMARA, P. F. and ELSON, M. J. (1981) op. cit.; SCLSERP *The Philosophy and Implementation of Restraint Policies*, SC 1107 (Standing Conference: London, 1979).
4. South East Joint Planning Team (SEJPT) *Strategic Plan for the South East* (HMSO: London, 1970), p. 9.
5. DoE *Development of Strategic Plan for the South East: Interim Report* (HMSO: London, 1976), p. 13.

6. SEJPT *Strategy for the South East: 1976 Review* (HMSO: London, 1976), p. 62.
7. Hertfordshire County Council (HCC) *Structure Plan: Written Statement* (Submitted Plan) (HCC: Hertford, 1976).
8. ELSON, M. J. (1982) op. cit., pp. 8–11.
9. This was the criterion, from 1980, for an adequate supply of housing land in a county or district area; DoE *Land for Private Housebuilding*, Circular 9/80 (HMSO: London, 1980).
10. ELSON, M. J., HEALEY, P. and TERRY, S. *Local Needs in Areas of Restraint*, WP 42 (Oxford Polytechnic: Department of Town Planning, 1979).
11. ELSON, M. J. et al. (1980) op. cit., pp. 12–14.
12. ibid, pp. 9–11.
13. HEALEY, P., TERRY, S. and EVANS, S. *The Implementation of Selective Restraint Policy*, WP 45 (Oxford Polytechnic: Department of Town Planning, 1979).
14. DoE *Local Government and the Industrial Strategy*, Circular 71/77 (HMSO: London, 1977).
15. See CADDY, C. 'Local Planning in an Area of Restraint', in FUDGE, C. (ed.) *Approaches to Local Planning 2*, WP 17 (School for Advanced Urban Studies, University of Bristol, 1981), pp. 1–20.
16. ELSON, M. J. 'Containment in Hertfordshire: Changing Attitudes to Land Release for New Employment-Generating Development', in BARRETT, S. and HEALEY, P. (eds.) *Land Policy: Problems and Alternatives* (Gower: Farnborough, 1985) pp. 127–50.
17. McNAMARA, P. F. Towards a Classification of Land Developers, *Urban Law and Policy*, 1983, vol. 6, pp. 87–94.
18. TERRY, S. and ELSON, M. J. *Restraint and Employment: An Analysis of Development Control Decisions in Dacorum and North Hertfordshire: 1974 –1979*, Restraint Policies Project Paper No. 4 (Oxford Polytechnic: Department of Town Planning, 1981).
19. WOOD, M. (1982), op. cit. p. 29.
20. TERRY, S. and ELSON, M. J. (1981) op. cit., p. 25.
21. ELSON, M. J. (1982) op. cit., pp. 28–9.
22. For a detailed account of similar processes around 1970 see HALL, P. et al. (1973), op. cit.; vol. 2, pp. 97–125.
23. Planning controls on manufacturing were dealing with less than one per cent of jobs present in Dacorum District per annum. Between 1971–6 some 950 jobs were contained in manufacturing *permissions* yet the number of manufacturing jobs in the District declined by ten over the period. TERRY, S. and ELSON, M. J. (1981) op. cit., p. 31.
24. WOOD, M. (1982) op. cit., pp. 7–9.
25. McNAMARA, P. F. and ELSON, M. J. *Restraint and Housing: An Analysis of Development Control Decisions in Dacorum and North Hertfordshire: 1974 –1979*, Restraint Policies Project Paper No. 3 (Oxford Polytechnic: Department of Town Planning, 1981).
26. WOOD, M. (1982), op. cit. pp. 23–4.
27. McNAMARA, P. F. *Restraint Policy in Action: Housing in Dacorum and North Hertfordshire*, WP 77 (Department of Town Planning, Oxford Polytechnic, 1984a), pp. 58–62.

28. DoE *Hertfordshire County Structure Plan: EIP: Report of Panel* (DoE: London, 1977).
29. See McNAMARA, P. F. *Restraint Policy and Development Interests*, WP 76 (Oxford Polytechnic: Department of Town Planning, 1984b), p. 56. However Ball suggests 'the change in the price of residential land is dependent on the change in gross development profitability rather than the other way round'. See BALL, M. *Housing Policy and Economic Power* (Methuen: London, 1983), p. 113.
30. Bedfordshire County Council *House Sales Survey: Bulletin No. 4* (Bedfordshire County Council: Bedford, 1980).
31. ELSON, M. J. and McNAMARA, P. F. *Local Needs and New Dwellings*, WP 64 (Oxford Polytechnic: Department of Town Planning, 1982), pp. 44–9.
32. McNAMARA, P. F. 'The Role of Local Estate Agents in the Residential Development Process', *Land Development Studies*, 1984, vol. 1, pp. 101–12.
33. See McNAMARA, P. F. (1984b) op. cit., pp. 53–63 for a wider discussion.
34. North Hertfordshire District Council *How Rapidly Does the Development of Large Housing Sites Proceed?* (NHDC: Letchworth, 1982).
35. See Peak District National Park (PDNP) *Rural Housing: Problems and Solutions* (PDNP: Bakewell, 1983); SHUCKSMITH, M. *No Homes for Locals?* (Gower: Farnborough, 1981); DUNN, M., RAWSON, M. and RODGERS, A. *Rural Housing: Competition and Choice* (Allen and Unwin: London, 1981) for further discussion of alternative methods.
36. East Hertfordshire District Council *East Hertfordshire District Plan: Written Statement* (EHDC: Hertford, 1981).
37. North Hertfordshire District Council *The 'Pool of Planning Permissions' Policy* (NHDC: Letchworth, 1982).
38. A term coined by a member of the EIP Panel into the Alterations to the West Midlands Structure Plan in the context of the West Midlands Green Belt.
39. CADMAN, D. *The Growth of Institutional Investment in the UK Commercial –Industrial Market in the Post-War Period.* (Paper delivered to Regional Science Association Meeting, Reading, September 1982).
40. FOTHERGILL, S., KITSON, M. and MONK, S. *Industrial Land Availability in Cities, Towns and Rural Areas*, Industrial Location Research Project, WP 6 (University of Cambridge: Department of Land Economy, 1983).
41. PROCTOR, S. 'The Impact of the M25', *Town and Country Planning*, 1983, vol. 52, no. 8, pp. 201–3.
42. DoE *Industrial Development*, Circular 16/84 (DoE: London, 1984).
43. ELSON, M. J. (1985) op. cit., p. 145.
44. DoE *Planning Conditions*, Draft Circular (DoE: London, 1983), paras 29 and 68. Further relaxations are recommended in DoE *Planning Conditions*, Circular 1/85 (DoE: London, 1985).
45. Mole Valley District Council *Dorking Local Plan: Written Statement* (MVDC: Leatherhead, 1983).
46. Tandridge District Council *South of the Downs Local Plan* (TDC: Oxted, 1984).
47. Hertfordshire County Council (HCC) *Annual Monitoring and Position Statement* No. 9 (HCC: Hertford, 1983), p. 9., Surrey County Council *Annual Monitoring Report: 1982* (SCC: Kingston, 1982), has a discussion of similar issues.

48. HCC *Hertfordshire: The County of Opportunity* (HCC: Hertford, 1983).
49. Address to Regional Studies Association meeting, Stevenage, December 1982, by R. D. Dennis of the South East Regional Office of the Department of Industry.
50. ELSON, M. J. *Planning Policies in the Western Arc of the M25*, pp. 492–5, in HCEC (1984b) op. cit.
51. LICHFIELD, N. and GOLDSTEIN LEIGH ASSOCIATES *The Property Market Effects of the M25* (Lichfield and Goldstein Leigh: London, 1981); SCLSERP *The Impact of the M25*, SC 1706 (SCLSERP: London, 1982); SCLSERP *The Impact of the M25: Responses of Member Authorities*, SC 1800 (SCLSERP: London, 1983); Surrey County Council *The Control of Development Associated with the Strategic Road Network in Surrey* (SCC: Kingston, 1983).
52. Department of Industry *The Location, Mobility and Finance of New High Technology Companies in the UK Electronics Industry* (DoI: London, 1983).
53. DoE *The M25 and Land Use Planning in the South East* (DoE: London, 23 March 1984).
54. HCEC (1984b) op. cit., pp. 429–31.
55. The 1983 Hertfordshire Monitoring Report refers to this phenomenon (Hertfordshire County Council (1983) op. cit., p. 8), and SERPLAN in discussing losses of land in the London Green Belt over the 1979–82 period refer to local authorities 'taking a narrow view of the local interest from time to time'. (HCEC (1984b) op. cit.), p. 412.

CHAPTER 6: DEVELOPMENT CONTROL AND RURAL SETTLEMENTS

1. THOMAS, D. (1970) op. cit., pp. 130–3.
2. MHLG *Green Belts*, Circular 42/55 (MHLG: London, 1955), para. 5.
3. MHLG *Green Belts*, Circular 50/57 (MHLG: London, 1957), Appendix b.
4. For a period in the early 1970s the hotel 'boom' resulted in a number of permissions in Green Belt locations near London Airport. See Hillingdon Borough Council *Heathrow A4/M4 District Plan* (HBC: Uxbridge, 1982), vol. 2, pp. 71–88 for an analysis of appeals in Green Belt. Attempts to circumvent the 'open–rural' criterion have included proposals for a 500,000 sq. ft. *underground* warehouse near London Airport, and a privately-sponsored underground nuclear shelter in the Green Belt in South Buckinghamshire. In the latter case the Inspector ruled that the shelter was an 'urban-type' development not appropriate in the Green Belt. The Secretary of State saw no special need as 'the Government does not regard nuclear conflict involving the United Kingdom as either inevitable, imminent, or even probable' (APP/5133/A/80/14682(E)).
5. DoE *Memorandum on Structure and Local Plans, Draft for Consultation* (DoE: London, 1982a).
6. DoE *Green Belt Local (Subject) Plan for Warwickshire, Report of PLI into Objections* (DoE: Bristol, 1982b), paras. 88–92.
7. DoE *Gypsy Caravan Sites*, Circular 28/77 (DoE, 1977), Appendix, para. 32.
8. UNDERWOOD, J. 'Development Control: A Review of Research and Current Issues', *Progress in Planning*, 1981, vol. 16, pp. 179–242 (Pergamon: Oxford, 1981).

9. MHLG *Green Belts*, Circular 42/55 (HMSO: London, 1955), para. 6.
10. MASSER, F. I. and STROUD, D. C. 'Metropolitan Villages', *Town Plann. Rev.*, 1965, vol. 36, pp. 111–24.
11. MARTIN AND VOORHEES ASSOCIATES (MVA) *Review of Rural Settlement Policies 1945–1980* (MVA: London, 1981). For a similar profile in the Green Belt in Surrey see Tandridge District Council *South of the Downs Local Plan*, Consultation Draft (TDC: Caterham, 1983).
12. PACIONE, M. *Rural Geography* (Harper and Row: London, 1984), pp. 167–82.
13. PAHL, R. E. 'Class and Community in English Commuting Villages', in PAHL, R. E. (Ed.), *Whose City?* (Longman: London, 1970), pp. 19–39.
14. Macclesfield District Council *Knutsford Housing Study* (MCD: Macclesfield, 1977).
15. CONNELL, J. *The End of Tradition: Country Life in Central Surrey* (Routledge and Kegan Paul: London, 1978); CONNELL, J. 'Green Belt Country', *New Society*, 1971, vol. 439, pp. 304–6; SHUCKSMITH, D. M. (1981) op. cit.; DUNN, M. et al. (1981) op. cit.; SHAW, M. 'The Development of Statutory Rural Planning in the 1970s', *Countryside Planning Yearbook*, 1982, vol. 3, pp. 50–74.
16. The choice is *not* between concentrating development in key settlements or allowing dispersal among small rural settlements, but between development in rural settlements or satisfying local housing needs in nearby *urban* areas.
17. MHLG *Development in Rural Areas*, DCPN 4 (MHLG: London, 1969), para. 6.
18. Cheshire County Council *Structure Plan: Written Statement* (CCC: Chester, 1977), para. 6.40.
19. Berkshire County Council *Green Belt Local Plan for Berkshire* (BCC: Reading, 1982), para. 4.28.
20. Information by courtesy of Staffordshire County Council Planning Department.
21. Nottinghamshire County Council *Green Belt Local Plan: Statement of Public Consultation* (NCC: Nottingham, 1982).
22. DoE *Report on Objections to the Berkshire Green Belt Local Plan* (DoE: Bristol, 1983a), pp. 86–92.
23. See Tandridge District Council (1983) op. cit. for a good example of this process.
24. McLOUGHLIN, J. B. *Control and Urban Planning* (Faber and Faber: London, 1973).
25. McAUSLAN, P. *The Ideologies of Planning Law* (Pergamon: Oxford, 1980), chapter 6.
26. UNDERWOOD, J. 'Development Control: A Case Study of Discretion in Action' in BARRETT, S. and FUDGE, C. (eds.) *Policy in Action* (Methuen: London, 1981), pp. 143–61; BRUTON, M. J. 'Public Participation, Local Plans and Conflicts of Interest', *Policy and Politics*, 1980, vol. 8, pp. 423–4; BRUTON, M. J. *Bargaining in the Development Control Process* Papers in Planning Research No. 60, (Department of Town Planning, University of Wales Institute of Science and Technology, 1983).
27. UZELL, P. C. *The Oxford Green Belt – Success or Failure?* Part-time Diploma Special Study, (Oxford Polytechnic, Department of Town Planning, 1977).
28. CHERRETT, T. *The Implementation of Green Belt Policy* Gloucestershire Papers in Local and Rural Planning No. 15, (GLOSCAT, Cheltenham, 1982);

see also SMITH, K. 'The Application of Green Belt Policy', *Jnl. Plann. Environ. Law*, December 1983, pp. 777–85.

29. HAGUE, G. *Village Housing Policy – A Review of Policies 4 and 5 of the Dacorum District Plan*, MSc Options Project Report, (Oxford Polytechnic, Department of Town Planning, 1984).
30. Hertfordshire County Council *The Administrative Problems of the Green Belt* (HCC: Hertford, 1960), p. 10; also DOUBLEDAY, E. 'Planning Control by Reference to Characteristics of the Applicant', *J. Plann. and Property Law*, February 1958, pp. 80–2.
31. Hertfordshire County Council (1960) op. cit., p. 15.
32. DoE (1982b) op. cit., pp. 58–61.
33. O'GRADY, S. *An Assessment of Planning Policies for Local Housing Needs With Particular Reference to Stratford-on-Avon District* M.Phil. Dissertation, Oxford Polytechnic, Department of Town Planning, 1985.
34. Dacorum District Council *Dacorum District Plan* (DDC: Hemel Hempstead, 1984), pp. 7–9.
35. HAGUE, G. (1984) op. cit.
36. Wrekin District Council *Wrekin Rural Areas Local Plan: Draft Written Statement* (WDC: Telford, 1981), pp. 25–6 and map after p. 32.
37. HARDING, M. *Local Needs for Housing in Wrekin District* BA Special Study, (Oxford Polytechnic, Department of Town Planning, 1983).
38. DoE *Wrekin Rural Area District Plan: Report of Public Local Inquiry* (DoE: Bristol, 1981), pp. 2–4.
39. NEWCOMBE, J. L. 'The Control of Private Hospital Developments in the Green Belt', *Jnl. Plann. Environ. Law*, December 1983, pp. 786–9.
40. DoE. *Historic Buildings and Conservation Areas*, Circular 12/81 (DoE: London, 1981).
41. Hertfordshire County Council *Change of Use of Country Houses in Hertfordshire* (HCC: Hertford, 1978).
42. Department of Health and Social Security *Under-Used and Surplus Property in the National Health Service: Report of the Inquiry Team* (HMSO: London, 1983).
43. DoE (1983a) op. cit., p. 125.
44. Sheffield City Council *Green Belt Subject Plan: Written Statement* (SCC: Sheffield, 1981).
45. DoE *Sheffield Green Belt Subject Plan: Report of Public Inquiry* (DoE: Bristol, 1983b).
46. DoE (1983a) op. cit., p. 127.
47. NEWCOMBE, J. L. (1983) op. cit., p. 788.
48. Berkshire County Council (1982) op. cit., pp. 62, 66.
49. MARTIN AND VOORHEES ASSOCIATES (1981), op. cit. pp. 120–1.
50. ROWE, A. *Somewhere to Start* (Conservative Party Political Centre: London, 1980).
51. Joint Unit for Research on the Urban Environment (JURUE) *The Planning Problems of Small Firms in Rural Areas* (JURUE: Birmingham, 1983a).
52. DoE *Development Control: Policy and Practice*, Circular 22/80 (HMSO: London, 1980).
53. Berkshire County Council (1982) op. cit., p. 59.

54. COLLINS, J. 'Green Belts – How Sacrosanct?' *Planning*, 482, 1982, p. 8.
55. Cheshire County Council (1982) op. cit., p. 8.
56. See HCEC Memorandum by Cheshire County Council, 1984c, pp. 660–3.
57. YATES, P. 'Green Belt Business Health Scores a Miss with Districts', *Planning*, 567, 1984, p. 10.
58. JURUE (1983a) op. cit.
59. ibid.
60. JURUE *An Evaluation of the Effects of Development Commission Activities in Selected Rural Areas* (JURUE: Birmingham, 1983b).
61. Country Landowners Association *Employment in the Countryside: Letting Redundant Farm Buildings Outside Agriculture* (CLA: London, 1981).
62. DoE *Industrial Development*, Circular 16/84 (DoE: London, 1984).
63. Merseyside County Council *Green Belt Local Plan* (MCC: Liverpool, 1983).
64. Tyne and Wear County Council *Submitted Structure Plan* (TWCC: Newcastle upon Tyne, 1979), p. 47.
65. HALL, P. et al. (1973) op. cit., vol. 1, p. 543.
66. MILLER, C. and WOOD, C. *Planning and Pollution* (OUP: Oxford, 1983), pp. 189–211.
67. HCEC (1984b) op. cit.,, Evidence by Bolton Metropolitan Borough Council, pp. 273–9.

CHAPTER 7: AGRICULTURAL AND MINERAL PRODUCTION

1. DAVIDSON, J. and WIBBERLEY, G. P. *Planning and the Rural Environment* (Pergamon: Oxford, 1977), chapter 8.
2. BRYANT, C. R., RUSSWORM, L. H. and McLELLAN, A. G. *The City's Countryside* (Longman: London, 1982), especially chapter 2.
3. HEALEY, P. (1983) op. cit., chapter 8.
4. Nature Conservancy Council *Objectives and Strategy for Nature Conservation in Great Britain:* (Nature Conservancy Council: London, 1983).
5. LOWE, P. and GOYDER, J. (1983) op. cit.
6. ELSON, M. J. *Open Land Policies and Programmes in the Metropolitan Counties*, WP 14 (Countryside Commission: Cheltenham, 1979).
7. SCLSERP *The Improvement of London's Green Belt: A Second Report*, SC 860R (SCLSERP Standing Conference: London, 1978).
8. Countryside Review Committee *The Countryside: Problems and Policies* (HMSO: London, 1976).
9. Friends of the Earth *Proposal for a National Heritage Bill* (FOE: London, 1983).
10. COX, G. and LOWE, P. 'The Wildlife and Countryside Act 1981: The Battle Not the War', in GILG, A. (ed.) *Countryside Planning Yearbook 1983*, vol. 4, (Geo Books: Norwich, 1983) pp. 48–76.
11. CAIRNS, C. *An Experiment Continued: Countryside Management in the Urban Fringe of Barnet and South Hertfordshire*, CCP 148 (Countryside Commission: Cheltenham, 1983a).
12. This structure has been developed from that in HEBBERT, M. 'Green Belt Policy and the Farmer', in ELSON, M. J. (ed.) *Perspectives on Green Belt Local Plans*, WP 38 (Oxford Polytechnic, Department of Town Planning, 1978), pp. 73–100.

13. DoE *Green Belts*, Circular 14/84 (1984a), para. 6.
14. Greater Manchester Council *Structure Plan: Alternative Strategies* (GMC: Manchester, 1977).
15. DoE *Development Involving Agricultural Land*, Circular 75/76 (HMSO: London, 1976).
16. National Economic Development Office (NEDO) *Agriculture into the 1980s: Land Use* (NEDO: London, 1977).
17. MAFF *Farming and the Nation*, Cmnd. 7458 (HMSO: London, 1979).
18. *Local Government, Planning and Land Act 1980*, Schedule 14.
19. A good example is found in West Midlands County Council *Sandwell Wedge Subject Plan: Report of Survey and Issues* (WMCC: Birmingham, 1978).
20. BODDINGTON, M. A. B. *The Classification of Agricultural Land in England and Wales: A Critique* (Rural Planning Services: Ipsden, 1978); WORTHINGTON, T. R. 'Agricultural Land Quality and Planning', *Jnl. Plann. Environ. Law*, September 1982, pp. 561–5.
21. MAFF *Agriculture and the Countryside, (Strutt Report)*, (HMSO: London, 1978).
22. MAFF *Agriculture in the Urban Fringe: Slough/Hillingdon Area*, ADAS Tech. Rep. 30 (HMSO: London, 1973); MAFF *Agriculture in the Urban Fringe: Metropolitan County of Tyne and Wear*, ADAS Tech. Rep. 30/1 (HMSO: London, 1976); Rural Planning Services *The Oxford Green Belt: A Study for the Oxford Preservation Trust* (Rural Planning Services: Ipsden, 1978).
23. BOND, R. 'Reaping the Penalties of the Urban Fringe', *Surveyor*, 1984, vol. 163, pp. 24–6.
24. Merseyside County Council *Merseyside Structure Plan* (MCC: Liverpool, 1982).
25. ELLIOTT, A. H. and BELL, M. 'Farming and Practical Survival in the Urban Fringe', in PTRC Ltd., *Structure and Regional Planning Practice* (PTRC: London, 1982), pp. 1–10.
26. Countryside Commission *Local Authority Countryside Management Projects: A Guide to their Organization*, Advisory Series No. 10 (Countryside Commission: Cheltenham, 1978).
27. See FEIST, M. *A Study of Management Agreements*, CCP 114 (Countryside Commission: Cheltenham, 1978) for examples of this approach.
28. ELLIOTT, A. H. and BELL, M. (1982) op. cit., p. 8.
29. DoE *Development for Agricultural Purposes*, Circular 24/73 (HMSO: London, 1973); WELLER, J. *Agricultural Buildings: Planning and Allied Controls* (Capital Planning Information: Edinburgh, 1981).
30. LOUGHLIN, M. *Local Needs Policies and Development Control Strategies*, WP 42 (University of Bristol, School for Advanced Urban Studies, 1984), section 2.
31. Congleton District Council (1975) *The Provision of Accommodation in the Countryside for Agricultural Workers* (CDC: Sandbach, 1975).
32. BOURNE, F. J. B. 'Class VI – Yet Again!', *Jnl. Plann. Environ. Law*, March 1983, pp. 156–9.
33. Humberside County Council *Intensive Livestock Units Subject Plan* (HCC: Beverley, 1984).
34. DoE *Proposed Amendments to the General Development Order*, Draft for Consultation (DoE: London, 1983a).

35. Royal Town Planning Institute *Response to Proposed Amendments to General Development Order* (RTPI: London, 1984), para. 1.
36. BLAIR, A. M. *Spatial Effects of Urban Influences on Agriculture in Essex: 1960–1973* (Unpubl. PhD thesis, University of London, 1978); MUNTON, R. J. C. (1983) op. cit., chapter 6.
37. ELLIOTT, A. H. and BELL, M. op. cit. (1982), p. 9.
38. Surrey County Council *The Keeping and Riding of Horses in Surrey* (SCC: Kingston, 1982).
39. Countryside Commission *Report of Horses and Bridleways Working Group: Herts–Barnet Green Belt Management Experiment* (Countryside Commission: Cheltenham, 1979).
40. TURRALL-CLARKE, R. T. F. 'Horses and Planning: Recent Developments', *Jnl. Plann. Environ. Law*, November 1981, pp. 2–4.
41. Windsor and Maidenhead District Council *Horses, Stables and Riding Schools* (WMDC: Maidenhead, 1981).
42. Rochford District Council *Horse Riding Facilities: A Planning Policy* (RDC: Southend-on-Sea, 1984).
43. Hertfordshire County Council *A Code of Practice for Horse Owners and Riders* (HCC: Hertford, 1982).
44. DoE (1983a) op. cit., para. 22c.
45. PROCTOR, S. 'Belting for Horse Riding', *Planning*, 564, 1984, p. 9.
46. Windsor and Maidenhead District Council (1981) op. cit.
47. Buckinghamshire County Council *Minerals Subject Plan*, Draft (BCC: Aylesbury, 1980).
48. See THOMAS, D. (1970) op. cit., pp. 168–70; BLUNDEN, J. *The Mineral Resources of Great Britain* (Hutchinson: London, 1975), p. 49.
49. BATE, R. 'The Demand for Aggregates: The Rise and Fall of the DoE Forecasts', *Mineral Planning*, 1983, vol. 16, pp. 3–5.
50. DoE *Guidelines for Aggregates Provision in England and Wales*, Circular 21/82 (DoE: London, 1982a).
51. SCLSERP *Policy Guidelines to meet the South East Regions Need for Aggregates in the 1980s*, SC 1151R (SCLSERP: London, 1979), p. 16.
52. ROBERTS, P. W. and SHAW, T. *Mineral Resources in Regional and Strategic Planning* (Gower: Farnborough, 1982), p. 98.
53. BATE, R. 'Demand for Aggregates', *Mineral Planning*, 1983, vol. 17, pp. 3–5.
54. Advisory Committee on Aggregates *Aggregates: The Way Ahead* (Verney Report) (HMSO: London, 1976).
55. DoE (1982) op. cit., para. 3.4.
56. DoE *Hertfordshire County Structure Plan: Alterations 1980, Report of the Panel* (DoE: London, 1983b); DoE *The Hertfordshire County Structure Plan: Proposals for Alteration No. 1: Statement Relating to the Secretary of State's Proposed Modifications* (DoE: London, 1983c), pp. 8–11.
57. Berkshire County Council *Minerals Subject Plan* (Deposited) (BCC: Reading, 1982); DoE *Berkshire County Minerals Subject Plan, Report of the Inspector* (DoE: Bristol, 1983d).
58. Surrey County Council *North West Surrey Minerals (Extraction and Restoration) Subject Plan* (Deposited) (SCC: Kingston, 1983).

59. DoE *Town and Country Planning (Minerals) Act 1981*, Circular 1/82 (HMSO: London, 1982b).
60. BATE, R. 'The Minerals Bill in the House of Commons', *Mineral Planning*, 1981, vol. 8, pp. 2–3.
61. DoE *Buckinghamshire Minerals Subject Plan: Report of a PLI into Objections and other Representations* (DoE: Bristol, 1981).
62. DoE *Report of PLI into Objections to the North West Surrey Minerals Plan* (DoE: Bristol, 1983e), p. 1.
63. KELLETT, J. E. *Minerals and Structure Plans* (Department of Urban and Regional Studies, Sheffield City Polytechnic, 1982).
64. DoE (1983d) op. cit., p. 11.
65. DoE (1981) op. cit., para. 137.
66. DoE (1976) op. cit., Annexe B, para. 1.
67. Sand and Gravel Association (SAGA) *Joint Agricultural Land Restoration Experiments: Progress Report No. 2, 1977–82 for Bush Farm, Upminster, Essex* (SAGA: London, 1982).
68. DoE *Report of the Committee on Planning Control Over Mineral Working*, Circular 58/78 (HMSO: London, 1978), para. 7.
69. DoE (1982a) op. cit., para. 24.
70. Buckinghamshire County Council (1980) op. cit., p. 61.
71. loc. cit.
72. DoE (1983c), op. cit.
73. CLEAL, R. 'Bonds – An Anomaly to be Resisted', *Mineral Planning*, 1983, vol. 18, pp. 7–11; see PARRY, D. R. 'An Operators View of the Minerals Planning System', *Mineral Planning*, 1984, vol. 19, pp. 6–8 where enterprise zones for minerals are mooted.
74. The 1976 *Greater London Development Plan* contains such policies.
75. DoE (1983d), op. cit. p. 11.

CHAPTER 8: ACCESS FOR LEISURE

1. ABERCROMBIE, P. (1945) op. cit., chapter 1.
2. SHOARD, M. 'Metropolitan Escape Routes', *The London Journal*, 1979, vol. 5, pp. 87–112.
3. DAVIDSON, J. 'Recreation and the Urban Fringe', *The Planner*, 1976, vol. 60, pp. 889–93.
4. Ministry of Land and Natural Resources *Leisure in the Countryside: England and Wales*, Cmnd. 2938 (HMSO: London, 1966).
5. House of Lords Select Committee on Sport and Leisure *Second Report, 193-1* (HMSO: London, 1973).
6. DoE *Sport and Recreation*, Cmnd. 6200 (HMSO: London, 1975), p. 14.
7. Countryside Review Committee *Leisure and the Countryside: A Discussion Paper*, Topic Paper No. 2 (HMSO: London, 1977), p. 11.
8. HCEC (1984b) op. cit., p. 191.
9. These are evaluated in ELSON, M. J. *The Leisure Use of Green Belts and Urban Fringes* (SSRC and Sports Council: London, 1979).
10. SHOARD, M. (1979), op. cit.
11. Countryside Commission *A Comparison of the 1977 and 1980 National Surveys*

(Countryside Commission: Cheltenham, 1982). See also SIDAWAY, R. and DUFFIELD, B. S. 'A New Look at Countryside Recreation in the Urban Fringe', *Leisure Studies*, 1984, vol. 3, pp. 249–71.

12. Chairmen's Policy Group *Leisure Policy for the Future* (Sports Council: London, 1983). See also PATMORE, A. *Recreation and Resources: Leisure Patterns and Leisure Places* (Basil Blackwell: Oxford, 1983).
13. Countryside Review Committee (1976), op. cit.
14. South Yorkshire County Council (SYCC) *County Structure Plan: Written Statement* (SYCC: Barnsley, 1977).
15. SYCC *County Environment Study* (SYCC: Barnsley, 1978).
16. Hertfordshire County Council *County Structure Plan: Written Statement* (HCC: Hertford, 1979).
17. ELSON, M. J. 'Recreation, Green Belts and Green Belt Local Plans', in ELSON, M. J. (ed.) *Perspectives on Green Belt Local Plans*, WP 38 (Oxford Polytechnic, Department of Town Planning, 1979), pp. 34–72.
18. GAULT, I. (1981) op. cit., sections 3 and 4.
19. West Midlands County Council *Green Belt Subject Plan: Draft Written Statement* (WMCC: Birmingham, 1981), p. 4; WMCC *Green Belt Subject Plan: Revised Draft Written Statement* (WMCC: Birmingham, 1983), pp. 12–17; Warwickshire County Council *Green Belt Subject (Local) Plan* (WCC: Warwick, 1980), p. 12.
20. SCLSERP *Policy for Recreation in London's Green Belt*, SC 1111R (SCLSERP: London, 1979), p. 4.
21. Berkshire County Council *Countryside Recreation Local Plan*, Draft (BCC: Reading, 1983).
22. DoE *Report of PLI into Objections to the North-West Surrey Minerals Subject Plan* (DoE: Bristol, 1983), p. 7.
23. DoE *Sheffield City Council: Green Belt Plan: Report on Objections* (DoE: Bristol, 1983), pp. 13–14.
24. Tyne and Wear County Council *Green Belt – Open Land Subject Plan* (TWCC: Newcastle Upon Tyne, 1982).
25. Tyne and Wear County Council *Leisure Plan: Report of Survey* (TWCC: Newcastle Upon Tyne, 1978).
26. ELSON, M. J., BULLER, H. and STANLEY, P. A. *Motorsports: From Image to Reality*, Sports Council Research Report No. 30, (Sports Council: London, 1986).
27. Countryside Commission and Sports Council *Access to the Countryside for Recreation and Sport: Issues for Consultation*, CCP 166 (Countryside Commission: Cheltenham, 1984).
28. ELSON, M. J. 'Recreation Demand Forecasting: A Misleading Tradition?', in PTRC Ltd., *Planning for Leisure* (PTRC: London, 1975) pp. 75–81.
29. ELSON, M. J. 'Land Use and Management in the Urban Fringe', *The Planner*, 1979, vol. 64, pp. 52–4.
30. DoE *Derelict Land Guidance Notes* (DoE: Birmingham, 1983).
31. Staffordshire County Council (SCC) *South Cannock Land Renewal Plan* (SCC: Stafford, 1981); SCC *North Staffordshire Land Renewal Plan*, Draft (SCC: Stafford, 1982).
32. ibid., p. 64.

33. South Yorkshire County Council *Rother Valley Park: Prospect Report* (SYCC: Barnsley, 1977).
34. Greater London Council (GLC) *Greater London Development Plan* (GLC: London, 1976).
35. GLC *Beddington Farmlands Draft Planning Brief* (GLC: London, 1984).
36. Buckinghamshire County Council *Minerals Subject Plan* (BCC: Aylesbury, 1980), p. 121.
37. Town and Country Planning Association 'Green Belts – Ministers Reply', *Town and Country Planning*, 1956, vol. 24, pp. 151–3.
38. MHLG *The Green Belts* (HMSO: London, 1962).
39. Countryside Review Committee (1977) loc. cit.
40. SCLSERP (1979), op. cit.
41. Berkshire County Council *Green Belt Subject Plan* (BCC: Reading, 1982).
42. GREGORY, D. *Green Belts and Development Control: A Case Study in the West Midlands*, Occ. Pap. No. 12 (University of Birmingham, Centre for Urban and Regional Studies, 1970), pp. 49–53.
43. Permission to use development control data for secondary analysis, granted by Hertfordshire County Council, is gratefully acknowledged.
44. Land Use Consultants *Recreation in London's Green Belt*, A Report to the Sports Council (Sports Council: London, 1984).
45. SLEE, W. *An Evaluation of Country Park Policy*, Gloucestershire Papers in Local and Rural Planning No. 16, (GLOSCAT: Cheltenham, 1982).
46. A variety of arrangements are mentioned in: Surrey County Council *The Surrey Countryside*, Newsletter No. 1 (SCC: Kingston, 1983).
47. Countryside Commission *Rufford Park Marketing Study*, CCP 129 (Countryside Commission: Cheltenham, 1979).
48. Land Use Consultants *Chasewater Park* (LUC: London, 1984).
49. Countryside Commission for Scotland and Countryside Commission *Guide to Countryside Interpretation. Part One: Principles of Countryside Interpretation and Interpretive Planning* (HMSO: London, 1975).
50. Dartington Amenity Research Trust *Feasibility Study of Croxteth Park* (DART: Totnes, 1977).
51. Essex County Council *Marsh Farm Park Management Plan* (ECC: Chelmsford, 1982).
52. Civic Trust for the North West *The Tame Valley Interpretation Project* (CTNW: Salford, 1979).
53. WILLIAMS, H. *The Management of Publicly-Owned Land in the Hertfordshire–Barnet Experiment Area*, WP 17 (Countryside Commission: Cheltenham, 1979).
54. MATTINGLY, A. *Access to the Countryside* (Ramblers Association: London, 1982).
55. British Trust for Conservation Volunteers *Footpaths: A Practical Conservation Handbook* (BTCV: Wallingford, 1983).
56. Countryside Commission *Management Agreements: Policy Statement and Grants*, CCP 156 (Countryside Commission: Cheltenham, 1983).
57. FEIST, M. (1978), op. cit.
58. FERGUSON, M. J., SLOANE, B. and WARREN, A. *Styles of Site Management in the South London Green Belt*, WP 6, Land for Informal Recreation (University College: London, 1980).

59. FITTON, M. 'The Urban Fringe and the Less Privileged', *Countryside Recreation Review*, 1976, vol. 1, pp. 25–34; HARRISON, C. M. 'A Playground for Whom?: Informal Recreation in London's Green Belt', *Area*, 1981, vol. 13, pp. 109–14.
60. BANISTER, C. and GROOME, D. (eds.) *Out and About* (Manchester University, Department of Town and Country Planning, 1984).
61. See GRIGG, A. O. and SMITH, P. G. *An Opinion Survey of the Yorkshire Dales Rail Service in 1975*, LR 769 (TRRL: Crowthorne, 1977).
62. GREENING, P. A. K. and SLATER, P. *Rural Recreational Transport: The Sunday Bus Experiment*, TRRL Report 1026 (TRRL: Crowthorne, 1981).
63. SPEAKMAN, C. 'Public Transport and the Countryside', in BANISTER, C. and GROOME, D. (eds.) (1984), op. cit.

CHAPTER 9: GREEN BELT MANAGEMENT

1. SHOARD, M. *Theft of the Countryside* (Temple Smith: London, 1980).
2. Nature Conservancy Council, (1984), op. cit.
3. O'RIORDAN, T. 'Putting Trust in the Countryside', in Programme Organizing Committee of the Conservation and Development Programme for the U.K. (eds.) (1983) op. cit., pp. 171–260.
4. WORTH, J. 'What We Think of the Countryside', *Ecos*, 1984, vol. 5, no. 1, pp. 35–7.
5. Nature Conservancy Council *Nature Conservation and Agriculture* (NCC: Shrewsbury, 1977).
6. BOWERS, J. K. and CHESHIRE, P. C. *Agriculture, the Countryside and Land Use* (Methuen: London, 1983); BODY, R. *Agriculture: The Triumph and the Shame* (Temple Smith: London, 1982).
7. Countryside Commission *Management Agreements, Policy Statement and Grants*, CCP 156 (Countryside Commission: Cheltenham, 1983).
8. Himsworth, K. S. *A Review of Areas of Outstanding Natural Beauty*, CCP 140 (Countryside Commission: Cheltenham, 1981).
9. Forestry Commission *Forestry Grant Scheme* (Forestry Commission: Edinburgh, 1983).
10. ELSON, M. J. *Open Land Policies and Programmes in the Metropolitan Counties*, WP 14 (Countryside Commission: Cheltenham, 1979).
11. MUNTON, R. J. C. (1983) op. cit., p. 83.
12. WESTMACOTT, R. and WORTHINGTON, T. *Agricultural Landscapes: A Second Look*, CCP 168 (Countryside Commission: Cheltenham, 1984).
13. COBHAM, R. *Agricultural Landscapes: Demonstration Farms* CCP 170 (Countryside Commission: Cheltenham, 1984).
14. CARTER, E. 'The Work of FWAG', in BREAKELL, M., CLATWORTHY, M. and HOGG, I. (eds.) *Caring for the Countryside*, WP 79 (Oxford Polytechnic, Department of Town Planning, 1984), pp. 4–6.
15. MUNTON, R. J. C. (1983), op. cit.
16. SCLSERP *The Improvement of London's Green Belt: A Second Report*, SC 860R (SCLSERP: London, 1978); SCLSERP *The Metropolitan Green Belt*, SC 1816 (SCLSERP: London, 1983).

17. Greater London Council (GLC) *The Colne Valley Park – A New Prospect* (Colne Valley Regional Park Standing Conference: London, 1972).
18. See Colne Valley Countryside Management Project *Third, Fourth, and Fifth Annual Reports 1980–1, 81–2, 82–3* (CVCMP: Slough, 1981–3).
19. Colne Valley Standing Conference *Draft Proposals for the Regional Park* (CVSC: Hillingdon, 1983).
20. GLC *Colne Valley Park – New Initiatives*, Report to Arts and Recreation Committee, 1.9.82 (GLC: London, 1982).
21. ibid., p. 11.
22. WEBSTER, P. 'Local Authority Action in the Urban Fringe', *Countryside Recreation Review*, 1976, vol. 1, pp. 13–20.
23. MAUND, R. 'The Greater Manchester Adventure: An Exercise in Strategic Environmental Improvement', *Environmental Education and Information*, 1982, vol. 2, pp. 79–96; GMC *Management of River Valleys and Country Parks: A Discussion Paper* (GMC: Manchester, 1975).
24. For example, GMC *Medlock Valley Subject Plan*, Draft, (GMC: Manchester, 1981); GMC *Mersey Valley Subject Plan*, Draft (GMC: Manchester, 1981).
25. Civic Trust for the North West *Twenty Years of Success* (CTNW: Salford, 1982).
26. GMC *Annual Structure Plan Monitoring Report* (GMC: Manchester, 1983).
27. TRAVIS, A. S. 'Urban Fringe Recreation in Other Countries: Some Examples', in TRAVIS, A. S. and VEAL, A. J. (eds.) (1976) op. cit., pp. 31–41.
28. HIRSCH, W. G. 'Social Service and Business: Provision for Recreation in Kentucky, USA and in the Ruhrkohlenbezirk, West Germany', in ELSON, M. J. and HIRSCH, G. P. (eds.) 'Planning for Recreation', *Planning Outlook*, 1974, Special Issue, pp. 97–105.
29. Civic Trust *A Lea Valley Regional Park* (Civic Trust: London, 1964); Lea Valley Regional Park Authority (LVRPA) *Park Plan and Proposals* (LVRPA: Enfield, 1969).
30. LVRPA *Park Plan Review: Objectives and Issues* (LVRPA: Enfield, 1983); LVRPA *Annual Report 1982–3* (LVRPA: Enfield, 1983).
31. Countryside Review Committee (1977), op. cit.
32. HOOKWAY, R. J. S. 'The Management of Britain's Rural Land', pp. 63–45, in TCPSS, *Report of Summer School Proceedings* (RTPI: London, 1967).
33. HOOKWAY, R. J. S. 'Countryside Management: The Development of Techniques', pp. 7–13, in TCPSS, *Report of Summer School Proceedings* (RTPI: London, 1977).
34. See for example STEELEY, G. and COLEMAN, D. *Hertfordshire Countryside Management Service: Project Report 1976–1981* (HCC: Hertford, 1981), p. 2; Operation South Cannock *Annual Report 1983* (OSC: Great Wyrley, 1983), p. 1.
35. Countryside Commission *The Bollin Valley: A Study in Land Management in the Urban Fringe*, CCP 97 (Countryside Commission: Cheltenham, 1976); Countryside Commission *Countryside Management in the Urban Fringe*, CCP 136 (Countryside Commission: Cheltenham, 1981).
36. WILLIAMS, H. (1979), op. cit.
37. CAIRNS, C. *A Management Plan for the Green Belt Management Area in Barnet and South Hertfordshire 1982–1987*, CCP 147 (Countryside Commission: Cheltenham, 1983b).

38. CAIRNS, C. (1983a), op. cit.
39. LAVERY, P. 'Countryside Management Schemes in the Urban Fringe', *Planning Outlook*, 1983, vol. 25, pp. 52–9.
40. Leeds District Council *Tong-Cockersdale: Draft Local Planning Policy* (LDC: Leeds, 1975).
41. McGLUE, T. and JUNIPER, B. 'Development Plans and the Control of Landscape Change', *Planning Outlook*, 1983, vol. 25, pp. 59–66.
42. West Midlands County Council *Barr–Beacon–Sandwell Wedge Local Plan*, Draft (WMCC: Birmingham, 1983).
43. FERGUSON, M. J. and MUNTON, R. J. C. *Informal Recreation in the Urban Fringe: The Provision and Management of Sites in London's Green Belt*, WP 2 Land for Informal Recreation, (University College: London, 1978).
44. CAIRNS, C. (1983b) op. cit., p. 46.
45. HEBBERT, M. and GAULT, I. (1978) op. cit.
46. LOWE, P. et al. *Land Use Conflicts in the Urban Fringe: A Case Study of Aggregate Extraction in the London Borough of Havering*, WP 11 (Countryside Commission: Cheltenham, 1979), p. 10.
47. CAIRNS, C. (1983a), op. cit. p. 90.
48. DoE *Groundwork North West*, Press Notice NW 33/83 (DoE: Manchester, 1983).
49. Groundwork North West Unit *Groundwork North West* (GNWU: Manchester, 1983).
50. Operation Groundwork *Operation Groundwork: Making Good Between Town and Country* (Pamphlet) (Operation Groundwork: St. Helens, 1983).
51. STANSFIELD, K. 'Turning the Black Belt Green', *Local Government News*, July–August 1982, pp. 30–1.
52. Groundwork North West Unit *Newsletter*, No. 2 (GNWU: Manchester, 1984).
53. Macclesfield Groundwork Trust *Linking Town and Country* (MGT: Bollington, 1984).
54. Land Use Consultants *The Evolution of Countryside Management*, A Report to the Countryside Commission, (1982).

CHAPTER 10: THE POLITICS OF THE 1984 CIRCULAR

1. DoE *Streamlining the Cities*, Cmnd. 9063 (HMSO: London, 1983).
2. BALL, M. (1983) op. cit., chapters 7 and 8.
3. HCEC (1984b) op. cit., pp. 383–4.
4. DoE *Local Government Planning and Land Act 1980: Town and Country Planning: Development Plans*, Circular 23/82 (HMSO: London, 1981); DoE *Industrial Development*, Circular 16/84 (DoE: London, 1984).
5. HOOPER, A. 'Estimating Land Availability for Housebuilding: Some Methodological Issues', pp. 10–26, in BARRETT, S. and HEALEY, P. (eds.) *Land Policy: Problems and Alternatives* (Gower: Farnborough, 1985).
6. See 'Baron's Business', *The Builder*, 9 October 1983.
7. DoE *Private Sector Land: Requirements and Supply*, Circular 44/78 (HMSO: London, 1978).
8. DoE and House Builders Federation *Study of the Availability of Private Housebuilding Land in Greater Manchester 1978–1981* (DoE: London, 1979).

9. DoE *Land for Private Housebuilding*, Circular 9/80 (HMSO: London, 1980), paras. 4–5.
10. CHIDDICK, D. 'Planning Policies and the Housebuilding Industry', in PTRC Ltd., *Structure and Regional Planning Practice* (PTRC: London, 1981), pp. 27–34.
11. HUMBER, R. 'This Green and Pleasant Land', *House Builder*, 1982, vol. 41, (6), pp. 2–3.
12. loc. cit.
13. HCEC (1984b) op. cit., p. 385 has an unconvincing explanation.
14. Housing Research Foundation (HRF) *Is There Sufficient Housing Land for the 1980s?: Paper I: How Many Houses Should We Plan For?* (HRF: London, 1982).
15. HRF (1983), op. cit.
16. But see SMYTH, H. *Land Banking, Land Availability and Planning for Private House Building*, WP 23 (School for Advanced Urban Studies, University of Bristol, 1982); SMYTH, H. *Land Supply, Housebuilders and Government Policies*, WP 43 (School for Advanced Urban Studies, University of Bristol, 1984).
17. See HCEC (1984b), 'Memorandum Submitted by CPRE', p. 174.
18. Housebuilders Federation (HBF) *Study of Publicly-Owned Land Register Sites in the Greater London Area Designated as Green Belt or Open Land* (HBF: London, 1983).
19. SCLSERP *Housing Land in South East England*, SC 1600 (SCLSERP: London, 1981); SCLSERP Housing Land Supply in the South East (Outside London), SC 1891 (SCLSERP: London, 1983); SERPLAN *Housing Land Supply in the South East*, RPC 88 (SERPLAN: London, 1984).
20. See *The Builder*, 9 October 1983, op. cit., and BARON, T. 'Plannings' Biggest and Least Satisfied Customer – Housing', in TCPSS, *Proceedings of Town and Country Planning Summer School* (RTPI: London, 1980), pp. 34–40.
21. CPRE *'Disturbing' New Figures Suggest Countryside Losses*, Press Release, 4 April 1983 (CPRE: London).
22. CPRE *Planning: Friend or Foe?* (CPRE: London, 1981).
23. DoE *Memorandum on Structure and Local Plans*, Draft for Consultation (DoE: London, 1982), para. 4.49.
24. HBF *The House Builders Federation: Comments on Draft Development Plans Memorandum*, HD 82.409 (HBF: London, 1982).
25. Association of District Councils (ADC) *Comments on Draft Development Plans Memorandum* (ADC: London, 1982).
26. DoE *Memorandum on Structure and Local Plans and Green Belt*, Draft Circular (DoE: London, 1983a).
27. HCEC (1984b) op. cit., p. 388.
28. DoE *Land for Housing*, Draft Circular DoE: London, 1983).
29. HBF *HBF Response to Draft Circular on Memorandum on Structure and Local Plans and Green Belt*, HD 83.473 (HBF: London, 1983).
30. HBF *HBF Response to Draft Circular: Land for Housing*, HD 83.368A (HBF: London, 1983).
31. DoE *Guidance on Green Belts*, Press Notice 338 (DoE: London, 1983).
32. DoE. *Green Belt – Patrick Jenkin Responds to GLC*, Press Notice 521, 23 November 1983, (DoE: London, 1983).

33. CPRE letter to Minister dated 10 October 1983.
34. CPRE 'CPRE's Battle for the Belts: Diary of a Victory', *Countryside Campaigner* (CPRE: London, 1983), pp. 4–5.
35. See for example *Green Belt: Patrick Jenkin Sets the Record Straight*, Press Notice 376, 9 September 1983, and *Green Belt and Land for Housing*, Press Notice 595, 20 December 1983 for the accusation of deliberate misinterpretation.
36. Hansard (weekly), vol. 47, no. 1286, cols. 277–9, 26 October 1983.
37. Hansard 598, col. 1158, 18 November 1983.
38. Hansard 601, col. 1164, 18 November 1983.
39. DoE, *Circular on Land for Housing*, Press Notice 555, 2 December 1983, (DoE: London, 1983).
40. HCEC (1984b) op. cit., p. 1.
41. DoE *Green Belts*, Draft Circular (DoE: London, 1984).
42. DoE *Green Belt and Land for Housing*, Press Notice 595, 20 December, 1983 (DoE: London, 1983).
43. DoE *Land for Housing*, Draft Circular (DoE: London, 1984).
44. DoE *Green Belts and Land for Housing: Revised Draft Circulars Published*, Press Notice 73, 9 February 1984, (DoE: London, 1984).
45. HRF *Housing and Land 1984–1991: 1992–2000: How Many Houses Will We Build?: What will be the Effect on our Countryside?* (HRF: London, 1984).
46. HCEC (1984b) op. cit., pp. 227–59.
47. Appeal to the national interest is a common tactic among *all* sectoral groups; see NEWBY, H. (1979) op. cit., p. 257.
48. HCEC (1984b) op. cit., pp. 180–98.
49. The following paragraphs are based on HCEC (1984a) op. cit., pp. xi–xx and xxxv.
50. DoE *First Memorandum of Response by the Department of the Environment to the First Report from the Environment Committee, Session 1983–4, HC 275-I* (DoE: London, 1984).
51. HCEC (1984a) op. cit., paras. 68–71.
52. ELSON, M. J. *Necessary Ambiguity?: Central–Local Relations and the Definition of Green Belts in Local Plans*, Paper presented to Local Plans Research Conference, Oxford Polytechnic, May 1985, 12 pp.
53. CPRE *Green Belts Sacrosanct: Key Conservationists Applaud Commons Report*, Press Release 13 June 1984, (CPRE: London, 1984).
54. MERCER, R. 'Green Belt Policy – Part I', in RICS, *Current Problems in Property Law*, Blundell Memorial Lectures (RICS: London, 1984), p. 81.
55. Interview with T. Baron reported in *Countryside Campaigner*, Spring 1984, p. 9.
56. HUMBER, R. 'Green Belt Policy – Part II', in RICS, *Current Problems in Property Law*, Blundell Memorial Lectures (RICS: London, 1984), pp. 83–104.
57. See *House Builder*, vol. 43, no. 3, p. 44.
58. *Countryside Campaigner*, op. cit., Spring 1984.

CHAPTER 11: WHAT FUTURE FOR THE GREEN BELT?

1. The final structure plan to be approved for England and Wales is that for the County of Avon (Bristol area).
2. HCEC (1984a–c), op. cit.

3. DoE *Green Belts*, Circular 14/84 (HMSO: London, 1984).
4. Institute for Employment Research *Review of the Economy and Employment* (IER: University of Warwick, 1983).
5. This suggests the views of Barker may be overstated. See BARKER, A. 'Public Participation and Central Control of Structure Planning', in CROSS, D. T. and BRISTOW, M. R. (eds.) op. cit. (1983), pp. 257–85.
6. RHODES, R. A. W. *Control and Power in Central–Local Government Relations*', (Gower and SSRC, Aldershot, 1981).
7. HCEC (1984c), 'Memorandum by Dr. R. J. C. Munton' pp. 560–7.
8. HCEC (1984b), 'Memorandum by Dr. Martin J. Elson' pp. 61–76.
9. HCEC (1984c), 'Memorandum by K. G. Willis and M. C. Whitby' pp. 577–88; WILLIS, K. G. 'Green Belts: An Economic Appraisal of a Physical Planning Policy', *Planning Outlook*, 1982, vol. 24, pp. 62–9.
10. HCEC (1984b), 'Examination of DoE Witnesses' p. 38, para. 22.
11. DoE *Land for Housing*, Circular 15/84 (HMSO: London, 1984).
12. HUMBER, R. (1984), op. cit.
13. Paper delivered by M. Dobson to Regional Studies Association Conference 'Green Belts, Land Supply and Open Land Control', University of Manchester, December, 1983.
14. The words 'checking sprawl' were specifically omitted from plans containing Green Belts in the South and West Yorkshire Conurbations, suggesting a different emphasis.
15. RYDIN, Y. 'The Struggle for Housing Land: A Case of Confused Interests', *Policy and Politics*, 1984, vol. 12, pp. 431–6.
16. Thus the discussion in Northern Ireland, following a proposal by central Government to rename 'Areas of Special Control' as Green Belts, was only symbolic.
17. READE, E. 'The Effects of Town and Country Planning in Britain', Unit 23, in Open University, *Urban Change and Conflict* (Open University: Milton Keynes, 1983).
18. Note for example the mismatch between HBF views on the Greater Manchester Green Belt in Chapter 10 and the assessment in Chapter 4.
19. SCLSERP *Development Trends in the South East Region*, SC 1504 (SCLSERP: London, 1981).
20. STONE, P. A. *The Structure, Size and Cost of Urban Settlements* (Cambridge University Press: Cambridge, 1973); SEJPT *Strategic Plan for the South East Review: Report of the Urban Economy Study Group* (HMSO: London, 1976).
21. HCEC (1984c), 'Memorandum by Wokingham District Council' p. 573.
22. MERCER, R. (1984), op. cit. pp. 57–82.
23. Portland Planning Consultants *Needs and Opportunities for Travellers on the M25* (ETB: London, 1984). Between the draft and final Government advice on the M25 the need to allow for tourist developments was added to the document.
24. Daily Telegraph, 21 September 1984.
25. The GLC are placing great emphasis on the need to keep new development around towns in the London Green Belt to a minimum. See HCEC (1984c) 'Memorandum by the Greater London Council', p. 80.
26. CLARKE, S. *Green Belts and the Inner City Problem*, Thesis for MSc in Public Sector Management (Management Centre, University of Aston, 1983).

27. HCEC (1984b) 'Memorandum by Birmingham City Council', p. 615.
28. DoE *The M25 and Regional Planning in the South East* (DoE: London, 1984).
29. DoE *Industrial Development*, Circular 16/84 (HMSO: London, 1984).
30. SERPLAN *Regional Trends in the South East: The South East Regional Monitor 1983–4*, RPC 45 (SERPLAN: London, 1984), p. 37.
31. KNIGHT FRANK AND RUTLEY *Office Developments in the M25 Corridor North* (KFR: London, 1984), p. 10.
32. FOTHERGILL, S. and GUDGIN, G. (1982) op. cit., p. 104.
33. LEIGH, R., NORTH, D., GOUGH, J. and SWEET-ESCOTT, K. *Monitoring Manufacturing Change in London: 1976–81, 1, The Implications of Local Economic Policy* (London Industry and Employment Research Group: Middlesex Polytechnic, 1983).
34. LAWLESS, P. *Britain's Inner Cities: Problems and Policies* (Harper and Row: London, 1981), p. 258.
35. HCEC (1984c), 'Memorandum by David G. Gregory', pp. 540–4.
36. Tyne and Wear County Council *Structure Plan: Annual Report* (TWCC: Newcastle on Tyne, 1982), p. 47.
37. BARON, T. 'The Challenge for the UK Housing Industry in the 1980s and the Planning System', *Construction Management and Economics*, 1983, vol. 1, (1), pp. 17–29.
38. DoE *Crown Land and Crown Development*, Circular 18/84 (HMSO: London, 1984).
39. See 'M25 North', *Estates Times*, 17 August 1984, pp. 7–25; 'M25 South', *Estates Times*, 24 August 1984, pp. 7–24.
40. DoE *The Transfer of the Greater London Council's Interest in Land Under the Green Belt (London and Home Counties) Act 1938*, Consultation Paper (DoE: London, 1984).
41. London Green Belt Council *Response to DoE Consultation Paper on Transfer of GLC Land Held Under the 1938 Act* (LGBC: Potters Bar, 1984).
42. National Farmers Union *Response to White Paper – Streamlining the Cities* (NFU: London, 1984).
43. DoE. *The Transfer of the Greater London Council's Interest in Land Under the Green Belt (London and Home Counties) Act 1938*, Decisions in Response to Consultations (DoE: London, 1984).
44. Dudley MDC *Southern Green Belt Study* (DMDC: Dudley, 1983).
45. DoE *The Re-Allocation of Planning Functions in the Greater London and Metropolitan County Council Areas* (DoE: London, 1984).
46. DoE *Streamlining the Cities*, Cmnd. 9063 (HMSO: London, 1983).
47. BODY, R. *Farming in the Clouds* (Temple Smith: London, 1984), pp. 16–17.
48. MUNTON, R. J. C. (1983), op. cit.
49. Friends of the Earth (1983), op. cit.
50. WESTMACOTT, R. and WORTHINGTON, T. (1984), op. cit.
51. MELCHETT, Lord 'While the Minister responsible for conservation may be acting more out of ignorance than malice, the same isn't true of the National Farmers Union', *Guardian*, 5 May 1984.
52. HCEC (1984c) appendix 9, para. 12.
53. Royal Town Planning Institute Study Group 'The Planning Response to Social and Economic Change', *The Planner*, 1984, vol. 70, (10), pp. 8–12.

54. TCPA *A New Prospectus: Policy Direction for the Next 20 Years* (TCPA: London, 1984).
55. HUMBER, R. 'Circular 15/84: 'Make or Break for Housebuilders', *House Builder*, 1984, vol. 43, (9), pp. 36–40.
56. CPRE *Countryside Campaigner Yearbook* (CPRE: London, 1984), pp. 6–9 and 26.
57. PATERSON, T. Conservation and the Conservatives, A Bow Paper, (Bow Group: London, 1985), pp. 16–17.

Index